All in One

Essential Music Theory

Mark Sarnecki

San Marco Publications

Elementary Music Theory © 2023 by San Marco Publications. All rights reserved.

All right reserved. No part of this book may be reproduced in any form or by electronic or mechanical means including Information storage and retrieval systems without permission in writing from the author.

ISNB: 9781896499406

Contents

Lesson 1:	Pitch and Notation	1
Lesson 2:	Time Values	16
Lesson 3:	Accidentals	25
Lesson 4:	Major Scales	40
Lesson 5:	Minor Scales	56
Lesson 6:	Other Scales	74
Lesson 7:	C Clefs	89
Lesson 8:	Modes	97
Lesson 9:	Intervals	104
Lesson 10:	Meter 1	132
Lesson 11:	Chords	161
Lesson 12:	Cadences	197
Lesson 13:	Meter 2	224
Lesson 14:	Transposition	268
Lesson 15:	Score Types	287
Lesson 16:	Melody	300
Lesson 17:	Music Analysis	340
Music Terms and Signs		369

1
Pitch and Notation

Sound - Good Vibrations!

Music is *sound*. Sound is all over the place, and you have two fantastic devices that let you hear it: your ears! Sound is created by a vibrating object, like a string, a drum head, a column of air, or a metal or wooden bar. These vibrations are sent to the ear as sound waves.

The ear is a complicated thing. The external or outer ear is called the ***pinna*** or ***auricle*** and acts like a funnel to bring sounds into your inner ear. The inner ear is called the ***cochlea*** and is a small curled tube filled with fluid that takes sound vibrations or waves and creates signals that the brain interprets as sound. You turn on the music, the vibrations go into your ears, your brain decodes them, and you hear your favorite song.

Figure 1.1

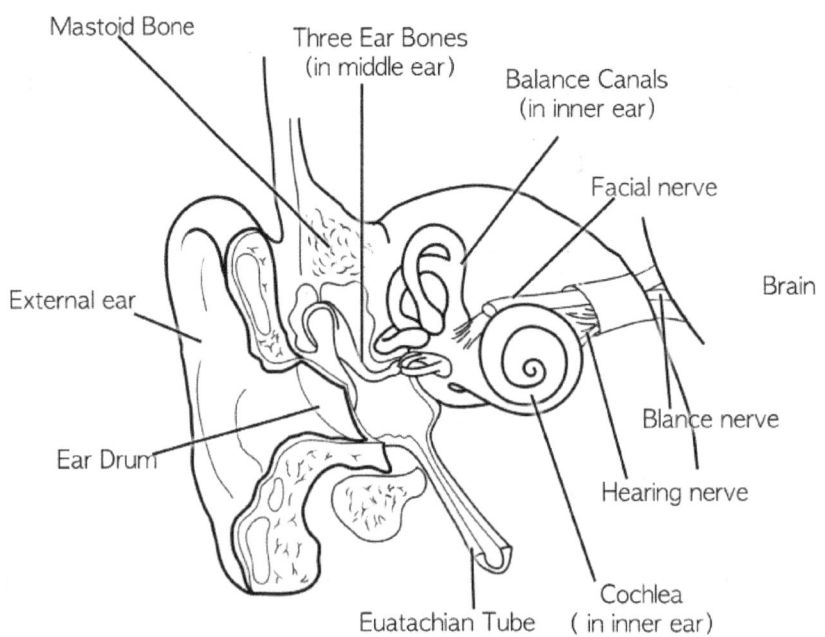

The Note

A *note* is the symbol we use to write or notate music. Each note can represent a specific sound.

The most important part of any note is the *note head*. The note head is the round part of the note. The note head is placed on the staff and gives us the pitch of the note. Note heads are all shaped the same. See Figure 1.2.

Figure 1.2

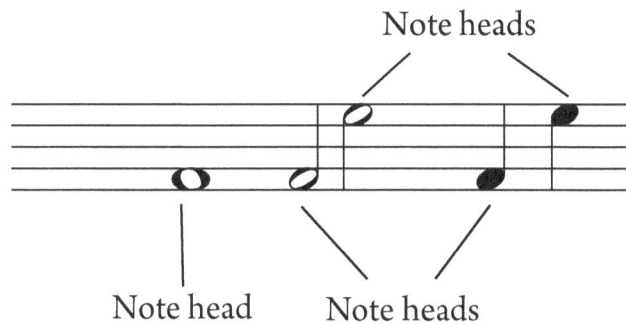

Some notes have stems. The stem is the line that goes up or down from the note head. When a stem goes up, it is placed on the right side of the note head, and when it goes down it is placed on the left side. See Figure 1.3.

Figure 1.3

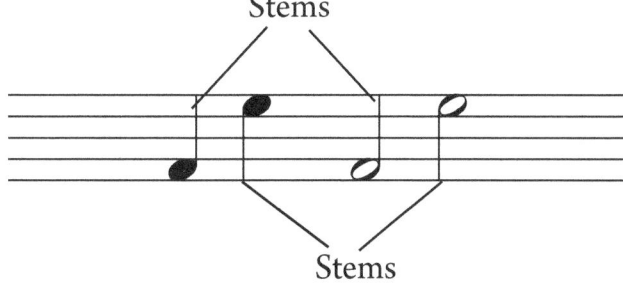

© San Marco Publications 2022

Pitch and Notation

Pitch and Intensity

Sounds can be heard as high or low. This is called ***pitch***. The faster an object like a string vibrates, the higher the pitch, the slower it vibrates, the lower the pitch. On a keyboard the higher pitched sounds are on the right and the lower pitched sounds are on the left (Figure 1.4). Understanding the keyboard when studying music theory is helpful.

Figure 1.4

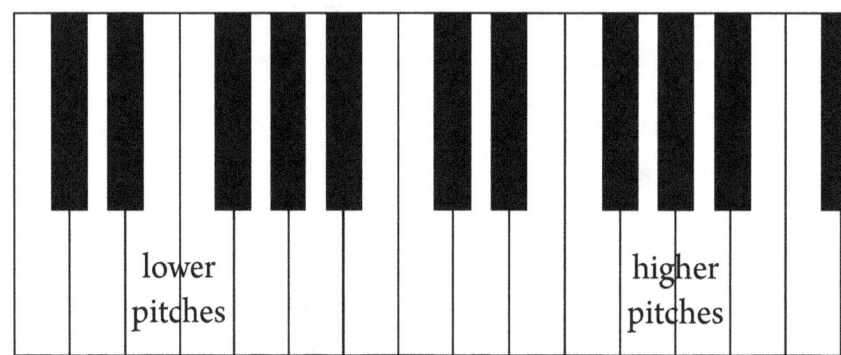

As well a pitch, music occurs in different degrees of loudness or softness. This is called ***intensity***. Intensity is determined by how much power is sent to the ear by the sound wave. If you play a really loud chord on the piano with all your strength, a powerful wave is sent to your ear, and the sound intensity is loud.

Pitch may also be defined as the name of the note that you play on your instrument. The system that we use to identify different pitches is achieved by placing notes on a set of lines or spaces called the ***staff***.

The Staff

Music has been written down for about 1000 years. This isn't very long in terms of world history. Around the year 500 AD we see the first examples of written western music. Monks in the monasteries of the Catholic church developed a system of writing notes called ***neumes*** (pronounced noomes). Neumes were small markings that were written above the words of a song that indicated the pitch of a note and how long to hold it. Eventually, neumes were placed on a system of lines. The line indicated a specific pitch. If the neume was above the line the pitch was higher, if the neume was below the line, the pitch was lower.

Over the years composers experimented with different ways of writing music, and around the year 1500 they came up with the system we still use today.

Figure 1.5 shows an early manuscript written with neumes.

Figure 1.5

The staff we use today is an outstanding invention. It is the home for music notes and consists of five lines with four spaces between them. The lines and spaces are numbered from the bottom up. As we study theory, we will learn that most things in music are counted from the bottom up (staff lines, notes in a scale, intervals). Figure 1.6 is a diagram of the staff lines and spaces.

Figure 1.6

The Musical Alphabet

Every note we play has a name. Music uses a system of seven letter names to identify pitches. They are:

A B C D E F G

There are no H's, W's or Z's. After G, the musical alphabet moves back to A. On the keyboard this can be found on the white keys. Figure 1.7 shows the musical alphabet on the keyboard.

Figure 1.7

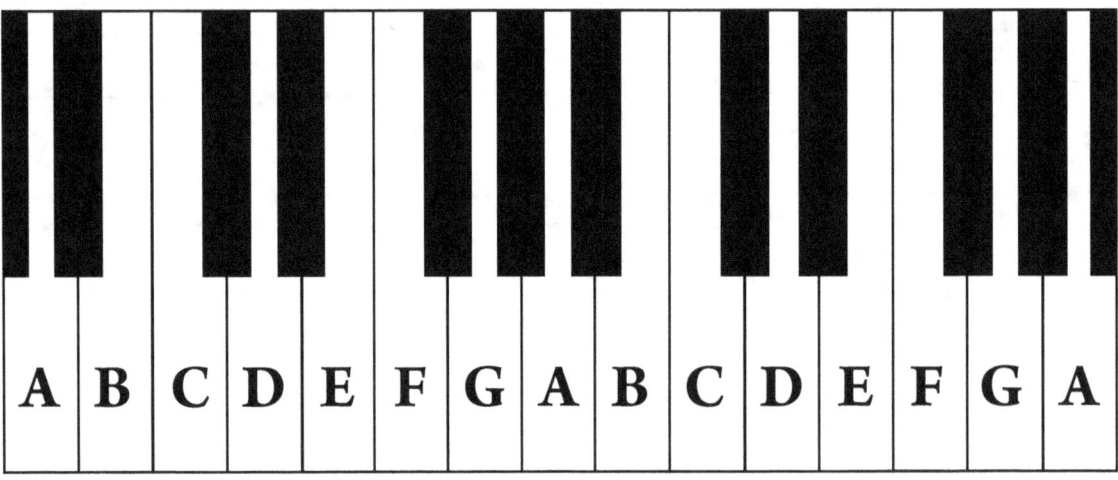

1. Number the lines and spaces on the staff.

2. Write the musical alphabet on the keyboard.

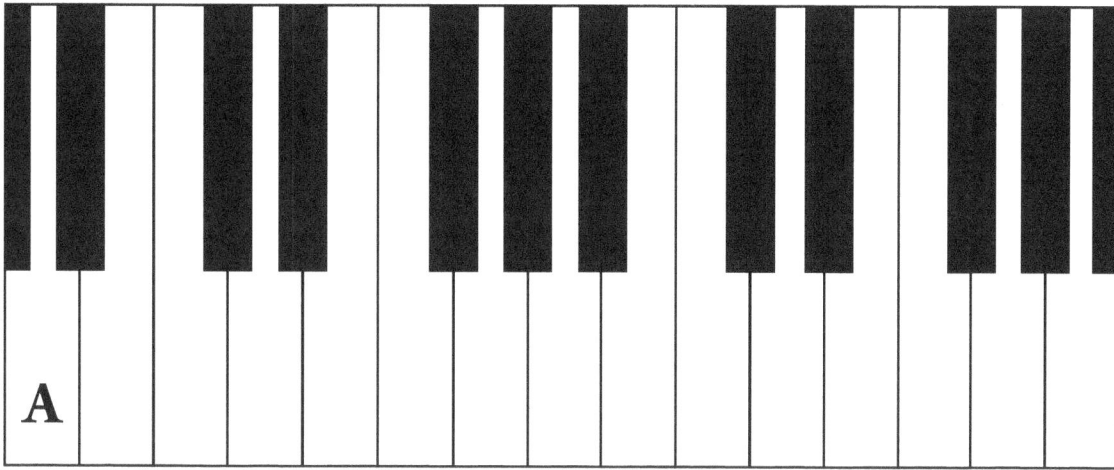

The Treble Staff

We know that the staff consists of five lines and four spaces, but how do we know where the notes are on the staff? To determine this, we need a symbol called a *clef* at the beginning of the staff. The clef defines where notes go on the staff, like a map.

The ***treble clef*** is the most common clef. It looks a little like a fancy letter G. The inner loop of the treble clef circles around the second line of the staff. The second line is where the note G is located. For this reason, the treble clef is sometimes called the ***G clef***.

Figure 1.8

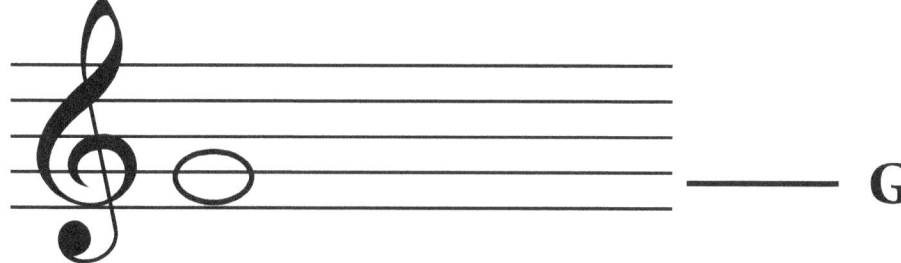

3. Draw several treble clefs in a row.

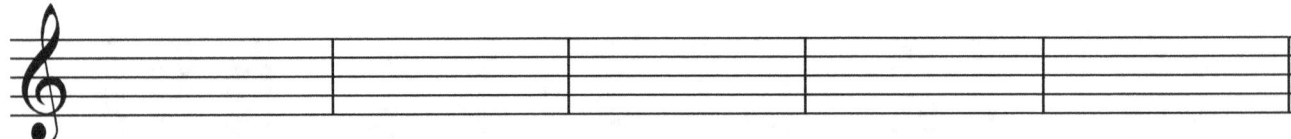

The treble clef is used by instruments with a higher pitch like the flute, guitar, violin, trumpet, clarinet, saxophone and piano.

Space Notes

A space note is a note that occurs within the spaces of the staff. They are placed between the lines without crossing over the lines. When we refer to space notes we say they are **in** a space. For example, in Figure 1.9, the first note is **in** the second space.

Figure 1.9

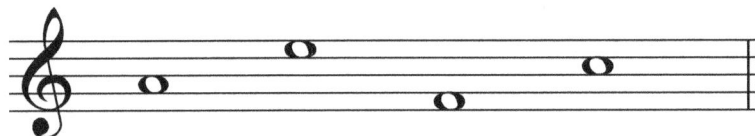

Line Notes

A line note has a line going through its middle. When drawing a line note be sure that the line goes directly through the middle of the note. Line notes are said to be **on** a line. In Figure 1.10, the first note is **on** line 3.

Figure 1.10

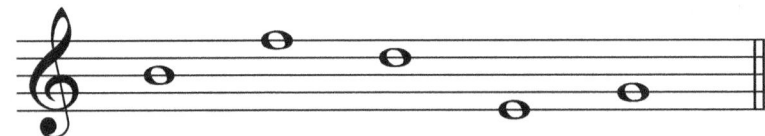

Knowing that G occurs on the second line of the treble staff, using the musical alphabet, it is easy to fill in the remaining notes of the treble staff.

Figure 1.11

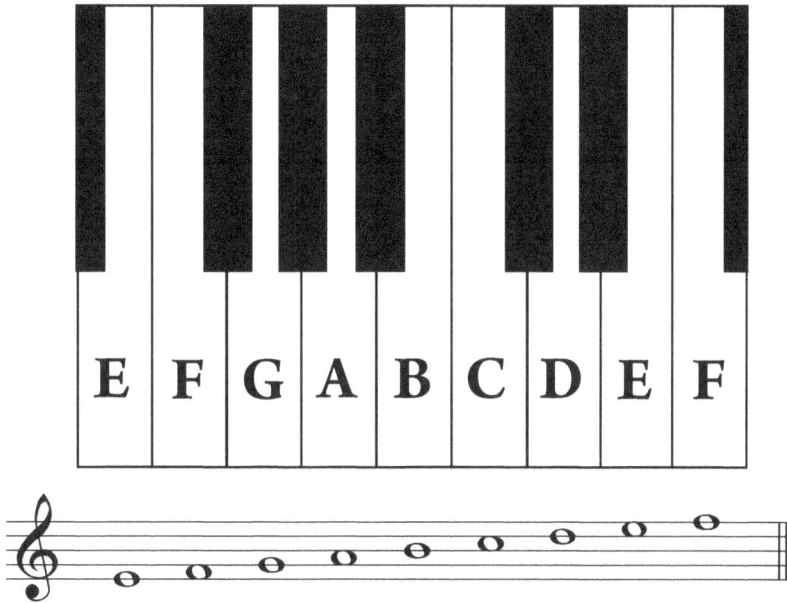

Figure 1.12 contains the line notes in the treble clef. Be careful when you draw a line note. The line must go right through the middle of the note. The line notes are EGBDF.

Figure 1.12

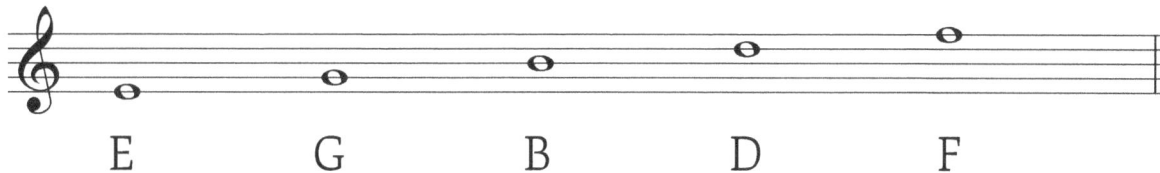

The space notes of the treble clef spell the word FACE. When drawing a space note keep it in the middle of the space and try not to go over the lines.

Figure 1.13

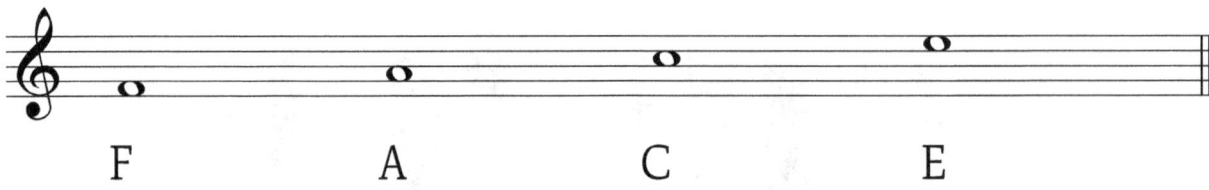

1. Name the following notes.

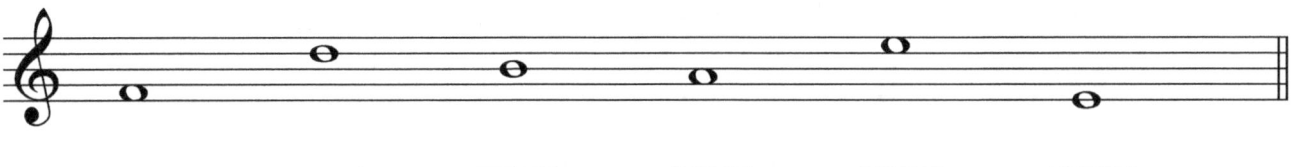

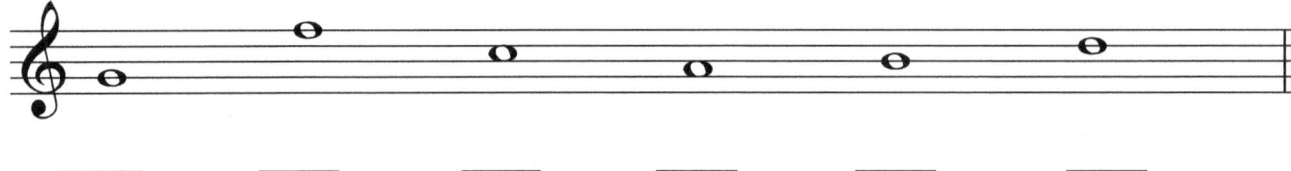

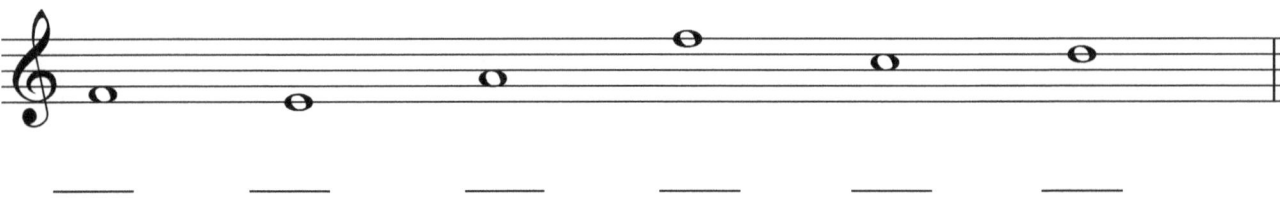

The Bass Staff

The ***bass staff*** uses the ***bass clef*** (pronounced: base) and covers the lower sounds in music. The bass clef is sometimes called the F clef because it looks like a fancy F and it has two dots that surround the fourth line which holds the note F.

Figure 1.14

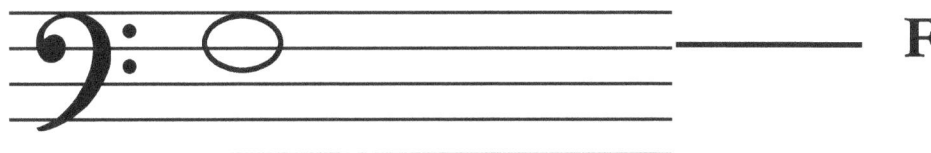

1. Draw several bass clefs in a row.

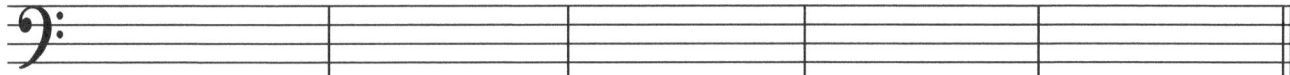

Many lower pitched instruments use the bass clef like the tuba, string bass, cello, trombone, and piano.
Since we know where F is on the bass staff, it is easy to find the other notes.

Figure 1.15

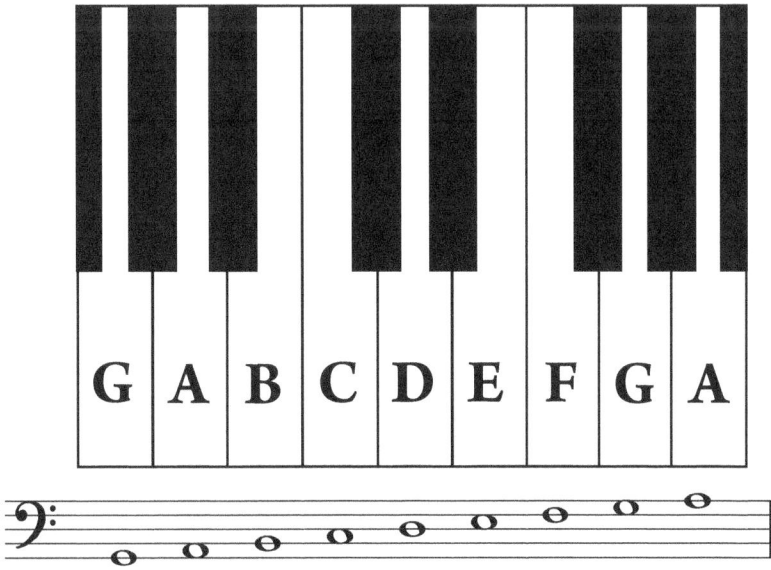

Figure 1.16 contians the notes on the lines and spaces of the bass clef.

Figure 1.16

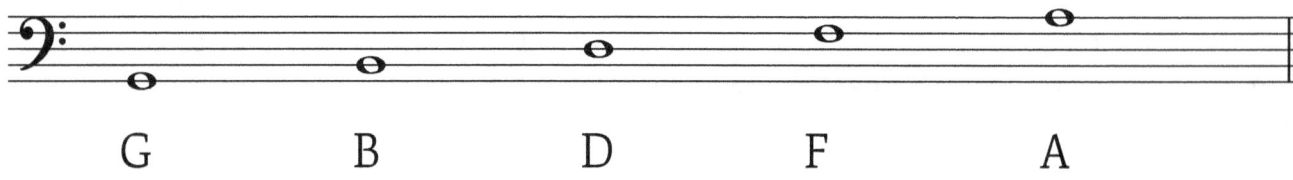

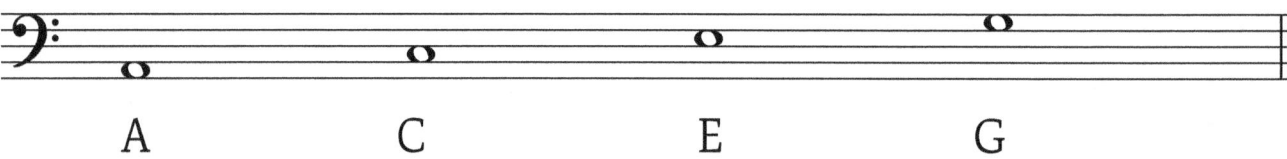

1. Name the following notes.

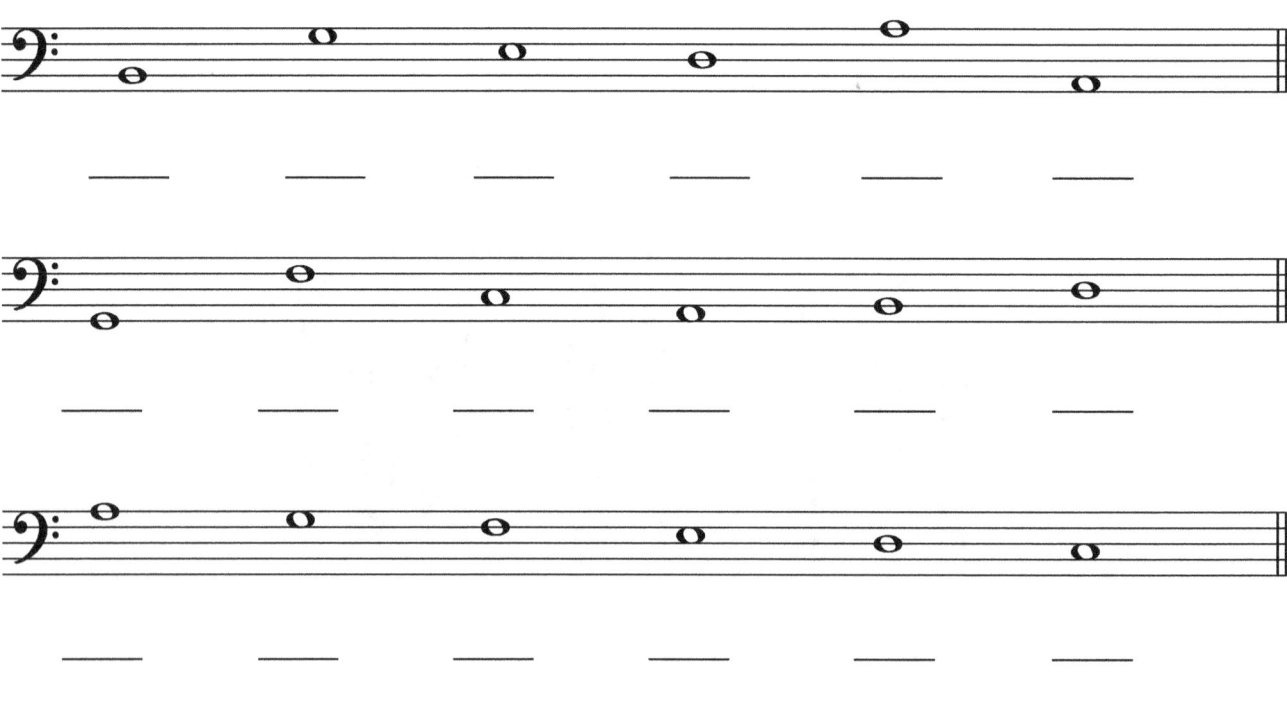

Ledger Lines - extending the staff.

The staff has five lines and four spaces and holds nine notes. However, there are a lot more than nine notes. The staff can be extended up and down using small lines called **ledger lines**. A ledger line is a short horizontal line spaced the same distance as the lines of the staff itself. It occurs above or below and holds the notes that are higher or lower than the staff.

Figure 1.17 shows that ledger lines are spaced the same distance vertically as the lines of the staff.

Figure 1.17

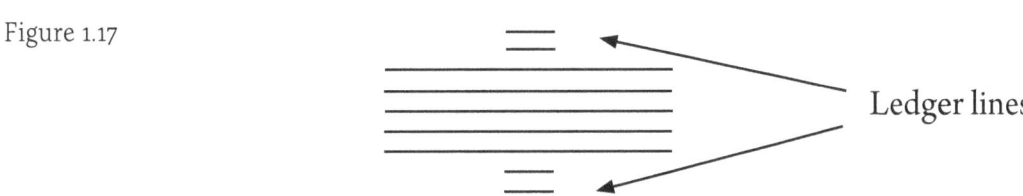

A ledger line is only as long as the note it is attached to, and is never used unless it is attached to a note (Figure 1.18).

Figure 1.18

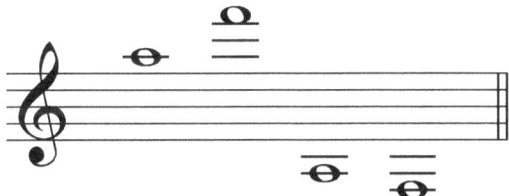

In this level we will study notes up to four ledger lines above and below the staff. Figure 1.19 shows these ledger line notes on the treble staff. The alphabetical order of the musical alphabet continues as you move above or below the staff using ledger lines. The notes move up and down in alphabetical order just like the notes on the staff.

Figure 1.19

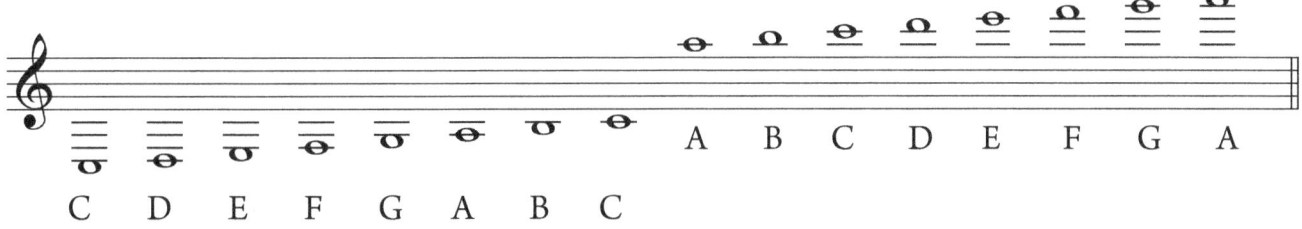

1. Write the following notes using ledger lines below the treble staff.

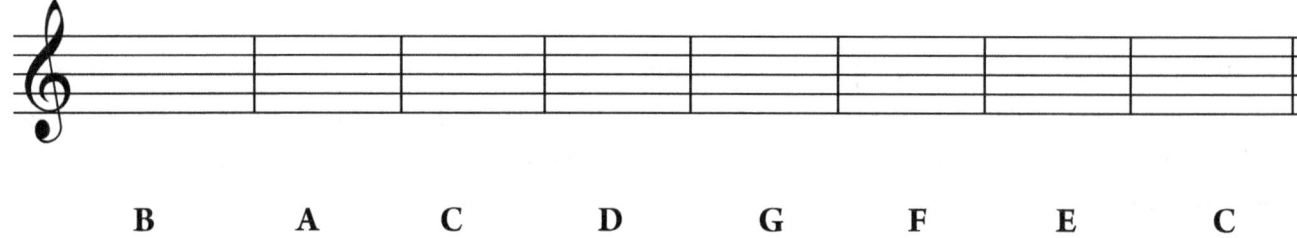

    B   A   C   D   G   F   E   C

2. Write the following notes using ledger lines above the treble staff.

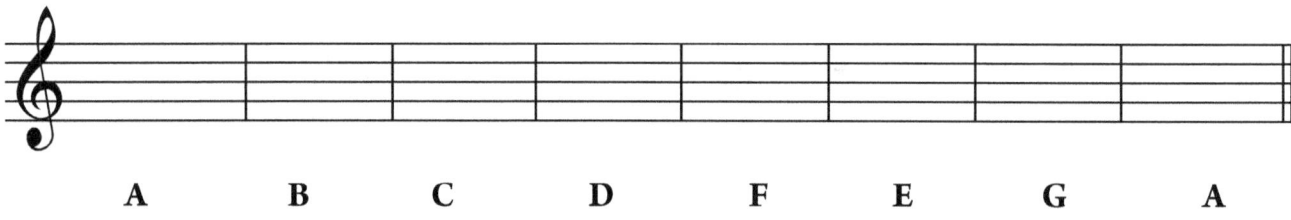

    A   B   C   D   F   E   G   A

Figure 1.20 shows the ledger line notes on the bass staff.

Figure 1.20

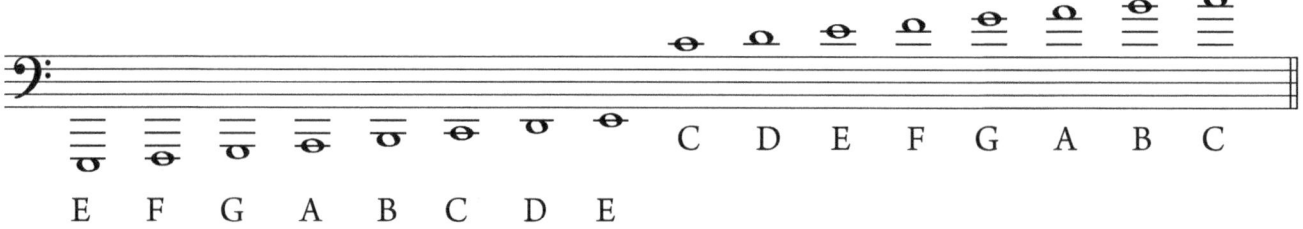

3. Write the following notes using ledger lines below the bass staff.

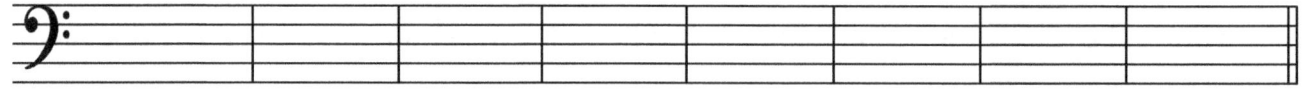

    A   B   D   C   E   G   F   E

4. Write the following notes using ledger lines above the bass staff.

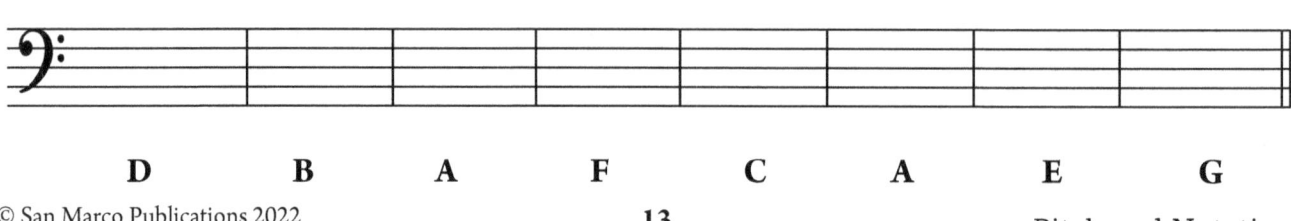

    D   B   A   F   C   A   E   G

© San Marco Publications 2022   Pitch and Notation

The Grand Staff

When you combine the treble and bass staves, you get the ***grand staff***. This staff is used by the piano because both clefs are needed to cover its extensive range. The treble clef is on the top and the bass clef is on the bottom. They are joined by a line and a brace or bracket. Figure 1.21 contains the grand staff with its notes. Notice that middle C occurs in both clefs in the middle of the grand staff.

Figure 1.21

1. Name the following notes on the grand staff.

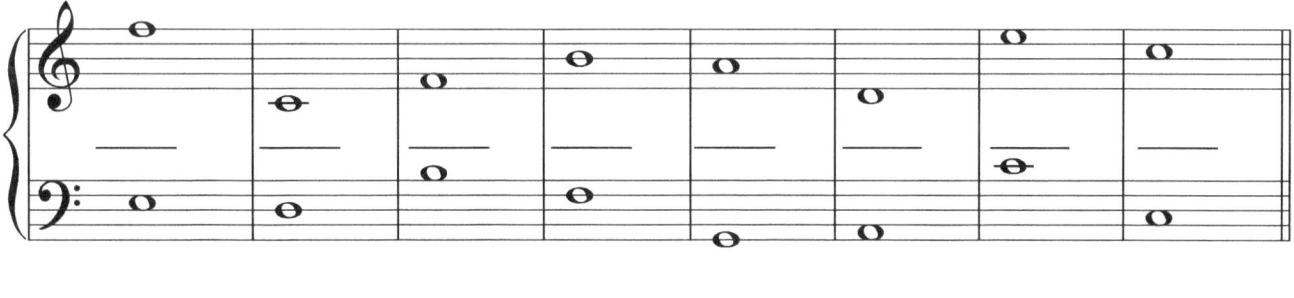

2. Write the following notes on the grand staff.

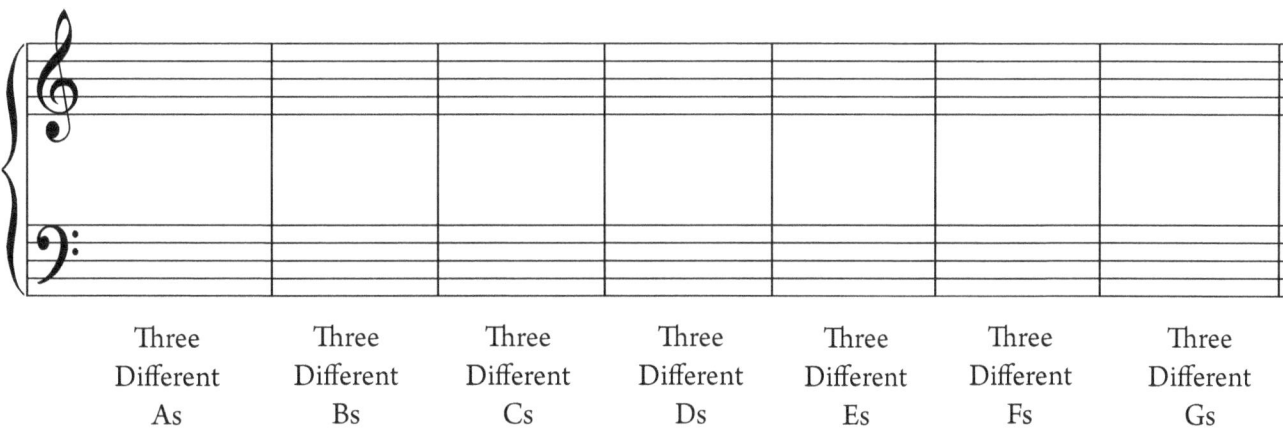

3. Name the notes and draw lines matching them with the keyboard.

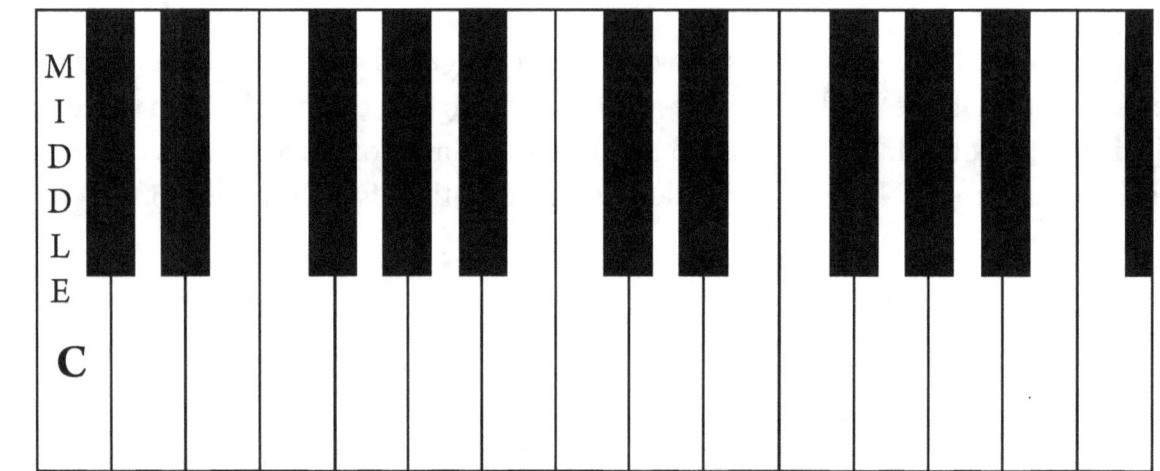

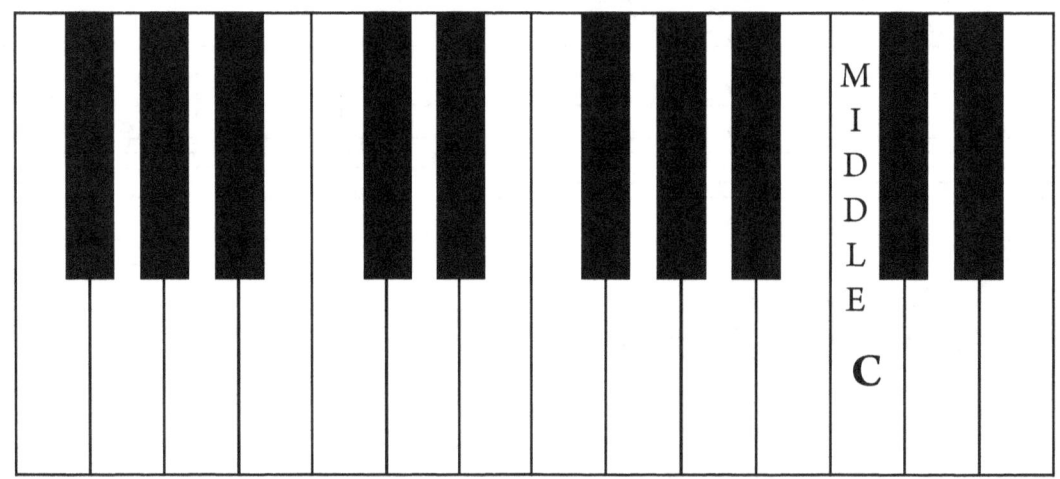

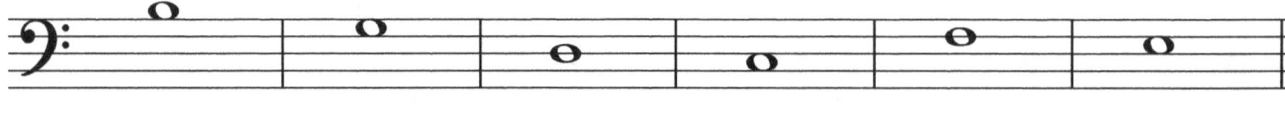

2
Time Values

In written music, where the note is placed on the staff indicates its pitch, but how the note looks indicates its duration, or how long you hold it. Every note has a value. It might be one beat, or four beats, or two beats.

The Whole Note

The note head of the ***whole note*** is hollow, and it has no stem. This note is easy to detect because it is the only one without a stem. The whole note receives four counts, and its duration is four beats.

Figure 2.1

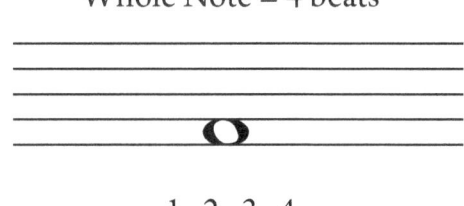

The Half Note

The ***half note*** is a hollow note with a stem attached. It receives two counts, and its duration is two beats.

Figure 2.2

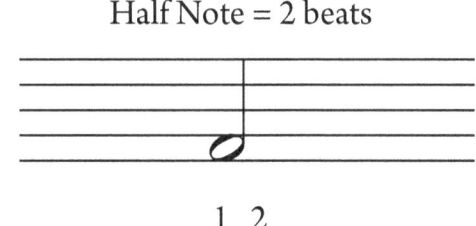

The Dotted Half Note

The ***dotted half note*** is a half note with a dot beside it. It receives three counts, and its duration is three beats. If the dotted note is in a space, the dot is placed in the same space as the note. If the dotted note is on a line, the dot is placed in the space above the note.

Figure 2.3

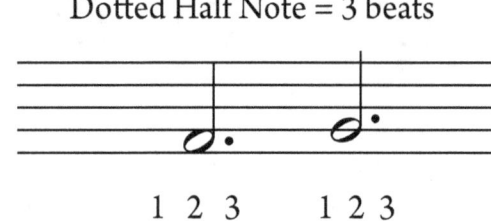

The Quarter Note

The ***quarter note*** has a solid note head and a stem attached. It receives one count, and its duration is one beat.

Figure 2.4

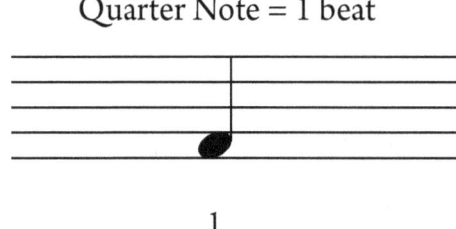

The Eighth Note

The ***eighth note*** looks similar to a quarter note, but its stem has an attached flag. When two or more eighth notes appear together, the flags are joined by a beam which connects the notes. If we divide the quarter note into two parts, we get eighth notes. Its duration is one half of a beat. Counting eighth notes is a little tougher than the other notes. If you have groupings of two eighth notes, you can count them "one and" with "one" for the first eighth note and "and" for the second eighth note.

Figure 2.5

Chart of Note Values - It's all relative!

Figure 2.6 shows that each note in the chart is twice the value of the one below it.

Figure 2.6

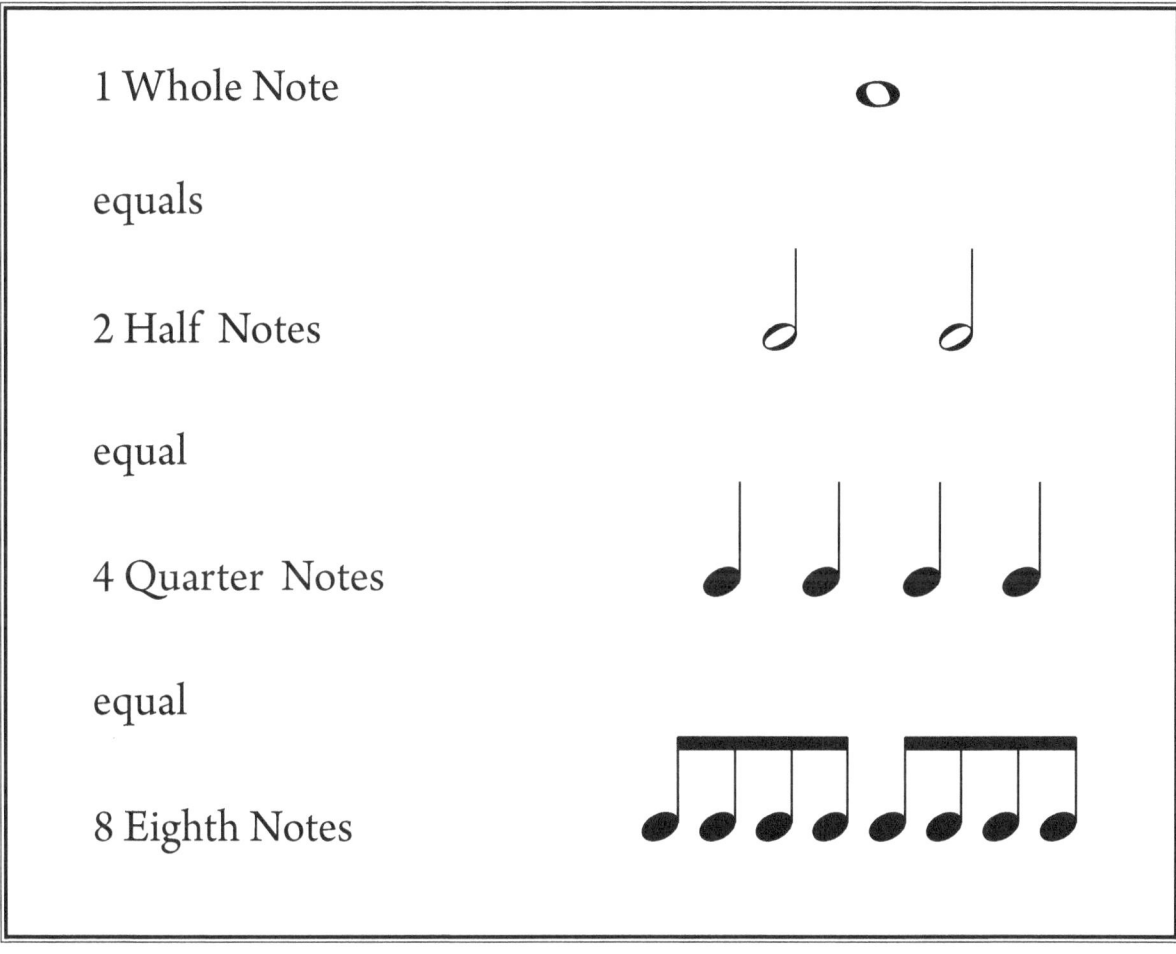

1. Name the type of note or notes.

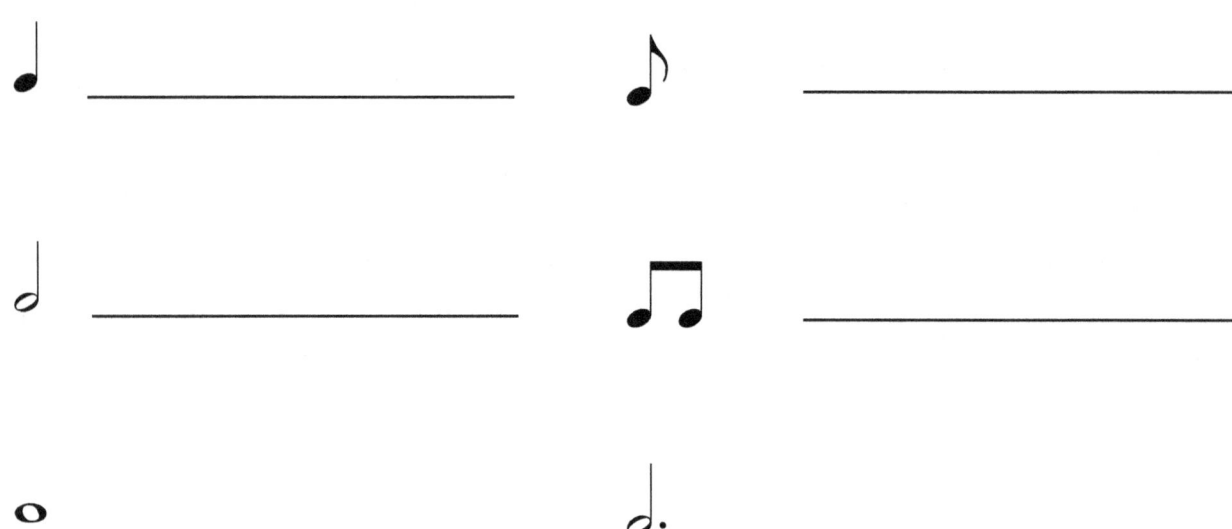

2. Write the number of beats the following notes receive.

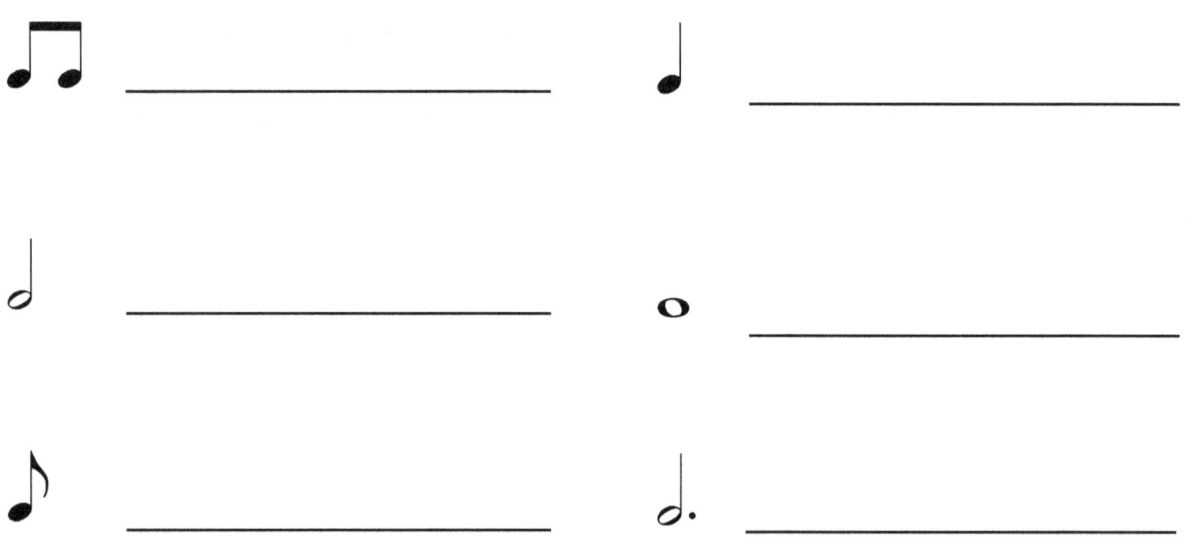

Time Values

3. Write one note which is equal to the following groups of notes.

Stems up? Stems down?

A note stem can go up, or a note stem can do down. For a note on the middle line, the stem may go in either direction. It usually depends on the other notes. If their stems are all going down the note on the middle line would go down. If they are going up, the note on the middle line would go up. Majority rules! However, if there is no clear majority, the stem of the note on the middle line can go in any direction you choose. Figure 2.9 shows notes on the third line with their stems going up and down. *The length of a stem is one octave or 8 notes.*

Figure 2.7

If a note is below the third line, its stem goes up. Be sure to place the stem on the right side of the note when it goes up. Figure 2.8 shows notes below the third line. The note on the third line has its stem going up. It follows the majority of the other notes whose stems also go up.

Figure 2.8

If a note is above the third line, its stem goes down. Be sure to place the stem on the left side of the note when it goes down. Figure 2.9 shows notes above the third line. The note on the third line has its stem going down. It follows the direction of the other notes whose stems go down.

Figure 2.9

1. Add stems to the following notes.

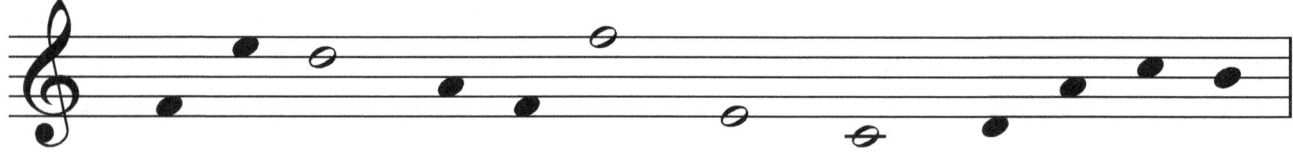

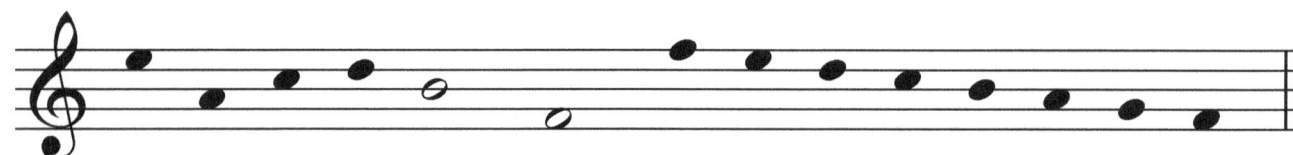

Rests

Silence is Golden

Mozart said: "Notes are silver, rests are golden." Silence in music is as important as sound. Silence in music is shown with **rests**. The name and length of the rests are the same as the name and length of the notes we studied in the last lesson.

The Whole Rest

A whole rest is four beats long and indicates four counts of silence. The whole rest hangs from the fourth line. It is also used to indicate one whole measure of rest.

Figure 2.10

Whole Rest = 4 beats

1 2 3 4

1. Draw a line of whole rests on the staff below.

The Half Rest

A half rest is two beats long and indicates two counts of silence. The half rest sits on the third line.

Figure 2.11

Half Rest = 2 beats

1 2

2. Draw a line of half rests on the staff below.

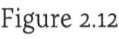

The Quarter Rest

A quarter rest is one beat long and indicates one count of silence. The quarter rest is tricky to draw. Study its shape.

Figure 2.12

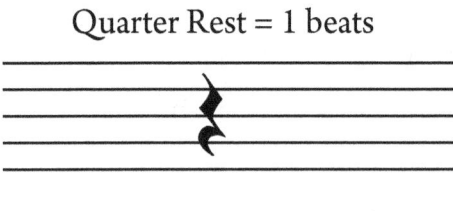

Quarter Rest = 1 beats

1

3. Draw a line of quarter rests on the staff below.

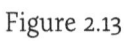

The Eighth Rest

An eighth rest is one half of a beat long and indicates one half of a count of silence. The eighth rest is placed in the middle of the staff and looks a little like the number 7.

Figure 2.13

Eighth Rest = ½ beat

4. Draw a line of eighth rests on the staff below.

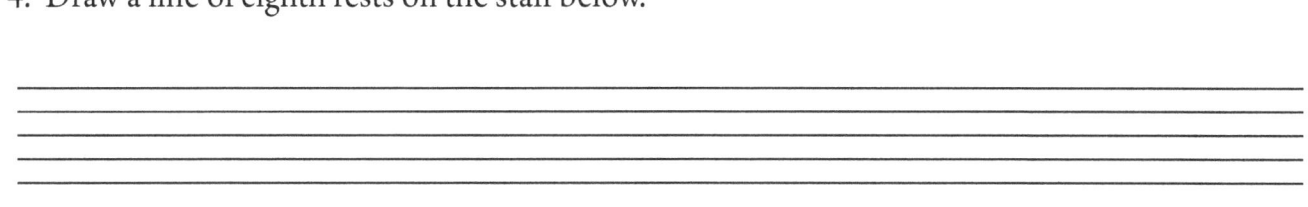

5. Draw one rest which is equal to the following notes.

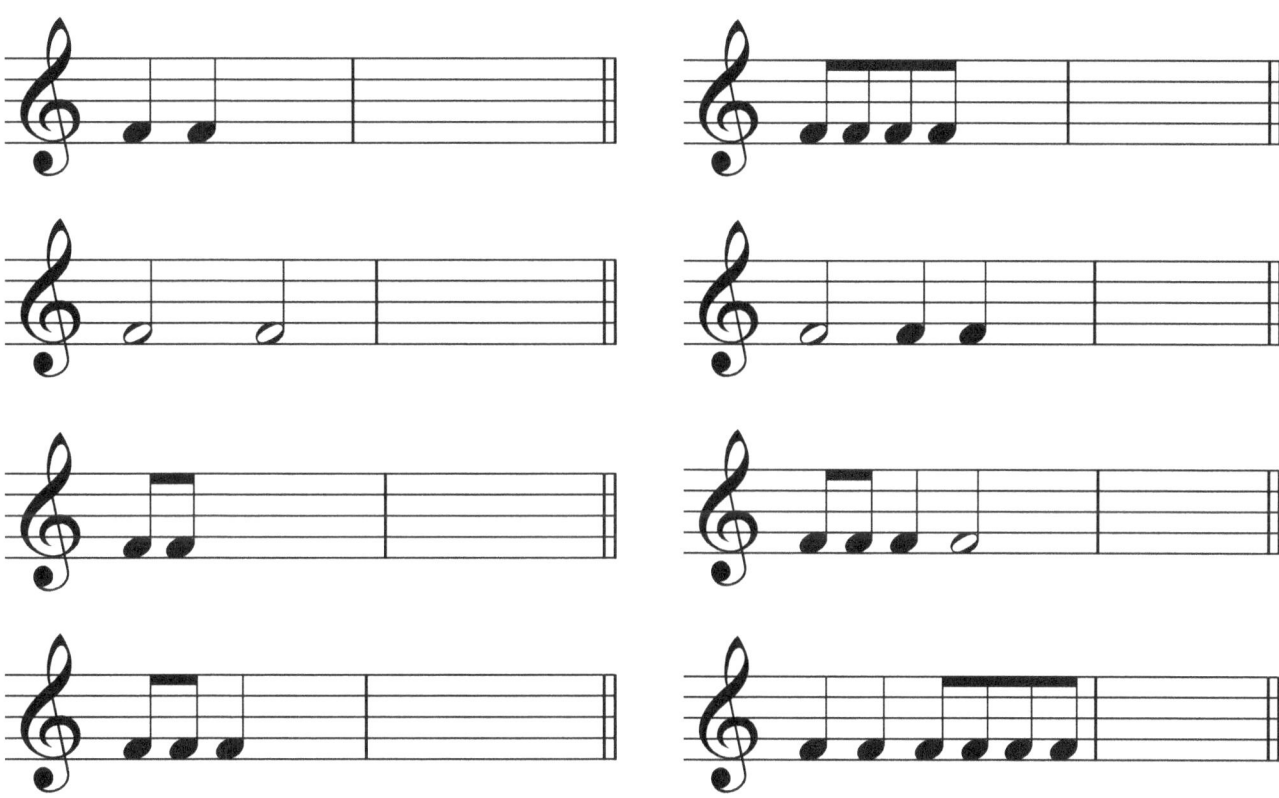

6. Name the following notes and write the number of beats each receives.

Name: ____   ____ ____   ____ ____ ____ ____   ____

Beats: ____   ____ ____   ____ ____ ____ ____   ____

Time Values

3
Accidentals

Whole Steps and Half Steps

In the music we are studying, the smallest distance between two notes is a ***half step***. On the keyboard, it is the distance from one key to the next closest key, black or white. This may mean a white key to a black key, a black key to a white key, or sometimes a white key to a white key. There is a natural semitone between the two white keys E and F and B and C. With these notes there is no black key involved.

A ***whole step*** is twice as big as a half step. A whole step consists of two keys with another key, black or white, between them.

Figure 3.1 shows a few half and whole steps on the keyboard. The reason we use the keyboard as a reference is because all the notes are arranged in a simple, easy to understand way. For example, a half step is two adjacent keys on the keyboard. We will learn that almost all white keys are natural notes and black keys are notes with accidentals.

Figure 3.1

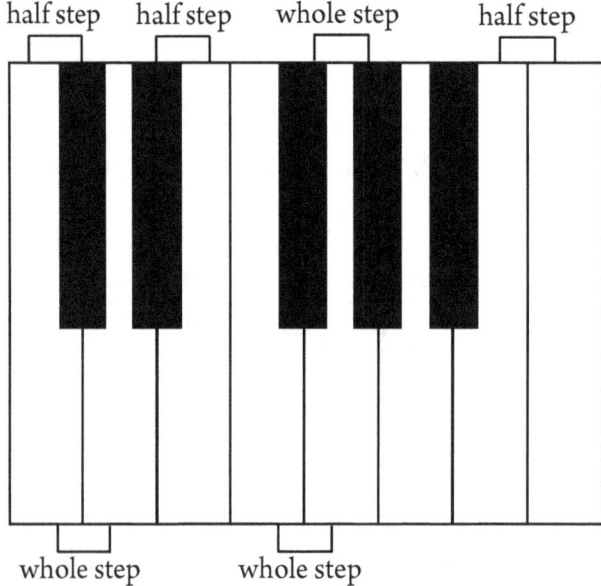

Pitch

The pitch (how high or low it sounds) of a note can be changed. We use symbols placed in front of the note called *accidentals* to raise or lower its pitch.

There are three types of accidentals: ***sharps, flats,*** and ***naturals***. These are shown in Figure 3.2.

Figure 3.2

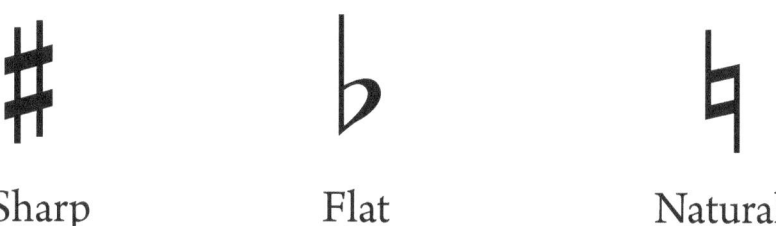

Accidentals are placed in front of the note that they alter. It is essential to place the accidental before the note, not after it. This can be confusing because when you talk about an accidental you say *"F sharp"*, but when you write it on the music score you write it sharp F. See Figure 3.3.

Figure 3.3

F sharp

When you write an accidental it should be written in the same space or on the same line as the note it is altering. Sharps, flats, and naturals have an open space that is placed in the same space or on the same line as the note they are altering.

The Sharp

A ***sharp*** is an accidental that raises the pitch of a note one half step. It looks like a number symbol. The square in the middle of the sharp should be centered on the same line or space as the note. A sharp sign can go in front of any note. Figure 3.4 contains the sharps located on the black keys of the keyboard.

Figure 3.4

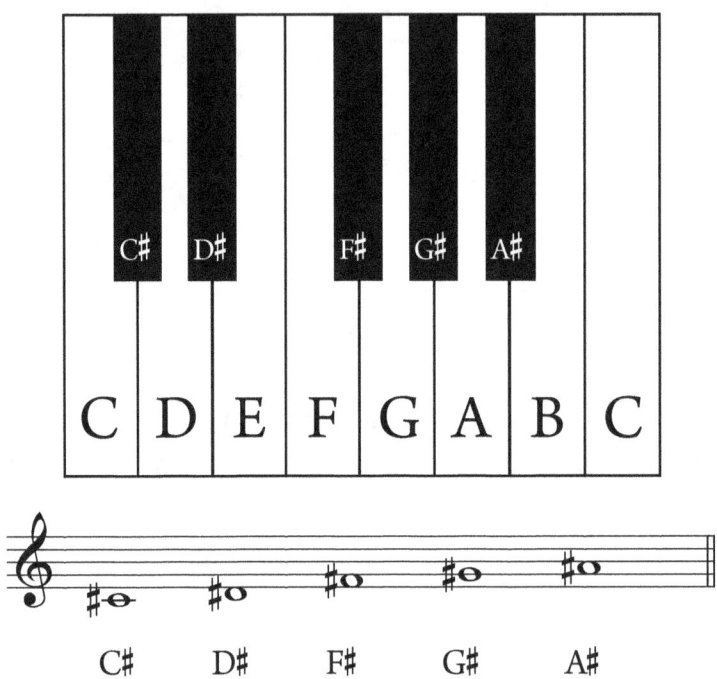

1. Write the following notes. Use whole notes.

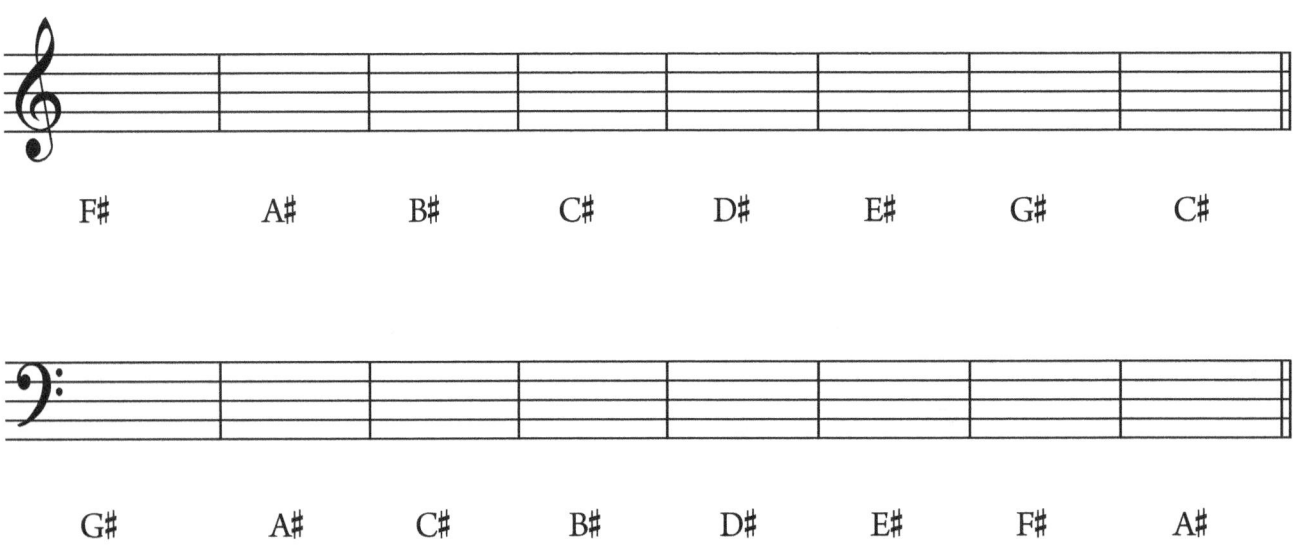

Accidentals

The Flat

A *flat* is an accidental that lowers the pitch of a note one half step. Flats look similar to the letter b. The open part of the flat sits directly on the same line or in the same space as the note that it is altering. Flat signs can be used on any note. Figure 3.5 contains the flats located on the black keys of the keyboard.

Figure 3.5

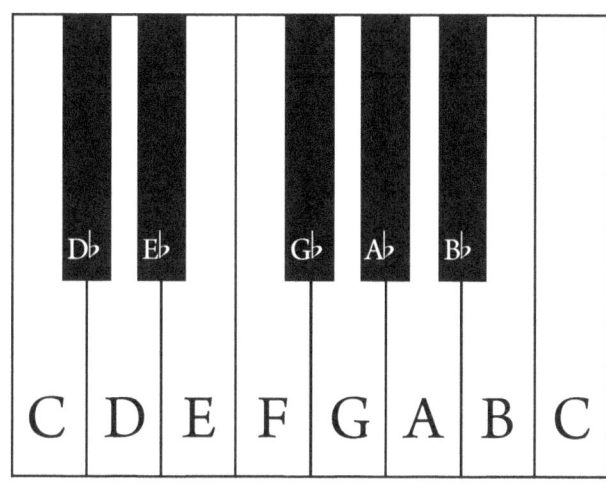

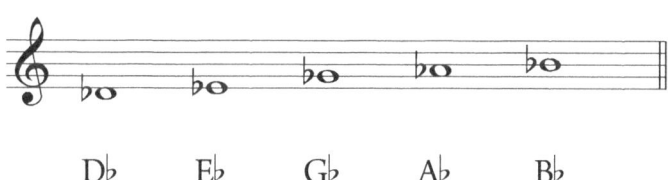

2. Write the following notes. Use whole notes.

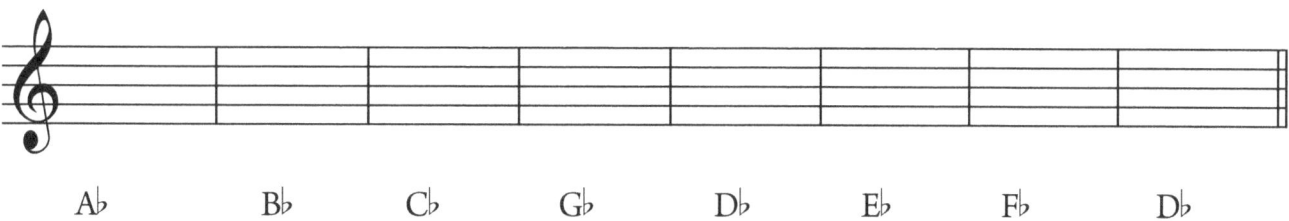

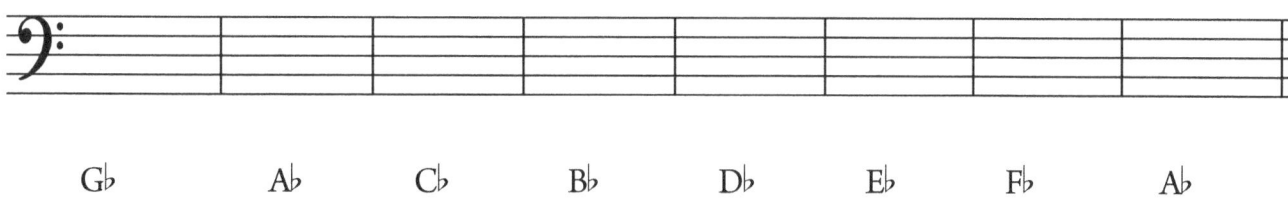

The Natural

A ***natural*** cancels a flat or sharp. If a note does not have an accidental, it is natural already. When there are no sharps or flats, the natural is not used. The natural can raise or lower the pitch of a note. If it cancels a flat, it raises a note. If it cancels a sharp, it lowers a note. A natural sign can be used on any note. Figure 3.6 contains naturals on the treble staff.

Figure 3.6

Enharmonic Notes

You can see that each black key can have two names. One sharp name and one flat name. When you have two notes that sound the same or have the same pitch, but different names, they are called ***enharmonic notes***. This also applies to some of the white keys. Figure 3.7 contains a keyboard showing enharmonic notes. Notice the enharmonic white keys.

Figure 3.7

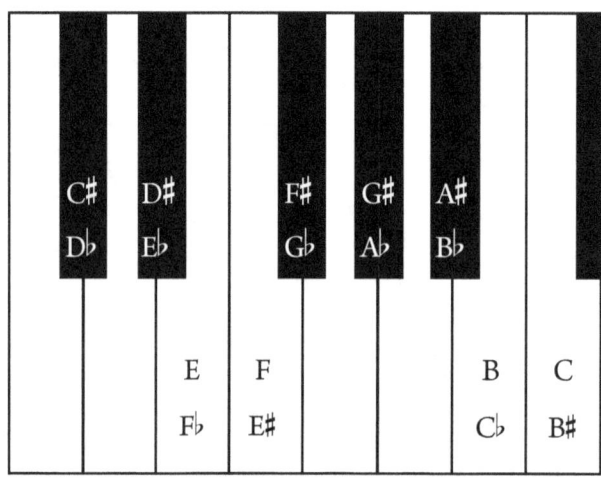

3. Draw lines matching the enharmonic notes.

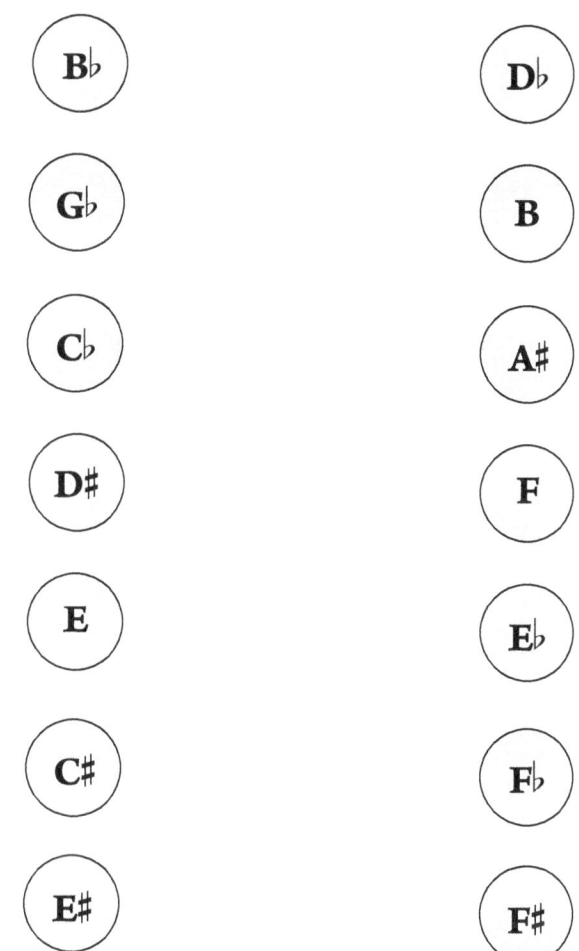

How to Use Accidentals

If an accidental occurs in a measure, it is good for the entire measure. However, a bar line cancels an accidental. In Figure 3.8 the B♭ lasts for the entire measure even though the flat sign is only written once. When the bar line occurs, the B is no longer flat.

Figure 3.8

When a note has the same letter name but is at a different pitch, the accidental is written again. In Figure 3.9 the F♯ an octave higher than the first one must be written again.

Figure 3.9

accidental written again

A note with an accidental tied over the bar line is not written again.

Figure 3.10

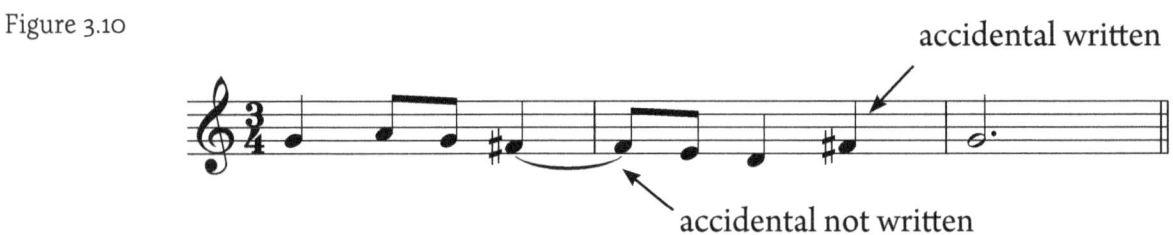

accidental written

accidental not written

Writing Half and Whole Steps

A half step can be written above or below a note using the same letter name for both notes.

F   F♯   G   G♯   A   A♭   C♯   C♮

A half step can be written above or below a note using different letter names for the notes.

G   A♭   B   C   A   G♯   F   E

A whole step is always written using two different letter names in alphabetical order.

G   A   B   C♯   A♭   G♭   C♯   D♯

1. Name the following notes.

2. Write these notes in both clefs. Use half notes.

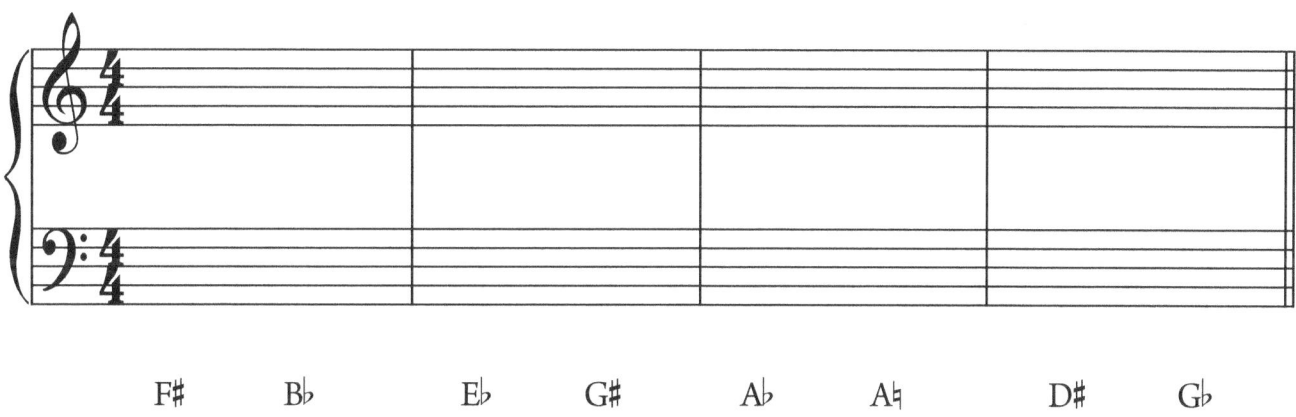

F# Bb Eb G# Ab A♮ D# Gb

3. Write these notes in both clefs. Use quarter notes.

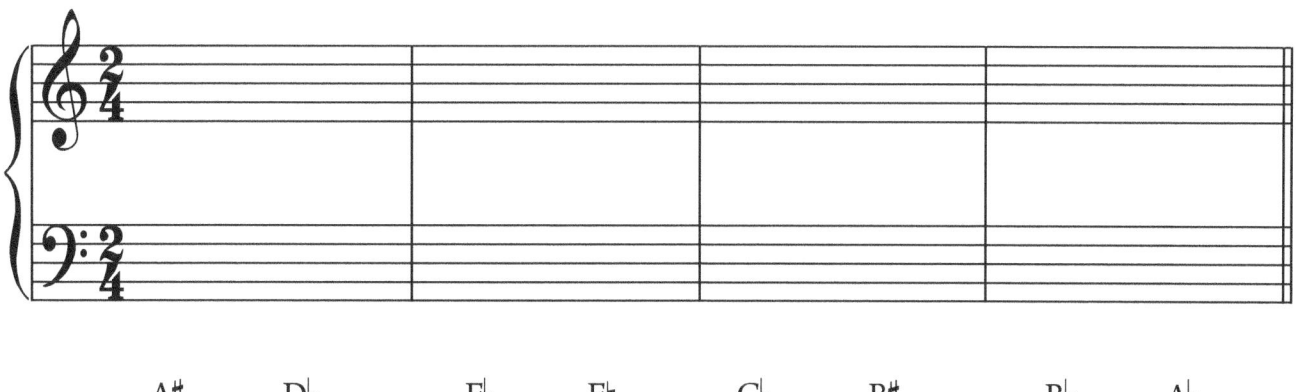

A# Db Fb F♮ Cb B# Bb Ab

4. Name each note and draw a line to the correct key on the keyboard.

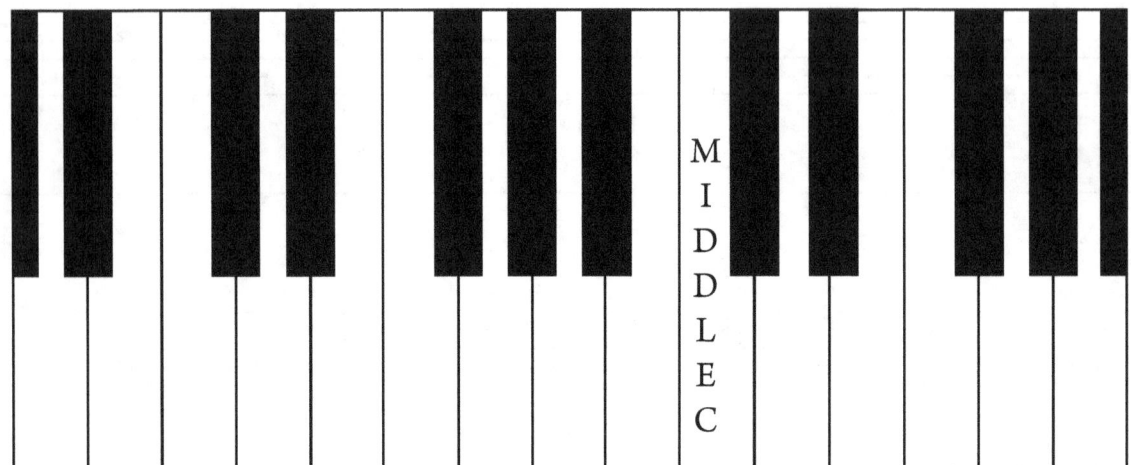

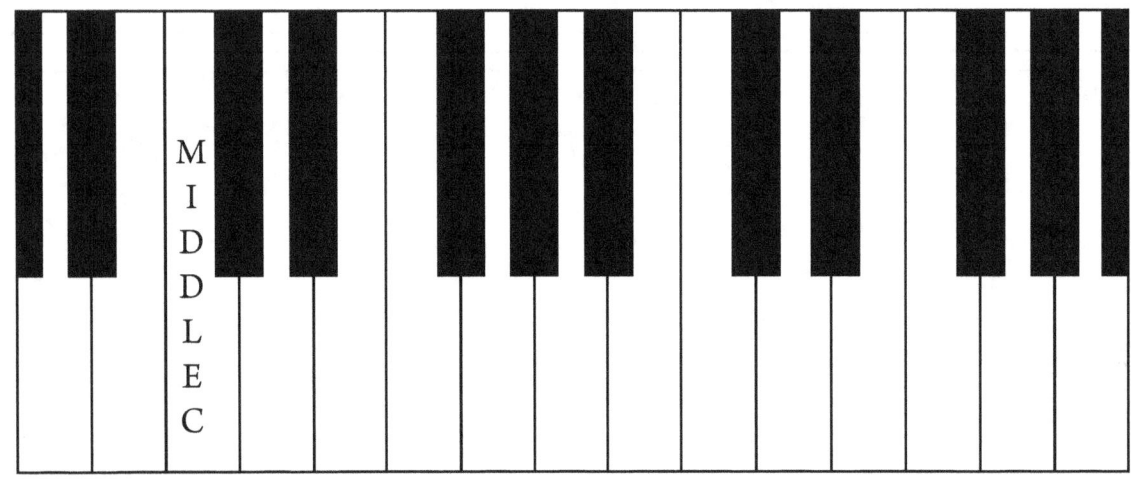

Accidentals

5. Describe the distance between the following pairs of notes as a half step or a whole step.

A _____ step   A _____ step   A _____ step   A _____ step

A _____ step   A _____ step   A _____ step   A _____ step

A _____ step   A _____ step   A _____ step   A _____ step

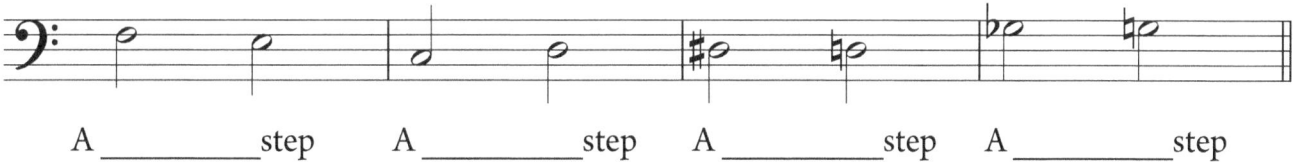

A _____ step   A _____ step   A _____ step   A _____ step

6. Write a note that is a half step above these notes.

7. Write a note that is a half step below the following notes.

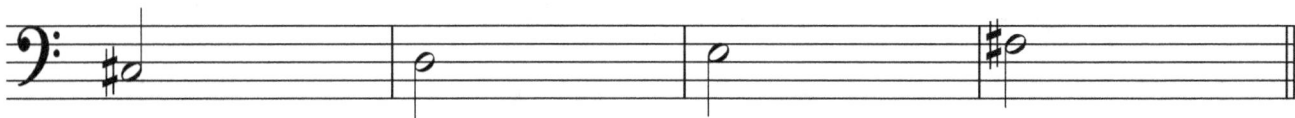

8. Write a note that is a whole step below the following notes.

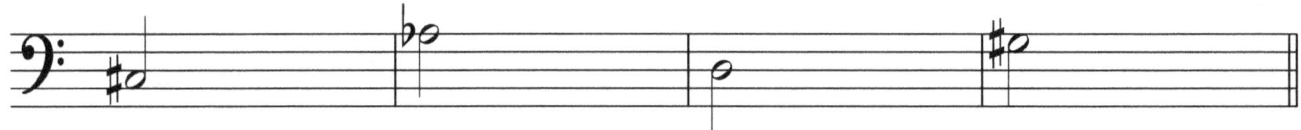

9. Write a note that is a whole step above the following notes.

More Accidentals

The Double Sharp

A ***double-sharp*** raises a note by a whole step or two half steps and looks like this: x . Double sharps are not very common but are sometimes required to spell a chord or interval correctly.

Figure 3.11

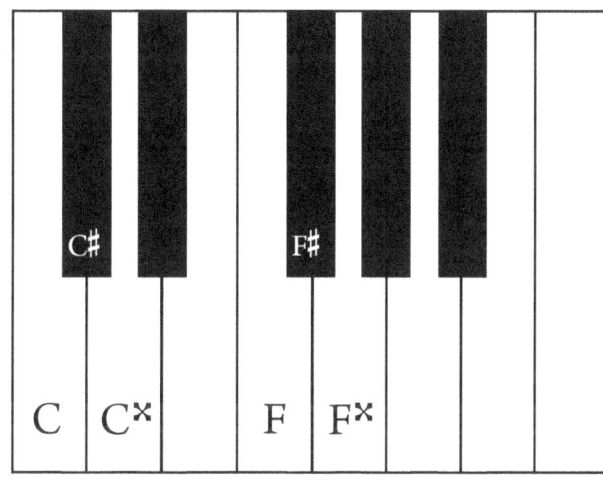

1. Apply double-sharps to each note

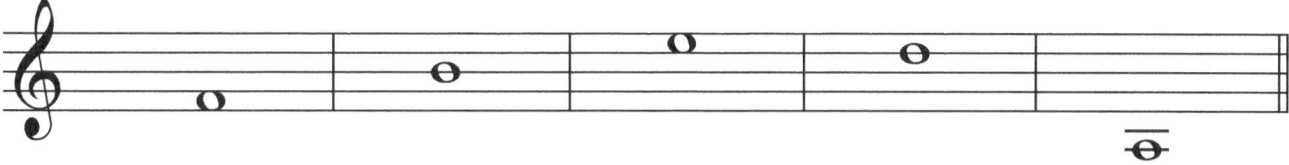

The Double Flat

A *double-flat* lowers a note by a whole step or two half steps and looks like this: ♭♭. Like double-sharps, double-flats occur rarely.

Figure 3.12

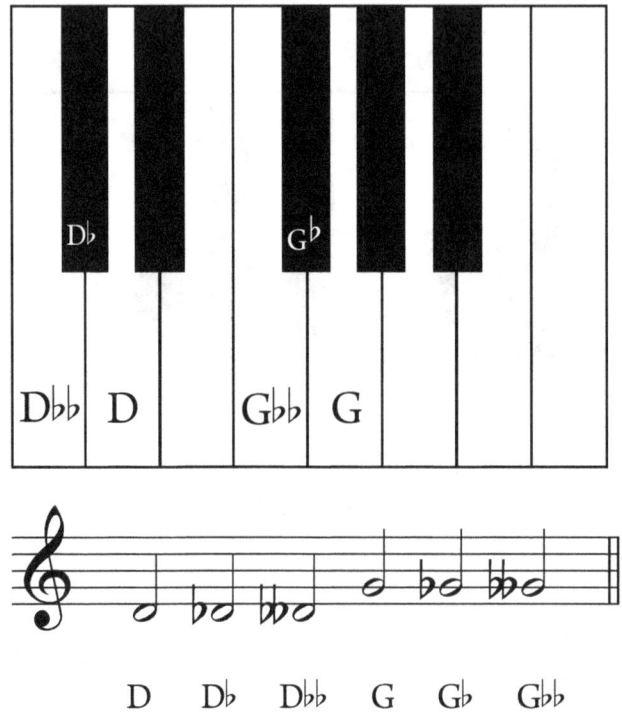

2. Apply double-flats to each note

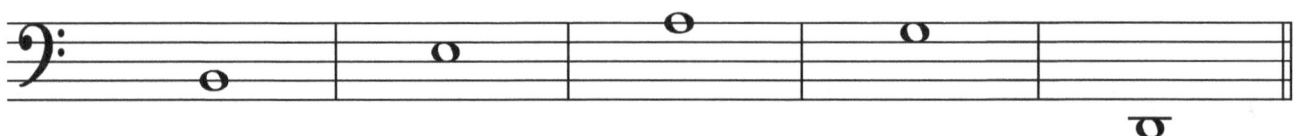

Enharmonic Equivalents

With the use of double-sharps and double-flats, every note except G♯/A♭ can have three names.

Figure 3.13 illustrates that the note G can be G, F𝄪, or A♭♭. These notes are considered *enharmonic equivalents*. This means that they are the same pitch but have different names, like F♯ and G♭.

Figure 3.13

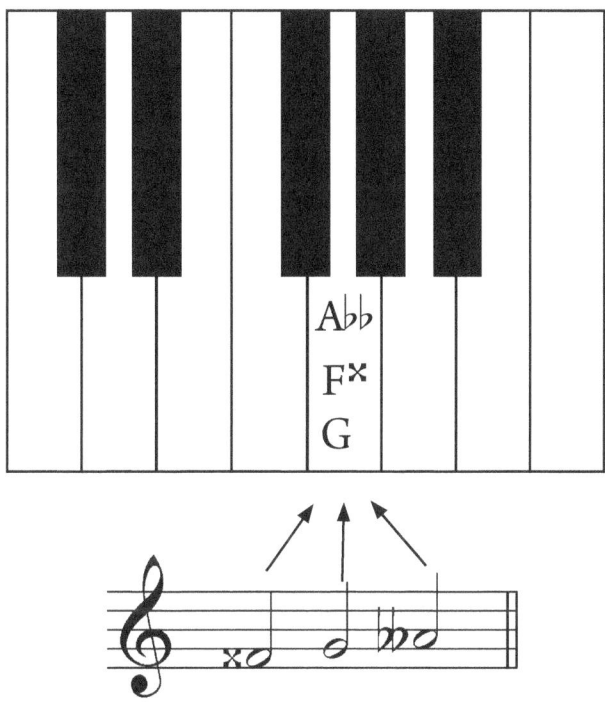

1. Write two enharmonic equivalents for each of the following notes.

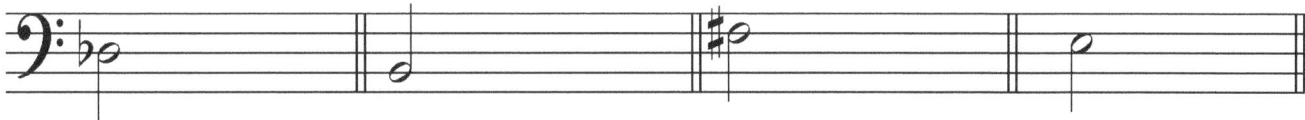

2. Rewrite the following melodies in the other clef without changing the pitch.

4
Major Scales

What is a scale?

Almost all music is based on a scale of some sort. Classical, country, rock, pop, hip-hop, jazz, and others are usually built in some way on some scale. The *major scale* is the most common scale.

A scale is a group of notes that occur in a specific order. The major scale is a series of eight notes (seven different pitches) that begin and end on the same note. The starting and ending note is called the ***tonic***. The major scale is named after the tonic. If the tonic is C, it is the C major scale. If the tonic is G, it's the G major scale. Figure 4.1 is the C major scale. It starts and ends on C and moves up every note in order. On the keyboard, it consists of all the white keys from C to C. It has seven different notes, C-D-E-F-G-A-B. The eighth note (C) is not counted as a new pitch because it is a repetition of the first note, but the major scale has eight notes in total. Each of these eight notes can be identified with a number with a small tent on top. This tent is called a caret ($\hat{1}$). When a number has a caret on top, it refers to ***scale degree***, which is just the number of the note as it occurs in the order of the scale. The first note is scale degree $\hat{1}$, the second is scale degree $\hat{2}$, etc.

Figure 4.1

Notice that the scale in Figure 4.1 goes from C to C, a distance of eight notes. This is the interval of an ***octave***. From one letter name to the next same letter name, up or down, is an octave. This scale is the C major scale, one octave, ascending.

Building the Major Scale

The major scale is constructed from a specific pattern of whole steps and half steps. All major scales follow the same pattern. Remember that a half step is the smallest distance between two notes. On the piano, it is the distance from any key to the next closest key.

If we examine the C major scale again (Figure 4.2) we can see a pattern of whole and half steps that happens in all major scales. Under the scale you can see whole, whole, half, whole, whole, whole, half. This is the same order for all major scales (WWHWWWH).

The scale can also be divided into two four note sections called tetrachords. Each tetrachord is WWH with a W between the two (WWH W WWH).

Figure 4.2

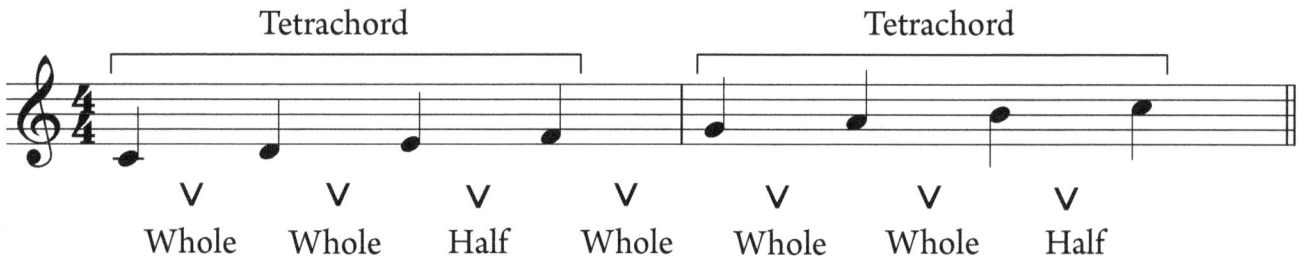

1. Mark the whole steps (W) and half steps (H) under the following scales. Above each one, label each scale degree with a number and caret. Mark the tonic note with a T.

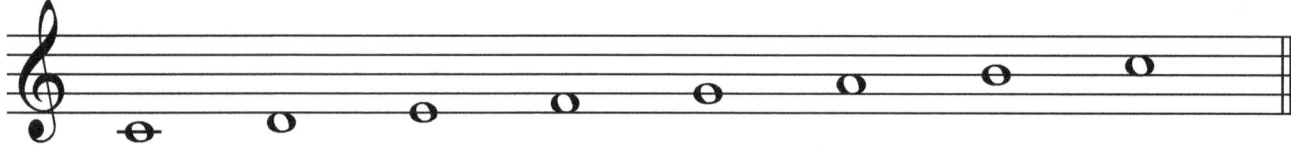

Major Scales

Scale degree one (1̂) is called the tonic. This is the most important note of any scale. The second most important note is scale degree five (5̂). This note is called the **dominant**. Major scales are usually written and played ascending and descending as in Figure 4.3. Here, the tonic and dominant notes are labeled with T and D.

Figure 4.3

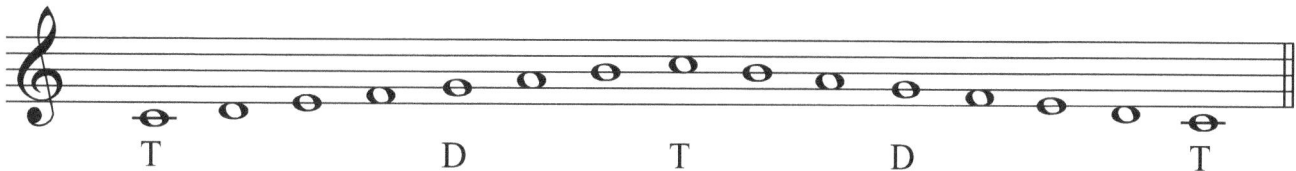

2. Write the C major scale ascending and descending using half notes. Mark the tonic (T) and dominant (D) notes.

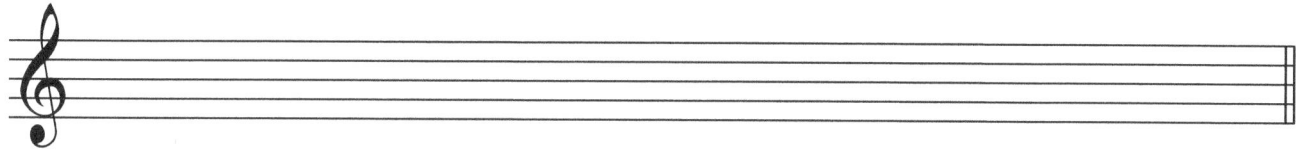

3. Write the C major scale ascending and descending using quarter notes. Mark the tonic (T) and dominant (D) notes.

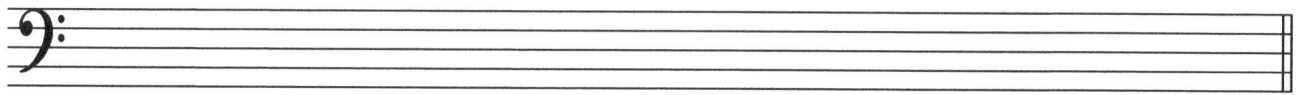

The G Major Scale

Using the same pattern of whole and half steps we can write major scales starting on any note. If we write a major scale starting on G, we must alter one note to get the correct pattern of whole and half steps (WWHWWWH). Figure 4.4 shows that an F♯ is necessary to get the correct pattern of whole and half steps. We need an F♯ between $\hat{7}$ and $\hat{8}$ to have a half step, which also gives us the whole step we need between $\hat{6}$ and $\hat{7}$. The G major scale contains one sharp, F♯.

Figure 4.4

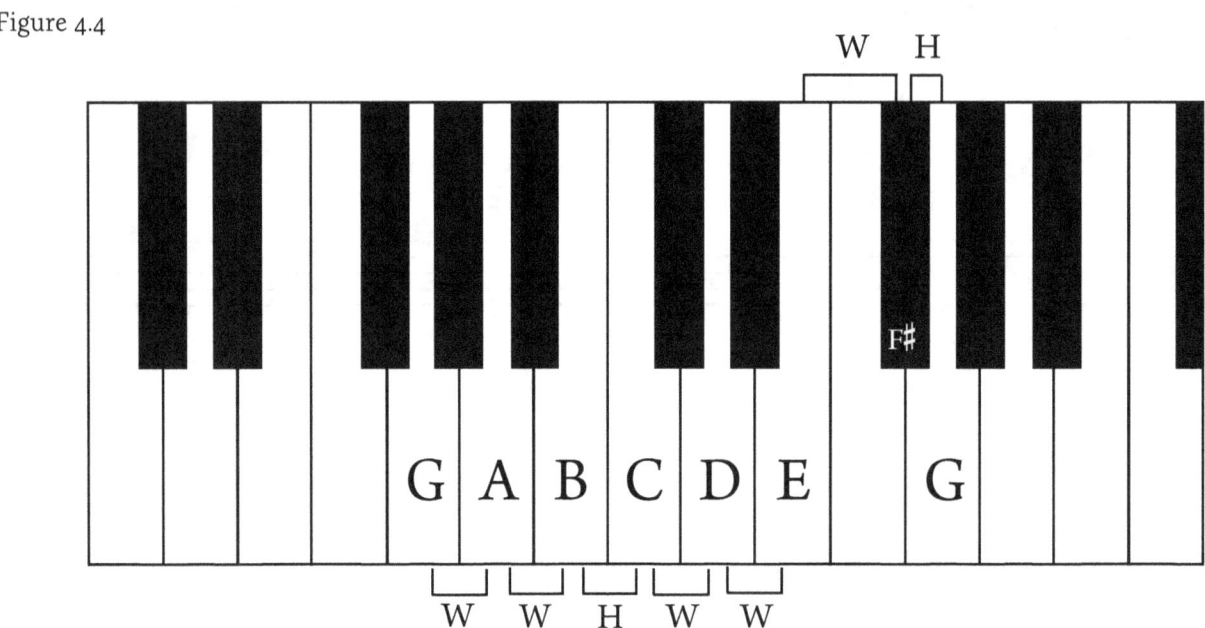

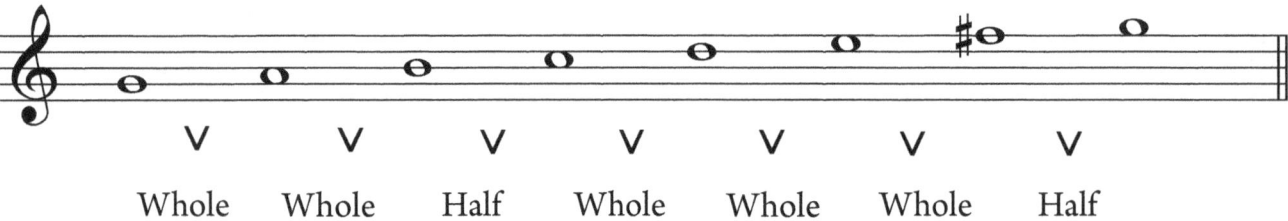

4. Write the G major scale ascending and descending using whole notes. Mark the tonic (T) and dominant (D) notes.

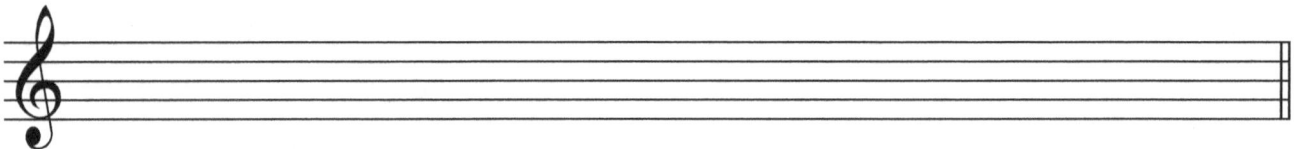

The F Major Scale

For the F major scale, a B♭ is required to have a half step between $\hat{3}$ and $\hat{4}$. The B♭ also creates the required whole step between $\hat{4}$ and $\hat{5}$. E to F is a natural half step between $\hat{7}$ and $\hat{8}$ so they do not need to be altered. This is shown in Figure 4.5. The F major scale has one flat, B♭.

Figure 4.5

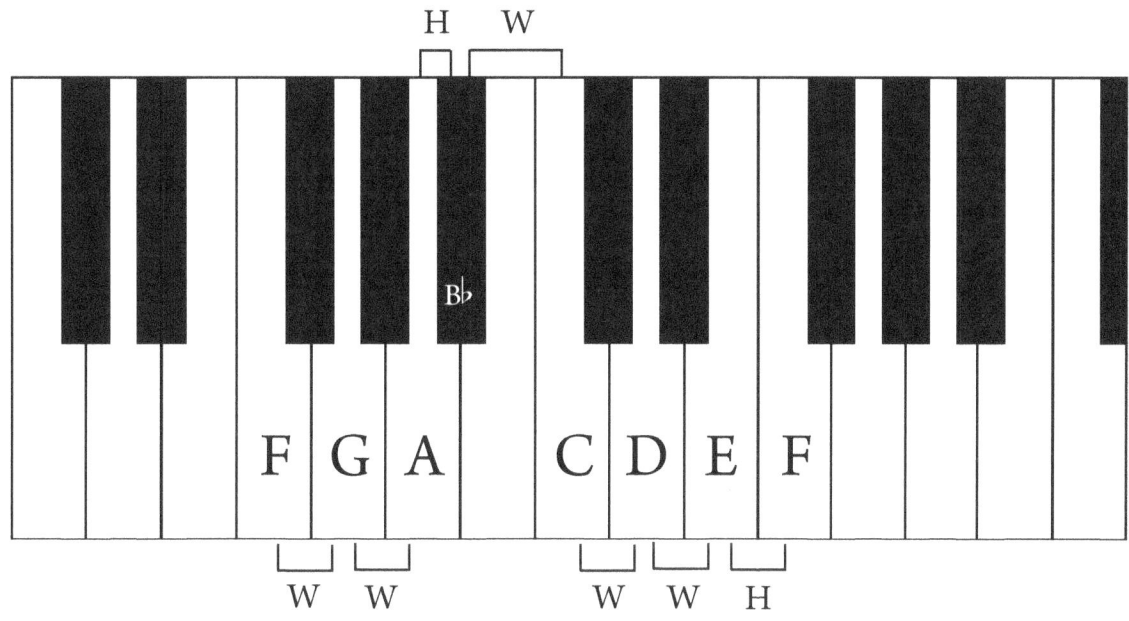

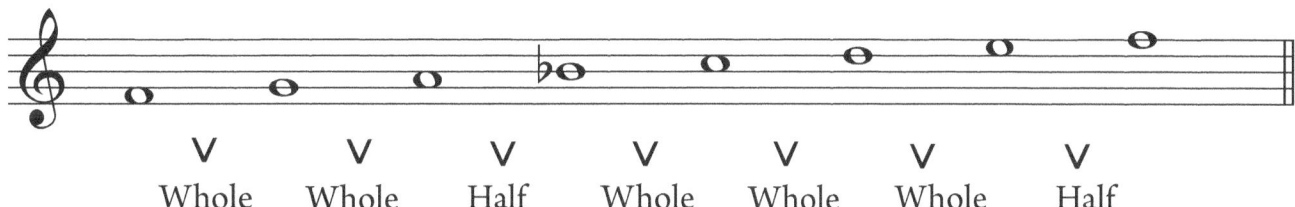

5. Write the F major scale ascending and descending using whole notes. Mark the tonic (T) and dominant (D) notes.

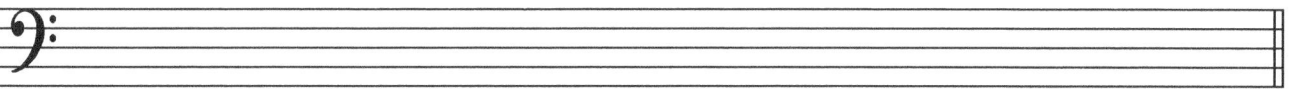

6. Write the following scales ascending and descending according to the instructions.

C major in whole notes

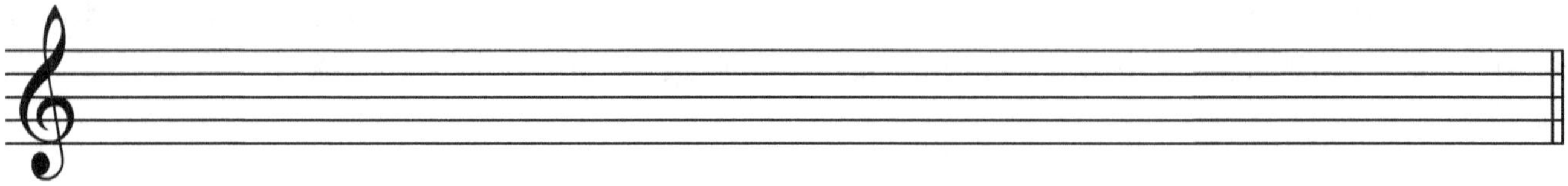

F major in quarter notes

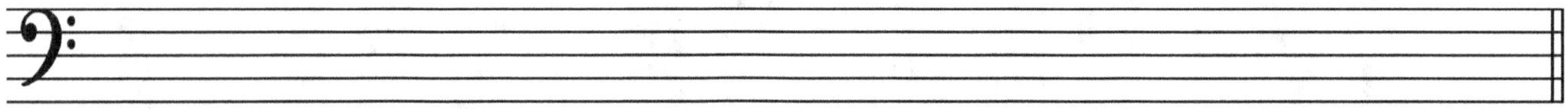

G major in whole notes

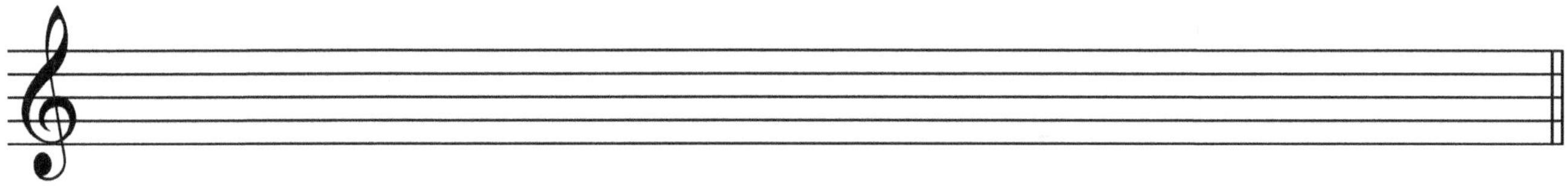

C major in half notes

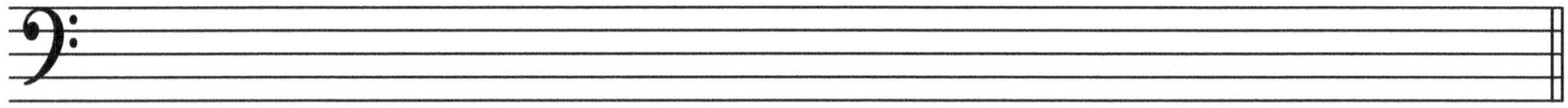

F major in whole notes

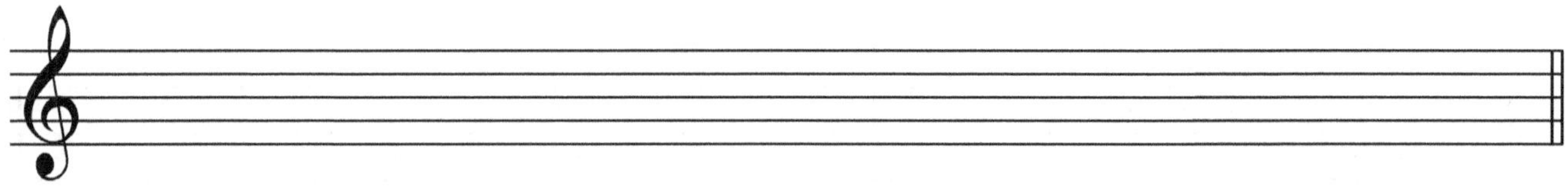

7. The following notes are all from the scale of C major. Label each with a scale degree number ($\hat{1}, \hat{2}, \hat{3}$, etc) above each note. Label the tonic (T) and dominant (D) notes.

8. The following notes are all from the scale of F major. Label each with a scale degree number ($\hat{1}, \hat{2}, \hat{3}$, etc) above each note. Label the tonic (T) and dominant (D) notes.

If you build a major scale starting on D you get a scale with 2 sharps. F♯ and C♯

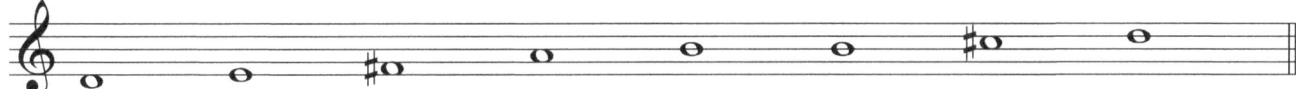

If you build a major scale starting on A you get a scale with 3 sharps. F♯, C♯, and G♯

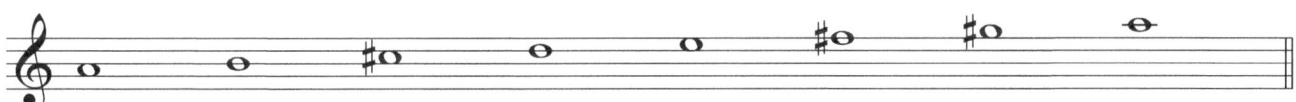

If you build a major scale starting on E you get a scale with 4 sharps. F♯, C♯, G♯, and D♯

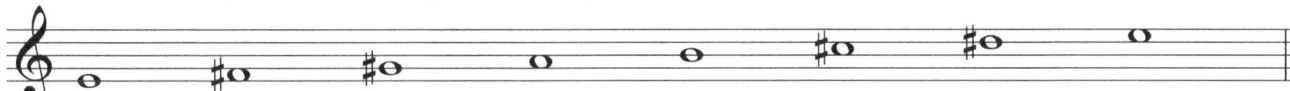

If you build a major scale starting on B♭ you get a scale with 2 flats. B♭ and E♭

If you build a major scale starting on E♭ you get a scale with 3 flats. B♭, E♭, and A♭

If you build a major scale starting on A♭ you get a scale with 4 flats. B♭, E♭, A♭, and D♭

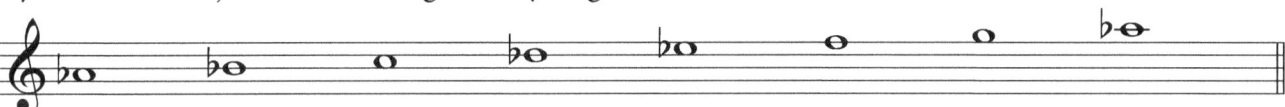

Key Signatures

The ***key signature*** is an essential element in the organization of music. Instead of writing all the accidentals throughout a piece of music, composers place them all at the beginning of the staff. The key signature contains the sharps and flats in a piece of music. It tells us the scale the music is based on, and often the starting and ending notes. It gives us the flats or sharps in a composition. Key signatures never contain both sharps and flats. They will contain all sharps or all flats or nothing at all.

When writing scales, we raise or lower certain notes with accidentals to get the correct pattern of whole and half steps. Every key signature has the same name as the scale. The key of G major will have the same accidentals as the G major scale (F♯). The key of F major will have the same accidentals as the F major scale (B♭).

The key signature at the beginning of a piece applies to the entire composition unless the composer changes it or adds accidentals. Figure 4.6 shows the F major scale first with accidentals, and then with a key signature. The key signature of F major is one flat (B♭). When it is placed at the beginning of the music there is no need to add B♭'s to the music. The key signature makes all the Bs flat automatically.

Figure 4.6

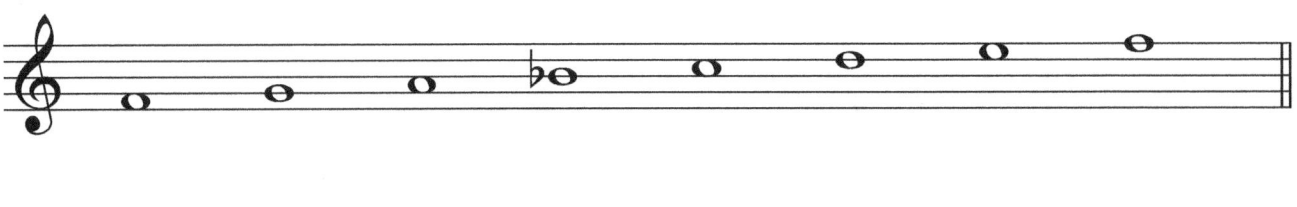

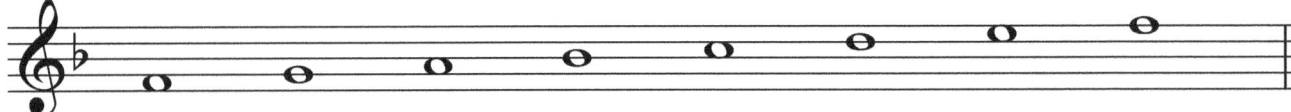

Major Scales

Circle of Fifths

Figure 4.7

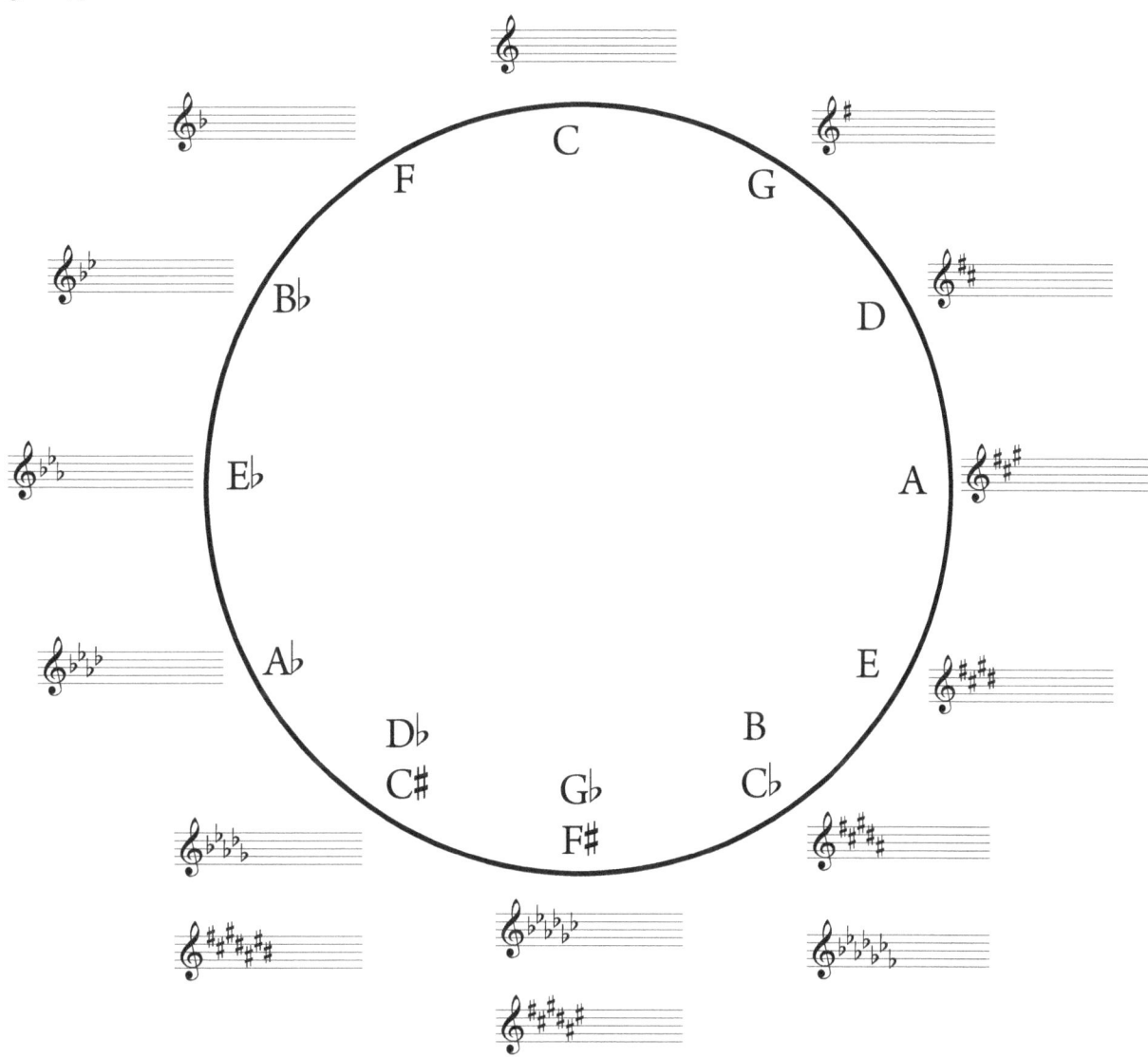

The *circle of 5ths* (Figure 4.7), is a chart organizing all of the keys into a system that can be used to relate them to one another. At the top, is the key of C major, which has no sharps or flats in its key signature. Each stop on the circle moving clockwise from C is a key with one more sharp than the previous key. Each stop moving counter-clockwise from C is a key with one more flat than the previous key. Each note is a perfect fifth away from another.

Sharp Keys

C major has no sharps or flats.

Figure 4.8 is a list of the sharp keys and where they are located on the staff. The order of sharps is **F C G D A E B**.

Here is a saying to help you remember the order of sharps:

Fat **C**ats **G**o **D**own **A**lleys **E**ating **B**irds.

Figure 4.8

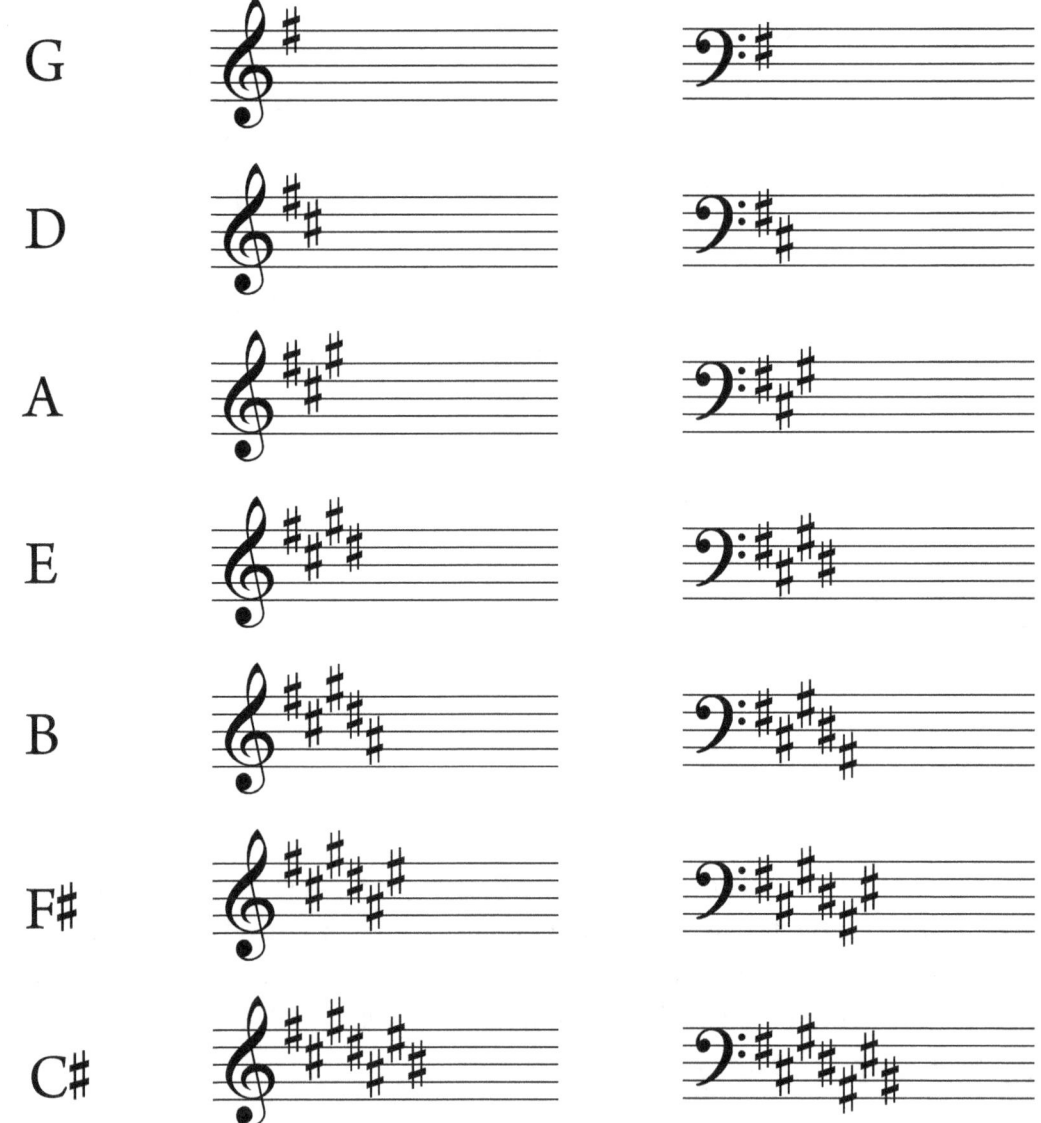

Major Scales

Flat Keys

Flats within a key signature always follow a specific order.

Figure 4.9 is a list of the flat keys and where they are located on the staff. The order of flats is **B E A D G C F**.

Here is a saying to help you remember the order of flats:

Big **E**lephants **A**lways **D**rive **G**olf **C**arts **F**ast

Figure 4.9

1. Name the following major keys and name the sharp and flats in each key.

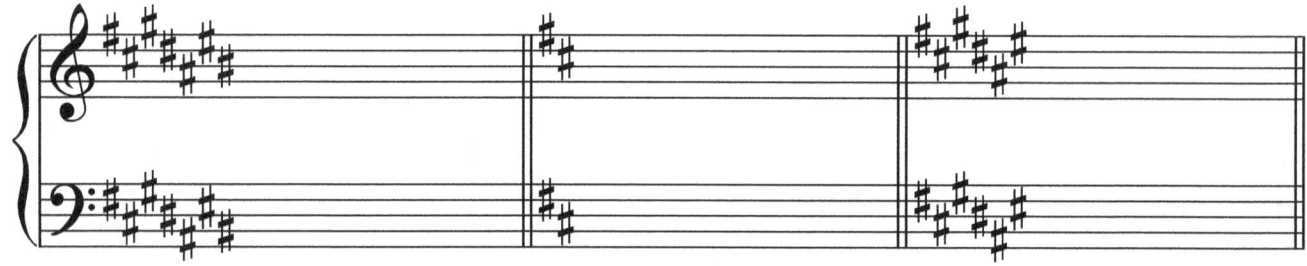

Key: _____   _____   _____

Sharps: _____   _____   _____

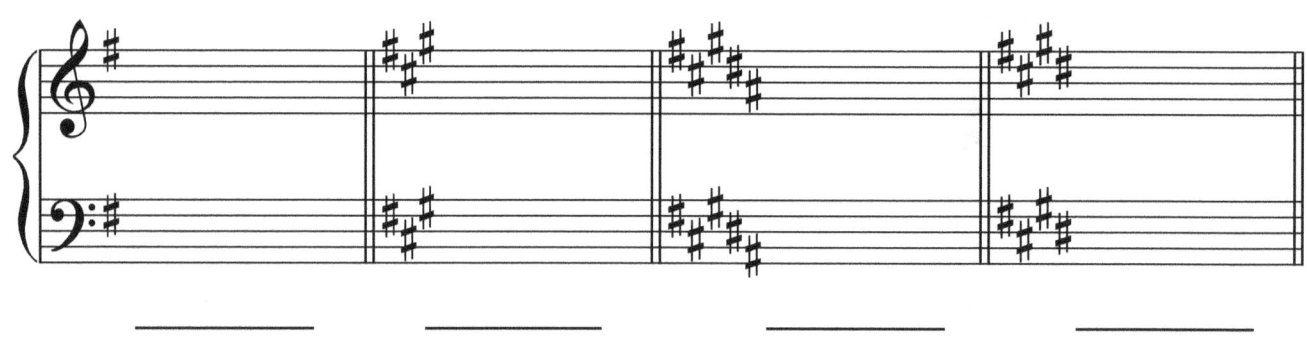

_____   _____   _____   _____

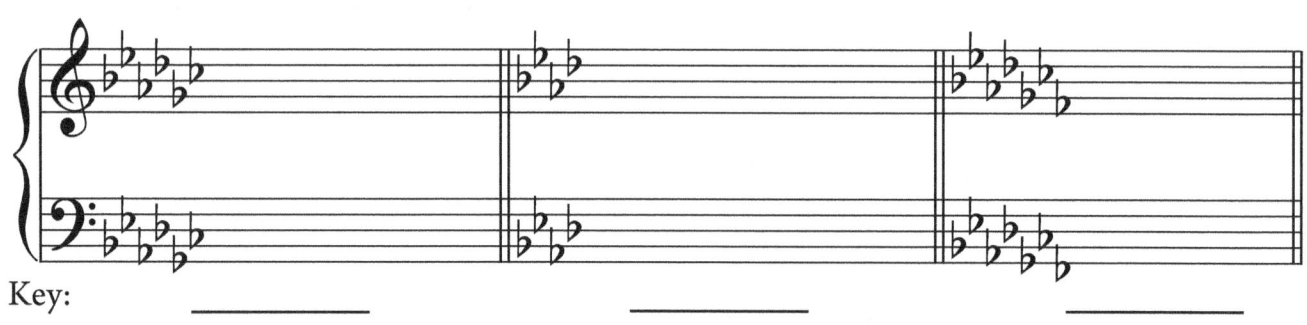

Key: _____   _____   _____

Flats: _____   _____   _____

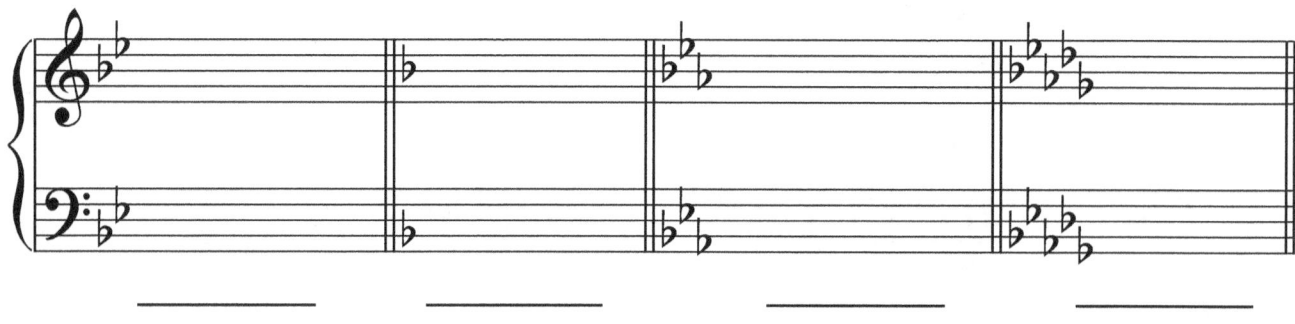

_____   _____   _____   _____

Technical Names for Scale Degrees.

Every scale degree has a technical name. These are the names for each scale degree.

$\hat{1}$ Tonic
$\hat{2}$ Supertonic
$\hat{3}$ Mediant
$\hat{4}$ Subdominant
$\hat{5}$ Dominant
$\hat{6}$ Submediant
$\hat{7}$ Leading tone

1. Write the following major key signatures and notes on the grand staves.

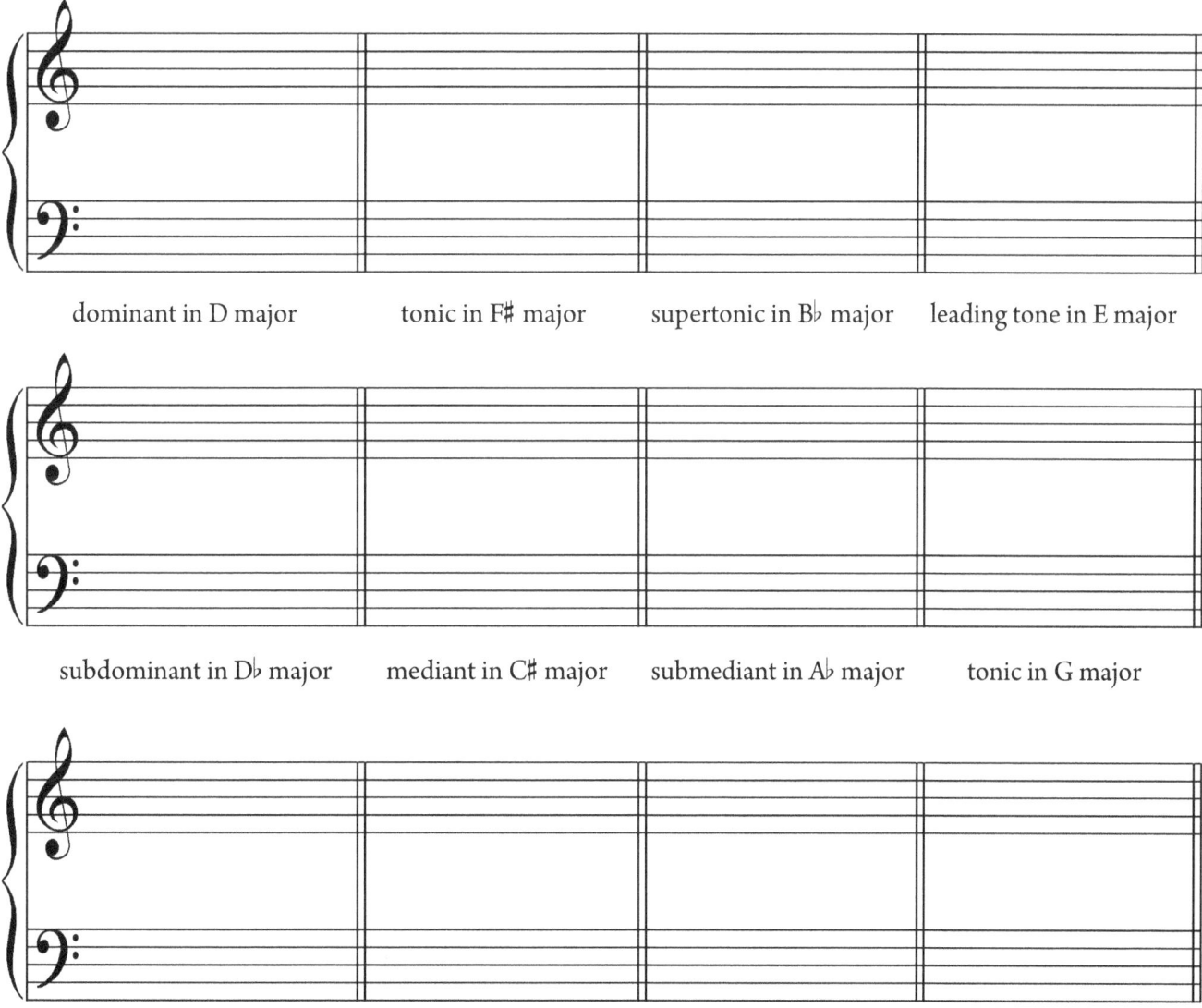

dominant in D major   tonic in F♯ major   supertonic in B♭ major   leading tone in E major

subdominant in D♭ major   mediant in C♯ major   submediant in A♭ major   tonic in G major

leading tone in B major   tonic in G♭ major   supertonic in E♭ major   dominant in A major

2. Write the following scales ascending and descending in wholes notes using a key signature for each.

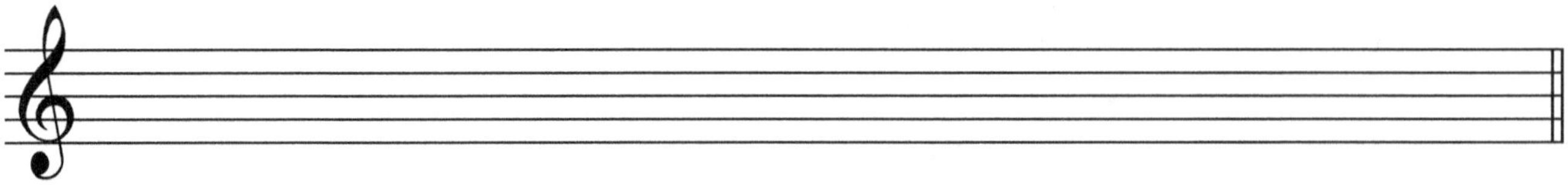

E major

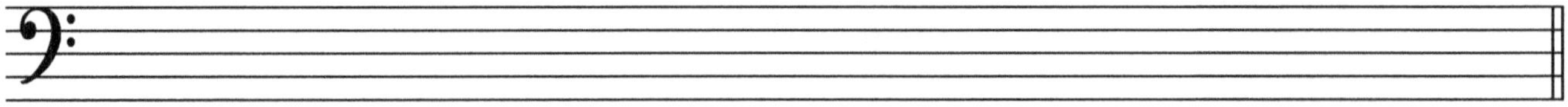

A♭ major

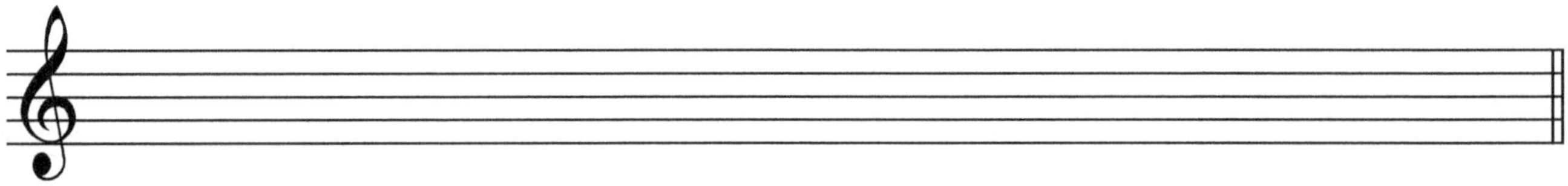

D♭ major

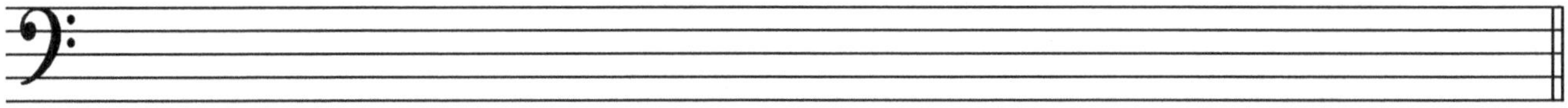

G major

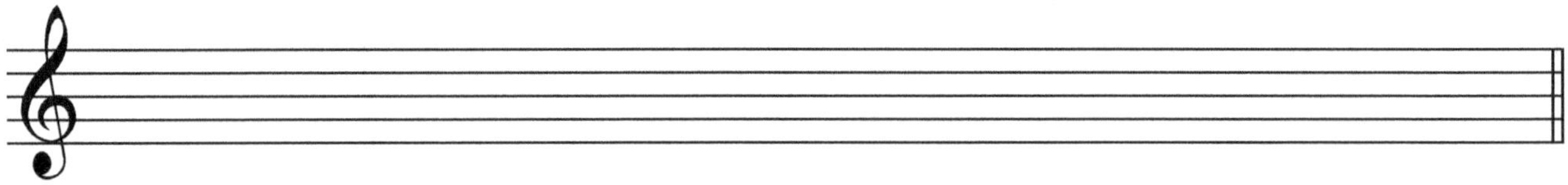

B major

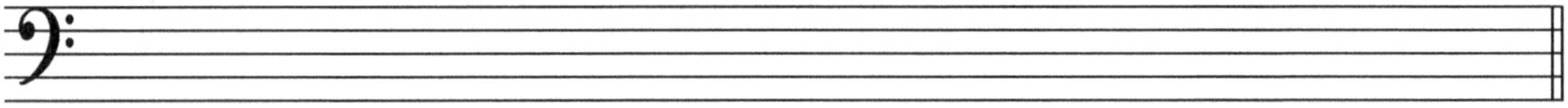

F major

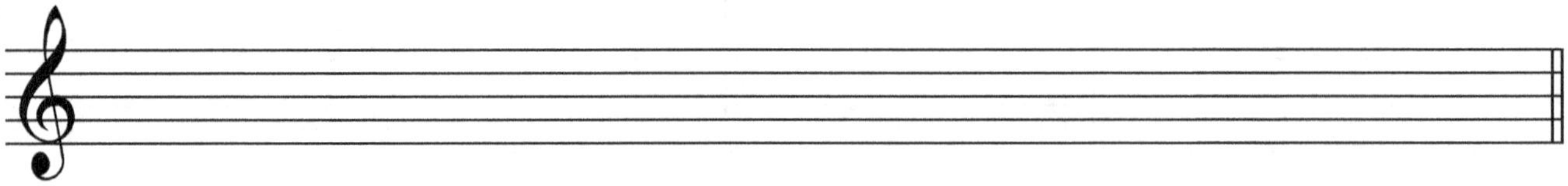

D major

Major Scales

3. Add clefs and accidentals to create the following major scales.

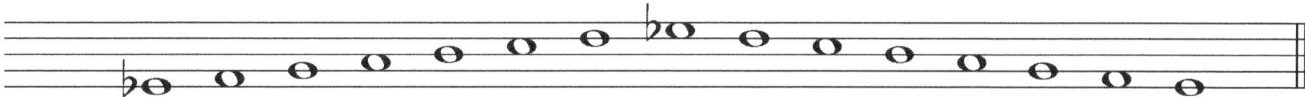

E♭ major

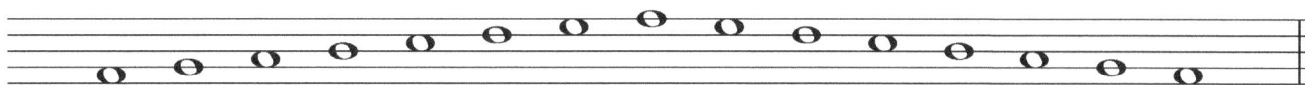

A major

F♯ major

B♭ major

C♯ major

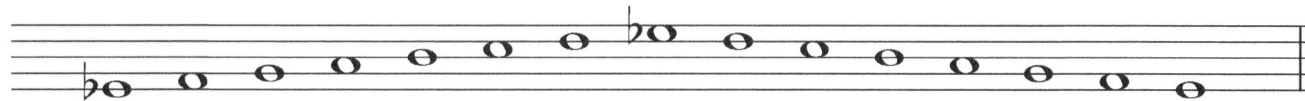

G♭ major

B major

4. Write the following scales ascending and descending using half notes.

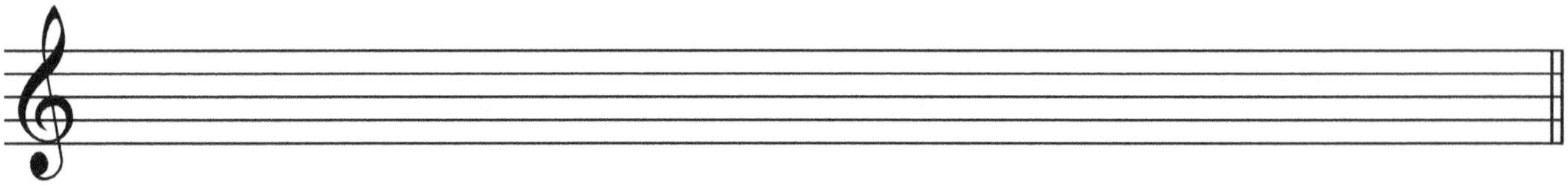

The major scale with 5 flats

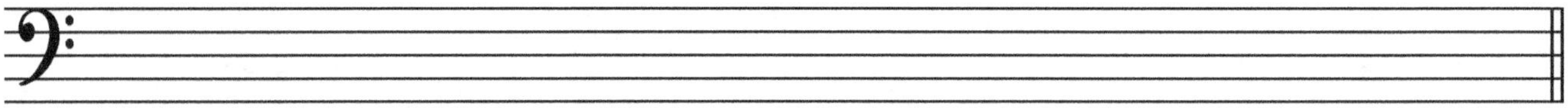

The major scale with D as the leading tone

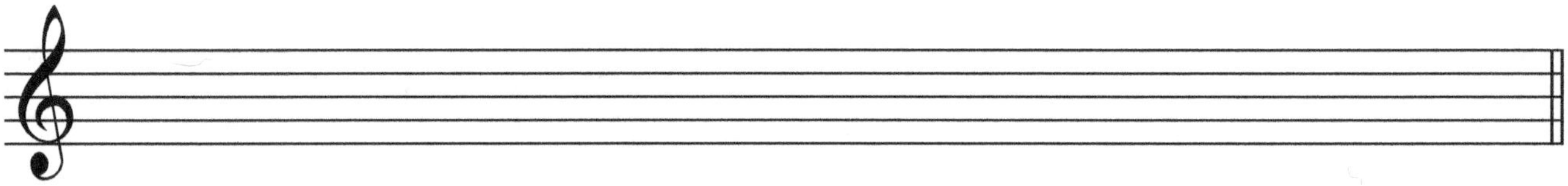

The major scale with C♯ as the supertonic

The major scale with D♯ as the submediant

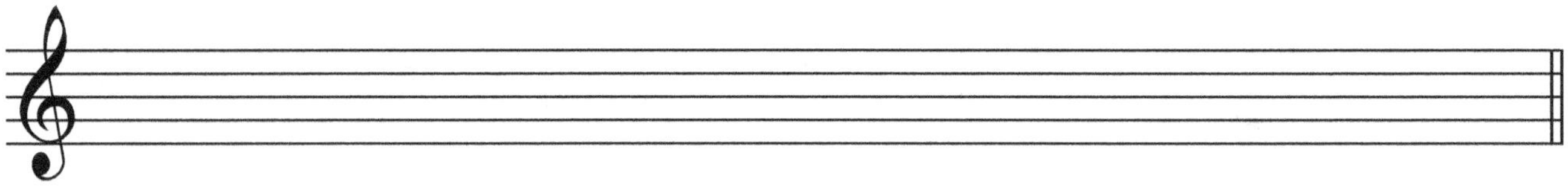

The major scale with one flat

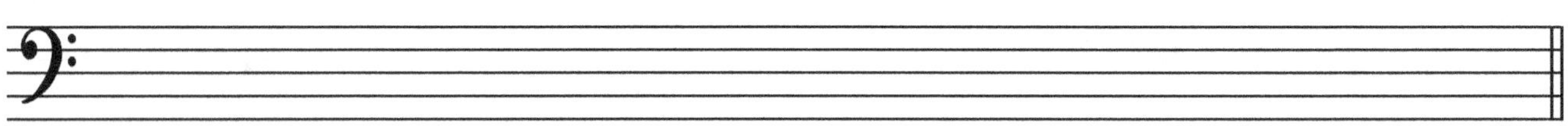

The major scale with A as the subdominant

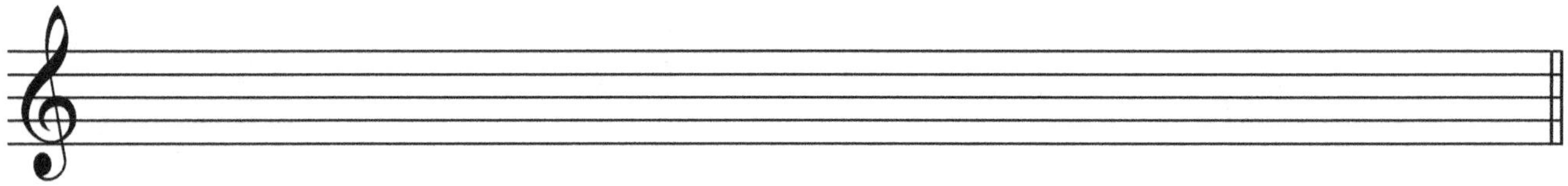

The major scale with F as the dominant

5
Minor Scales

A major scale evokes a particular color or character in sound. A *minor scale* has a different color or character. Some might say it has a sadder or darker sound, but that is a matter of opinion. The minor scale is another essential scale in music, and it occurs frequently.

If you play a major scale from the 6th note to the 6th note you get a natural minor scale. The C major scale played from A to A, produces the A natural minor scale (Figure 5.1). All of the notes in A natural minor come from the C major scale. A minor is the *relative minor* of C major. A minor and C major are related by key signature. They each have the same number of flats or sharps. C major's relative minor is A minor, and A minor's relative major is C major. Both keys have no sharps or flats in their key signature.

Figure 5.1

C major

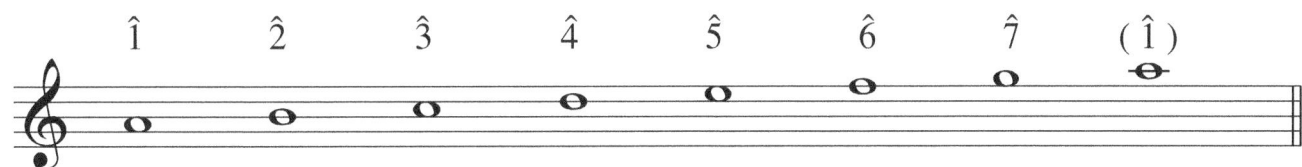

A minor

Relative Minor Keys

Major and minor scales are related by key signature. Every major key has a relative minor. They are related because they share the same key signature. To determine a minor key signature:

1. Name the major key.

2. Count up six notes (or down three) to get the relative minor key.

The 6th note of the D major scale is B. B minor has the same key signature as D major, two sharps, F♯ and C♯. Every key signature reflects two keys, one major and one minor.

Figure 5.2

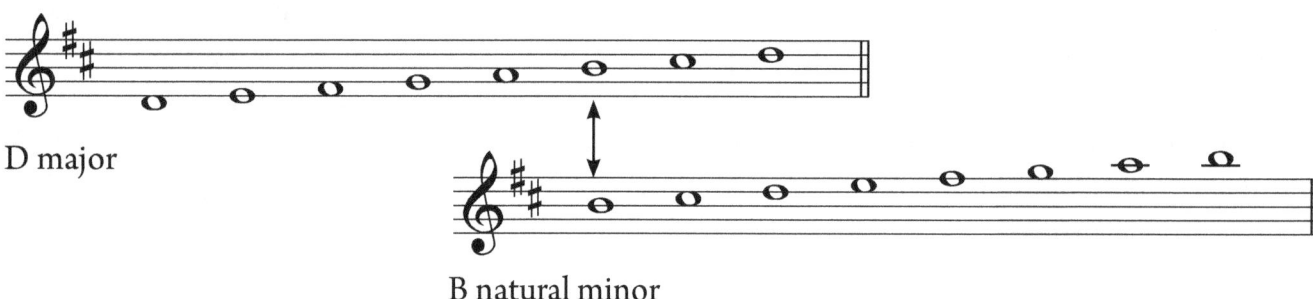

The relationship between these relative keys is shown in Figure 5.3. The tonic of the relative minor is located on scale degree $\hat{6}$ of the major scale. Scale degree $\hat{6}$ in C major is A. A minor is the relative minor of C major. They each have the same key signature, no sharps or flats.

Figure 5.3

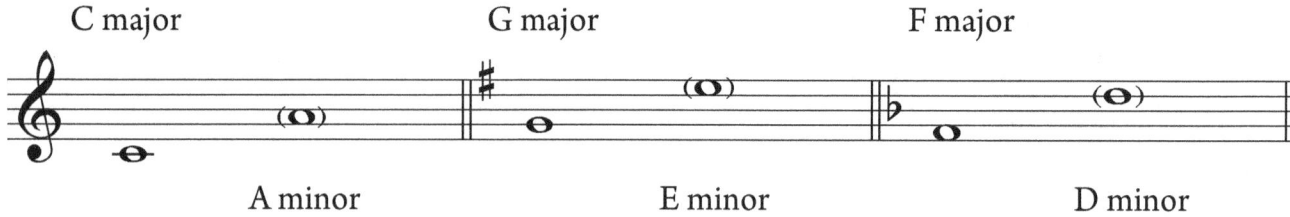

1. For the following examples: Name the major key. Write the tonic of the relative minor with a note in brackets. Name the relative minor key.

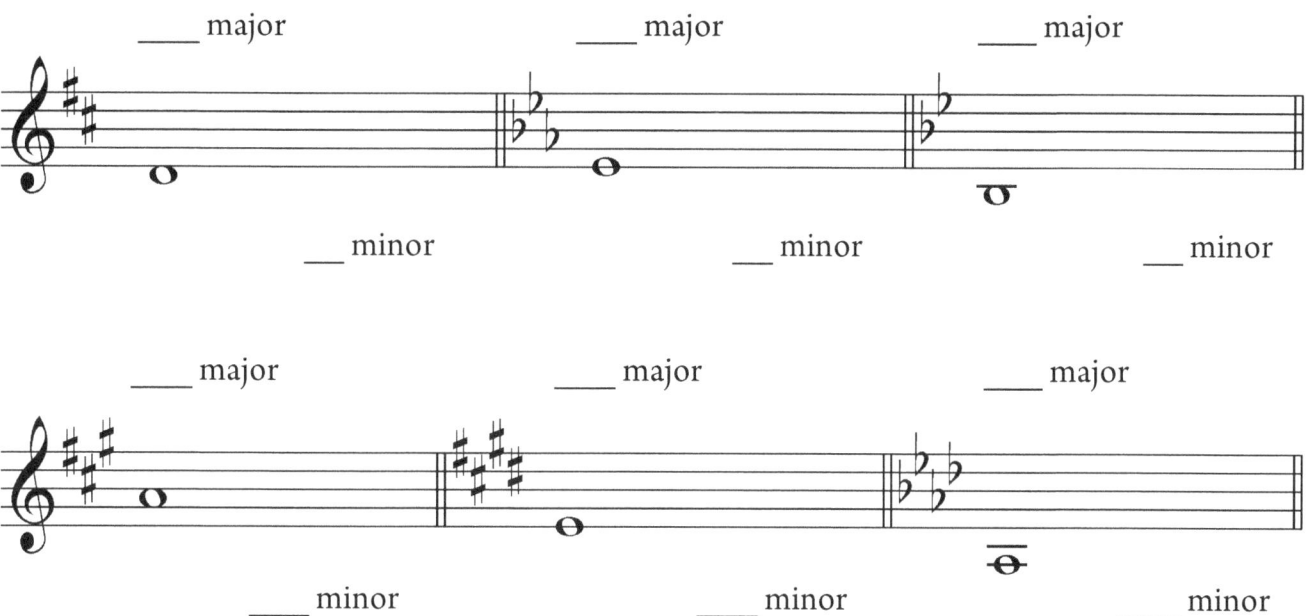

Figure 5.4 contains the key signatures of relative major and minor keys up to four sharps and four flats.

Figure 5.4

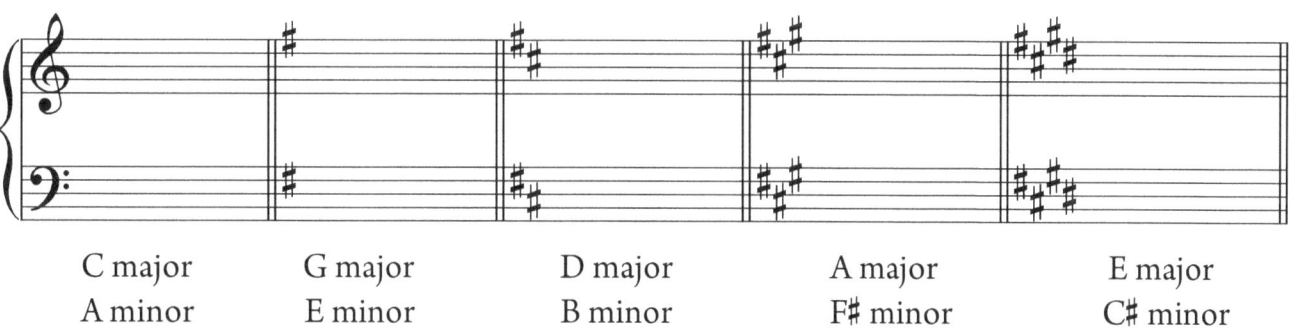

C major   G major   D major   A major   E major
A minor   E minor   B minor   F♯ minor   C♯ minor

F major   B♭ major   E♭ major   A♭ major
D minor   G minor   C minor   F minor

The Natural Minor Scale

The *natural minor scale* uses the same key signature as its relative major.

Figure 5.5 contains the D natural minor scale ascending and descending. The relative major of D minor is F major. F major has one flat (B♭), therefore D natural minor has one flat (B♭).

Figure 5.5

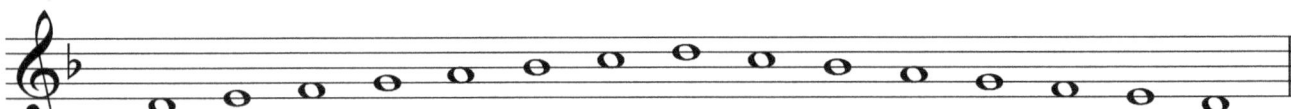

1. Write natural minor scales in the following keys ascending and descending using a key signature.

E natural minor

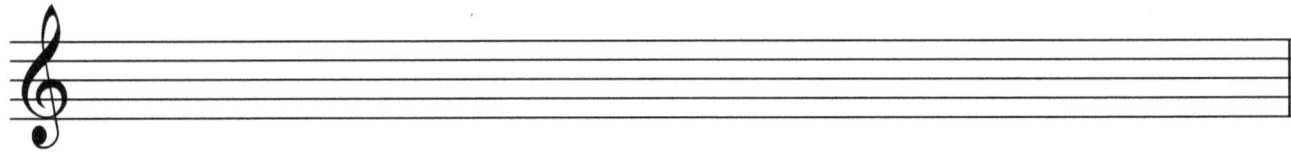

F natural minor

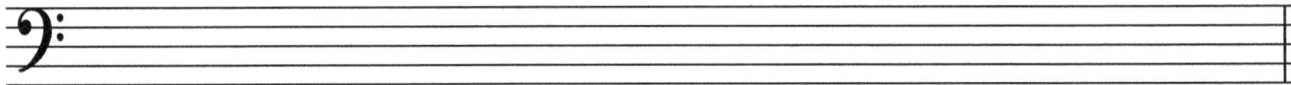

C♯ natural minor

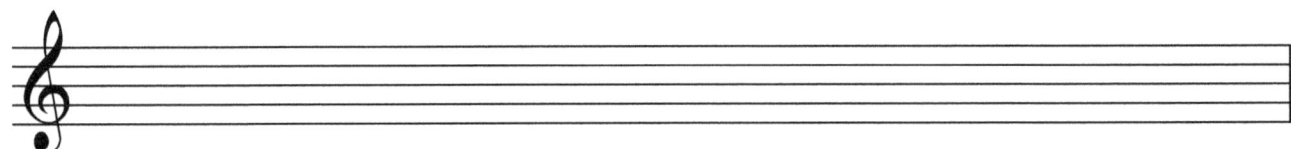

G natural minor

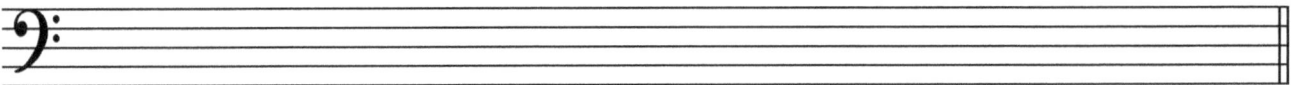

The Harmonic Minor Scale

The **harmonic minor scale** is the natural minor with $\hat{7}$ raised one half step.

Figure 5.6 contains the D harmonic minor scale ascending and descending. D harmonic minor has B♭ in its key signature and raised $\hat{7}$, which is C♯.

Figure 5.6

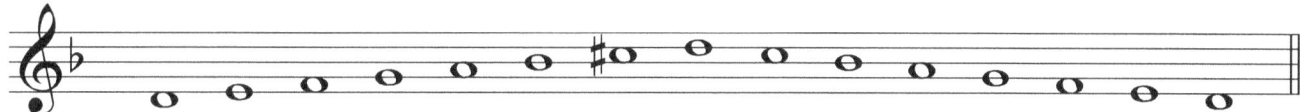

1. Write harmonic minor scales in the following keys ascending and descending using a key signature.

F harmonic minor

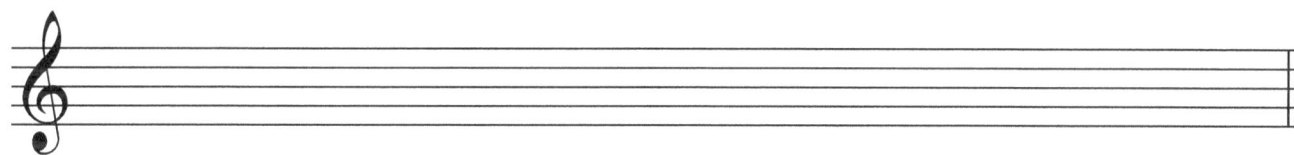

G harmonic minor

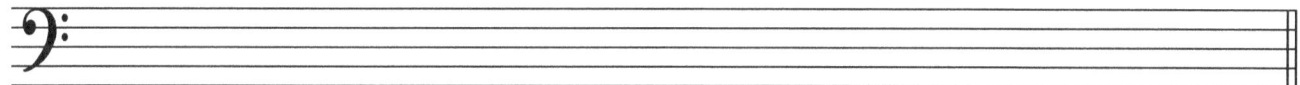

C♯ harmonic minor

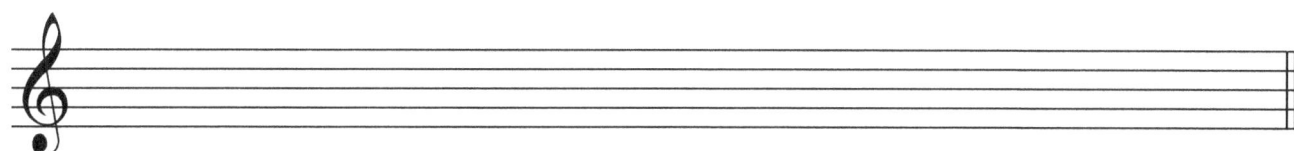

B harmonic minor

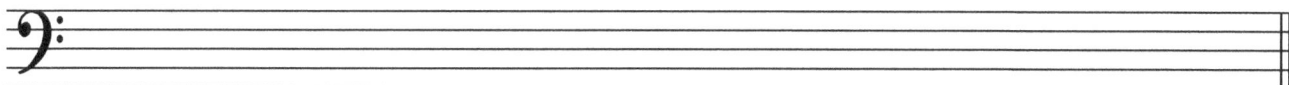

The Melodic Minor Scale

The ***melodic minor scale*** is the natural minor with $\hat{6}$ and $\hat{7}$ raised one half step ascending, and lowered one half step descending.

Figure 5.7 contains the D melodic minor scale ascending and descending. D melodic minor has B♭ in its key signature. $\hat{6}$ and $\hat{7}$ are raised to B♮ and C♯ in the ascending scale, and lowered to C♮ and B♭ in the descending scale.

Figure 5.7

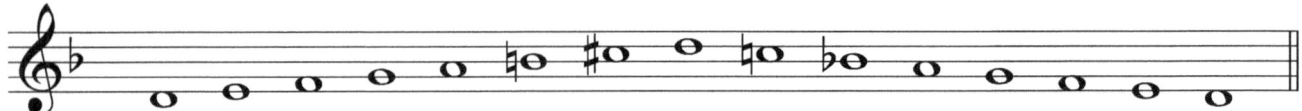

1. Write melodic minor scales in the following keys ascending and descending using a key signature.

E melodic minor

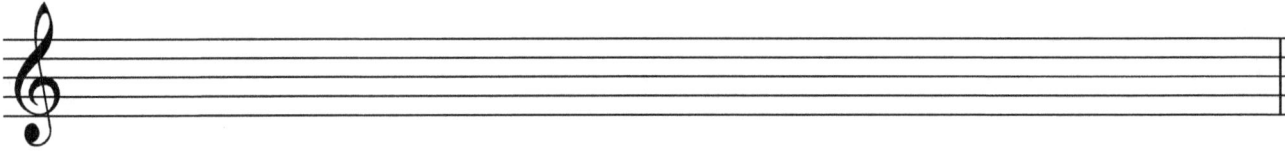

F♯ melodic minor

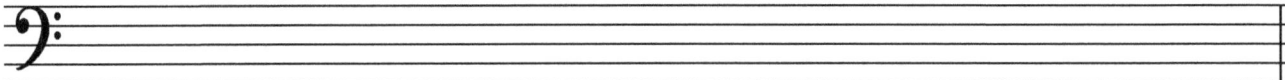

C melodic minor

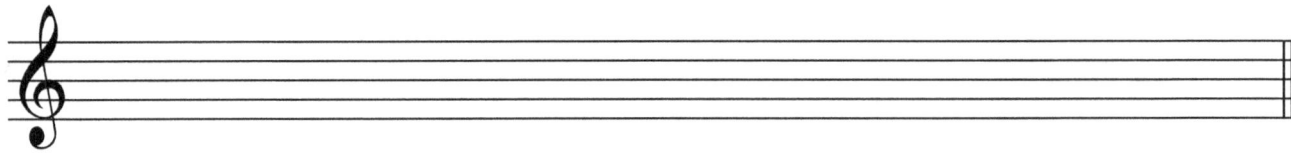

A melodic minor

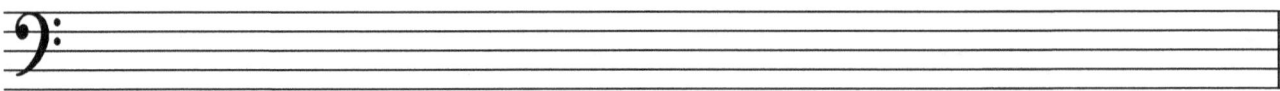

The Circle of Fifths With Minor Keys

Figure 5.8 is the circle of 5ths with added minor keys. The circle of 5ths shows that some of the flat keys sound the same as some of the sharp keys. The key of six flats (E♭minor, G♭major) sounds the same as the key of six sharps (D♯minor, F♯major). Keys which contain the same pitches but are notated differently are called *enharmonic keys* or *enharmonic equivalents*.

Figure 5.8

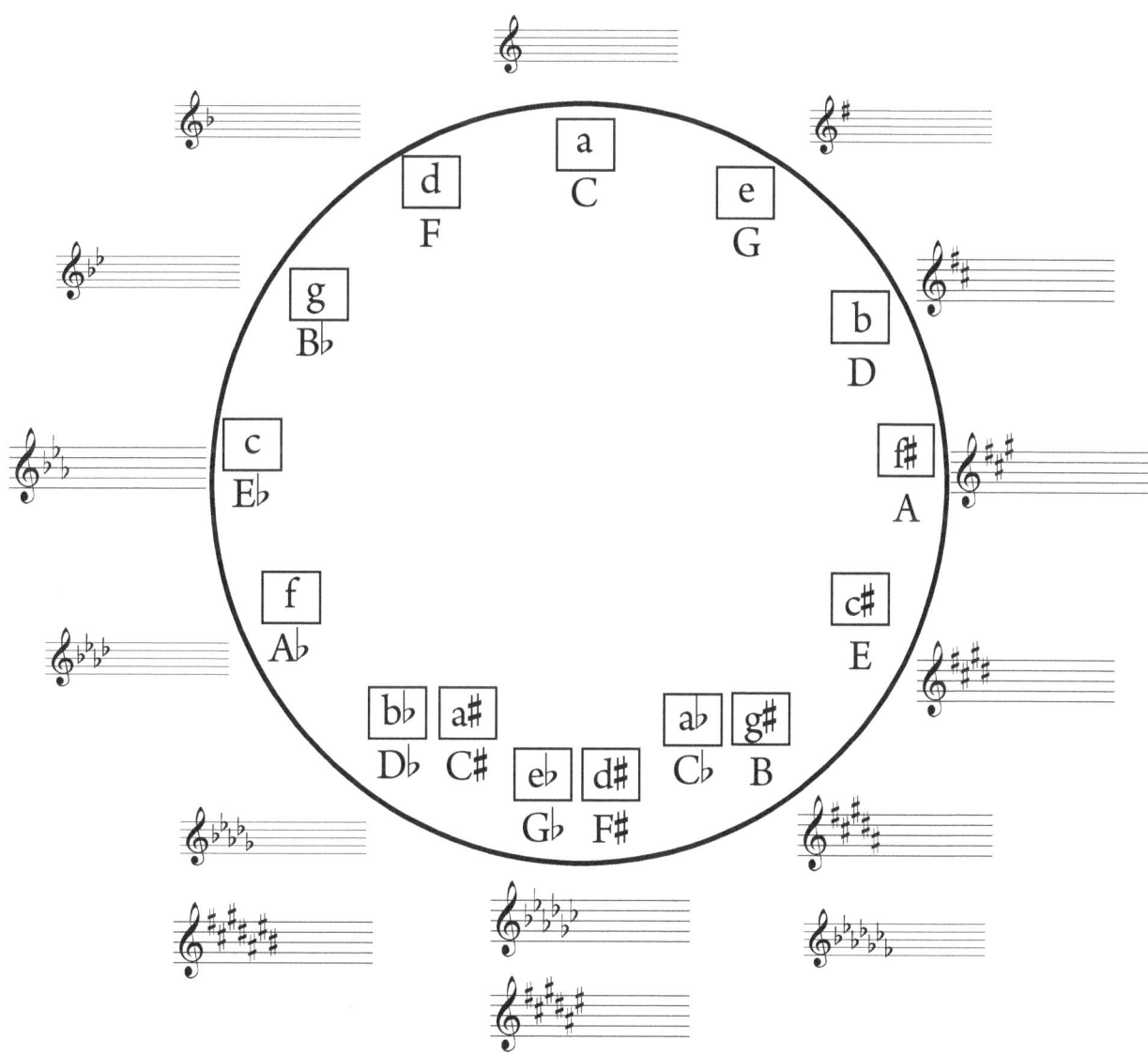

Minor keys are shown with lower case letters.

1. Name the key and following scales as natural, harmonic or melodic. e.g. *D harmonic minor.*

Scale: E natural minor

Scale: C harmonic minor

Scale: C# harmonic minor

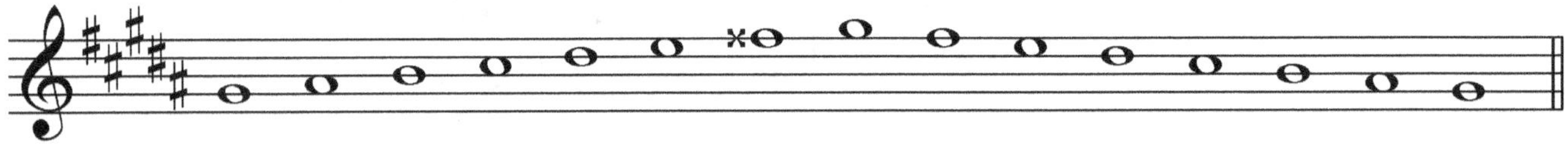

Scale: G melodic minor

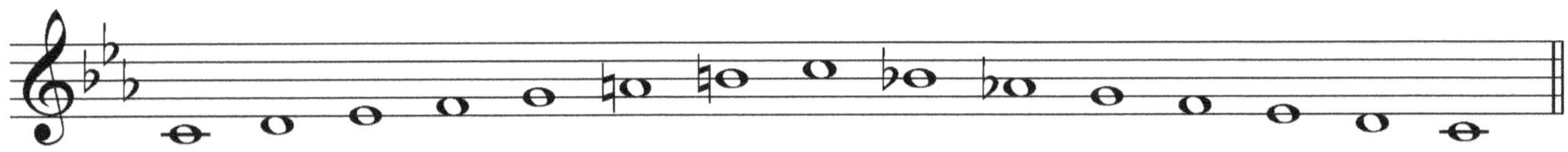

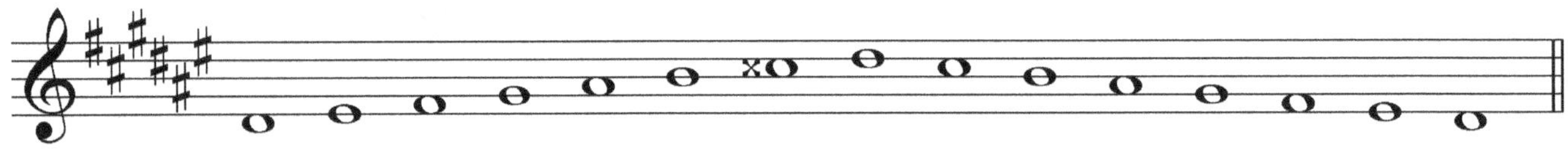

Scale: D# harmonic minor

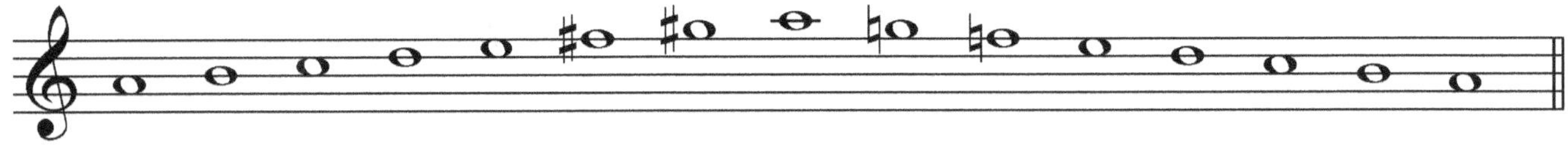

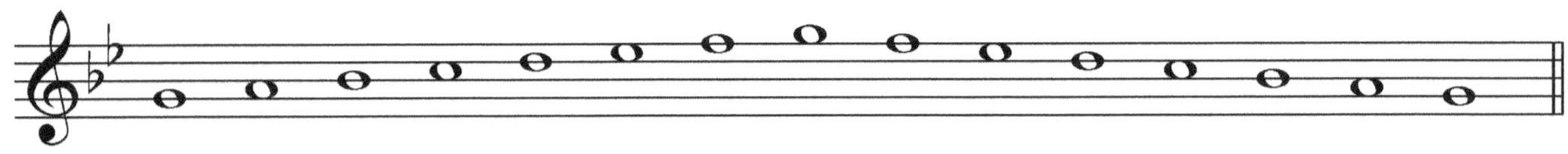

Scale: A melodic minor

Scale: G natural minor

2. Write the following scales ascending and descending in quarter notes using a key signature.

C# harmonic minor

E♭ melodic minor

D natural minor

F# harmonic minor

C melodic minor

B♭ natural minor

E harmonic minor

Parallel Major and Minor Keys

The scales covered to this point may also be known as **modes**. Mode is just another name for the word scale.

Thus far you have learned about the major mode and the three minor modes – natural, harmonic and melodic. Composers often move back and forth between the major and minor modes within the same piece to make their compositions interesting.

Because of the common notes and key signatures, composers may also change keys, or modulate back and forth between relative major and minor keys. For example, a piece in G minor often moves to the key of B♭ major. G minor and B♭ major are relative minor and major keys and share the same key signature of B♭ and E♭. Because of this, many notes are the same between the two keys, and it is easy to move between them.

Composers may also keep the tonic the same but change the mode of the piece from major to minor, or vice-versa. For example a piece in C major might change keys to C minor. These two keys are related because they share the same tonic, C.

Major and minor keys that use the same tonic are known as **parallel** major and minor keys. For example, F major and F minor are parallel keys. They both have F as the tonic.

Enharmonic Tonic Major and Minor Keys

Enharmonic major or minor keys are keys with the same tonic that have a different name. For example, C♯ major and D♭ major are enharmonic tonic majors. They are major scales that share the same tonic, but it has a different name. C♯ and D♭ are the same note.

The enharmonic tonic minor of G♭ minor is F♯ minor. Same tonic, named differently.

The tonic minor of G♭ major is G♭ minor.
The enharmonic tonic minor of G♭ major is F♯ minor. All this means is that it is the minor scale with the same tonic as G♭ major, but renamed. Its name has been changed enharmonically from G♭ to F♯.

1. Complete the following.

a. The enharmonic tonic major of C♯ major is _____

b. The enharmonic tonic minor of B♭ major is _____

c. The enharmonic tonic major of C♭ major is _____

d. The parallel minor of D major is _____

e. The tonic major of G minor is _____

f. The enharmonic tonic minor of E♭ major is _____

2. Write the following scales ascending and descending in whole notes using a key signature. Name each scale.

G major

G major's parallel minor, harmonic form

G major's relative minor, melodic form

G♯ minor's enharmonic tonic major

3. Write the following scales ascending and descending in half notes using a key signature.

The harmonic minor scale with the key signature of 4 flats

The melodic minor scale that is the parallel minor of D major

The natural minor scale with G as the subtonic

The harmonic minor scale with A as the leading tone

The melodic minor scale with E♭ as the tonic

The natural minor with G as the supertonic

The enharmonic tonic melodic minor, of D♭ major

The Leading Tone and the Subtonic

There are two technical names for $\hat{7}$ in minor keys. When $\hat{7}$ is raised and is a half step from the tonic, it is called the ***leading tone***. In the natural minor and the descending melodic minor where $\hat{7}$ is not raised and is a whole step away from the tonic, it is called the ***subtonic***. When it is a whole step away, it does not sound like it is leading to the tonic. That's why it is called the subtonic.

Figure 5.9 shows the A melodic minor scale. The leading tone (G♯) occurs in the ascending portion, and the subtonic (G♮) occurs in the descending portion.

Figure 5.9

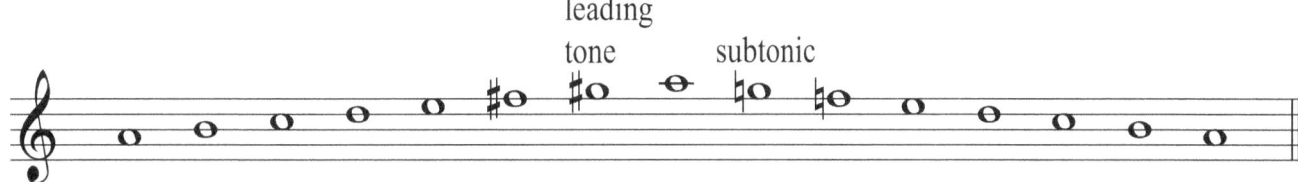

1. Write the following scales ascending and descending using key signatures. Label the leading tone (LT) and the subtonic (ST) where applicable.

B major's parallel minor, melodic form

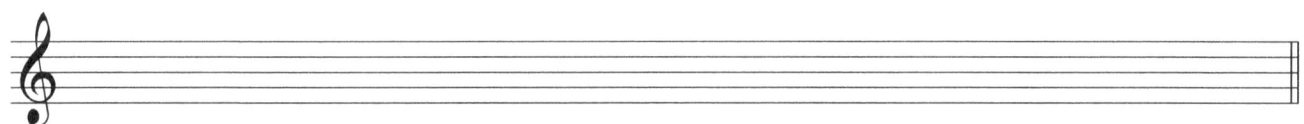

B major's relative minor, harmonic form

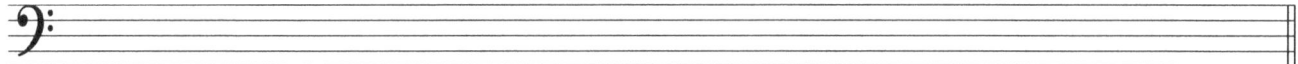

D♯ natural minor

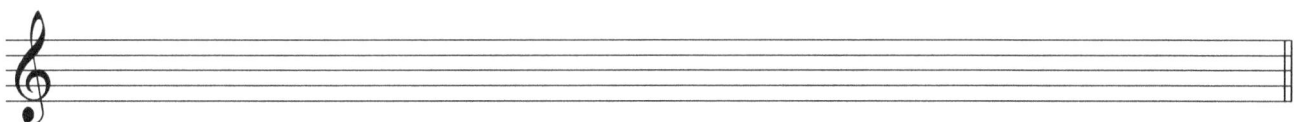

D♯ minor's enharmonic tonic minor, harmonic form

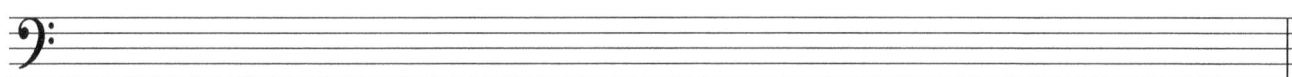

2. Name the key and following scales as natural, harmonic or melodic. e.g. *D harmonic minor.*

Scale:_____

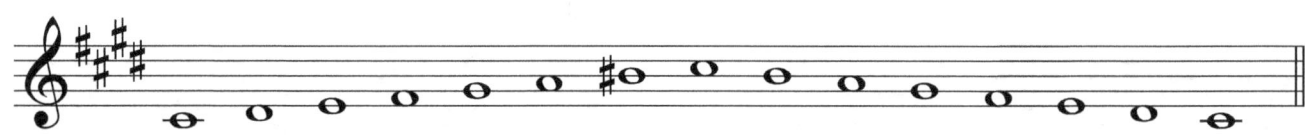

Scale:_____

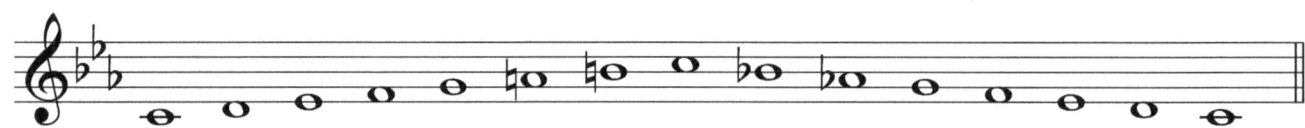

Scale:_____

Scale:_____

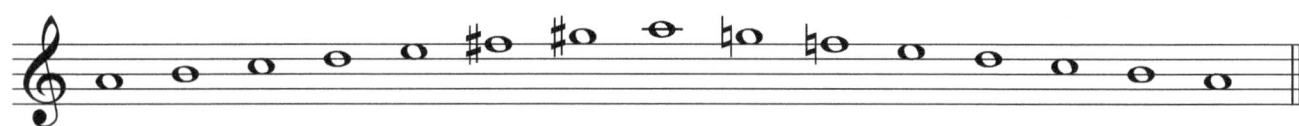

Scale:_____

Scale:_____

3. Write the following scales ascending and descending in quarter notes using a key signature. Label the leading tone (LT) and subtonic (ST) for each.

C# harmonic minor

F melodic minor

D natural minor

F# harmonic minor

C melodic minor

B natural minor

E harmonic minor

Minor Scales

4. Write the following scales ascending and descending in half notes using a key signature. Label the subtonic notes (ST).

The harmonic minor scale with the key signature of 4 flats

The melodic minor scale with the key signature of 2 sharps

The natural minor scale with G as the subtonic

The harmonic minor scale with F♯ as the leading note

The melodic minor scale with C♯ as the tonic

The natural minor with G as the dominant

The harmonic minor scale with A major as its relative major

Identifying the Key of a Melody

It is important to know the key of a piece of music. Identifying the key of a composition helps us to understand, analyze, perform and memorize it.

Study the melody in Figure 5.10.

This melody has a key signature of one sharp. This key signature suggests G major or it's relative minor, E minor. This melody also has the accidental D sharp. Often, music in a minor key will have accidentals indicating raised $\hat{7}$. In the key of E minor raised $\hat{7}$ is D♯. This melody ends on E, approached by the leading tone D♯. There is an E minor arpeggio in m.4. All of these elements point to the key of E minor. This melody is in E minor.

Melodies in minor keys may contain raised $\hat{6}$ as well as raised $\hat{7}$ since the melodic minor scale includes these notes. In fact, a melody in a minor key could be based on any of the three forms of the minor scale: natural, harmonic, or melodic minor.

Figure 5.10

Felix Mendelssohn
Quartet No. 4

The melody is Figure 5.11 has a key signature of three sharps. This key signature suggests A major or it's relative minor, F♯ minor. The melody starts and ends on A. There are no E♯'s suggesting the raised $\hat{7}$ of F♯ minor. Therefore, it is in the key of A major.

Figure 5.11

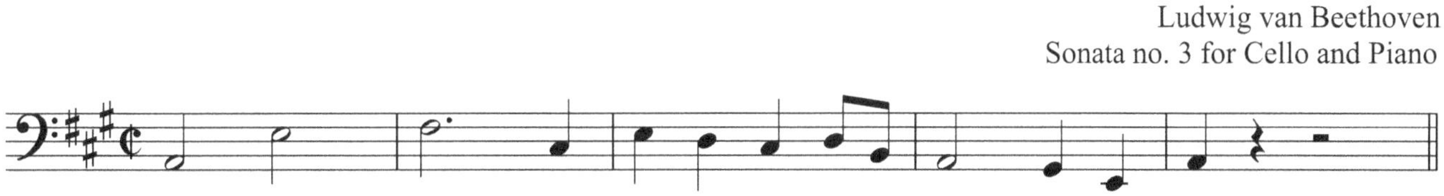

Ludwig van Beethoven
Sonata no. 3 for Cello and Piano

1. Name the keys of the following melodies.

6
Other Scales

The Chromatic Scale

The *chromatic scale* is made up of half steps. It has twelve pitches. Since it contains the same intervals throughout it is considered a *symmetric scale*. If you play a chromatic scale starting on C, you play every note ascending until you get to the next C, and then do the same descending. The notation of the chromatic scale may vary, but the simplest way to write a chromatic scale is to write sharps ascending and flats descending.

Figure 6.1 is an ascending chromatic scale starting on C. Sharps are used as the scale ascends. Half steps occur between E - F and B - C. When you write a chromatic scale notate these white key half steps using natural notes. For example, don't write F as E♯.

Figure 6.1

Figure 6.2 shows the C chromatic scale descending. Flats are used for the descending form of this scale. Flats are commonly used when notes move downward chromatically, and sharps are used for chromatic passages that ascend. The white key half steps C - B and F - E are notated as natural notes.

Figure 6.2

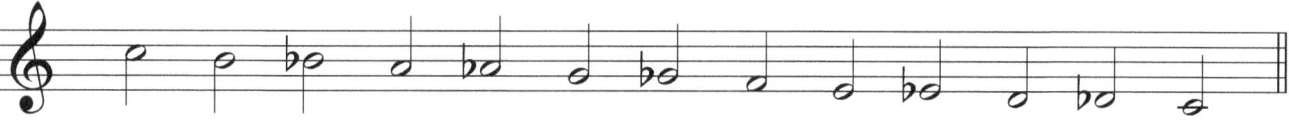

When writing the chromatic scale ascending and descending and it is a good idea to use a bar line at the top of the scale before moving down. This cancels all the previous accidentals. See Figure 6.3.

- When writing any chromatic scale do not use the same letter name more than twice.
- Never change the name of the tonic enharmonically. For example, if the scale starts on C♯ it must end on C♯, not on D♭.

Figure 6.3

When a chromatic scale starts on a flat, use sharps as soon as possible as you ascend. The A♭ chromatic scale in Figure 6.4 cannot change to sharps until C♯ because no letter name can be used more than twice. Notice that it does not end on G♯ at the top. It must end on the same note that it starts, in this case, A♭.

Figure 6.4

1. Write the following chromatic scales ascending and descending.

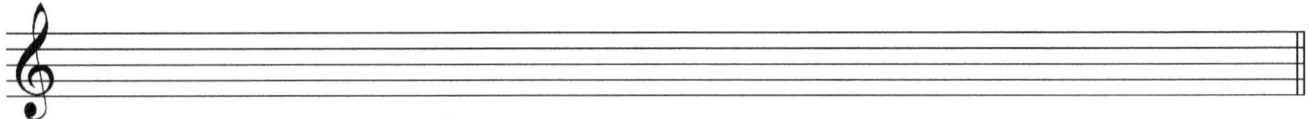

Chromatic scale on F

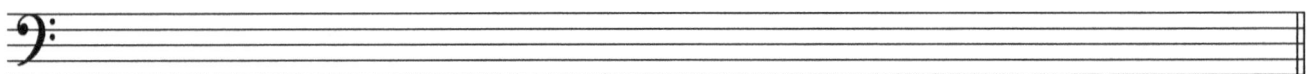

Chromatic scale on D♭

Chromatic scale on E

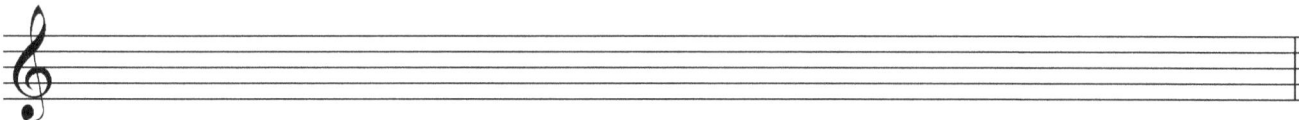

Chromatic scale on G#

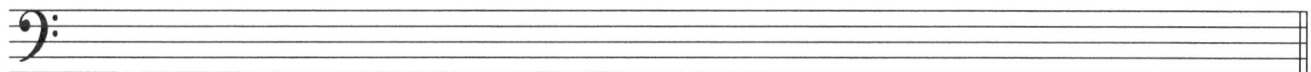

Chromatic scale on A

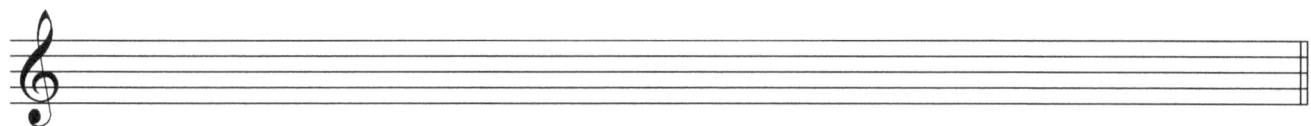

Chromatic scale on G♭

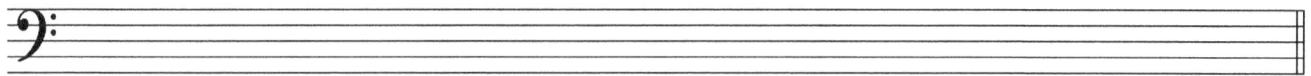

Chromatic scale on B

Chromatic scale on F#

The notation of a chromatic scale may vary if it is written in a specific key. In this case, the key signature will be the guide to the accidentals used in the chromatic scale.

For example, if a sharp-based key signature is used, sharps are used for the chromatic notes in the scale. The D chromatic scale in Figure 6.5 uses the key signature of D major. Since this is a key signature using sharps, the chromatic scale uses sharps. It is important to be aware of the key signature and adjust any notes accordingly.

Figure 6.5

The chromatic scale in the key of B♭ uses the key signature of B♭ major. This is a flat-based key signature. The added chromatic scale notes are not part of that key. However, since the key signature uses flats, the chromatic scale uses flats ascending and descending.

Figure 6.6 is the B♭ flat chromatic scale using a key signature. When writing this scale, begin with the key signature and the starting note. Since flats are used in the key of B♭ major, move each note up and down chromatically using flats. It is helpful to think of the keyboard when writing chromatic scales. Never use a letter name more than twice.

Figure 6.6

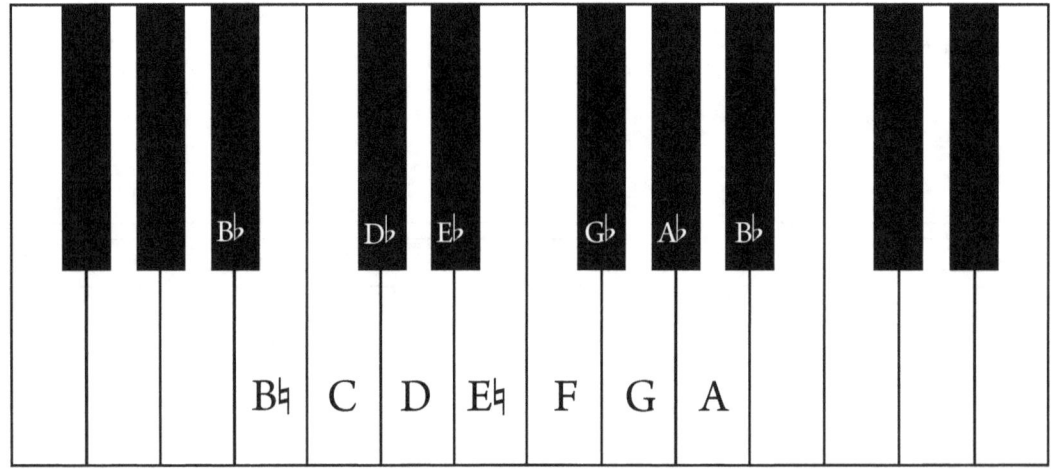

1. Write the following chromatic scales using key signatures for each.

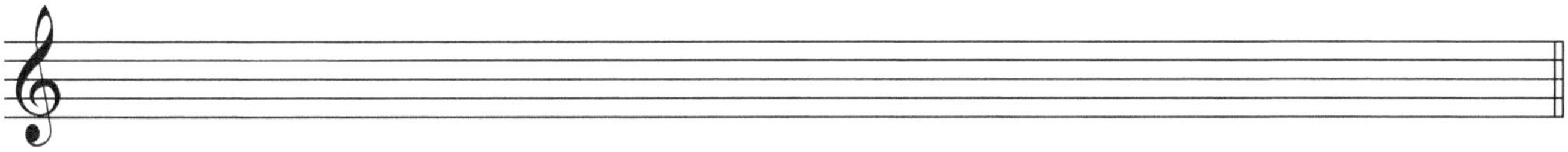

F chromatic scale

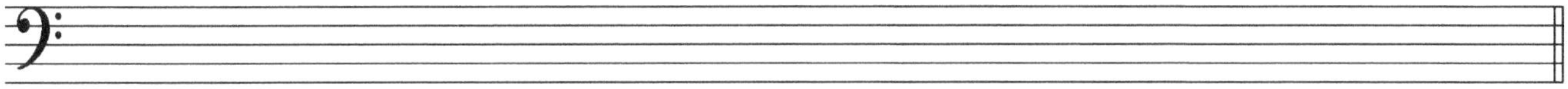

A chromatic scale

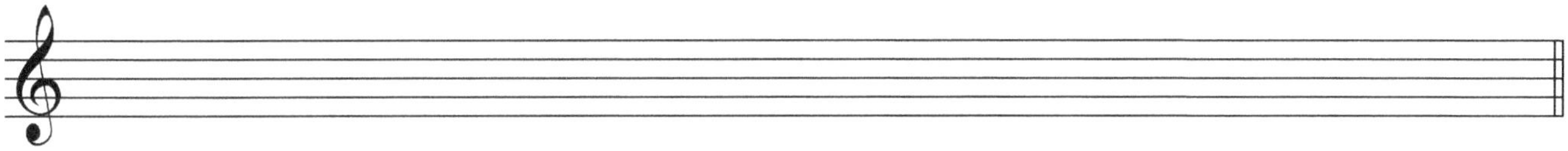

E♭ chromatic scale

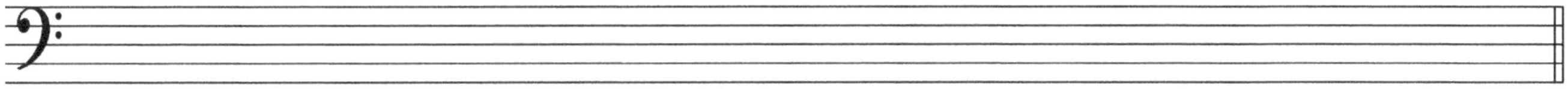

B chromatic scale

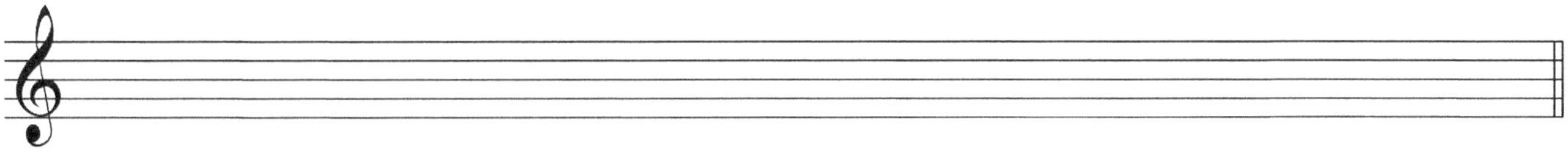

A♭ chromatic scale

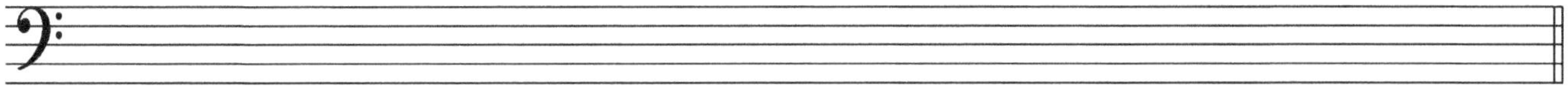

F♯ chromatic scale

©San Marco Publications 2022 — Other Scales

2. Circle any chromatic passages that occur in the following musical excerpts.

Henry Purcell
Dido and Aeneas, Didos Lament

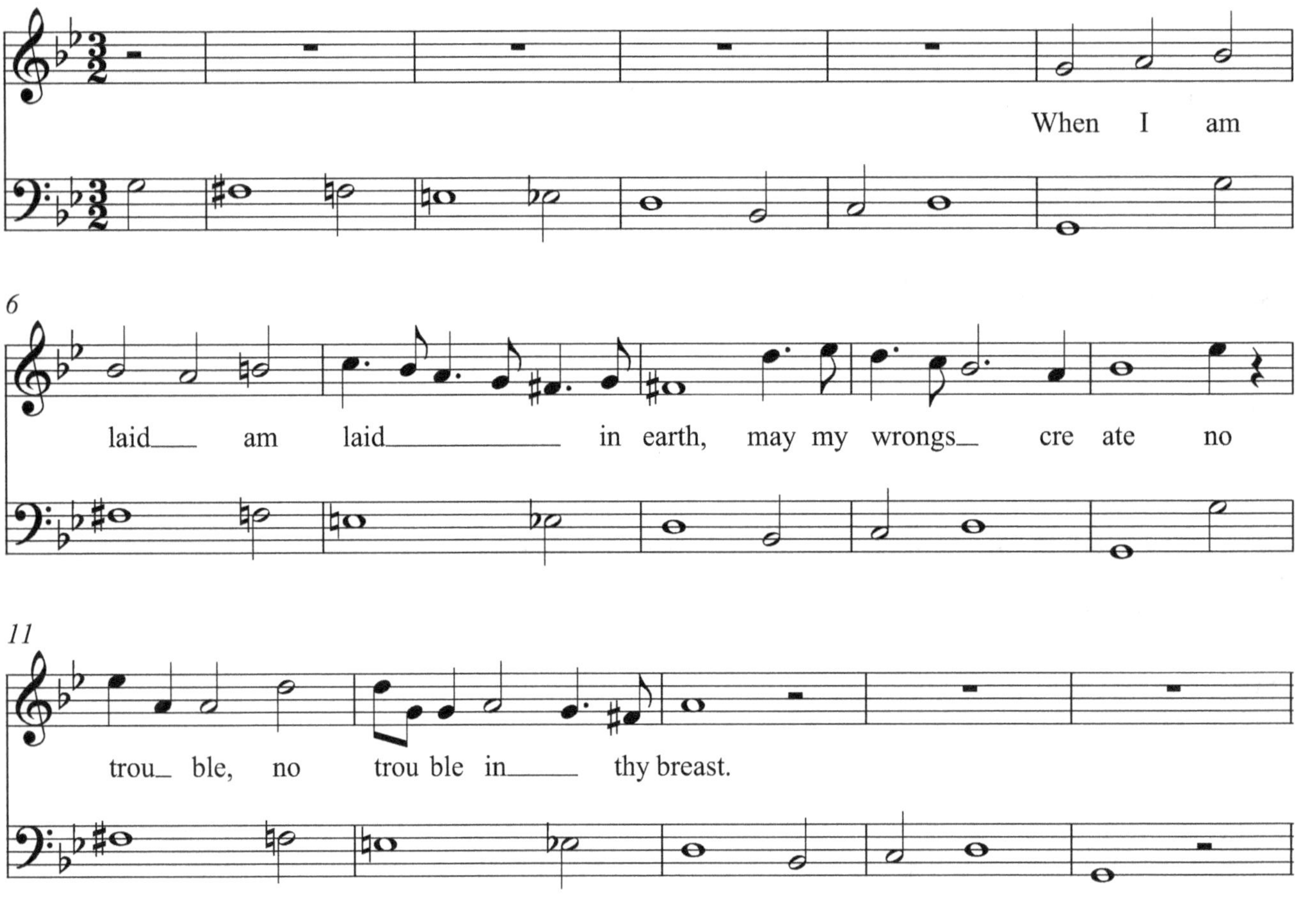

Ludwig van Beethoven
Sonata Op. 2, No. 2, IV

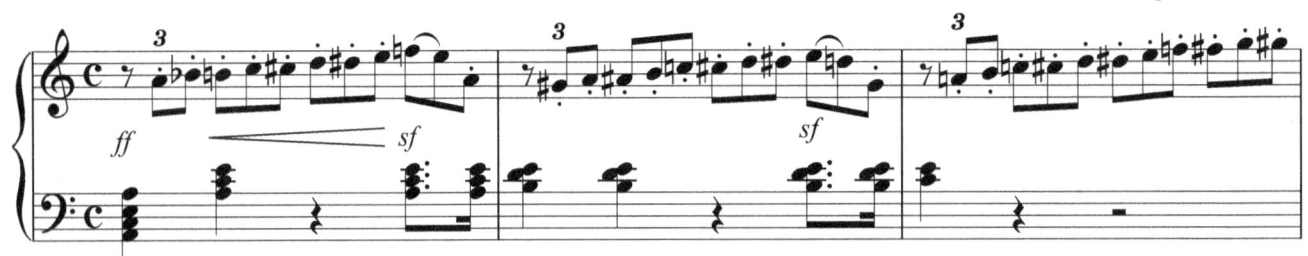

The Whole Tone Scale

The ***whole tone scale*** is a symmetric scale. It is constructed entirely of whole steps. This is a six-note scale. There are two different whole tone scales. One starting on C, and one starting on C♯. Starting on any other note will create the same pitches as those starting on C or C♯.

Figure 6.7 shows these whole tone scales. When writing this scale:

- Start and end on the same note. Do not change the tonic enharmonically.
- Use six different letter names.
- Do not mix sharps and flats. Use one or the other.

The whole tone scale is often used in movie music during dream sequences since it has a unique dreamy sound. Composers in the twentieth century, most notably Claude Debussy, used this scale in their compositions.

Figure 6.7

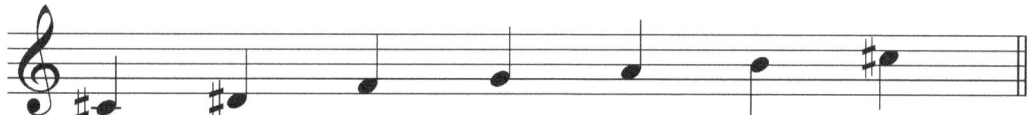

1. Add accidentals to the following to create whole tone scales.

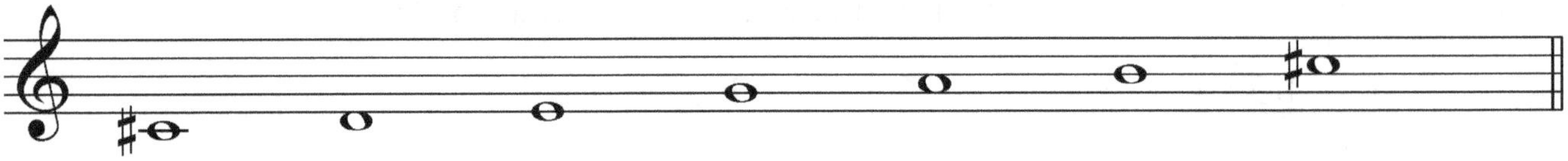

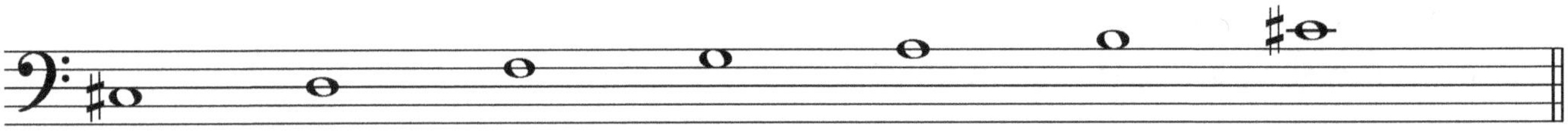

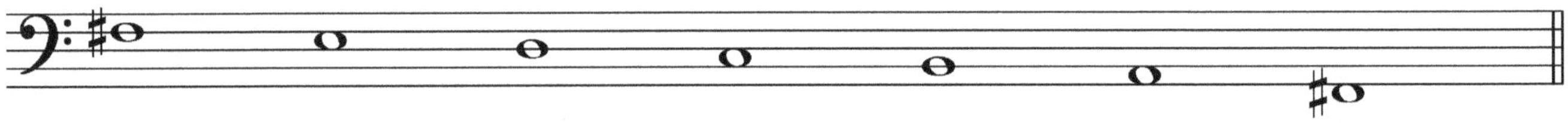

2. Write whole tone scales ascending and descending on the following notes.

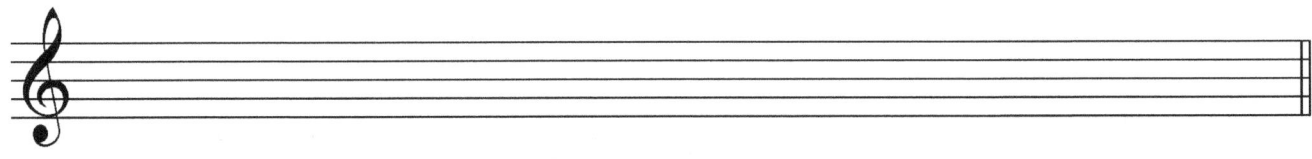
on G♭

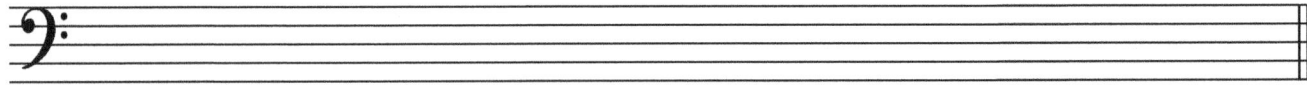
on B

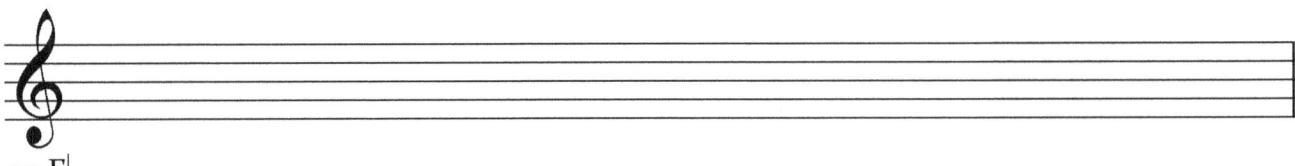
on E♭

The Octatonic Scale

The *octatonic* or *diminished scale*, as it is sometimes known, has eight different notes ("octa" means eight). The octatonic scale is a symmetrical scale. It is built using alternating whole and half steps. There are two forms of this scale. One starts with a whole step followed by a half step. The other starts with a half step followed by a whole step.

Figure 6.8 shows the two versions of this scale starting on C. Composers, like Stravinsky, Scriabin, and Bartok used this scale. It is common in jazz music as well.

Figure 6.8

Whole - Half Octatonic

Half - Whole Octatonic

There are only three octatonic scales. The octatonic scales built on C, C♯, and D are the only ones that use unique sets of notes. If you start an octatonic scale on any other note you will get scales with notes identical to those found on C, C♯, or D.

It is important not to change the first note of this scale enharmonically. For example, if it starts on C♯, it must end on C♯.

1. Add accidentals to create octatonic scales. Do not change the first note of each scale.

2. Write the following octatonic scales ascending and descending.

E octatonic, starting with a whole step

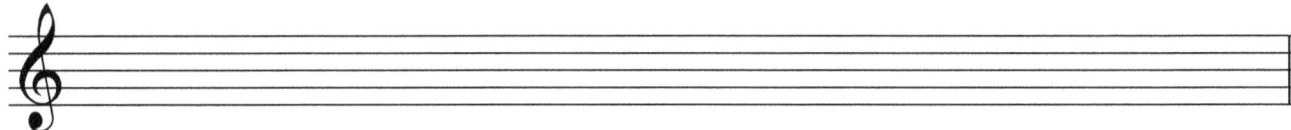

C♯ octatonic, starting with a half step

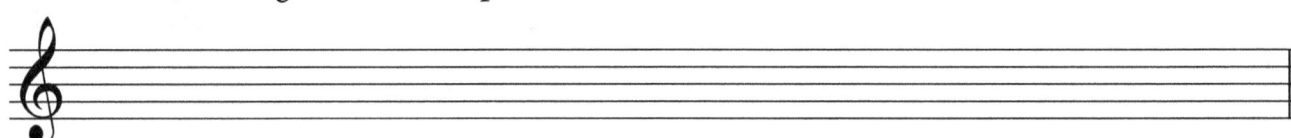

A♭ octatonic, starting with a whole step

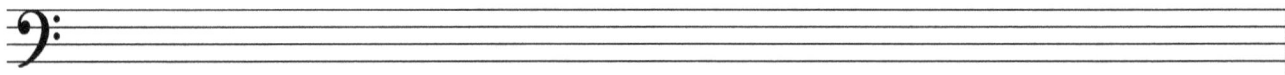

G octatonic, starting with a half step

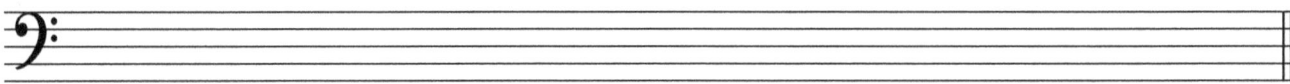

Other Scales

The Pentatonic Scale

Pentatonic scales are five note scales. The prefix "penta" is from the Greek meaning five, and tonic means tones or notes. Pentatonic scales are used in folk, rock, jazz and church music. There are two types of pentatonic scales: major and minor.

The Major Pentatonic Scale

The ***major pentatonic scale*** is a five-note scale that is related to the major scale. In the major pentatonic scale two notes are omitted from the major scale: $\hat{4}$ and $\hat{7}$.

The C major pentatonic scale is: C D E G A C. This is shown in Figure 6.9.

Figure 6.9

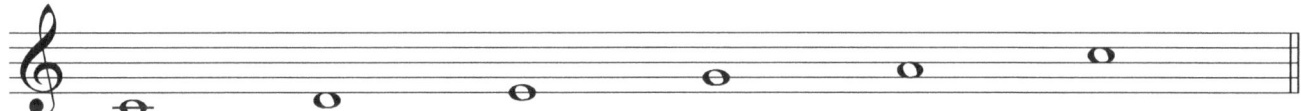

1. Write the following major pentatonic scales ascending only.

D major pentatonic

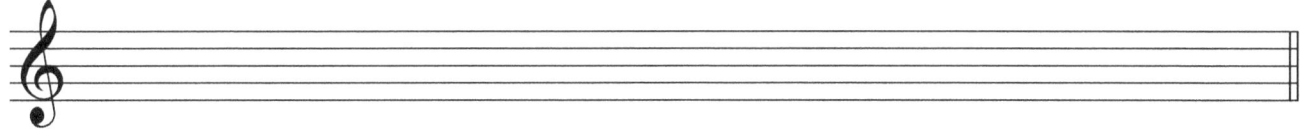

F major pentatonic

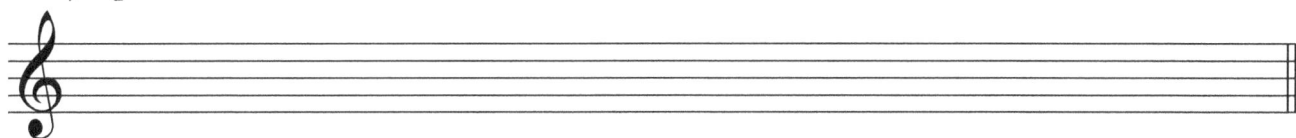

E♭ major pentatonic

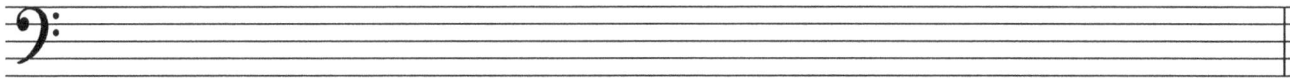

The Minor Pentatonic Scale

The **_minor pentatonic scale_** is another five note scale. This scale is a natural minor scale with two notes removed. To form a minor pentatonic scale, remove $\hat{2}$ and $\hat{6}$ from the natural minor scale. The A minor pentatonic scale is: A C D E G A. This scale is shown in Figure 6.10.

Figure 6.10

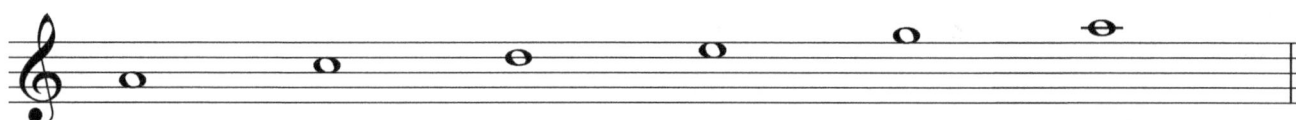

1. Write the following minor pentatonic scales ascending only.

G minor pentatonic

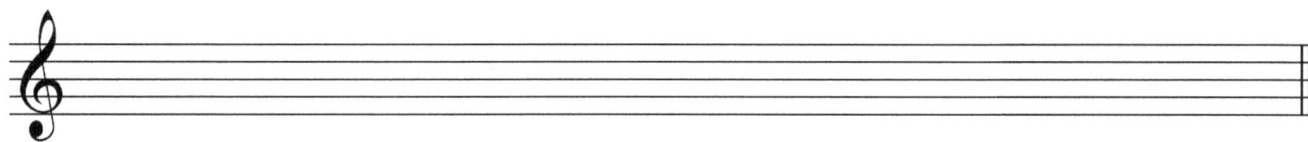

E minor pentatonic

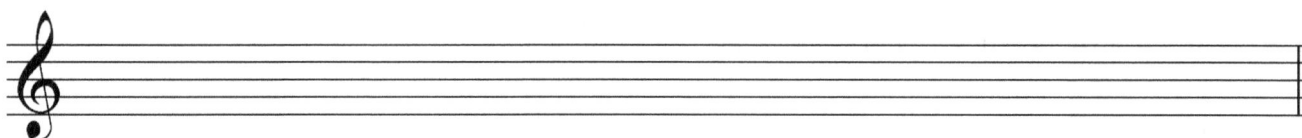

C minor pentatonic

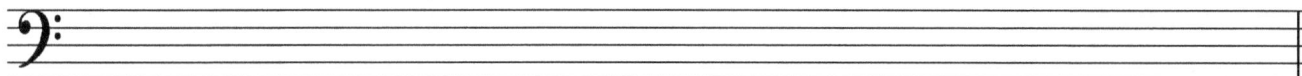

B minor pentatonic

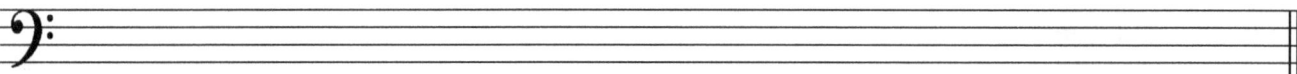

The Blues Scale

The **blues scale** can be created by altering notes of the major scale. The altered notes are called "blue" notes. These notes originated with African slaves brought to America. A blue note was created by bending the pitch of a note when singing.

The blues scale is the major scale with the $\hat{3}$, $\hat{5}$ and $\hat{7}$ lowered a half step. $\hat{5}$ occurs twice, once lowered and once in its original form. Scale degrees $\hat{2}$ and $\hat{6}$ are omitted.

Figure 6.11 contains the C blues scale.

Figure 6.11

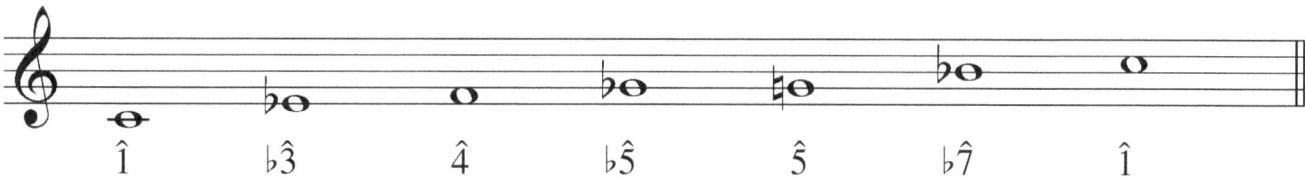

1. Add accidentals to the following to create blues scales.

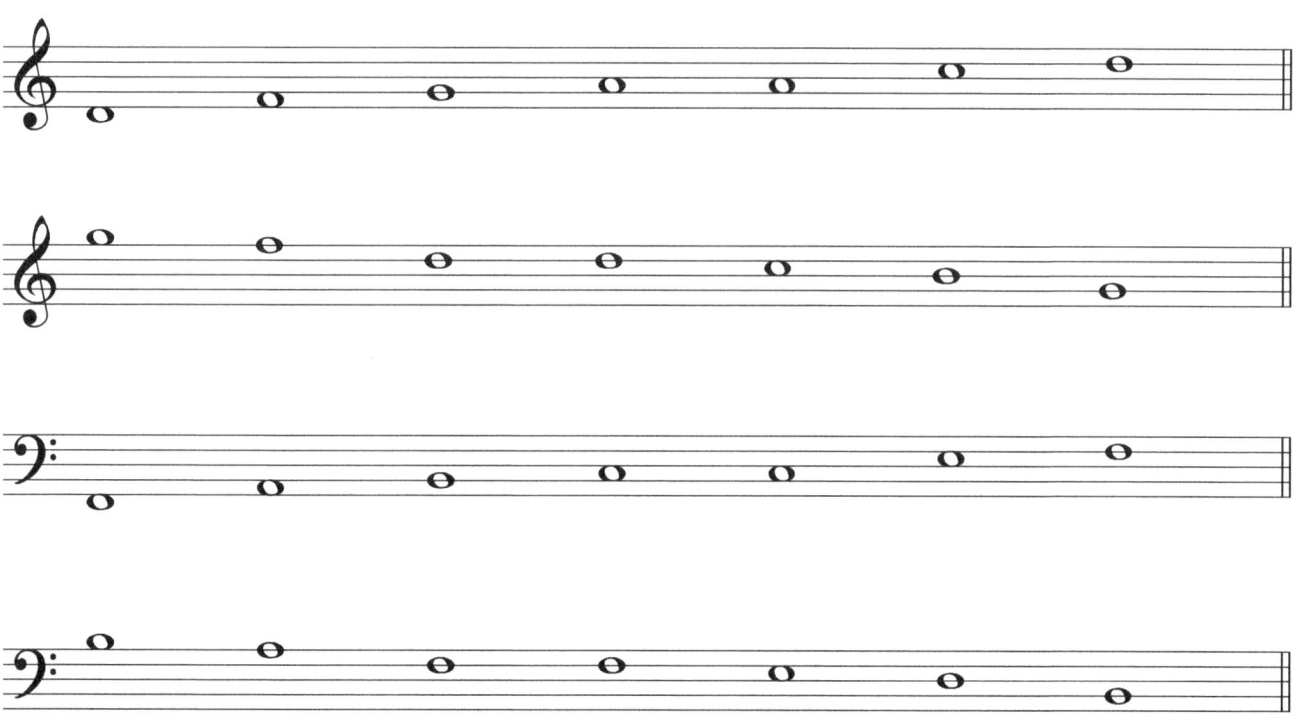

2. Write the following blues scales ascending.

E blues

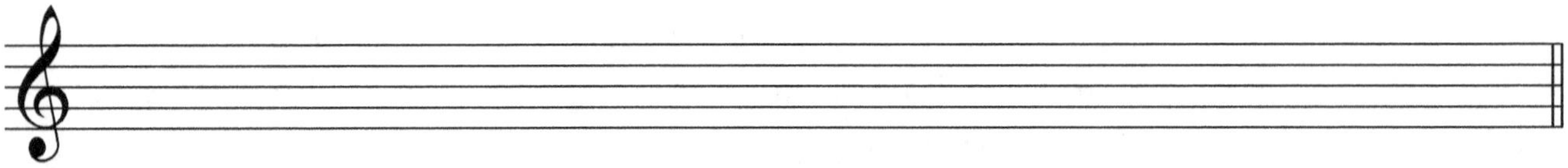

A♭ blues

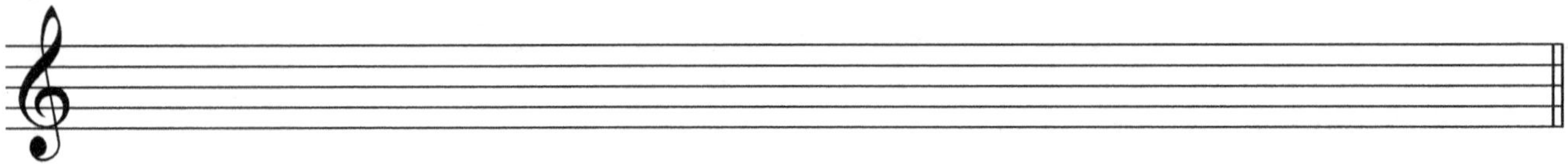

G blues

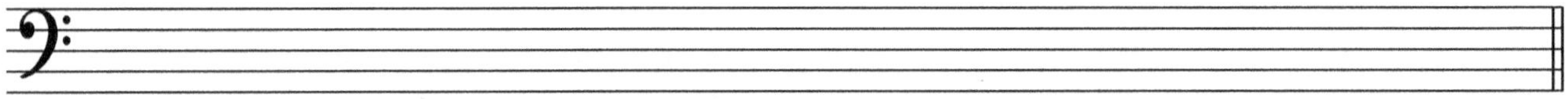

F blues

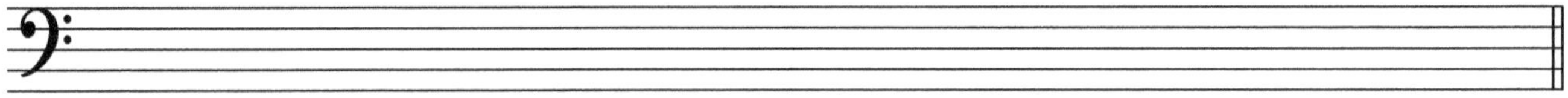

3. Write the following blues scales descending.

A blues

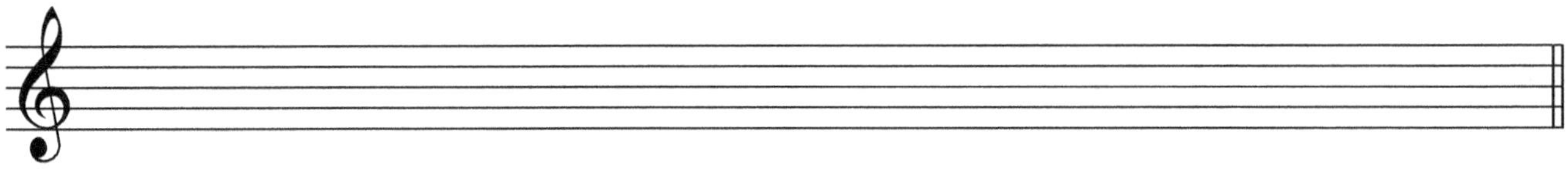

C blues

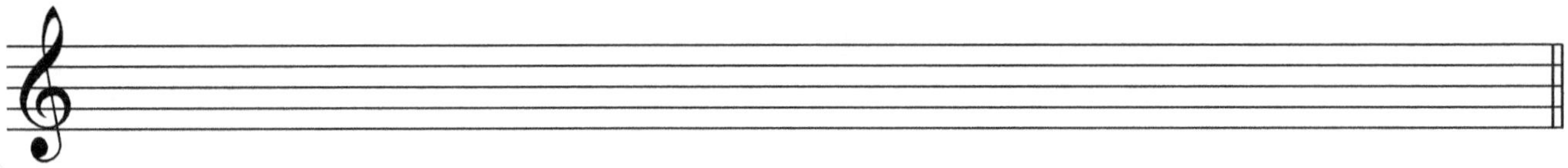

B blues

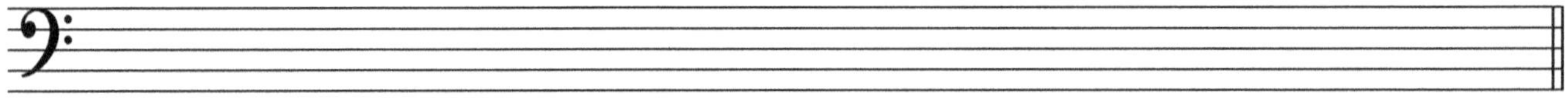

D blues

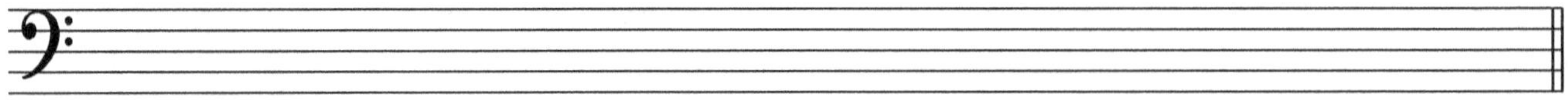

4. Identify the following scales as: major, natural minor, harmonic minor, melodic minor, chromatic, whole tone, octatonic, major pentatonic, minor pentatonic, or blues.

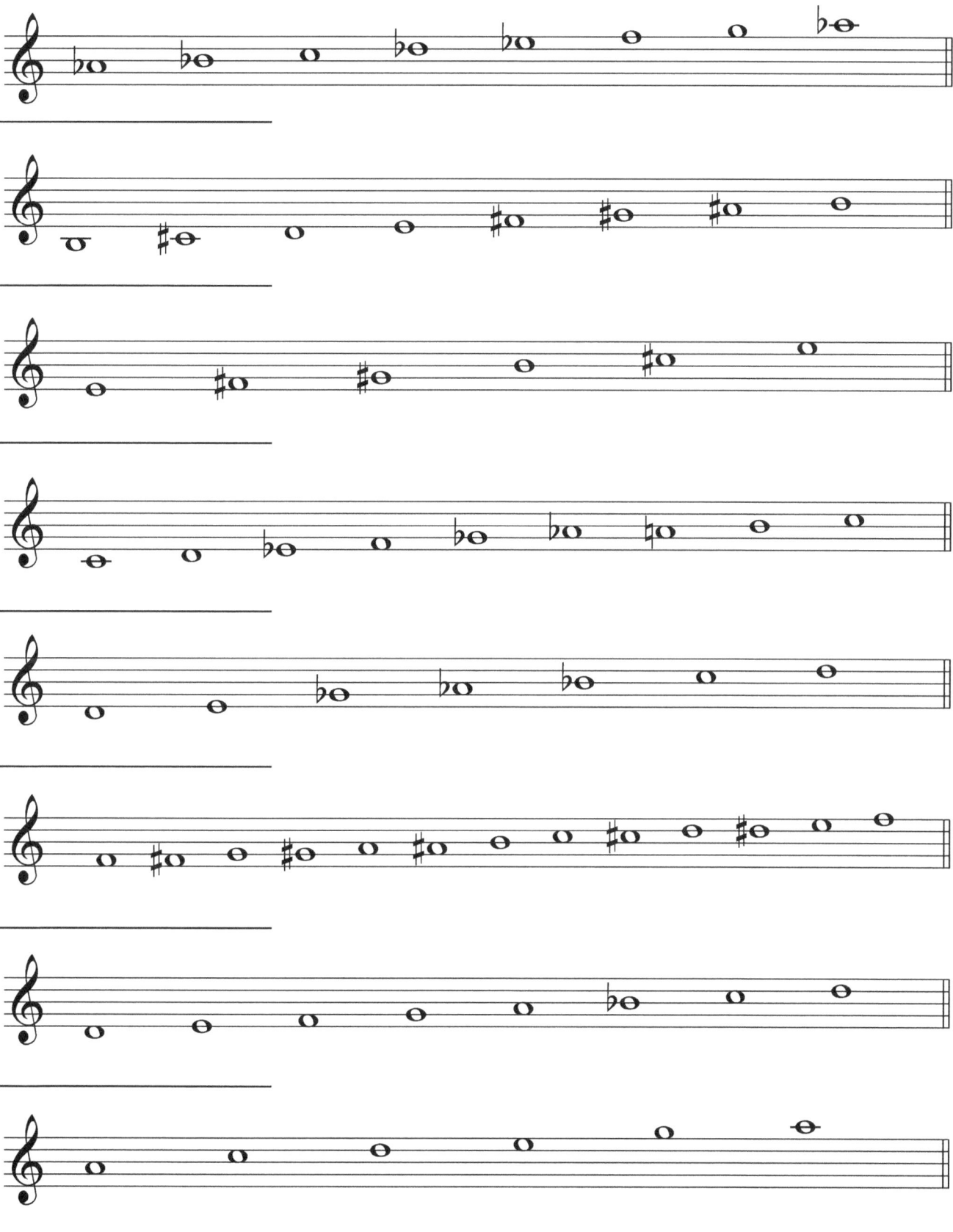

7
C Clefs

Why do we use different clefs? Wouldn't it be easier just to use one clef? To understand why we need different clefs look at Figure 7.1 and 7.2. Figure 7.1 is a melody in the treble clef. If we wanted to write this melody in the bass clef as shown in Figure 7.2, we would have to use a lot of ledger line notes, and they can be hard to read. Different clefs allow the notes to stay on and around the staff and make the music easier to read.

Figure 7.1

Figure 7.2

C Clefs

A *C clef* establishes the location of the note C on the staff. This is middle C on the piano. Wherever the little notch in the center of the clef occurs is where middle C is located. Figure 7.3 is a C clef with middle C on the third line.

Figure 7.3

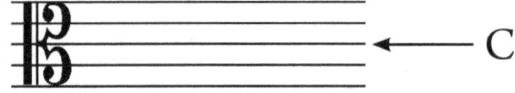

The C clef is different than other clefs because it is a ***movable clef***. Depending on which line the clef indicates, the name is different. The C clef can be placed on various lines of the staff.

Figure 7.4 shows four different C clefs. We will study the alto and tenor clef.

Figure 7.4

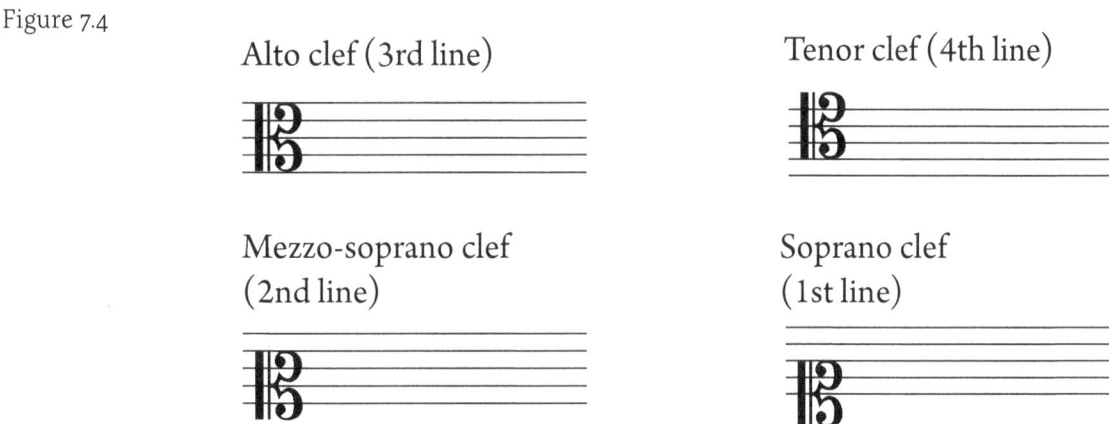

The Alto and Tenor Clef

The ***alto clef*** is used by the viola and the ***tenor clef*** is used by the 'cello, trombone, and bassoon. Other C clefs are not used today. Figure 7.5 shows the alto and tenor staves with notes.

Figure 7.5

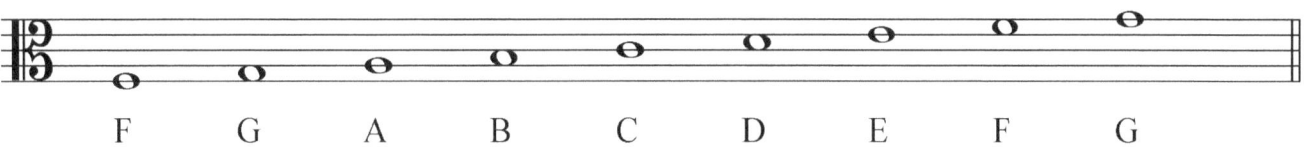

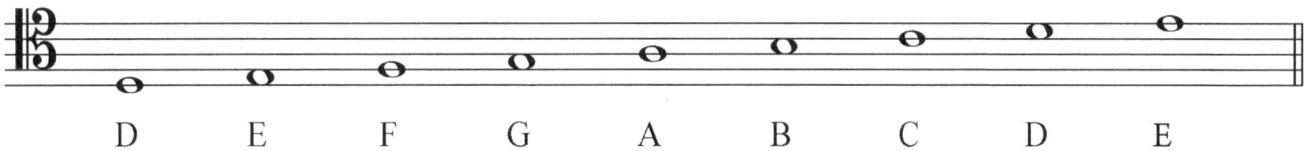

©San Marco Publications 2022   C Clefs

1. Name the following notes.

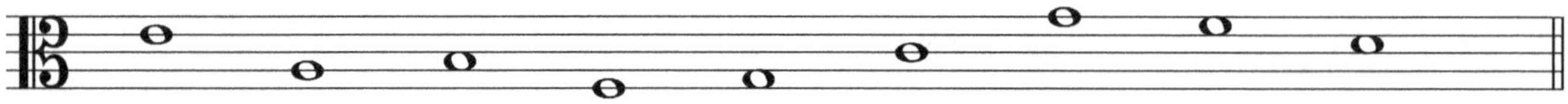

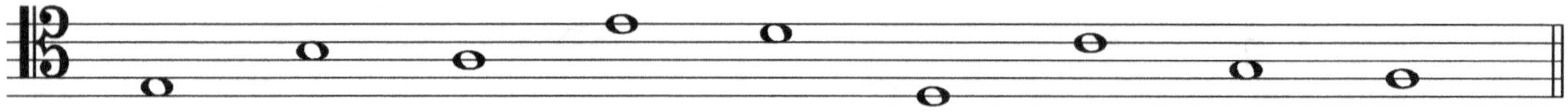

2. Draw an alto clef and write the following notes.

   a. E on a line
   b. B in a space
   c. D in a space
   d. F on a line
   e. middle C
   f. D on a line
   g. E in a space
   h. A in a space

   a.   b.   c.   d.   e.   f.   g.   h.

3. Draw a tenor clef and write the following notes.

   a. middle C
   b. D in a space
   c. E in a space
   d. F on a line
   e. G in a space
   f. D on a line
   g. B in a space
   h. A on a line

   a.   b.   c.   d.   e.   f.   g.   h.

4. Rewrite the following passage using the alto clef.

Wolfgang Amadeus Mozart
Cosi fan tutte

5. Rewrite the following passage using the tenor clef.

Gabriel Faure
Elegie, Op. 24

Alto and Tenor Clef Key Signatures

Figure 7.6 illustrates the placement of sharps and flats on the alto and tenor staff.

Figure 7.6

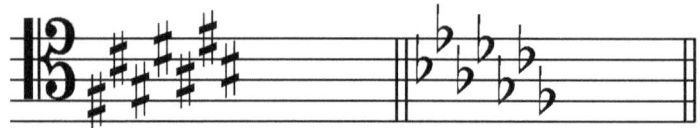

1. Write the following key signatures in the alto clef.

   D major   G minor   F minor   A major   E♭ major   B major

   C♯ major   B♭ minor   E minor   C♭ major   G♭ major   F♯ major

2. Write the following key signatures in the tenor clef.

   G major   C minor   F♯ minor   E major   D♭ major   D major

   B major   B minor   C♯ minor   C♯ major   C♭ major   E♭ minor

3. Add the correct clef and necessary accidentals to form the following scales.

a) F harmonic minor

b) C# melodic minor

c) E melodic minor

d) D blues

e) A♭ major pentatonic

f) G octatonic

g) B chromatic

h) D♭ major

i) C minor pentatonic

j) A whole tone

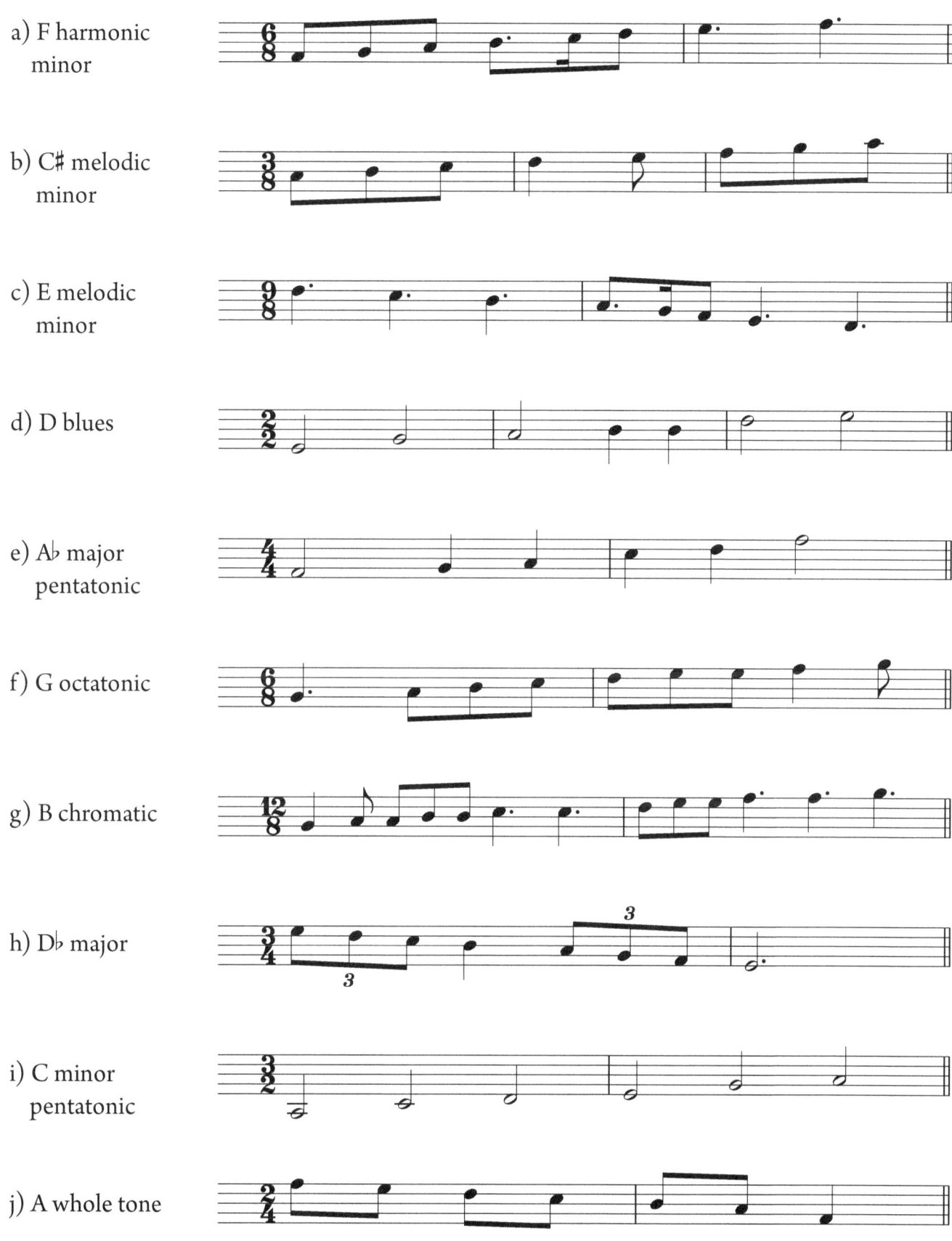

©San Marco Publications 2022

C Clefs

You may be asked to write a scale starting on a note other than the tonic. In this case, take care when writing a minor scale and raising or lowering $\hat{6}$ and $\hat{7}$. If you start on a note other than the tonic, these two notes will be in a different place within the scale. Figure 7.7 contains the D melodic minor scale starting on the dominant ($\hat{5}$). Scale degrees $\hat{6}$ and $\hat{7}$ become the second and third notes in this scale.

Figure 7.7

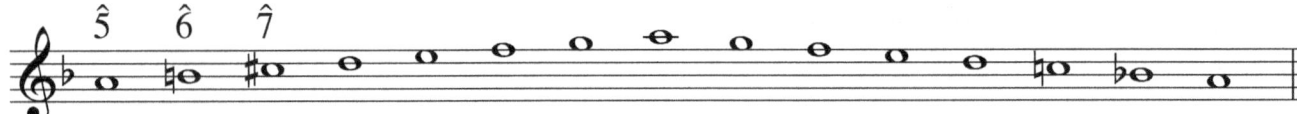

1. Write the following scales ascending and descending using a key signature for each.

E major from mediant to mediant

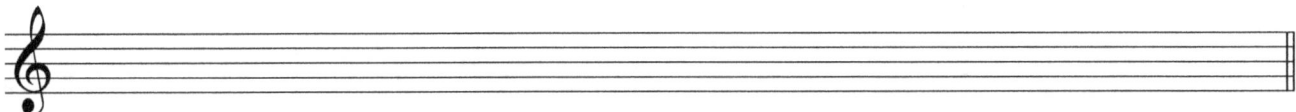

F♯ harmonic minor from supertonic to supertonic

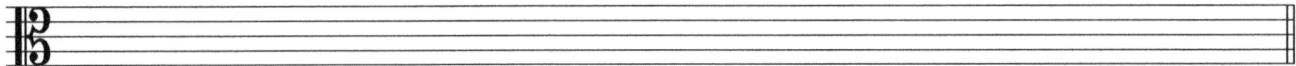

E♭ melodic minor from submediant to submediant

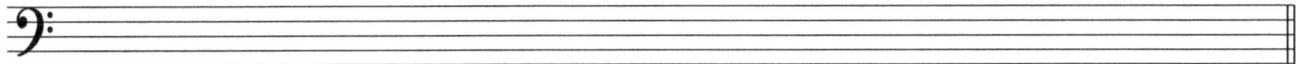

B major from subdominant to subdominant

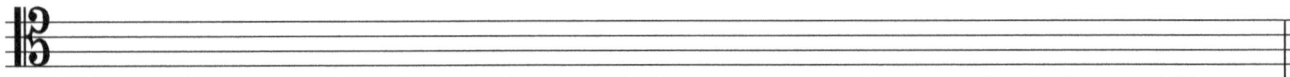

G harmonic minor from submediant to submediant

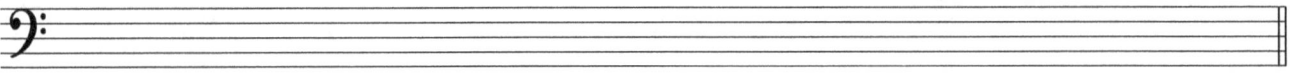

2. Write the following scales ascending and descending using a key signature for each.

G♭ major

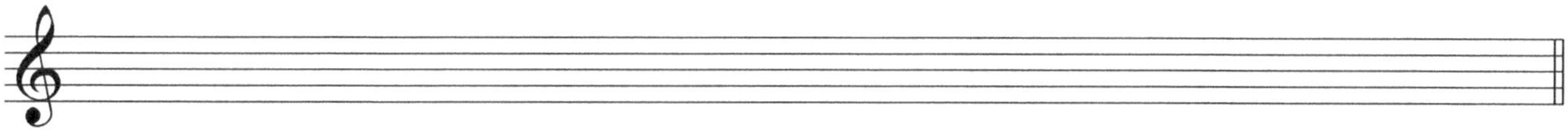

G♭ major's enharmonic tonic minor, harmonic form

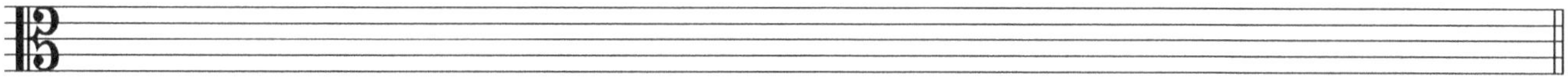

E♭ major

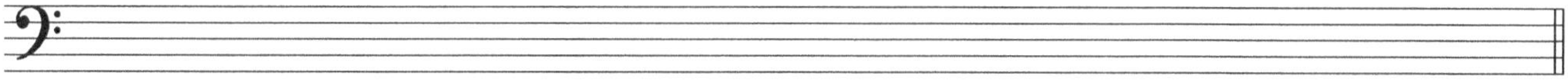

E♭ major's relative minor, melodic form

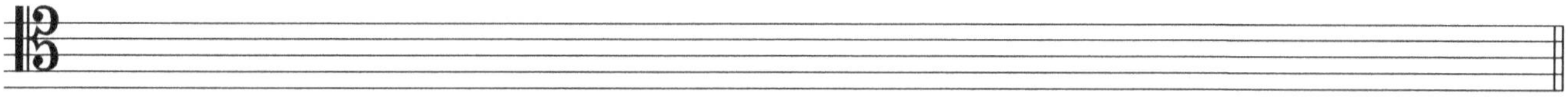

G♯ melodic minor

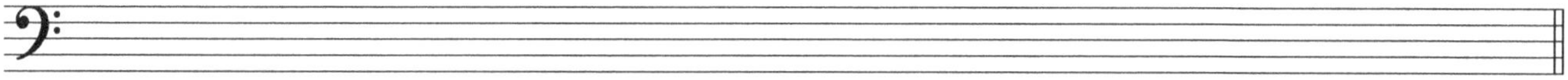

B♭ major

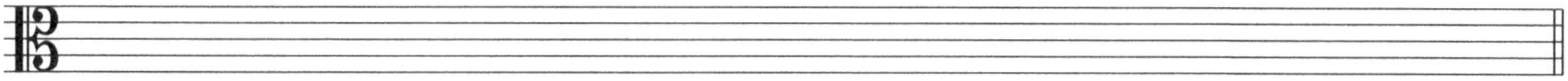

B♭ major's parallel minor, harmonic form

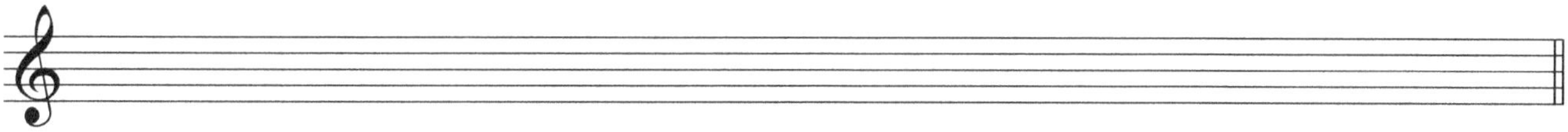

C♯ natural minor

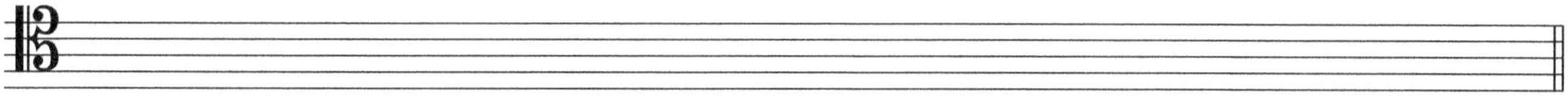

8
Modes

A *mode* is a type of scale. Modes are also called "church modes" because they were originally used by the Catholic church in Medieval times. Modes were used to compose the melodies of Gregorian chant and remained in use throughout the Middle Ages. With the rise of the major and minor tonal system in the Baroque era, modes were rarely used the Baroque, Classical, and most of the Romantic eras. They were revived by the Impressionist composers and are used most frequently today by rock and jazz players in improvisation and composition.

There are seven modal scales. Each major scale can be approached from seven different angles with one mode starting from each note of the scale. We will examine each mode using the key of C.

Ionian

The ***Ionian mode*** is the same as the major scale. All the white keys on the piano from C to C. It has the same patterns of whole and half steps as the major scale. It is used in all Western music from classical to rap. Figure 8.1 is the C Ionian mode.

Figure 8.1

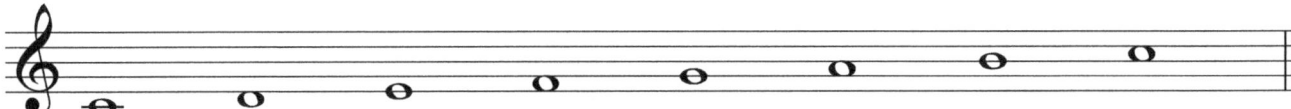

Dorian

The ***Dorian mode*** begins on the 2nd degree of the major scale. Using the scale of C it goes from D to D. This is the same as a natural minor scale with raised $\hat{6}$. This mode is used in rock, jazz, blues and fusion music. Figure 8.2 is the D Dorian mode.

Figure 8.2

Phrygian

The ***Phrygian mode*** begins on the 3rd degree of the major scale. Using the scale of C, it goes from E to E. This is the same as a natural minor with lowered $\hat{2}$. This mode has a Spanish sound and is used in Flamenco and fusion music. Figure 8.3 is the E Phrygian mode.

Figure 8.3

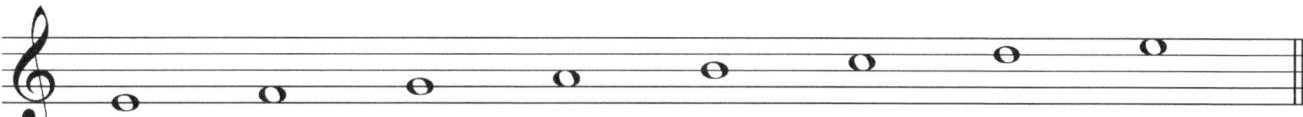

Lydian

The ***Lydian mode*** begins on the 4th degree of the major scale. Using the scale of C, it goes from F to F. This is the same as a major scale with raised $\hat{4}$. This mode is used in country, rock, jazz, blues and fusion music. Figure 8.4 is the F Lydian mode.

Figure 8.4

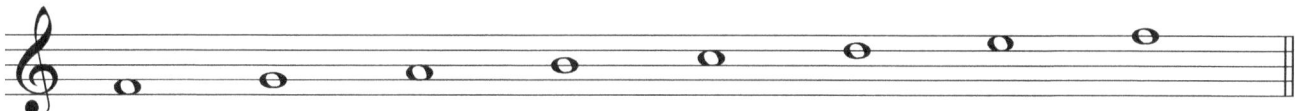

Mixolydian

The ***Mixolydian mode*** begins on the 5th degree of the major scale. Using the scale of C, it goes from G to G. This is the same as a major scale with lowered $\hat{7}$. This mode is used in rockabilly, country, rock, and blues music. Figure 8.5 is the G Mixolydian mode.

Figure 8.5

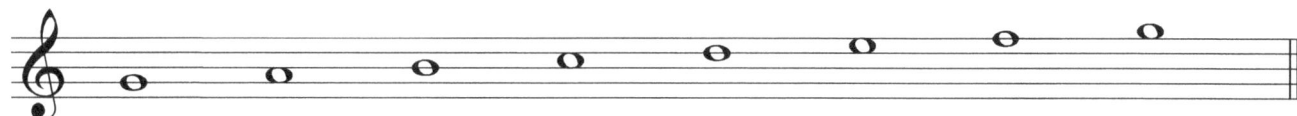

Aeolian

The ***Aeolian mode*** begins on the 6th degree of the major scale. This mode is also the natural minor scale. Using the scale of C, it goes from A to A. It is used in most music including pop, country, rock, jazz, blues, classical, hip-hop, rap, etc. Figure 8.6 is the A Aeolian mode.

Figure 8.6

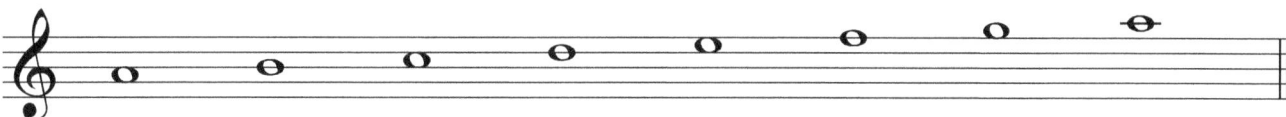

Locrian

The **Locrian mode** begins on the 7th degree of the major scale. Using the scale of C, it goes from B to B. This is the same as a natural minor scale with lowered $\hat{2}$ and lowered $\hat{5}$. It is the least commonly used mode but can be found in some jazz and fusion music. Figure 8.7 is the B Locrian mode.

Figure 8.7

Writing Modes

When writing modes, it is helpful know their order. Here is a saying to help you remember the order of modes: *I Don't Punch Like Muhammad Ali.*

Let's say we are asked to write the B♭ dorian mode.

1. First, the dorian mode starts on $\hat{2}$ of a major scale.
2. Determine what major scale has B♭ as scale degree $\hat{2}$, (A♭ major).
3. Write the mode from B♭ to B♭ using the key signature of A♭ major (4 flats).
4. You're done! See Figure 8.8.

Figure 8.8

A♭ major

B♭ dorian

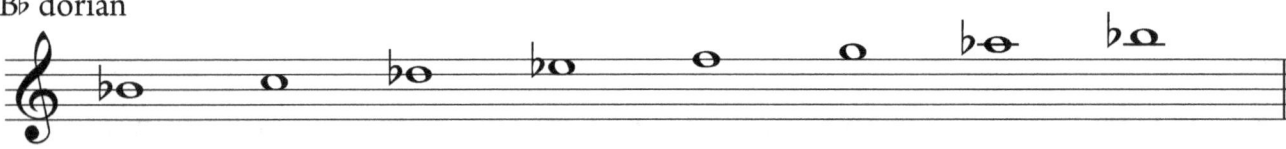

To write the A mixolydian mode.

1. The mixolydian mode starts on $\hat{5}$ of a major scale.
2. Determine what major scale has A as scale degree $\hat{5}$, (D major).
3. Write the mode from A to A using the 2 sharps of D major (F♯ and C♯).
4. Modes use accidentals. See Figure 8.9.

Figure 8.9

D major

A mixolydian

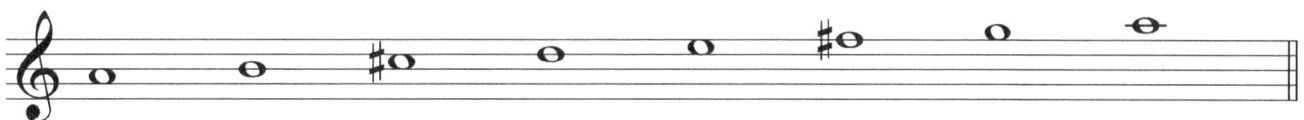

Another way to look at modes - an easier way!

There is an important aspect to understand about modes. Even though modes look like they are derived from notes within a major scale, you should learn and know the modes as their own entities. For example, the G Mixolydian mode (G-A-B-C-D-E-F-G) looks a lot like the traditional G major scale (G-A-B-C-D-E-F#-G). The only difference is the G Mixolydian mode contains an F♮, and the G major scale contains an F#. You could look at this mode as an altered type of major scale. In other words, a major scale with a lowered $\hat{7}$.

Looking at modes as comparable to most major or minor scales can make them easier to understand. Here is a list of the modes and how they relate to major and minor scales.

1. **Ionian** is the major scale
2. **Dorian** is a natural minor scale with a raised $\hat{6}$
3. **Phrygian** is a natural minor scale with a lowered $\hat{2}$
4. **Lydian** is a major scale with a raised $\hat{4}$
5. **Mixolydian** is a major scale with a lowered $\hat{7}$
6. **Aeolian** is the natural minor scale
7. **Locrian** is a natural minor scale with lowered $\hat{2}$ and $\hat{5}$

It can help to remember the modes using the above method. In this way, you can learn them as distinct scales and write and identify them easily. For example, if you wanted to write the A Dorian mode, you would just write an A natural minor scale with a raised $\hat{6}$ (F#).

Figure 8.10

A dorian

1. Write the following modes ascending using accidentals instead of a key signature.

C lydian

G phrygian

E mixolydian

C dorian

D aeolian

F locrian

E♭ lydian

F# mixolydian

Modes

Identifying Modes

It is fairly simple to identify a mode. One way is to know the order of the modes, and on what degree of the major scale they occur. To identify the mode in Figure 8.11:

1. Collect the accidentals to determine the major scale. Here, there are three sharps indicating the scale of A major.
2. What is the starting note of the mode? Here it is D. D is the fourth note of the A major scale.
3. The Lydian mode begins on the fourth degree of the major scale. That makes this the D Lydian mode.

Figure 8.11

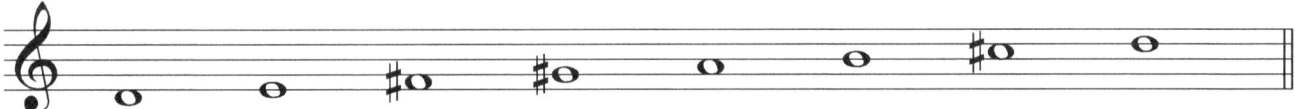

Modes can also be identified easily if you know the relationship between modes and the major and minor scales stated earlier. The Lydian mode is the major scale with a raised $\hat{4}$. Figure 8.11 is a D major scale with a G♯. This quickly identifies it as the D Lydian mode.

1. Identify the following modes.

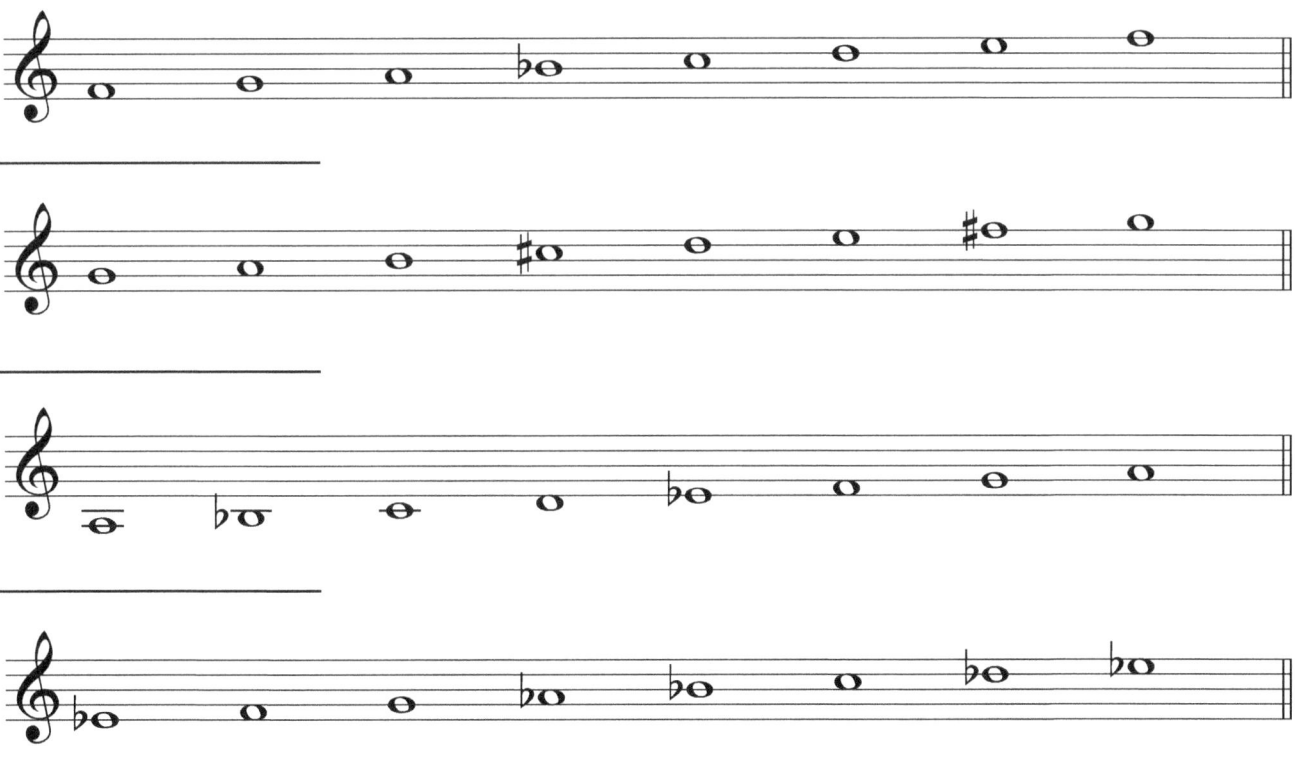

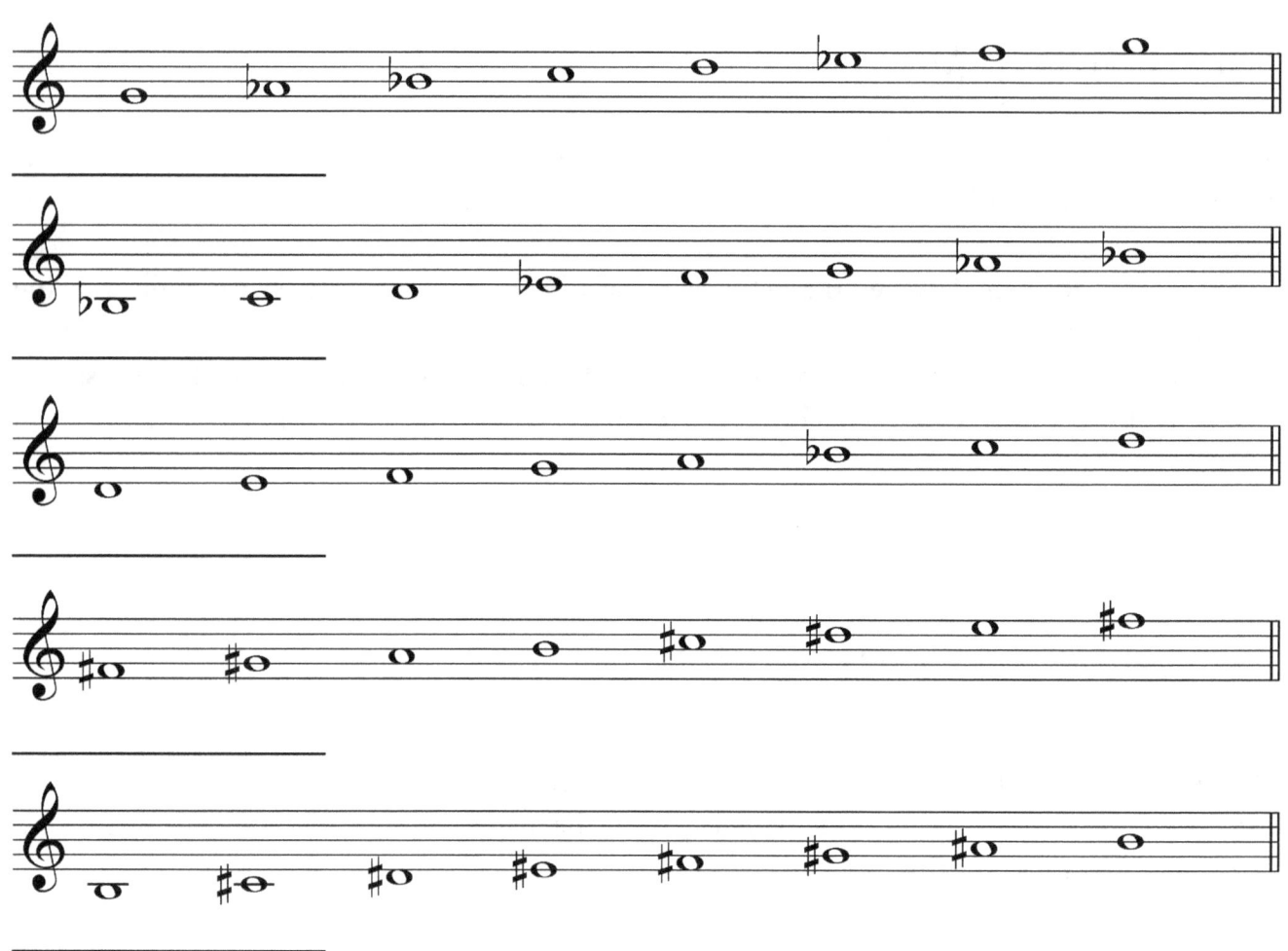

103

Modes

9
Intervals

Chromatic Half Steps

An *interval* can be defined as the distance from one note to the next. The smallest interval in the music we are studying is a half step.

Half steps may occur between two notes using the same letter name as shown in Figure 9.1. When a half step contains two notes with the same letter name, it is known as a **chromatic half step**. For example, a chromatic half step above F is F♯. A chromatic half step below A is A♭. These half steps use the same letter name.

Study how sharps, flats, and naturals can raise or lower a note without changing its letter name.

Figure 9.1

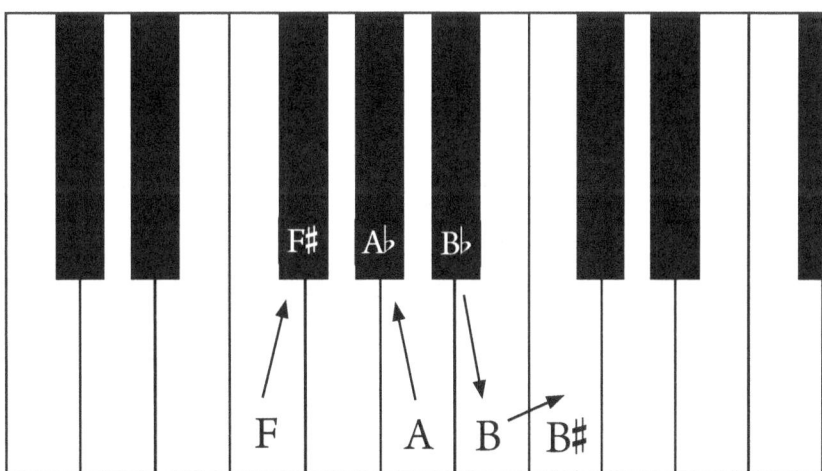

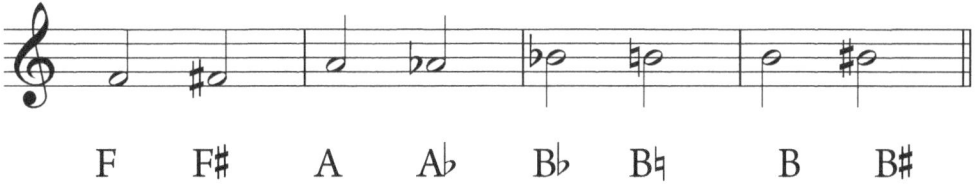

1. Write chromatic half steps above the following notes.

2. Write chromatic half steps below the following notes.

Diatonic Half Steps

Half steps may also occur between two notes with different letter names. Figure 9.2 shows half steps between notes using different letter names. When a half step contains two notes with different letter names it is known as a ***diatonic half step***. The notes names occur in alphabetical order. For example, E♭ - F♭, F♯ - G, A - B♭, etc.

Figure 9.2

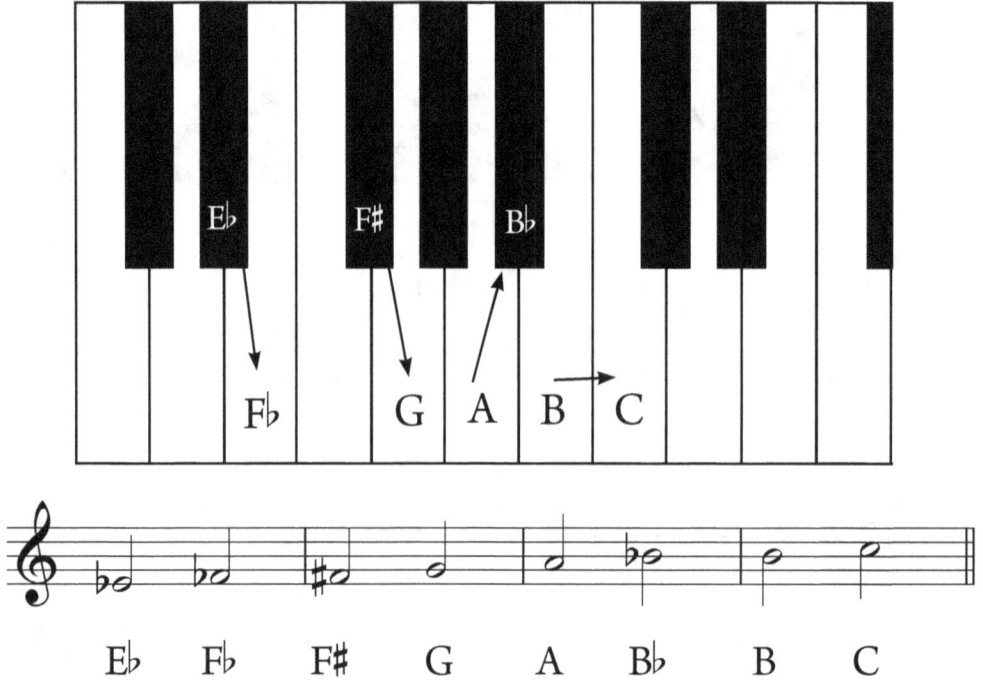

Intervals

1. Write diatonic half steps above the following notes.

2. Write diatonic half steps below the following notes.

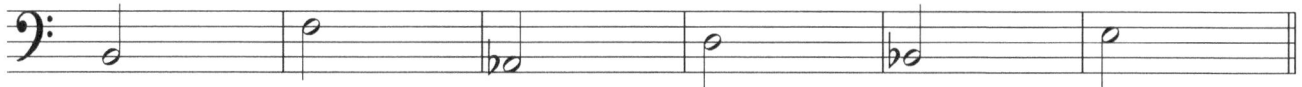

3. Name the following halfs steps as chromatic half steps (CHS) or diatonic half steps (DHS).

_____ _____ _____ _____ _____ _____

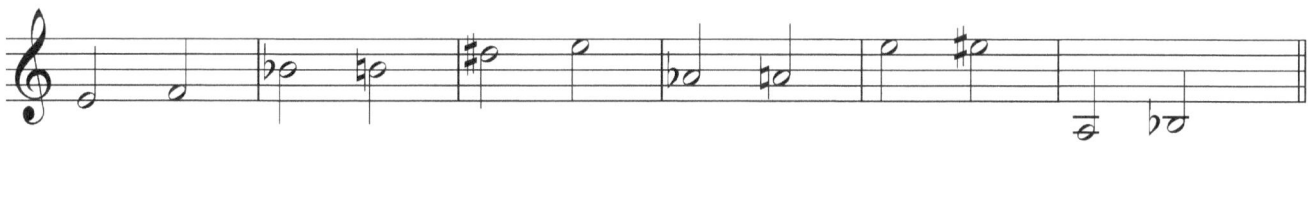

_____ _____ _____ _____ _____ _____

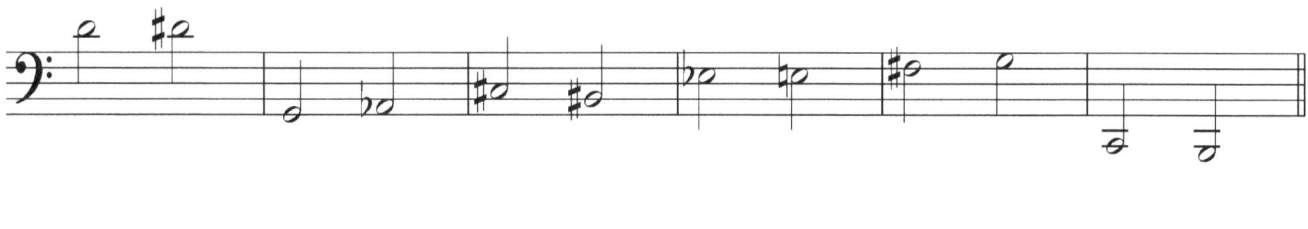

_____ _____ _____ _____ _____ _____

_____ _____ _____ _____ _____ _____

Whole Steps

A ***whole step*** is made up of two half steps. On the keyboard, there is always one key in the middle of a whole step. Sometimes the key is black, and sometimes it is white.

Figure 9.3 shows whole steps written on the score in music notation and where they occur on the keyboard. A whole step always contains two different letter names in alphabetical order. For example, F - G, A♭ - B♭, C♯ - D♯, or if it's a whole step below, D - C, B♭ - A♭, etc.

Figure 9.3

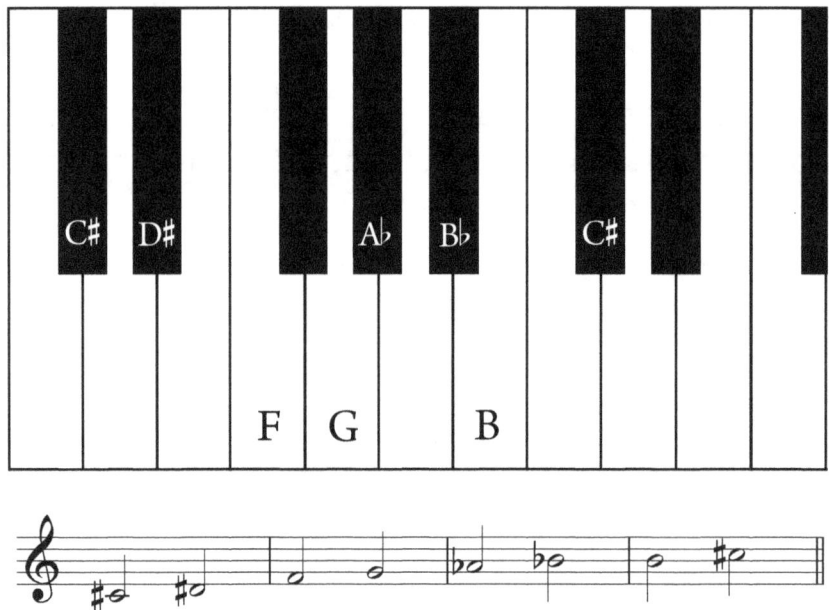

1. Write whole steps above the following notes.

2. Write whole steps below the following notes.

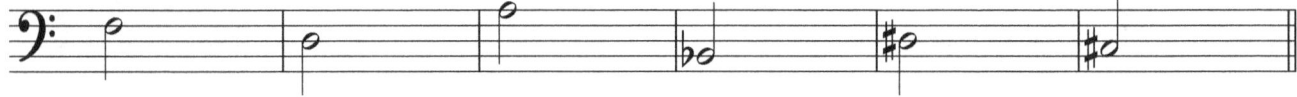

Numerical Intervals

Intervals larger than a half step are expressed as numbers. For now, we will deal with the intervals from 1 to 8. There are two basic types of intervals, **harmonic** and **melodic**.

- A harmonic interval occurs when two notes are played or sung at the same time.
- A melodic interval occurs when two notes are played or sung one after the other.

Figure 9.4

Harmonic   Melodic
Interval   Interval

Intervals are numbered. To determine the number of an interval, count up from the lowest note to the highest note. This is done even if the lowest note comes after the highest note.

Figure 9.5

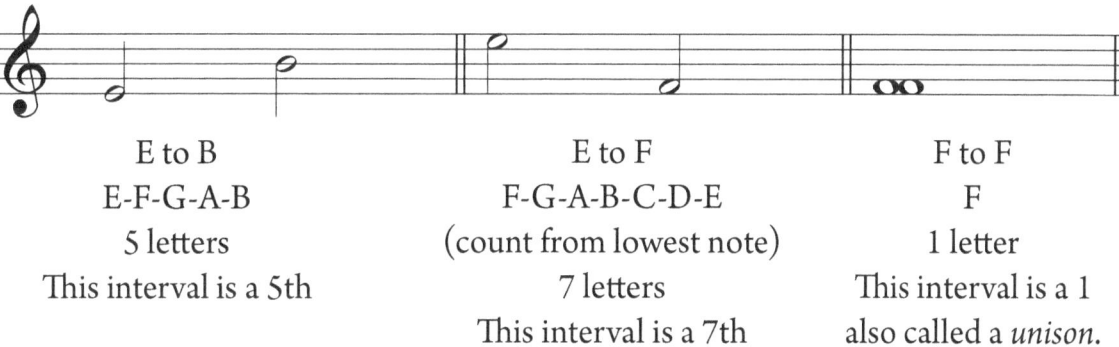

E to B	E to F	F to F
E-F-G-A-B	F-G-A-B-C-D-E	F
5 letters	(count from lowest note)	1 letter
This interval is a 5th	7 letters	This interval is a 1
	This interval is a 7th	also called a *unison*.

1. Write the following harmonic intervals above the given notes

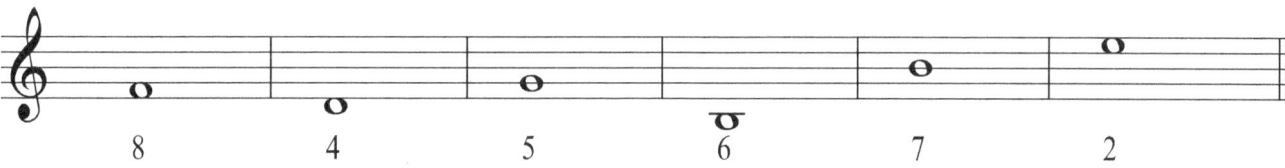

8   4   5   6   7   2

4   3   5   2   1   5

2. Write the following melodic intervals below the given notes

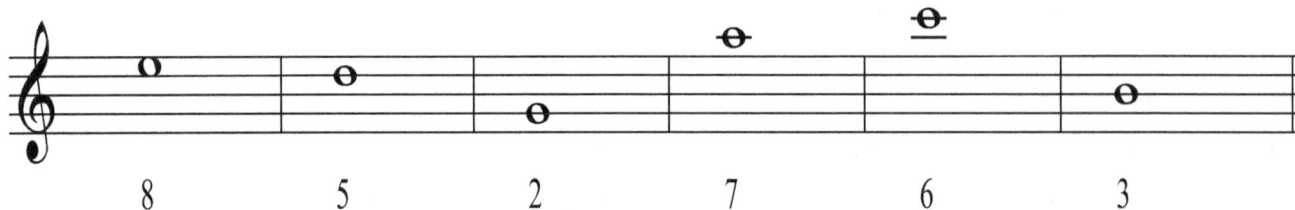

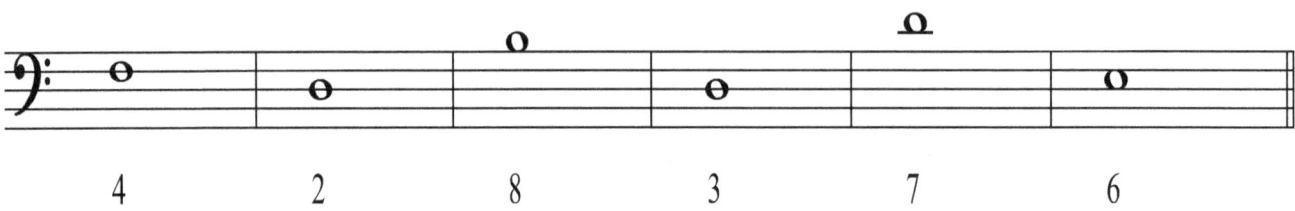

3. Name the following intervals.

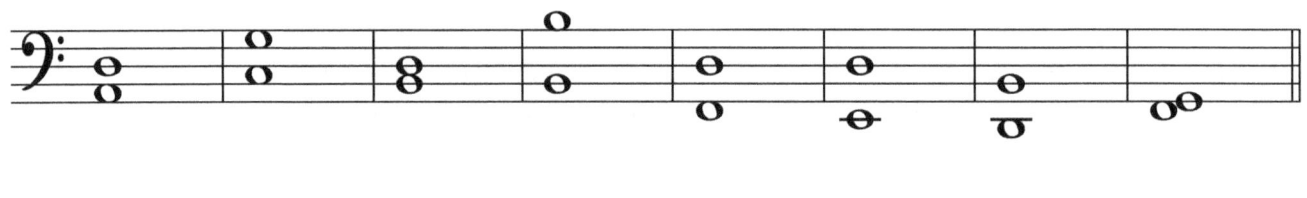

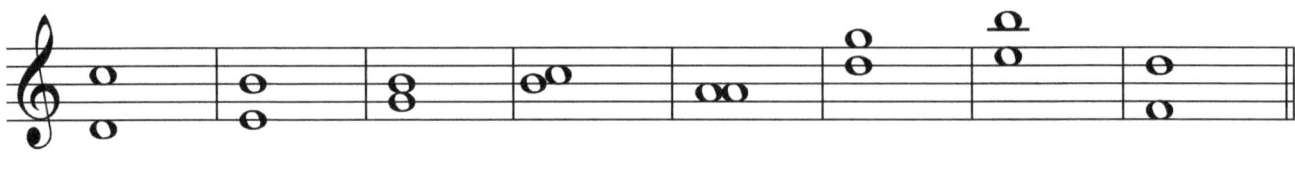

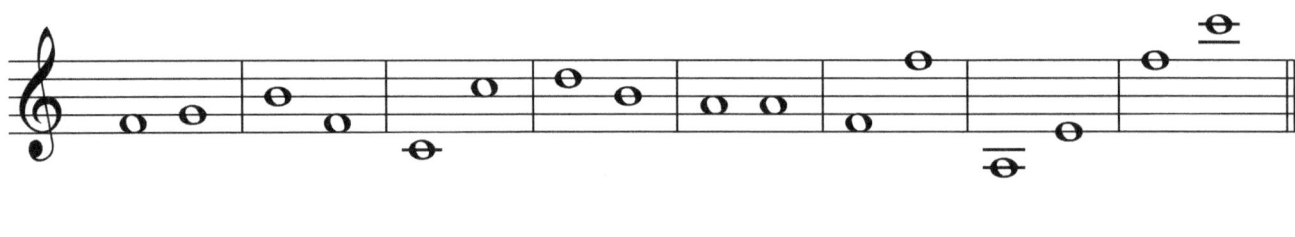

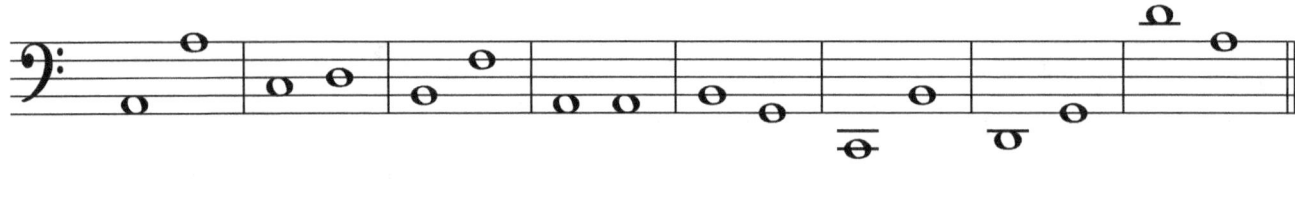

Major Intervals

Major intervals only occur on the following numbers: 2, 3, 6, and 7. In order for an interval to be major it must be one of these numbers, and the top note must be a member of the bottom notes major scale.

Figure 9.6 illustrates major intervals on different notes.

a. C to D is a major 2nd because D is the second note of the C major scale.
b. D to F♯ is a major 3rd. F must be sharp since it is the third note of the D major scale. F♮ would not be a major 3rd here.
c. E♭ to C is a major 6th because C is the 6th note of the E♭ major scale.
d. G to B is major 3rd since B is scale degree $\hat{3}$ of the G major scale.
e. D to C♯ is a major 7th since the scale of D major has C♯ as its 7th note.

When you write and solve intervals, the key signature of the bottom notes major scale is crucial. Knowing the key signatures is essential when dealing with intervals.

Figure 9.6

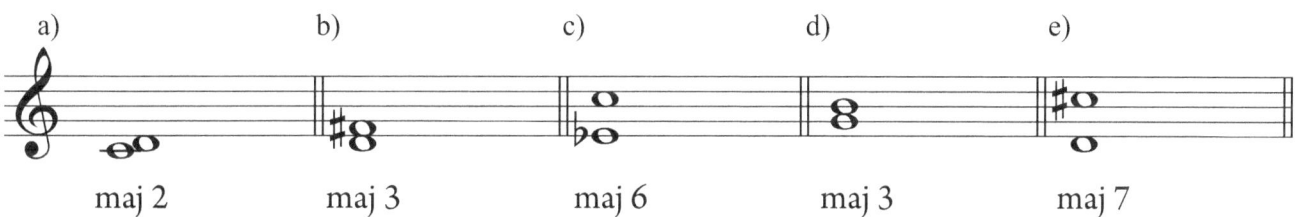

1. Name the following intervals. Think of the bottom note as the tonic of a major scale.

Perfect Intervals

The number of a perfect interval is always 1, 4, 5, or 8. Even though a unison (1) isn't really an interval, since there is no distance between its notes, it is still considered perfect. For an interval to be perfect the top note must be a member of the bottom notes major scale.

Figure 9.7 illustrates a number of perfect intervals. a) is a perfect unison. In b), A♭ is a perfect 4th above E♭ because A♭ is the fourth note of the E♭ major scale. A♮ would not be a perfect 4th here because it is not a member of E♭'s scale. When solving intervals always think of the major scale of the bottom note. Is the top note a member of the bottom notes major scale? If it is, the interval will be perfect, or major depending on the number.

Figure 9.7

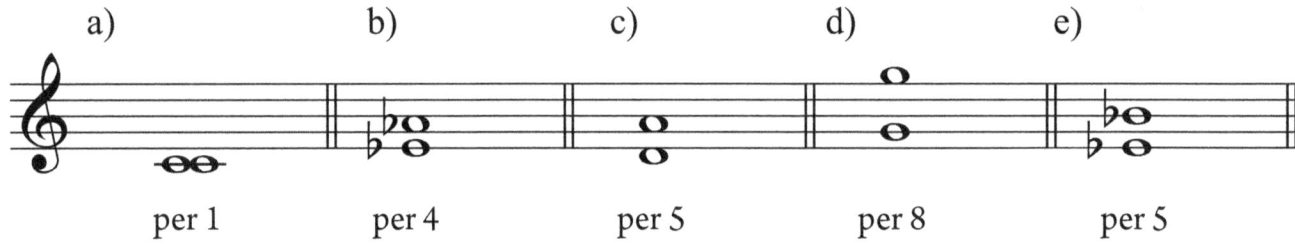

1. Name the following intervals. Think of the bottom note as the tonic of a major scale.

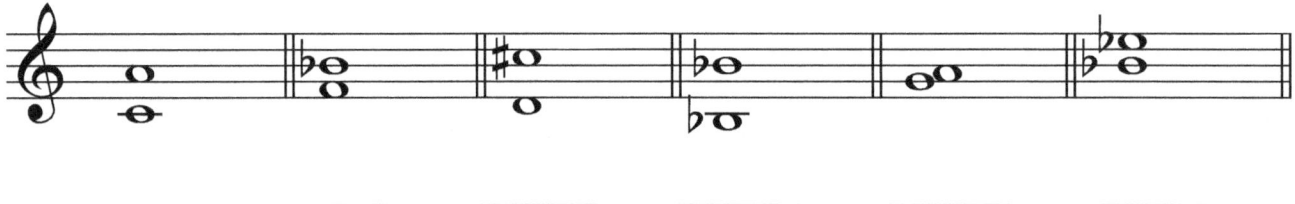

Intervals in a Major Scale

Major intervals use the numbers 2, 3, 6, and 7. Perfect intervals use 1, 4, 5, and 8. In order for an interval to be major or perfect the top note must be a member of the bottom notes major scale.

Figure 9.8 shows the major and perfect intervals formed between the notes of the C major scale.

Figure 9.8

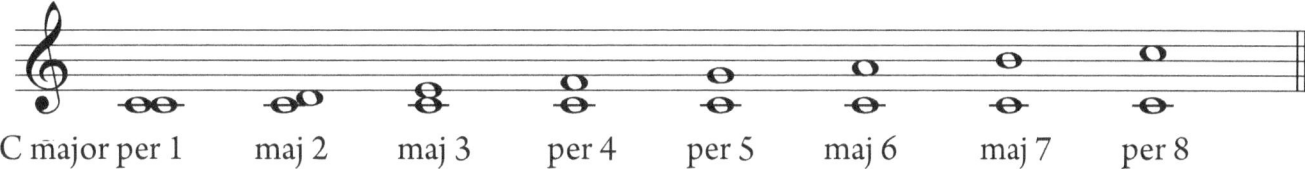

1. The following notes are written above E♭ using the notes of the E♭ major scale. Name the number (2, 3, etc.) and quality of each interval (maj or per).

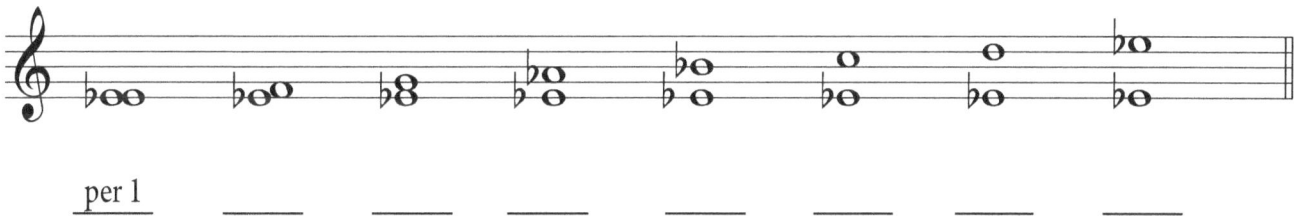

   per 1   ____   ____   ____   ____   ____   ____   ____

2. The following notes are written above A using the notes of the A major scale. Name the number (2, 3, etc.) and quality of each interval (maj or per).

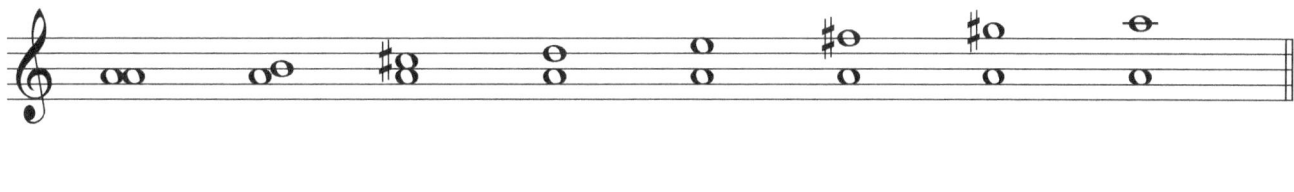

   ____   ____   ____   ____   ____   ____   ____   ____

3. Write each note of the A♭ major scale above each A♭ note. Name the size and quality of each interval.

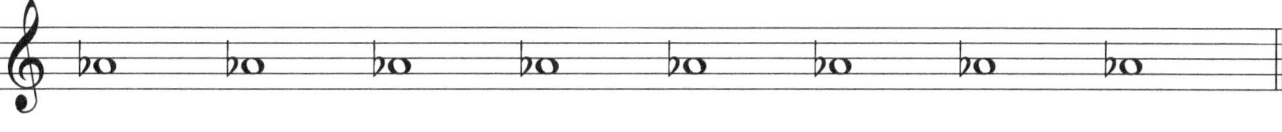

   ____   ____   ____   ____   ____   ____   ____   ____

Minor Intervals

Only 2nds, 3rds, 6ths, and 7ths can be *minor intervals*. They are always a half step smaller or closer together than a major interval that has the same number. A minor 2nd is the smallest interval. The half step is a minor 2nd.

Figure 9.9 shows the differences between major and minor intervals.

a. C to D is a major 2nd, because D is a note of the C major scale. C to D♭ is one half step smaller or closer together and is a minor 2nd. D♭ is not a note of the C major scale.
b. D to F♯ is a major 3rd because F♯ is a note of the D major scale. D to F♮ is a minor 3rd because it is one half step closer together than the major interval D- F♯.
c. F to D is a major 6th because D is the sixth note of the F major scale. F to D♭ is a half step closer together and is a minor 6th.
d. D to C♯ is a major 7th. D to C♮ is a half step closer togeher so it is a minor 7th.

A minor interval is one half step smaller or closer together than a major interval. Only major intervals (2nds, 3rds, 6ths and 7ths) can become minor intervals. Perfect intervals (1, 4, 5, and 8) never become minor intervals.

Figure 9.9

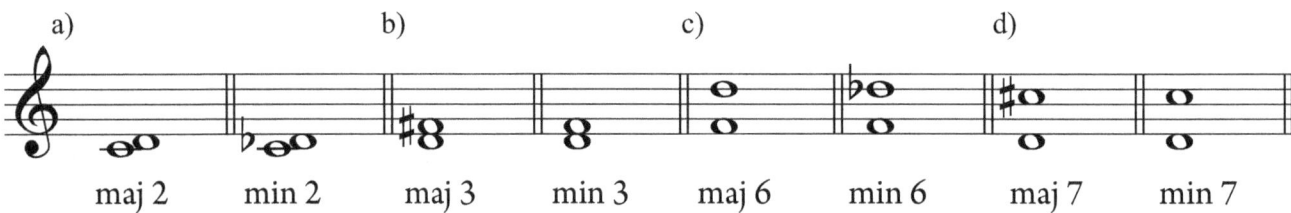

1. Name the following major intervals. Rewrite them making them minor intervals by lowering the top note one half step.

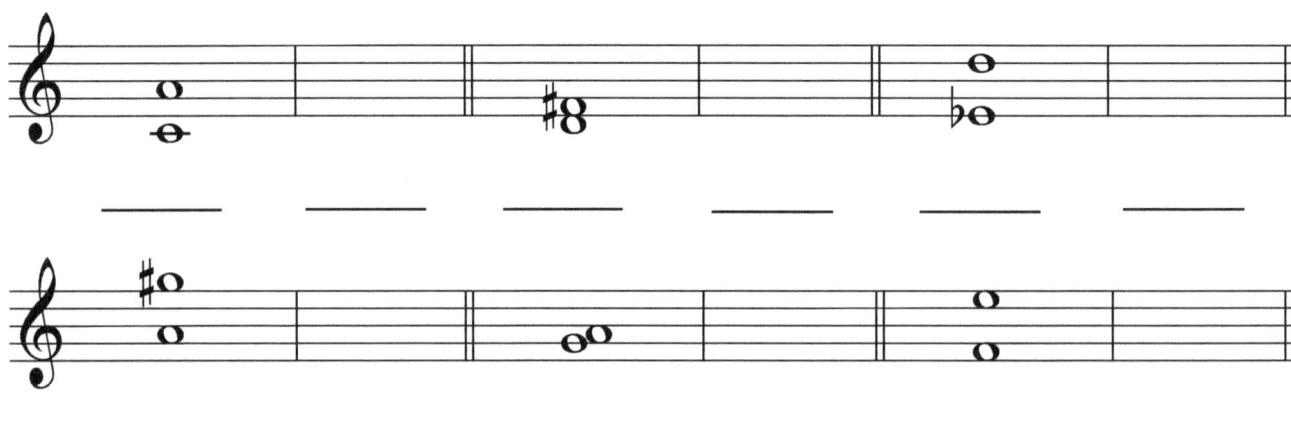

2. Name the following major intervals. Rewrite them, making them minor, by lowering the top note one half step. Rename each interval. The first one is done for you.

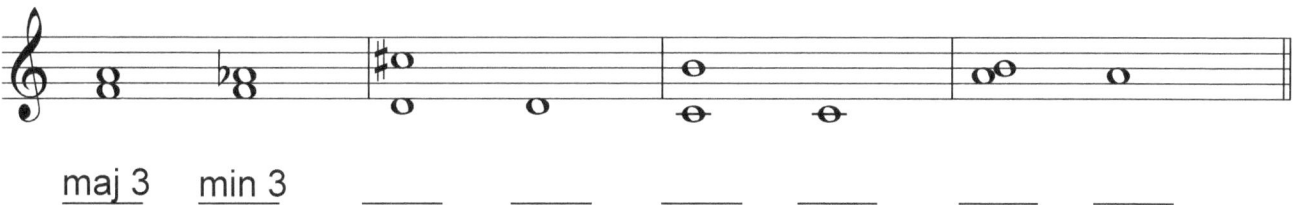

maj 3   min 3

3. Name the intervals under the brackets.

Carl Maria von Weber
Der Freischutz

Ludwig van Beethoven
Sonata Op. 10 No. 2

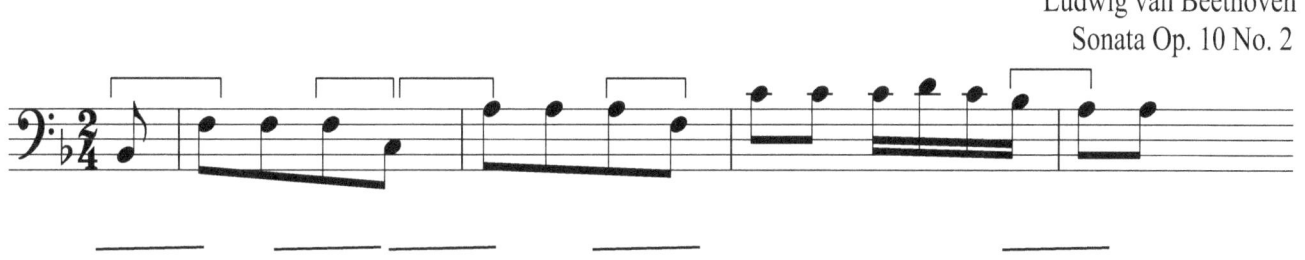

4. Name the following intervals.

_____   _____   _____   _____   _____   _____   _____

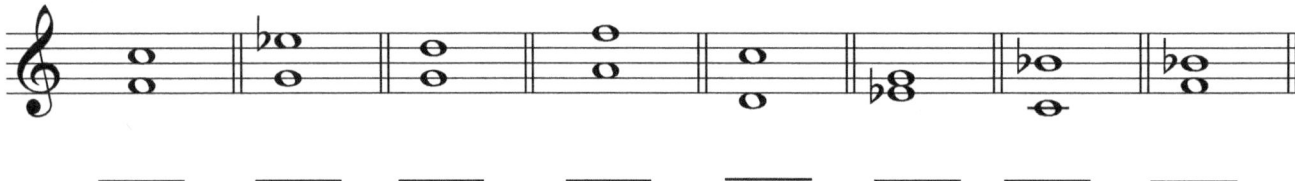

_____   _____   _____   _____   _____   _____   _____

5. Write the following harmonic intervals above the given notes.

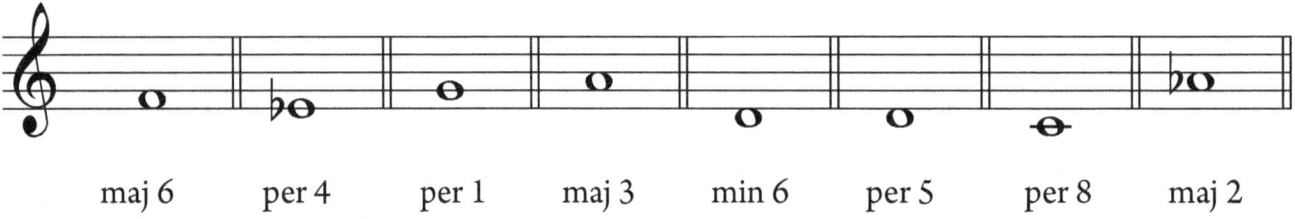

maj 6   per 4   per 1   maj 3   min 6   per 5   per 8   maj 2

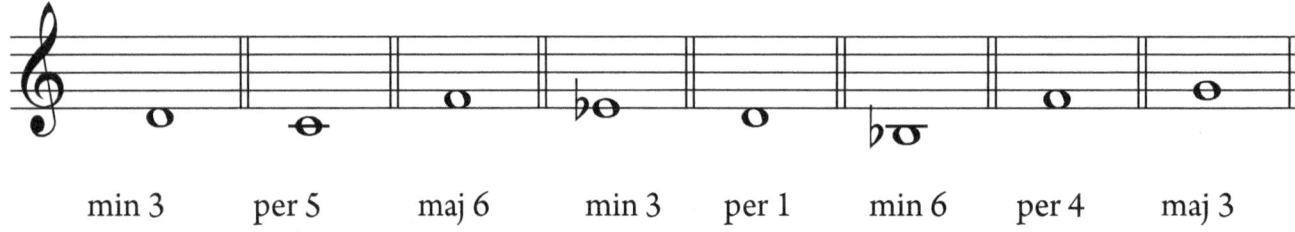

min 3   per 5   maj 6   min 3   per 1   min 6   per 4   maj 3

Augmented Intervals

An ***augmented interval*** is an interval that is a half step larger than a perfect or major interval. Another way to look at this is: the notes of the augmented interval are one half step further apart than the notes of a major or perfect interval.

Figure 9.10 shows that raising the top note of a major or perfect interval creates an augmented interval. Compare these intervals with those found in Figure 9.8.

Figure 9.10

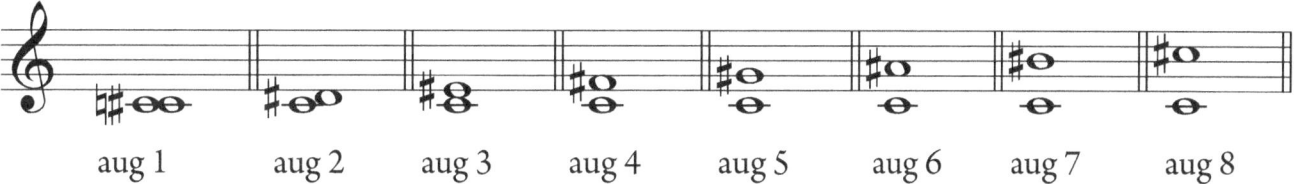

Another way to create an augmented interval is to lower the bottom note one half step. This makes the note one half step further apart and results in an augmented interval.

The intervals in Figure 9.11 are all augmented.

Figure 9.11

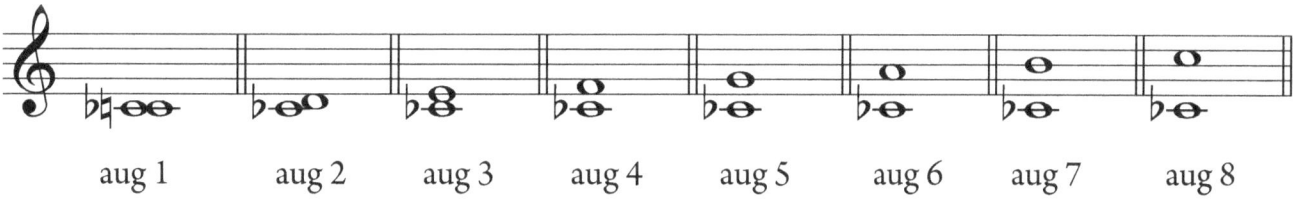

1. The following intervals are major or perfect. In the second measure, rewrite them and change the top note to make them augmented. Name each interval.

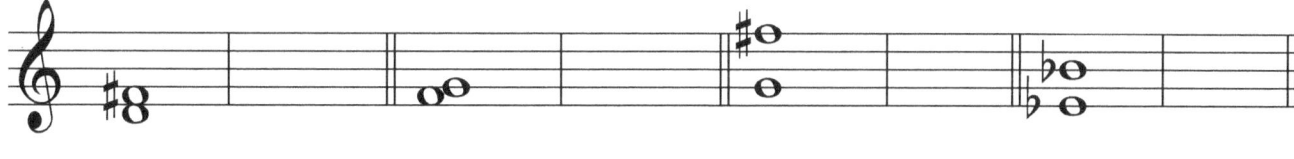

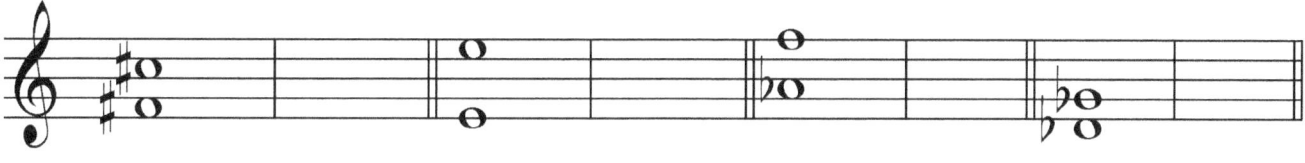

©San Marco Publications 2022

2. The following intervals are major or perfect. In the second measure, rewrite them and change the bottom note to make them augmented. Name each interval.

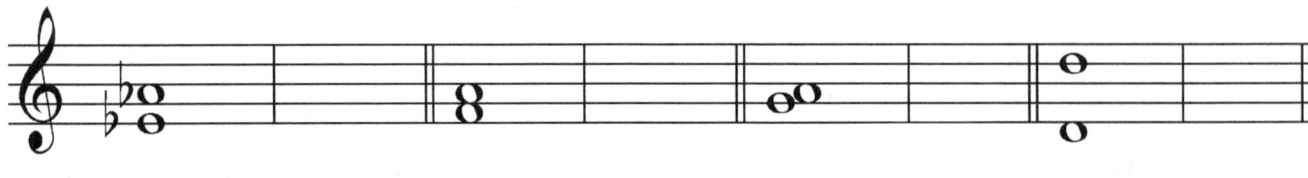

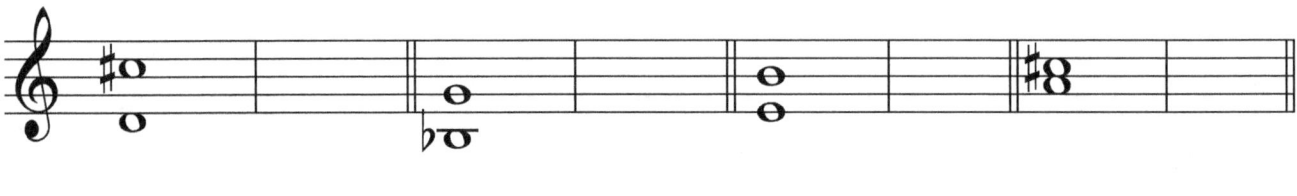

3. Write the following melodic intervals above the given notes.

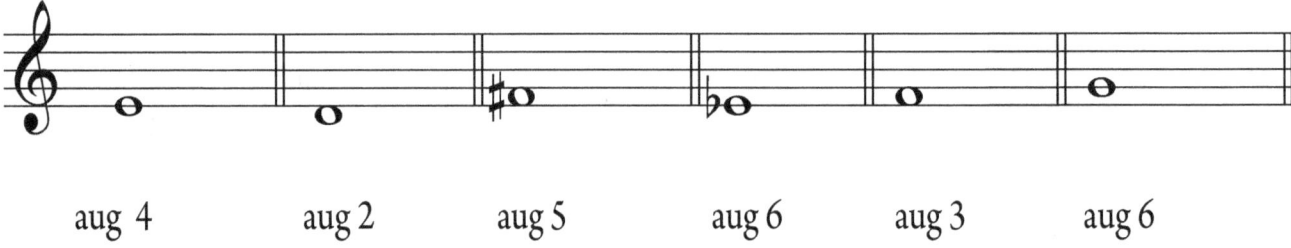

aug 4   aug 2   aug 5   aug 6   aug 3   aug 6

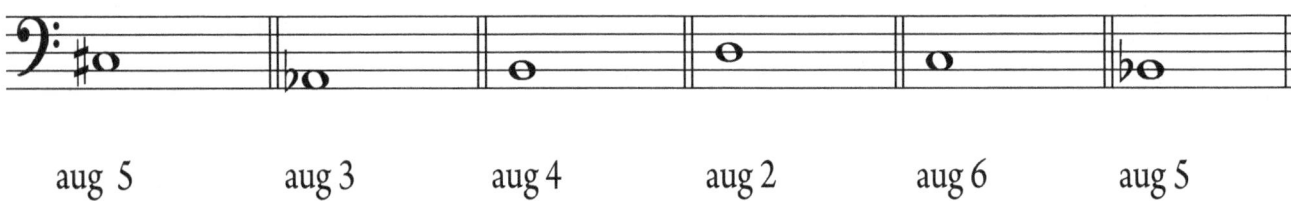

aug 5   aug 3   aug 4   aug 2   aug 6   aug 5

Diminished Intervals

A *diminished interval* is one half step smaller than a perfect interval. Lowering the top note or raising the bottom note of a perfect interval one half step results in a diminished interval.

Figure 9.12 contains diminished intervals.

Figure 9.12

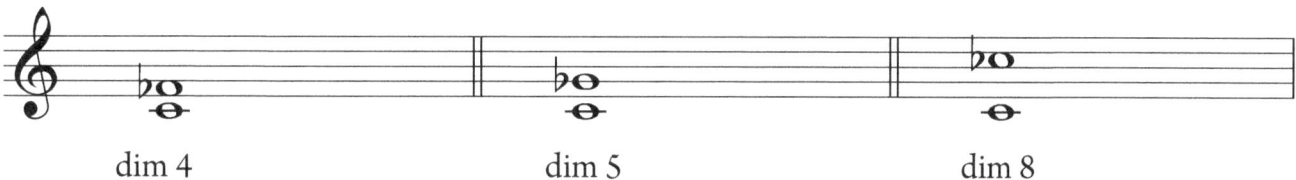

When the top note of a major interval is lowered one half step it becomes minor. When it is lowered two half steps the interval becomes diminished.

Figure 9.13 shows these interval relationships.

Figure 9.13

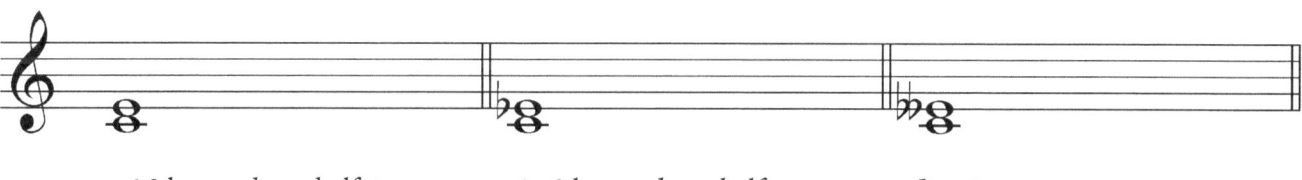

A major interval can be made diminished by raising the bottom note two half steps. Raising the bottom note brings the notes closer together.

Figure 9.14 shows that raising the bottom note of a major 3rd one half step produces a minor 3rd. Raising it two half steps produces a diminished 3rd.

Figure 9.14

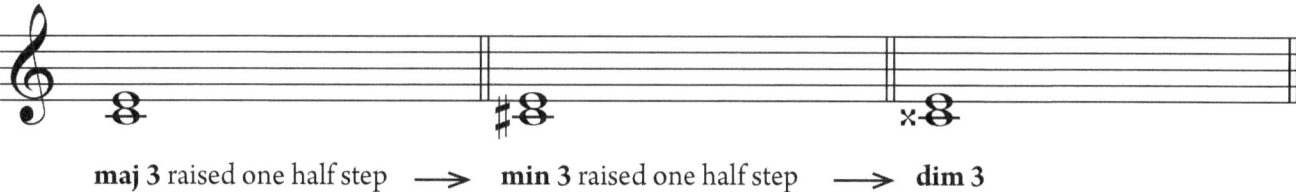

Intervals are always solved using the bottom note as the key note. This is true even if the bottom note comes after the top note in a melodic interval.

In Figure 9.15 both intervals are a minor 6th. The lowest note in the second interval comes after the highest note but the interval is still a minor 6th.

Figure 9.15

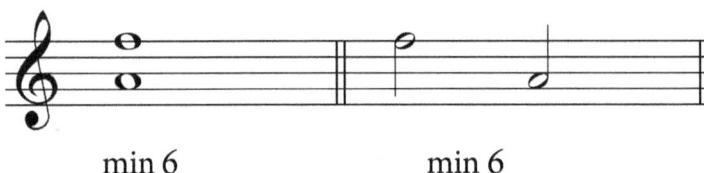

min 6   min 6

We consider the perfect unison the smallest interval, even though a unison is not really an interval. An interval is defined as the distance between two notes. There is no distance between the notes of a unison.

The unison requires special consideration. Since there is no distance between the notes of a unison, it cannot be made smaller. Unisons can never be diminished intervals. If any note of a unison is altered, the notes become further away from each other, and it becomes augmented.
Study Figure 7.16.

Figure 9.16

per 1   aug 1   aug 1   aug 1

This chart shows the relationship between intervals. The arrow indicates the movement of one half step.

diminished ← minor ← **major** → augmented

diminshed ← **perfect** → augmented

©San Marco Publications 2022

1. The following intervals are major or perfect. In the second measure, rewrite them and change the top note to make them diminished. Name each interval.

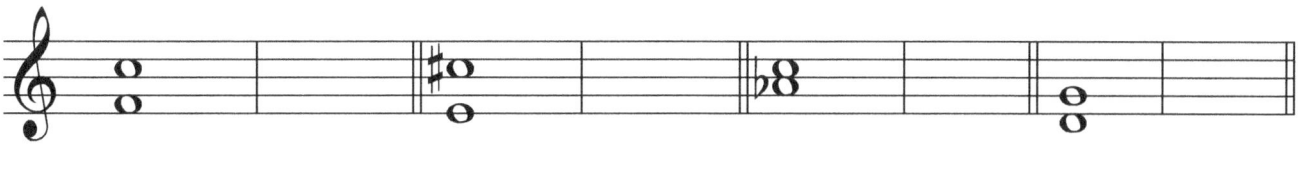

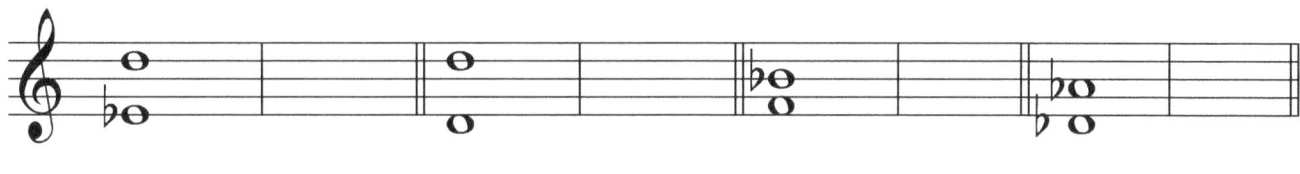

2. The following intervals are major or perfect. In the second measure, rewrite them and change the bottom note to make them diminished. Name each interval.

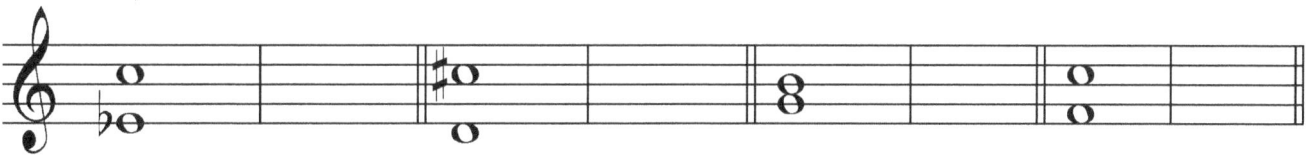

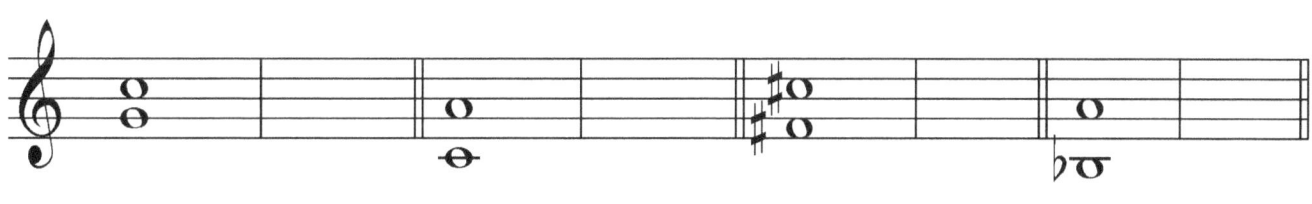

3. Write the following melodic intervals above the given notes.

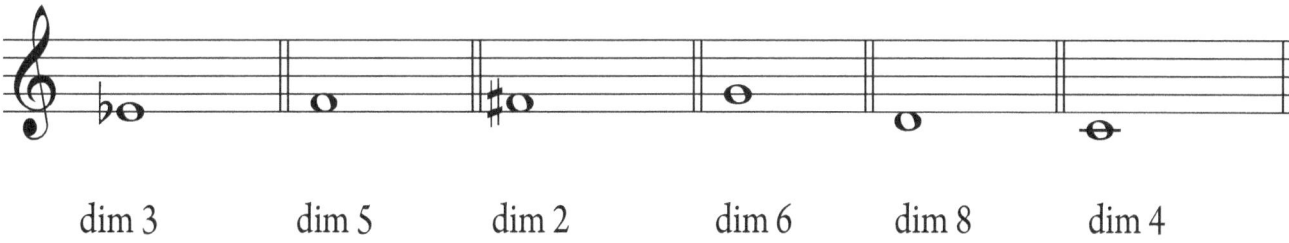

dim 3 dim 5 dim 2 dim 6 dim 8 dim 4

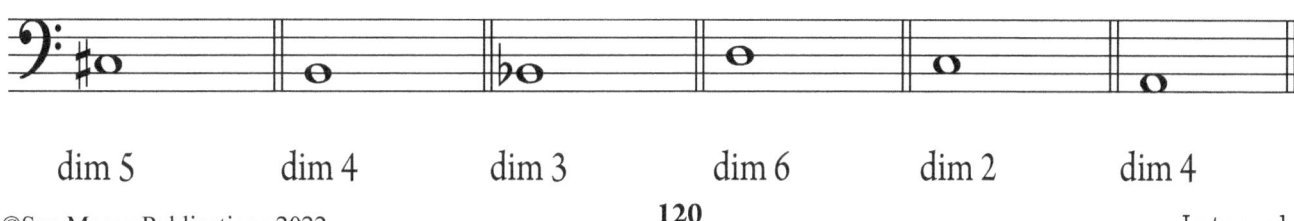

dim 5 dim 4 dim 3 dim 6 dim 2 dim 4

4. Name the following intervals.

5. Name the following melodic intervals.

Frederic Chopin
Ballade, Op 23, No. 1

6. Write the following melodic intervals.

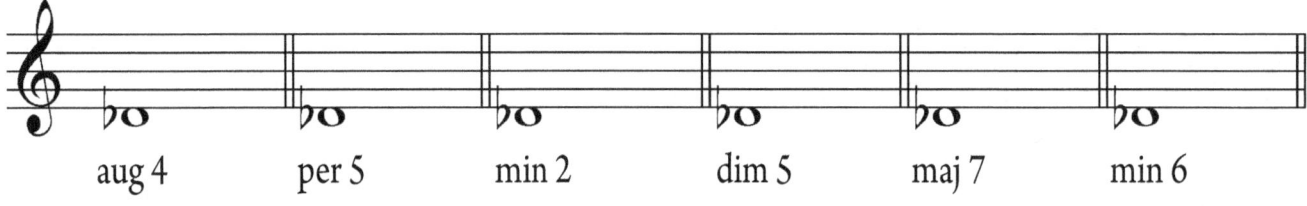

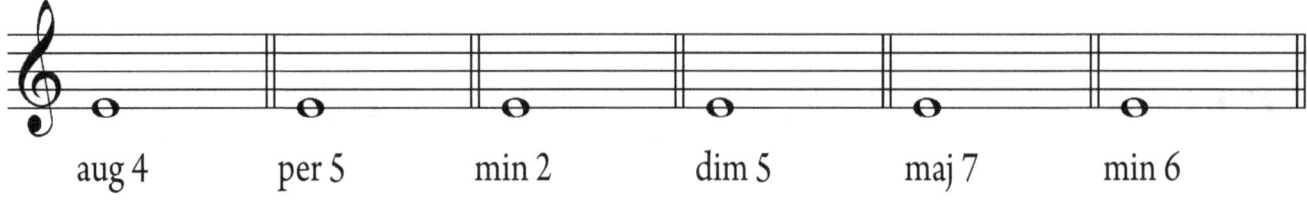

Solving Unusual Intervals

Sometimes the bottom note of an interval is not the tonic of a logical major key.

The lowest note in the interval in Figure 9.17 is a D♯. D♯ is not the tonic of a major key.

Figure 9.17

? 3

To solve this interval:
1. Since both notes have the same accidental, a sharp, remove both sharps (Figure 9.18).
2. With the sharps removed the bottom note is now D, a logical key.
3. The interval D to F is a minor 3rd. Since D♯ to F♯ is the same distance a half step higher, it is also a minor 3rd. The interval number and quality is the same with the added sharps. D♭ to F♭ is also a minor 3rd, being a half step lower than D to F. The movement up or down by half step does not change the interval quality.

Figure 9.18

min 3   min 3   min 3

The interval in Figure 9.19a has an A♯ as its lowest note. We know this interval is a 4th since the letter names are A to D (A-B-C-D = 1-2-3-4). A♯ is not the tonic of a major key. By lowering it a half step to A♮, we have the tonic of logical key (A major). Since we lowered the bottom note one half step, we must lower the top note one half step. D becomes D♭. A to D♭ is a dim 4th. Therefore, A♯ to D is also a dim 4th.

Figure 9.19b contains F♭ as its lowest note. When we raise it one half step, we get a logical major key, F major. Since we raised the bottom note a half step, we must raise the top note a half step from D to D♯. F to D♯ is the interval of an aug 6th. Therefore, F♭ to D is also an aug 6th.

Figure 9.19

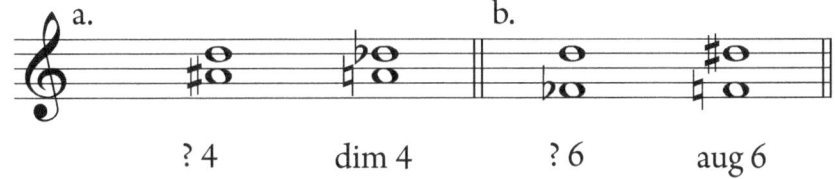

? 4   dim 4   ? 6   aug 6

1. Name the following intervals.

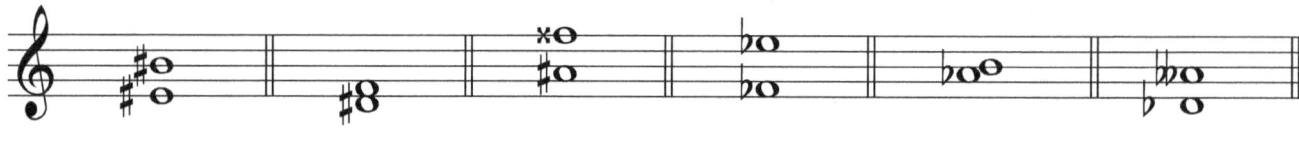

2. Name the following intervals.

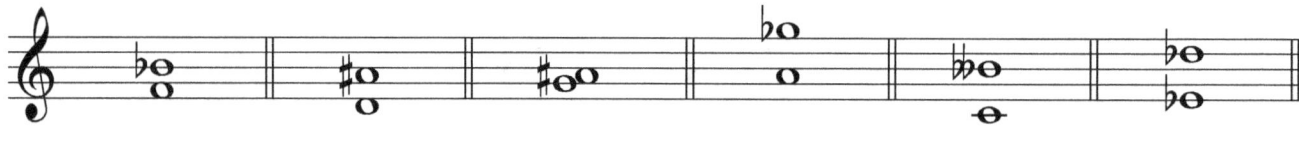

3. Rewrite the above intervals changing the upper note enharmonically. Rename them.

4. Name the intervals under the brackets.

Felix Mendelssohn
Trio in C minor

Antonin Dvorak
Trio in F minor, II

Ludwig van Beethoven
Symphony No. 9. III

Johann Sebastian Bach
Sonata No. 1 in B minor

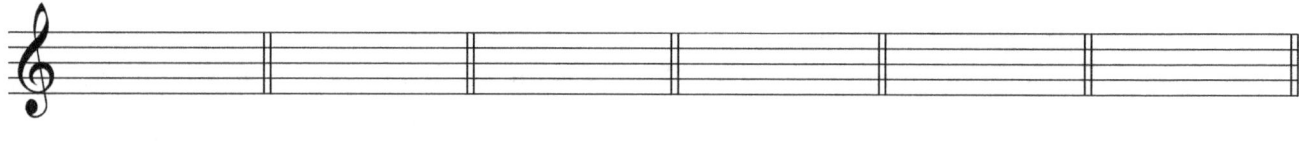

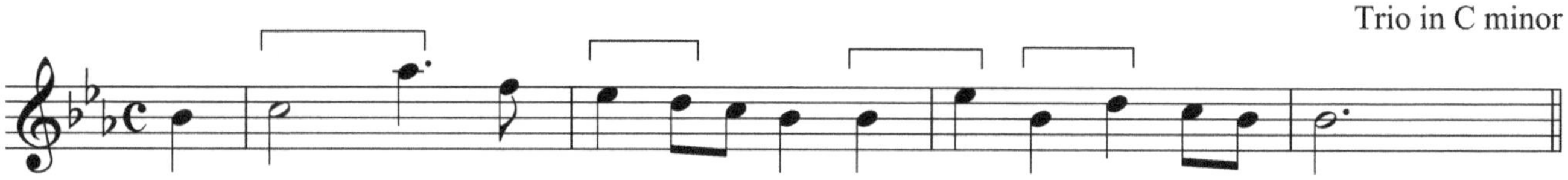

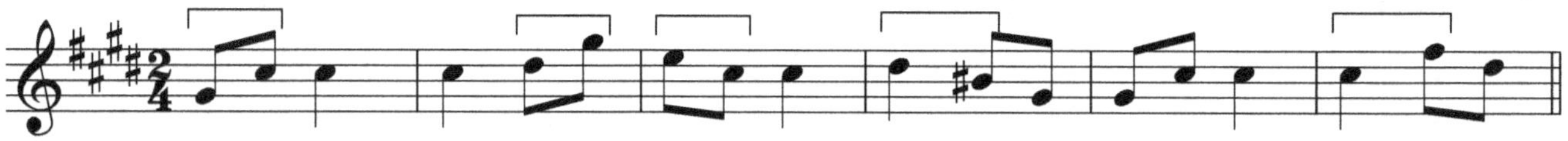

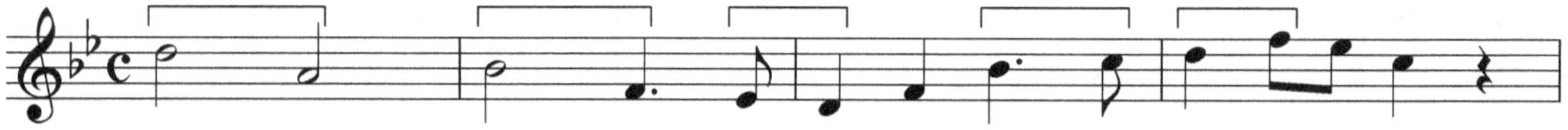

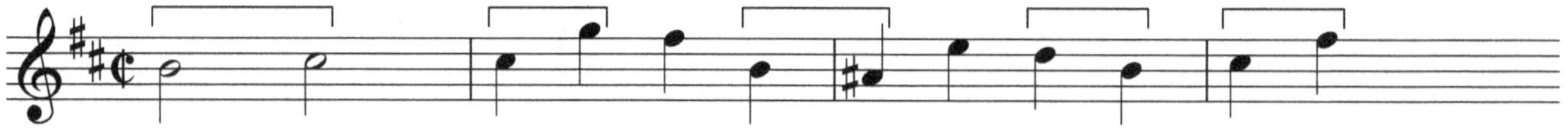

Writing an Interval Below a Given Note

You may be asked to write an interval below a given note. Let's say you have to write a major 6th below C. Figure 9.20. illustrates the following steps.

1. Write the note that is a 6th below C.
2. A 6th below C is E.
3. Check the interval quality. In this case E to C is a minor 6th. We need a major 6th, so you have to lower the E to E♭ in order to get a major 6th. Note: You cannot change the given note (C).

Figure 9.20

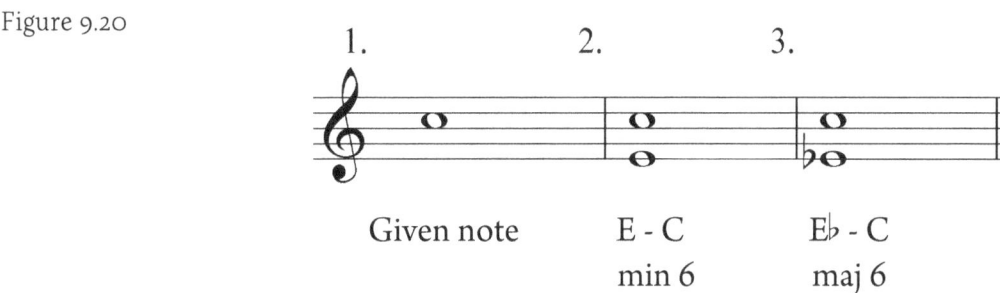

1. Write the following intervals below the given notes.

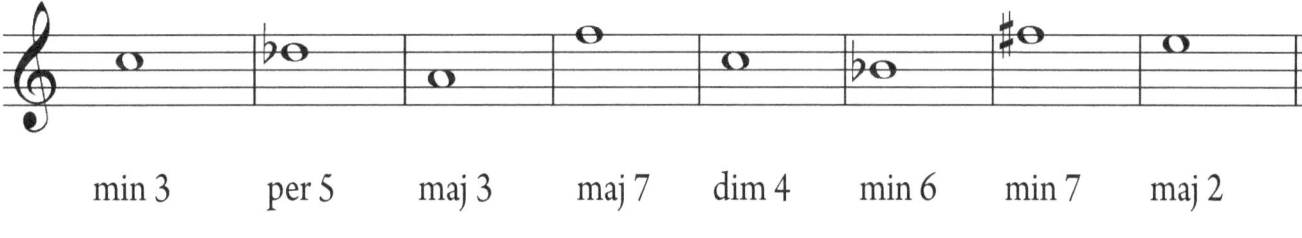

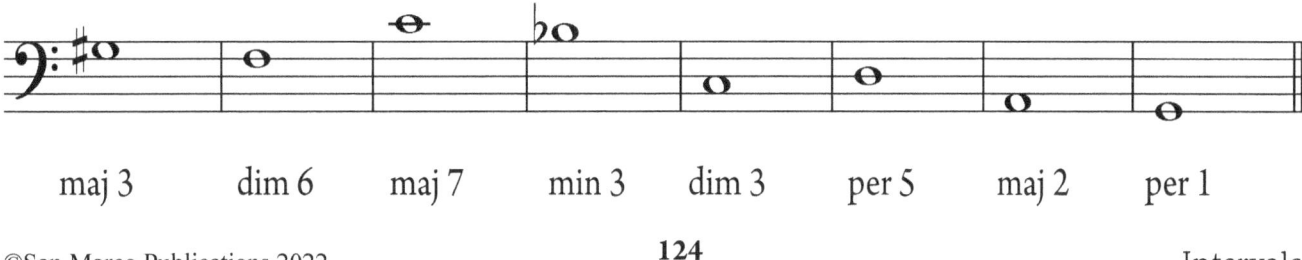

Inverting Intervals

Any interval can be inverted or flipped upside down. Figure 9.21 shows the perfect 4th G - C inverted in the second measure. When you invert a perfect 4th it becomes a perfect 5th. Here, C - G.

Figure 9.21

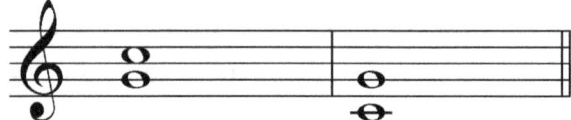

When an interval is inverted the sum of the original and the inverted interval equals nine. Using the intervals in Figure 9.21, G -C is a perfect 4th. When it is inverted it becomes C-G, a perfect 5th. When you add 4 and 5 you get 9. Study the interval inversions in Figure 9.22. They all add up to 9.

Figure 9.22

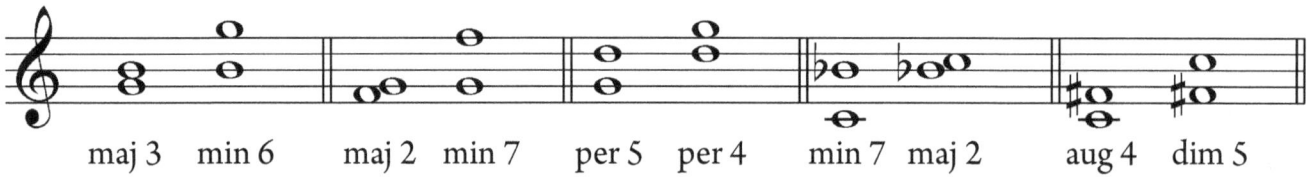

maj 3   min 6   maj 2   min 7   per 5   per 4   min 7   maj 2   aug 4   dim 5

Except for perfect intervals the interval quality changes when you invert them. Here is what happens to the interval qualities when you invert them:

- major becomes minor
- minor becomes major
- diminished becomes augmented
- augmented becomes diminshed
- perfect stays perfect

The augmented octave is a special case when inverting. An augmented octave is larger than an octave and when it is inverted the numbers do not add up to 9. Figure 9.23 shows the inversion of the augmented octave. An aug 8 becomes a dim 8 when inverted. However, since a dim 8 is smaller than an octave, it becomes and aug 1 when inverted.

Figure 9.23

aug 8   dim 8   dim 8   aug 1

1. Name the following intervals. In the staff below, invert them and rename them.

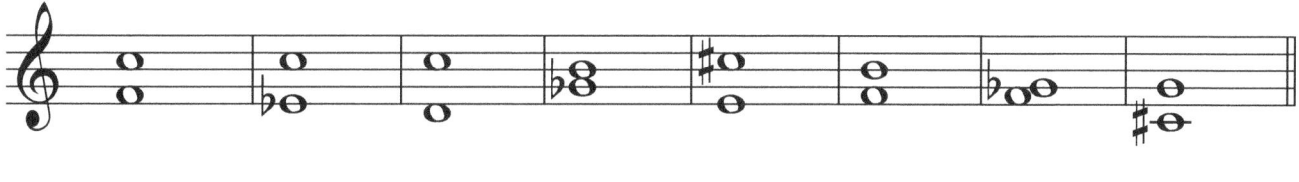

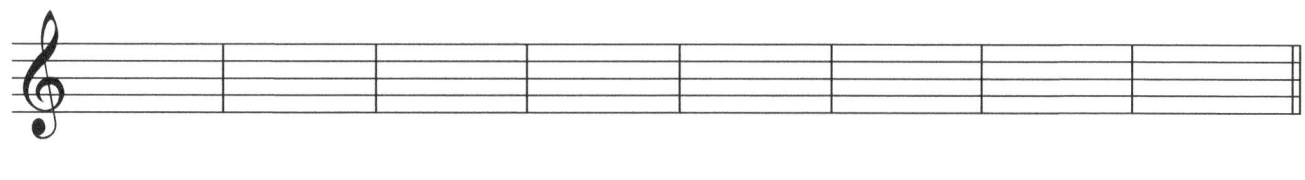

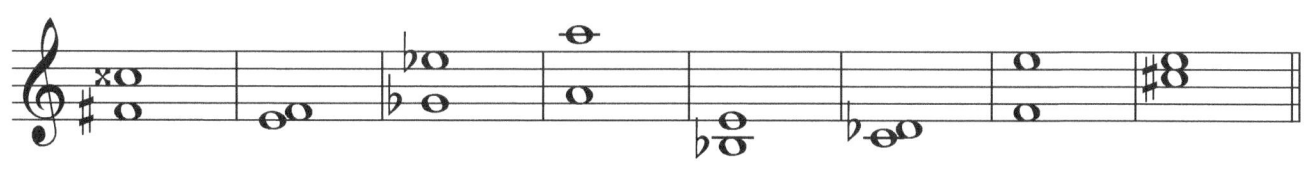

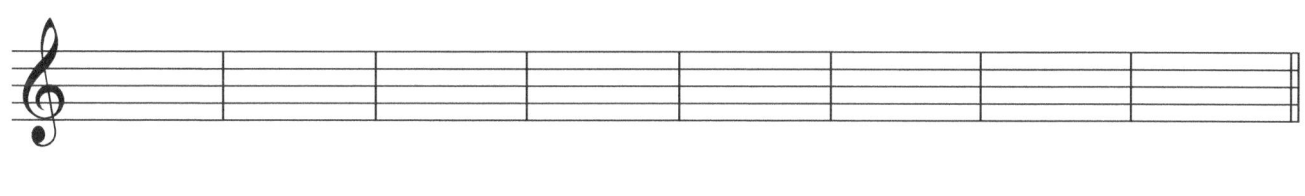

2. Name the following intervals.

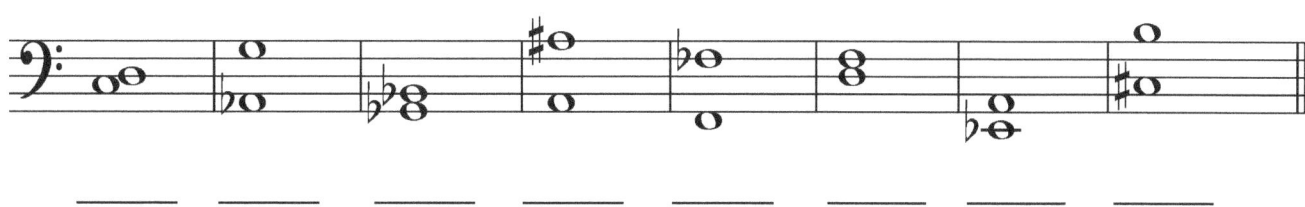

3. Write the following intervals above the given notes. Invert them and name the inversions.

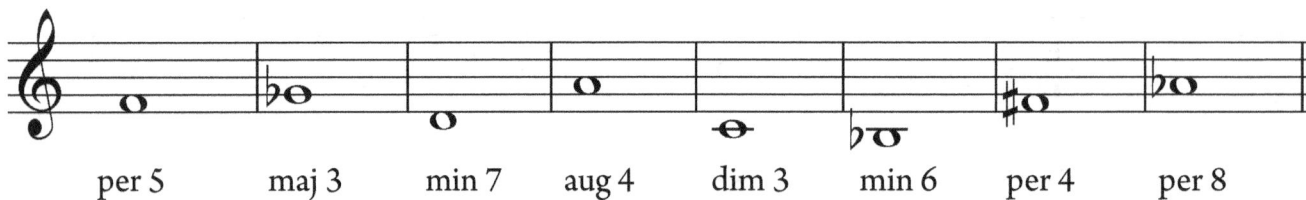

per 5   maj 3   min 7   aug 4   dim 3   min 6   per 4   per 8

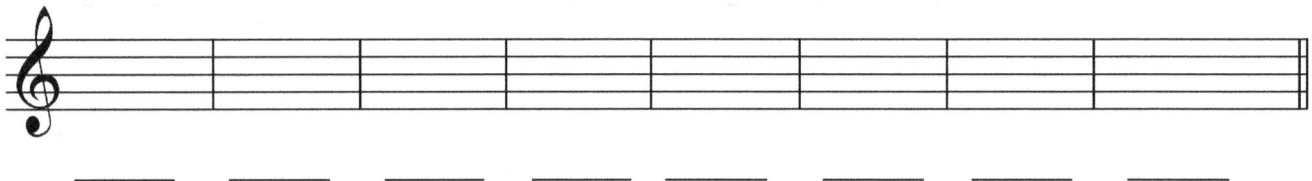

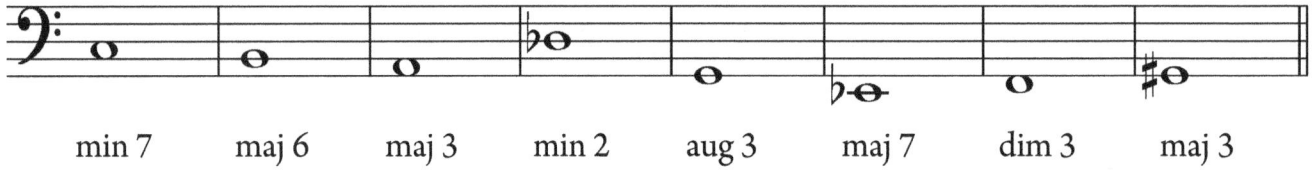

min 7   maj 6   maj 3   min 2   aug 3   maj 7   dim 3   maj 3

Enharmonic Change

If you change a note enharmonically, you change its name but not its pitch. Figure 9.24 shows enharmonic notes. Each measure contains two notes of the same pitch, but with a different name.

Figure 9.24

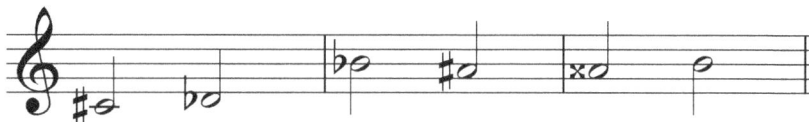

The intervals in each measure of Figure 9.25 sound exactly the same, but are named differently. The top note in example a) is changed enharmonically from B♭ to A♯, and the bottom note in example b) is changed enharmonically from A♭ to G♯. Even though the pitch does not change, the interval number and quality changes.

Figure 9.25

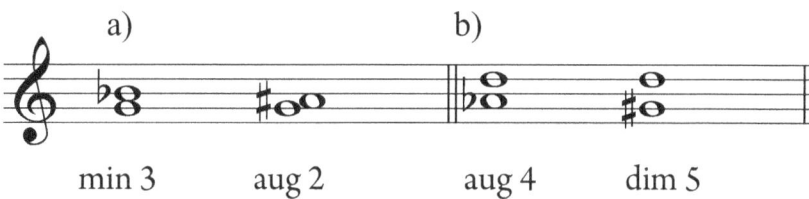

1. Name the following intervals. In the second measure change the lower note enharmonically and rename the interval. The first one is done for you.

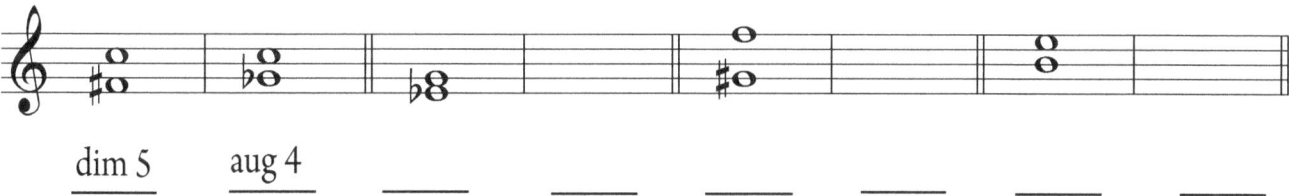

dim 5   aug 4   ____   ____   ____   ____   ____   ____

2. Name the following intervals. In the second measure change the upper note enharmonically and rename the interval.

____   ____   ____   ____   ____   ____   ____   ____

3. Name the following intervals. Invert them and rename them.

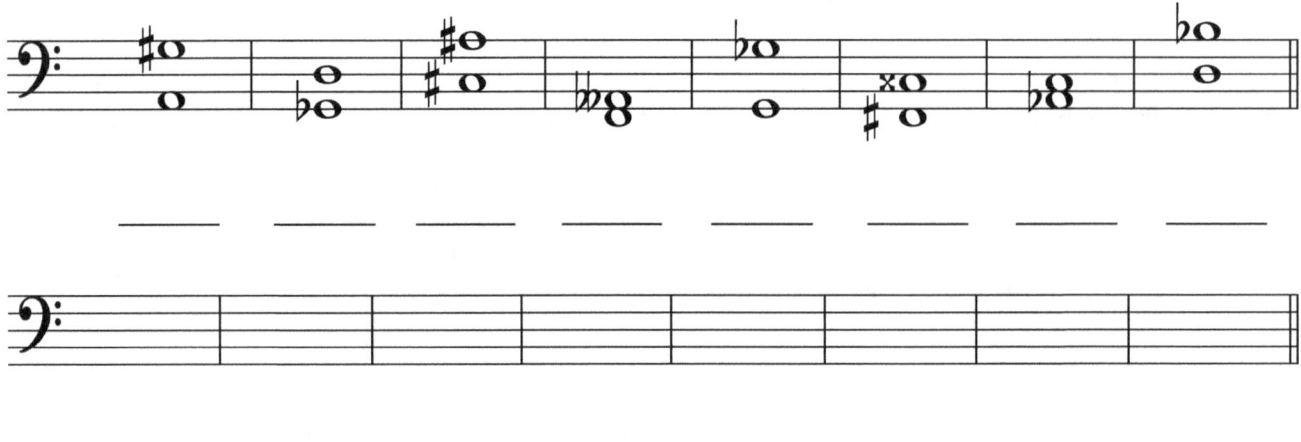

Compound Intervals

Intervals larger than an octave are called *compound intervals*.

Figure 9.26

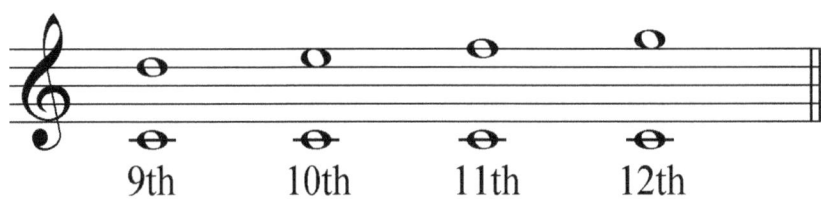

The easiest way to solve a compound interval is to bring the top note down an octave. This puts the interval in its simple form, which is an octave or less. The compound interval will be the same as the simple interval plus 7. The quality of the interval remains the same from simple to compound form.

Figure 9.27

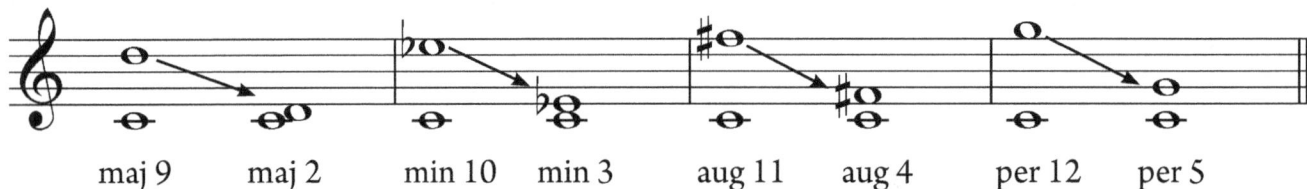

The compound interval can be inverted by moving the upper note down an octave and the lower note up an octave. This reverses the notes. See Figure 9.28. The size of the compound interval and its inversion will add up to 16.

Figure 9.28

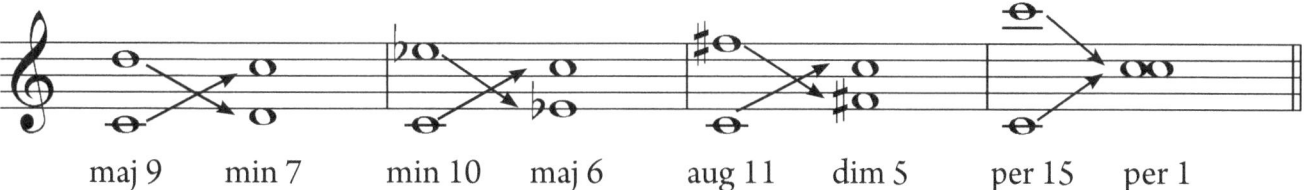

maj 9   min 7   min 10   maj 6   aug 11   dim 5   per 15   per 1

1. Name the following intervals. Invert and rename them.

2. Write the following intervals above the given notes.

3. Name the intervals under the brackets.

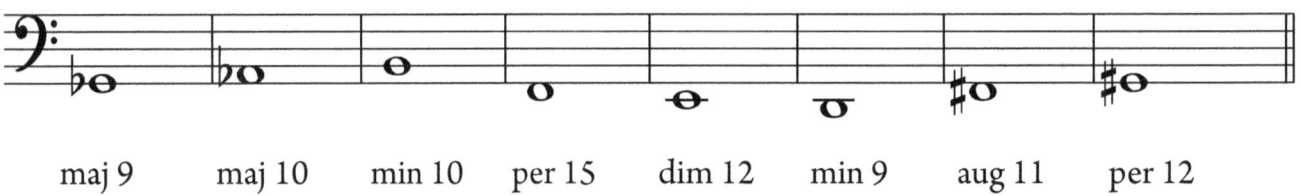

1. _____ 2. _____ 3. _____ 4. _____ 5. _____

4. Name the intervals indicated by the lines.

1. _____ 2. _____ 3. _____ 4. _____ 5. _____

6. _____ 7. _____

10
Meter 1

Bar Lines

The staff is divided into sections by vertical lines called **bar lines**. There are single bar lines and double bar lines. A double bar line indicates the end of a section or the end of a piece of music. You cannot hear a bar line. Its purpose is to make the music easier to read by dividing the music into smaller units or sections.

Figure 10.1

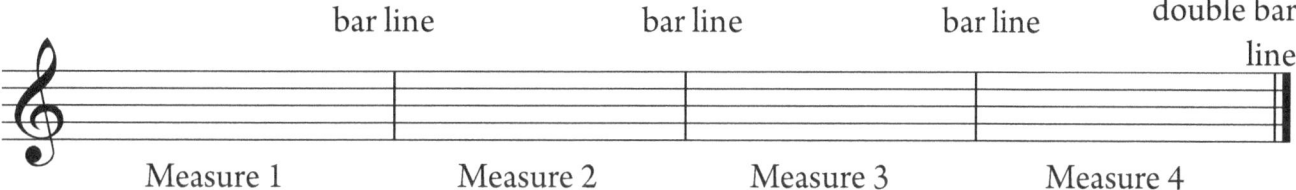

Measures

Bar lines divide the music into sections called **measures**. Figure 10.1 contains four measures. Measures may be different sizes depending upon the amount of beats and notes in the measure.

Time Signatures

Two numbers are placed at the beginning of every piece of music. These numbers are called the **time signature** or **meter**. The time signature tells you how many beats are in each measure. It also shows you which kind of note gets one beat.

Figure 10.2

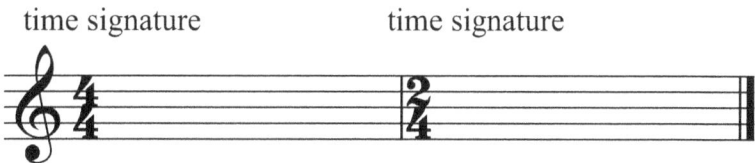

The Top Number

The top number of the time signature indicates how many beats will be in each measure. In the example in Figure 10.3, 4/4 time has four beats in each measure. In this level of theory, we will focus on two time signatures: 4/4 and 2/4.

Figure 10.3

The Bottom Number

The bottom number of the time signature indicates which note receives one beat. The 4 at the bottom of the time signature in Figure 10.3 means that the quarter note receives one beat. In 4/4 time every measure adds up to four quarter notes. In 2/4 time each measure adds up to two quarter notes. There can be different numbers at the bottom number of a time signature, but 4 is the most common. For now, we will be studying time signatures which have 4 on the bottom.

4/4 Time

There are many different time signatures. The most common is 4/4. The reason we have different time signatures or meters is that different types of music fall into different patterns. Sometimes words of a song help to shape the patterns in music. A four beat pattern indicates 4/4 time or a two beat pattern indicates 2/4 time. Figure 10.4 is an example where the words to the song help to dictate the time signature. This song has a definite four beats per measure pattern.

Figure 10.4

Common Time

4/4 time is so common you will often see it abbreviated with the letter "C" instead of the numbers 4/4. The C stands for **common** and is shown in Figure 10.5.

Figure 10.5

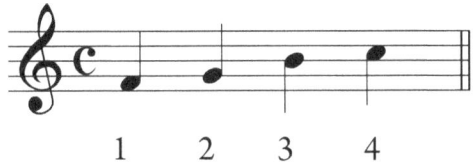

2/4 Time

For the time signature 2/4, there are two beats in each measure and the quarter note receives one beat. Figure 10.6 is an example of 2/4 time where the words to the song help to dictate the time signature. This song has a clear two beats per measure pattern.

Figure 10.6

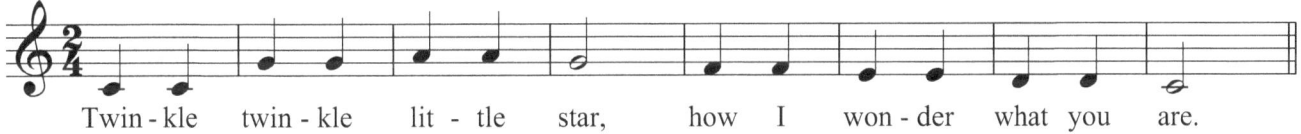

1. Write the beats according to the time signatures under each measure.

3/4 Time

In 3/4 time, there are three beats in each measure and the quarter note receives one beat. Figure 10.7 is an example of 3/4 time where the words to the song help to dictate the time signature. 3/4 time is sometimes known as waltz time because a waltz requires three beats per measure to dance to it.

Figure 10.7

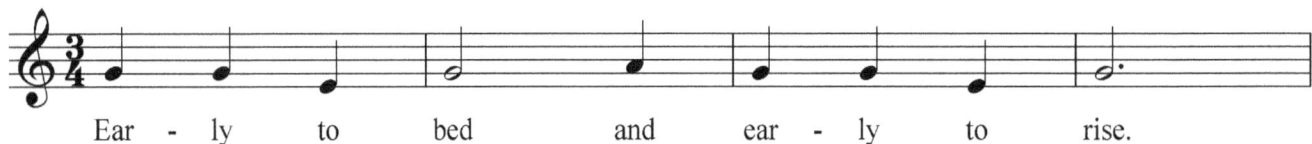

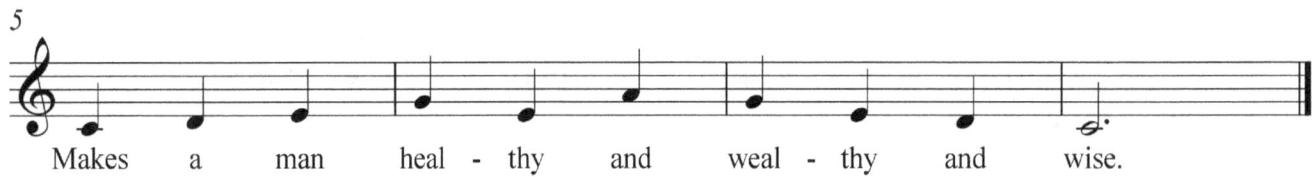

1. Add one note to complete each measure according to the given time signatures.

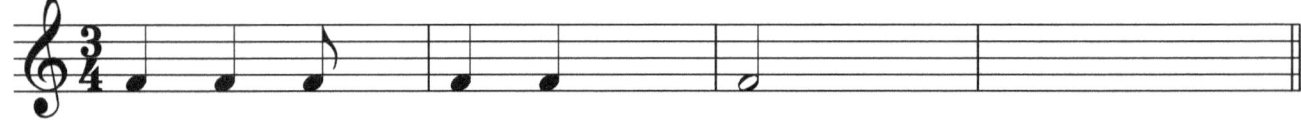

2. Add time signatures to the following lines.

3. Add bar lines according to the given time signatures.

4. Add one note to complete each measure according to the given time signatures.

5. Add one rest to complete each measure according to the given time signatures.

Tied Notes

A *tie* is a curved line which connects two notes of the same pitch. The time values of tied notes are added together to make a longer note - you only play the note once.

*Be careful not to confuse ties and slurs! A tie looks like a **slur** - but a slur connects two notes of a different pitch and indicates that the notes are to be played smoothly.* Figure 10.8 shows two tied Fs; the second example shows an F slurred to a G.

Figure 10.8

One reason we use a tie is to hold a note across a bar line. In Figure 10.9 the G is held for three beats.

Figure 10.9

Ties are usually written on the opposite side of a musical note to its stem. In Figure 10.10, the Fs are written stems up, so the tie is drawn below the notes. The Es have stems down, so the ties are drawn above the notes.

Figure 10.10

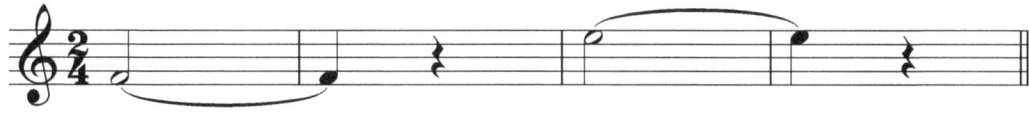

1. Write the counts under each measure. State how many beats each tied note receives. The first one is started for you.

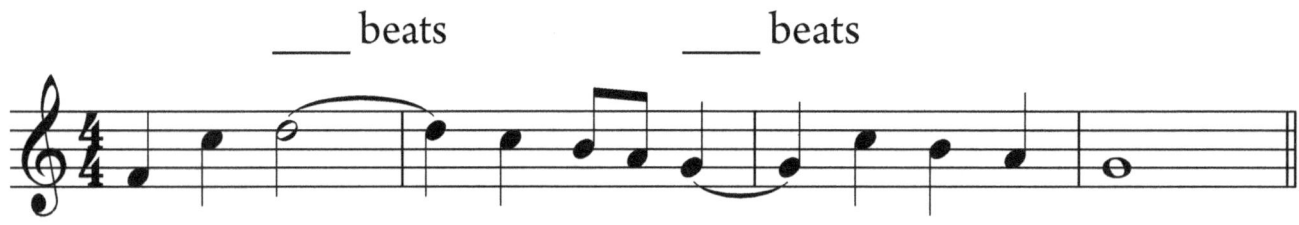

Dotted Notes

A dot to the right of a note makes it last longer. A dot adds half the value to a note.

The Dotted Half Note

A half note gets 2 beats. The dot is worth half of that. Half of 2 is 1 (2 + 1 = 3). This gives us a total of three. A ***dotted half note*** gets three beats. Figure 10.11 contains a dotted half note.

Figure 10.11

When drawing a dot beside a note in a space, the dot should be placed in the same space as the note. For a line note, the dot is placed in the space above the line note.
Figure 10.12 shows a dotted space and dotted line note.

Figure 10.12

The Dotted Quarter Note

A quarter note gets one beat. The dot is worth half of that. Half of 1 is ½ (1 + ½ = 1½). This is a total of one and a half. A ***dotted quarter note*** gets one and a half beats. When counting the dotted quarter it is easier to think of it as equal to three eighth notes. It helps to divide each beat using the word *and* to represent the eighth notes.

Figure 10.13

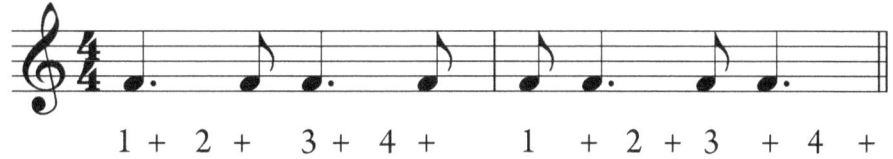

1. Add bar lines to complete the following according to the time signatures.

2. In the empty measure write one note that is equal to the following groups of notes.

Rest Review

Silence in music is as important as sound. A ***rest*** is used to show silence in music. Figure 10.14 shows the rests covered earlier. The whole rest is equal to one complete measure of rest. In 4/4 time it's value is 4 beats, in 3/4 time it is worth 3 beats, in 2/4 time it is worth 2 beats. This rest is used to represent one complete measure of silence no matter what the time signature.

Figure 10.14

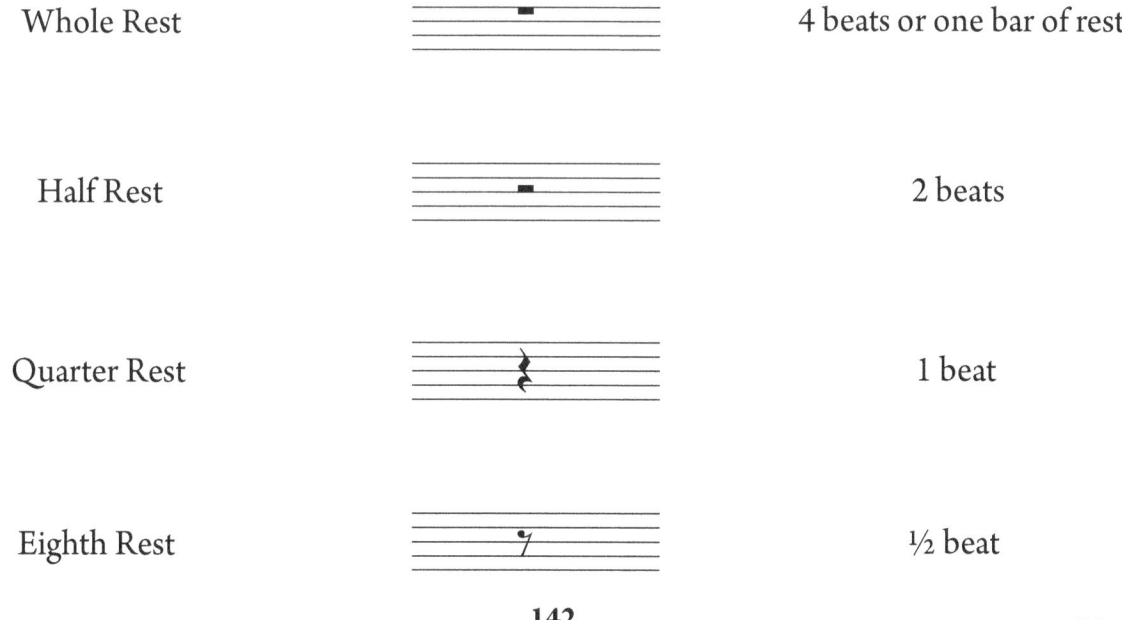

© San Marco Publications 2022

1. Add one rest to complete each measure according to the time signature.

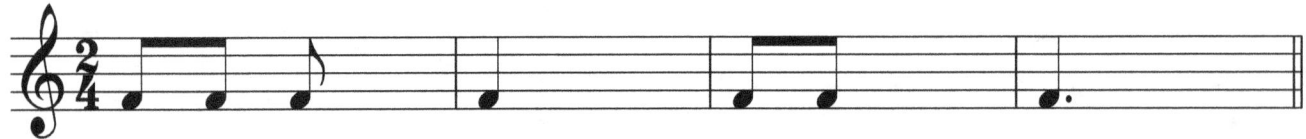

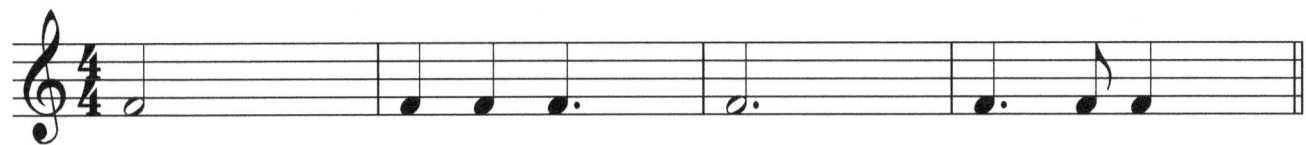

2. Add one note to complete each measure according to the time signature.

The Sixteenth Note

There are 16 sixteenth notes in a whole note. This makes the sixteenth note ¼ of a beat. One quarter note is equal to 4 sixteenth notes. A single sixteenth note has two flags attached to the stem. These flags are always placed on the right of the stem. When sixteenth notes are grouped together their stems are joined by two beams. Figure 10.15 show single sixteenth notes with flags and groups of sixteenth notes joined by beams.

Figure 10.15

Counting Sixteenth Notes

When we write sixteenth notes the beat is split up into four parts. We can assign each part a word or name. When you count say: 1 ee and ah (1 e + a). This divides the beat into four equal sections. Figure 10.16 shows a measure of sixteenth notes with counting.

Figure 10.16

Rest Placement

When writing rests be sure to place them in the correct place on the staff. The placement is the same for the treble and bass staff.

Figure 10.17

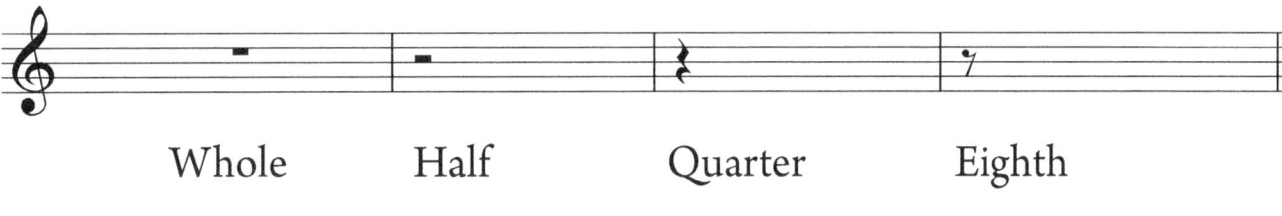

The Sixteenth Rest

A sixteenth rest looks like eighth rest with an extra flag on it. The flags are placed in the second and third space of the staff. This rest has the same value as a sixteenth note, ¼ of a beat

Figure 10.18

1. Circle the note or rest with the shortest duration.

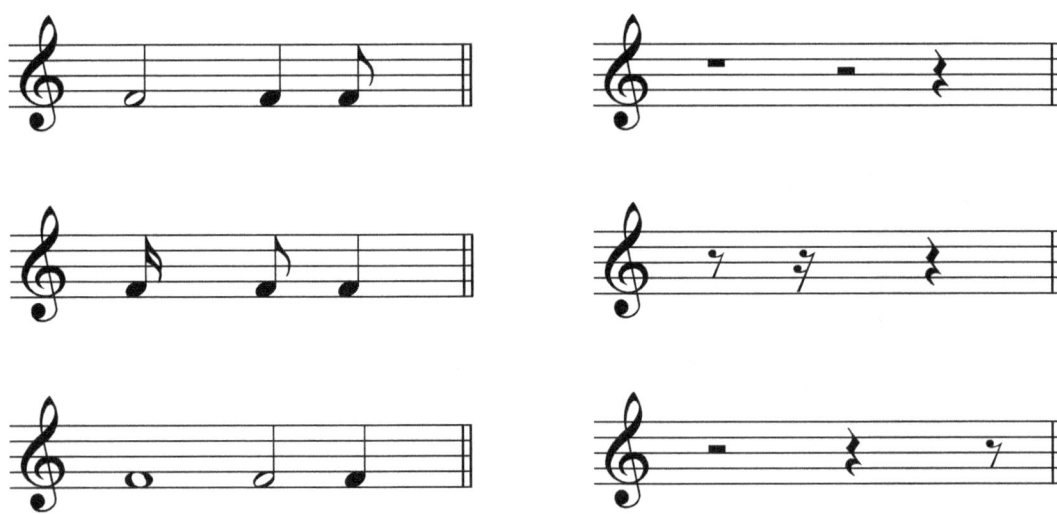

2. Circle the note or rest with the longest duration.

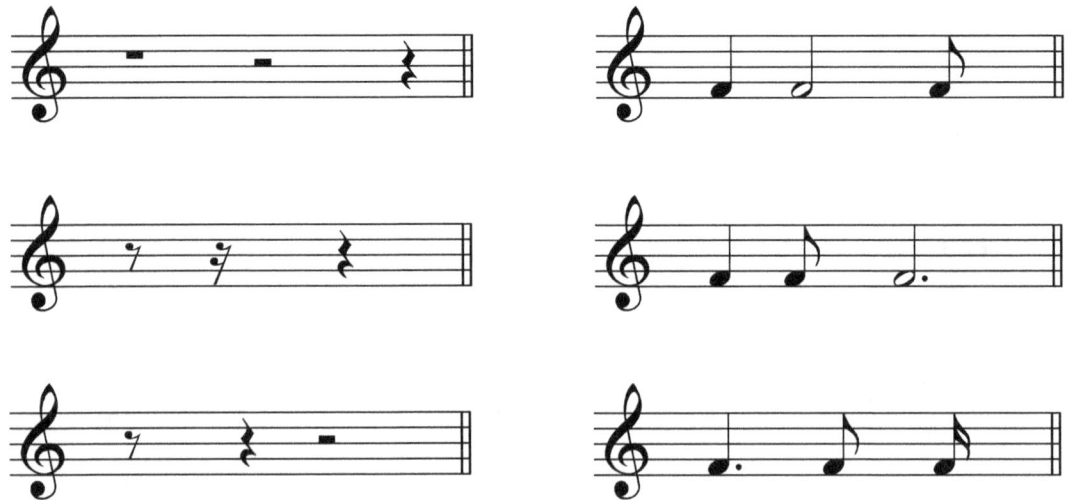

Joining Notes

Notes with flags are usually grouped together with beams to show one beat. Figure 10.19 shows how notes are grouped with beams to indicate one complete beat.

Figure 10.19

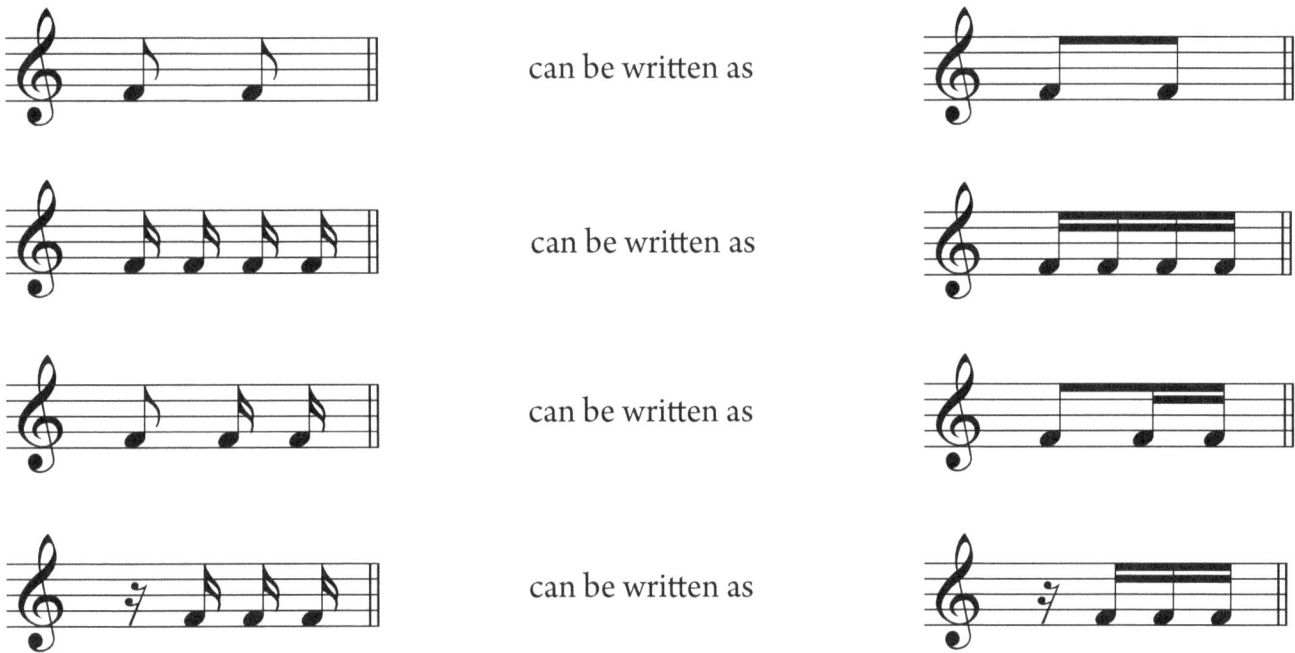

1. Rewrite the following joining the notes with beams wherever possible.

Review - Stem Direction and Beams

Eighth and sixteenth notes are grouped together with beams. When we beam these notes sometimes one or more of the stems are placed differently than would be the case if flags were used. If most of the notes are above the third (middle) line of the staff, stems go downward (Figure 10.20 a). If most of the notes are below the third line, the stems go upward (Figure 10.20 b). Here, majority rules.

Figure 10.20

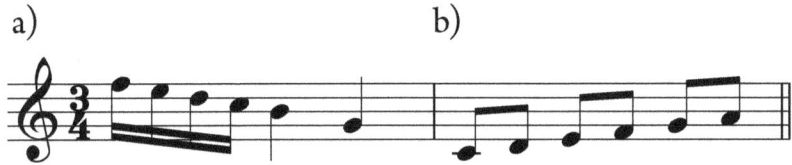

If the number of notes above the middle line of the staff is equal to the number below, the stem direction is determined by the note which is the farthest from the middle line (Figure 10.21).

Figure 10.21

1. Connect each group of four sixteenth notes with stems and beams.

2. Answer the following questions.

a) A whole note equals how many half notes? _____

b) A half note equals how many quarter notes? _____

c) A quarter note equals how many eighth notes? _____

d) A quarter note equals how many sixteenth notes? _____

e) An eighth note equals how many sixteenth notes? _____

3. Write one note which is equal to the following groups of notes.

4. Add time signatures at the beginning of each line.

5. Add one rest to complete each measure.

Dotted Eighth Notes

A dot after a note increases its value by half. Figure 10.22 contains a dotted half worth 3 beats and a dotted quarter worth 1 ½ beats.

Figure 10.22

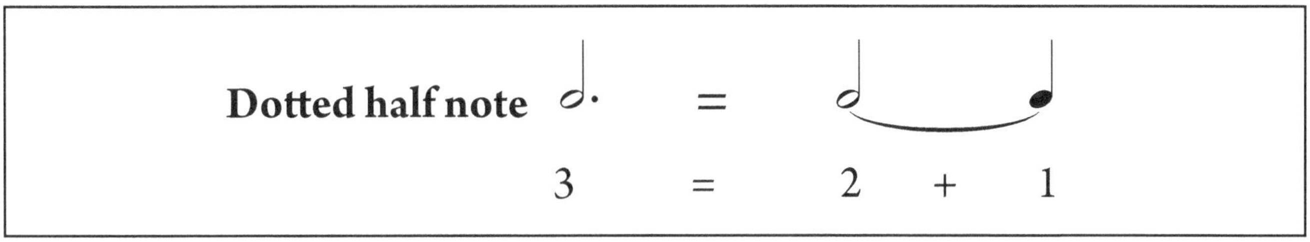

Dotted half note   𝅗𝅥.   =   𝅗𝅥 ⌣ ♩
    3   =   2   +   1

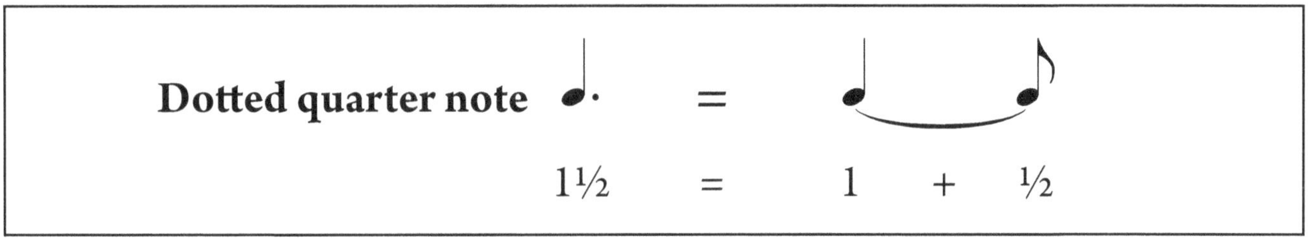

Dotted quarter note   ♩.   =   ♩ ⌣ ♪
    1½   =   1   +   ½

Figure 10.23 contains a dotted eighth note. An eighth note is worth ½ of a beat. The dot is equal to a sixteenth note. A sixteenth note is worth ¼ of a beat. The dotted eighth is equal to ¾ of a beat.

Figure 10.23

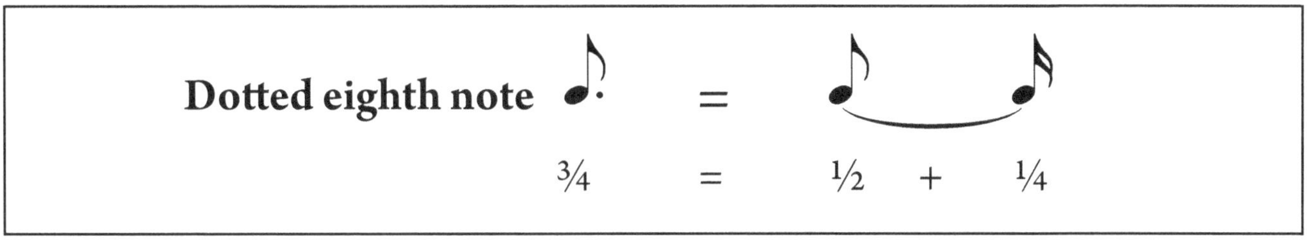

Dotted eighth note   ♪.   =   ♪ ⌣ ♬
    ¾   =   ½   +   ¼

Think of a dotted eighth note like a pie. The whole pie is 1 beat. An eighth note is ½ of the pie and a sixteenth note is ¼ of the pie. A dotted eighth (½ + ¼) is ¾ of the pie, or ¾ of a beat.

Figure 10.24

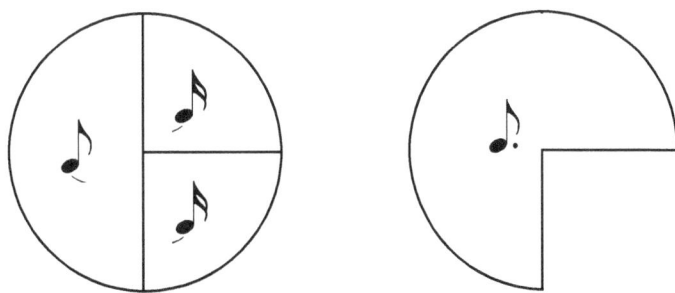

The dotted eighth note is often seen in combination with a sixteenth note as shown in Figure 10.25. The dotted eighth is connected by a beam to a sixteenth note. This creates one complete beat and is a common rhythmic figure.

Figure 10.25

1. Draw a line connecting each group of notes with its corresponding note value.

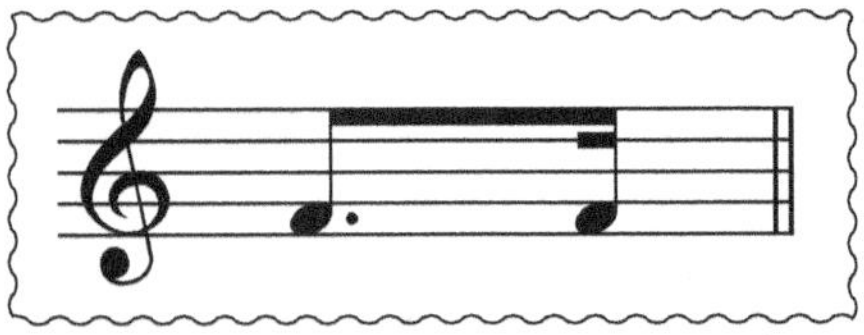

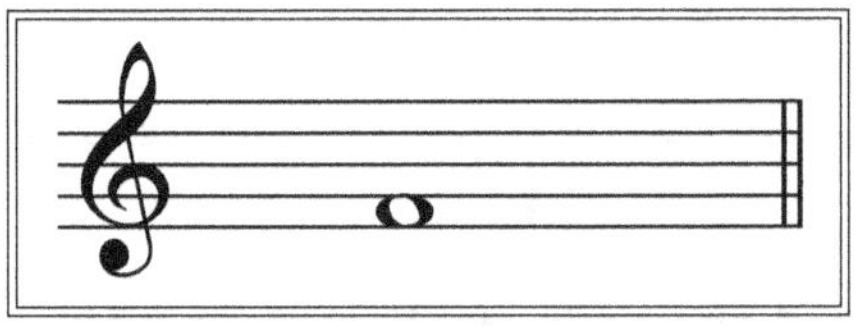

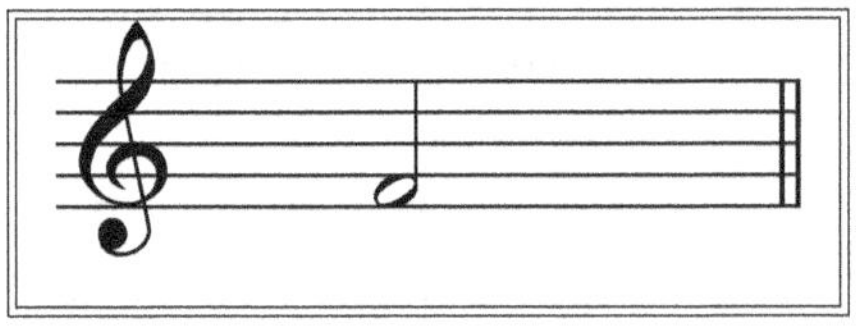

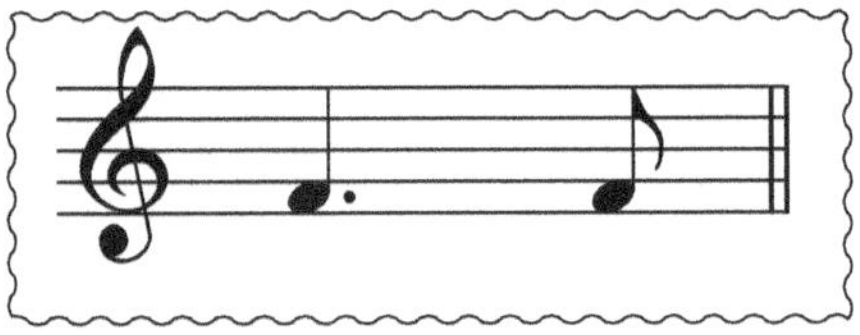

2. Add the missing bar lines to the following musical examples.

The Upbeat or Anacrusis

The first beat of a measure is the strongest and is called the **downbeat**. Some pieces begin on an unaccented or less strong beat. This is called an **upbeat, pickup,** or **anacrusis**.

When a melody begins on an upbeat, both the first and last measure will be incomplete. Figure 10.26 contains a melody that begins on an upbeat. It begins on beat 3, a weak beat. The first note of this melody is a quarter note upbeat. The first and last measures of this melody are incomplete. The third beat which is missing from the last measure is equal to the upbeat in the first measure. These two incomplete measures add up to one complete measure. No rests are needed with incomplete measures.

Figure 10.26

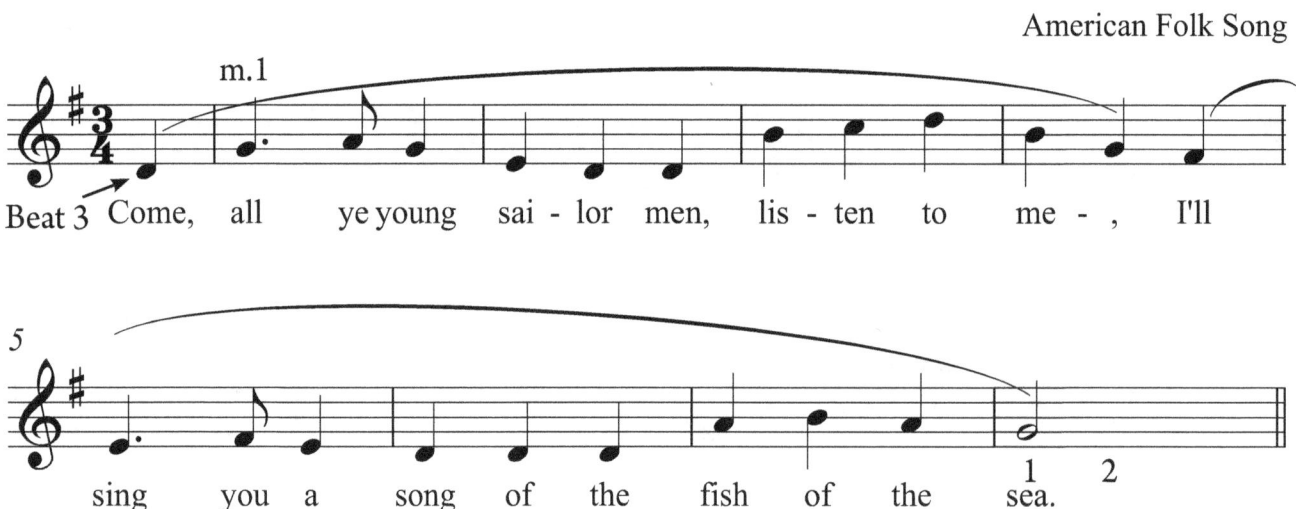

Review - The Phrase

Most traditional melodies move in four measure sections called **phrases**. A phrase is a musical sentence. Like the sentence in a story, a phrase represents one musical idea. Phrases are often indicated by a long curved line called a **phrase mark**. A phrase mark looks like a large slur. This line indicates the beginning and end of the phrase. Figure 10.26 contains phrase marks above the melody. This melody consists of two four measures phrases.

In Figure 10.26 each 4 measure phrase begins with an upbeat. When a piece begins with an upbeat, often each of the following phrases will also begin with an upbeat. This is a feature which unifies the music.

Measure numbers are an important feature in music. They help us when learning, analyzing, or rehearsing. In a piece that begins with an incomplete measure, the incomplete measure is not numbered. The first measure (m.1), is the bar after the anacrusis. This measure contains the first strong beat in the piece and is considered m.1. See Figure 10.26.

1. Name the key of the following melodies. Find and circle the upbeats (anacrusis) in each one. Mark the phrases with a slur.

Allegretto

key:

Allegro

key:

The Triplet

When the beat is divided into three equal parts the result is a **triplet**. Triplets fall into a category of notes we call **tuplets**. A tuplet is a group of notes that do not follow the normal rules of counting. In this lesson, we are going to cover triplets.

The Eighth Note Triplet

The most common triplets are eighth note triplets. The three notes of this triplet are beamed together and there is a small "3" over the beam indicating that it is a triplet. This triplet often occurs in 2/4, 3/4, and 4/4 time where it represents one complete beat. Figure 10.27 contains eighth note triplets. When writing eighth note triplets, the number must be positioned avoiding staff lines if possible. The number is placed in the middle of the beam no matter what the stem direction.

Figure 10.27

Triplets are played in the time of two notes of the same value. An eighth note triplet consists of three eighth notes played in the time of two eighth notes. In this case, one beat. Essentially, an eighth note triplet is equal to a quarter note or one beat in quarter time (2/4, 3/4, 4/4). Figure 10.28 shows triplet eighth notes with counting.

Figure 10.28

1. Add bar lines according to the time signatures.

2. Add time signatures to the following

Robert Schumann
Papillons Op. 2, No. 11

Joseph Haydn
Quartet, Op. 76, No. 5

Antonin Dvorak
Quartet in F

Ludwig van Beethoven
Symphony No. 5, III

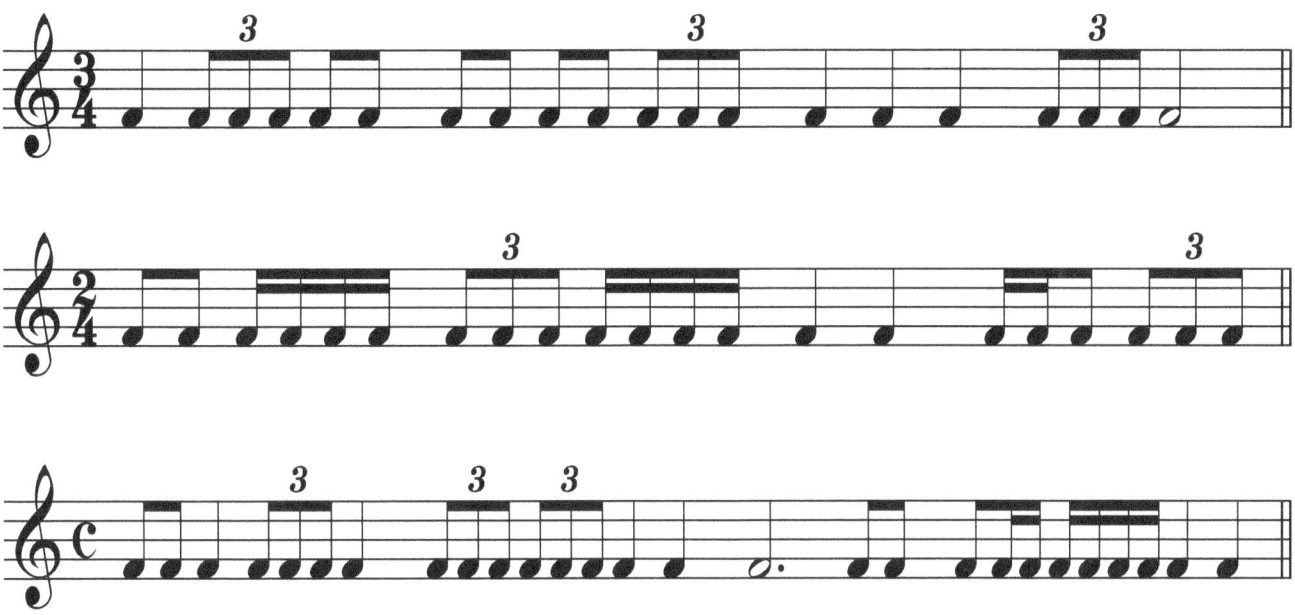

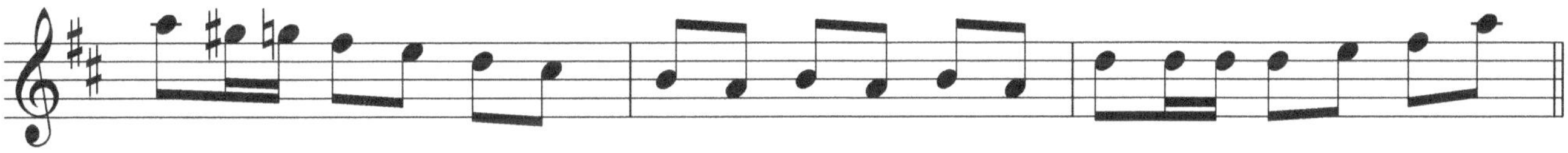

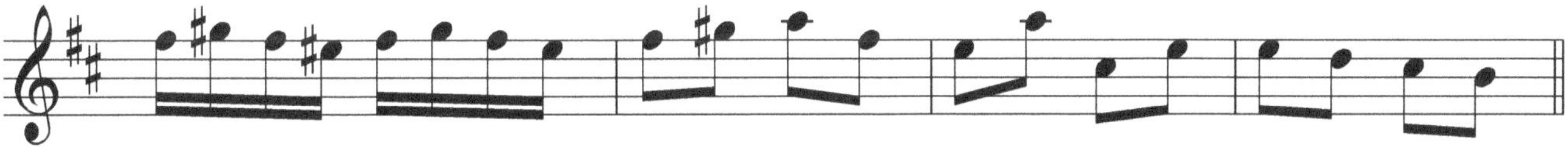

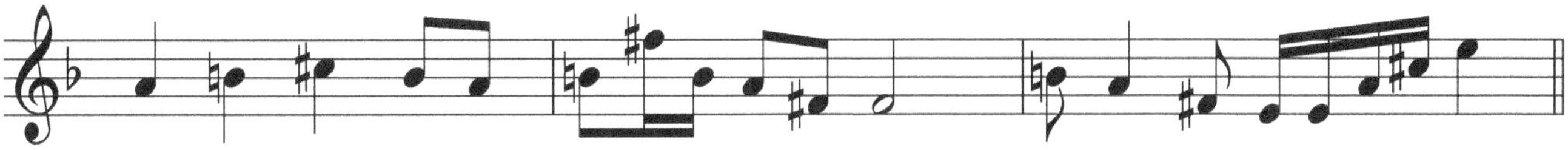

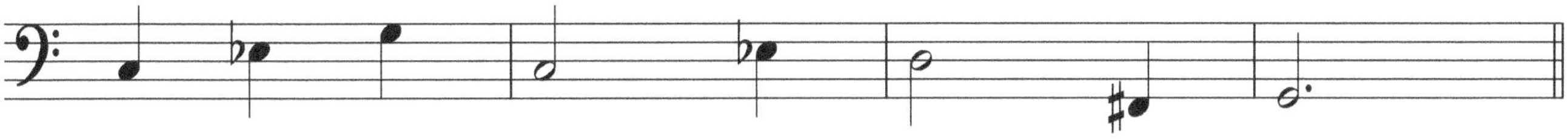

The Thirty-Second Note and Rest

A single thirty-second note is written with three flags (Figure 10.29). Thirty-second notes are grouped using three beams to join the notes (Figure 10.30). The thirty-second rest uses three hooks placed in the top three spaces of the staff (Figure 10.31). The thirty-second note is half the duration of a sixteenth note.

Figure 10.29

Figure 10.30

Figure 10.31

Figure 10.32

A thirty-second note triplet is equal to one sixteenth note.

Figure 10.33

1. Name one note which lasts as long as the number of thirty second notes in each of the following.

   a. 2 thirty-second notes last as long as a _____ note.

   b. 4 thirty-second notes last as long as an _____ note.

   c. 16 thirty-second notes last as long as a _____ note.

   d. 12 thirty-second notes last as long as a _____ note.

   e. 32 thirty-second notes last as long as a _____ note.

   f. 8 thirty-second notes last as long as a _____ note.

2. Write the correct time signature for the following.

A dot placed next to a sixteenth note increases its value by half. A dotted sixteenth note is usually connected to a thirty-second note as seen on beats 1 and 3 in Figure 10.34.

Figure 10.34

1. Add the missing rest or rests under each bracket.

2. Add the bar lines to the following according to the time signatures.

11
Chords

A chord is made up of three or more notes that are sounded at the same time. Chords may be played by a solo instrument like a piano or a guitar. They may also be played by many instruments at once, like an orchestra or a string quartet. The instruments work together to create chords. Like intervals, there are different qualities of chords. The quality is determined by the intervals that make up the chord.

Major Triads

A triad is a three note chord consisting of a root, third and fifth. Major triads are considered "major" because they are made up of certain intervals.

A major triad consists of a major third and a perfect fifth above the root.

Figure 11.1 contains a major triad built on the root D. There is a major third between D and F♯ and a perfect fifth between D and A. All major triads contain these intervals between the root and third and the root and fifth.

Figure 11.1

D - F♯ = major 3rd
D - A = perfect 5th

A triad can be written and played *solid* or *broken*. A triad is solid when all the notes are played together or at the same time as in Figure 11.2 Another word for solid is ***blocked***. A triad is broken when the notes are played one after the other as in Figure 11.3.

Figure 11.2

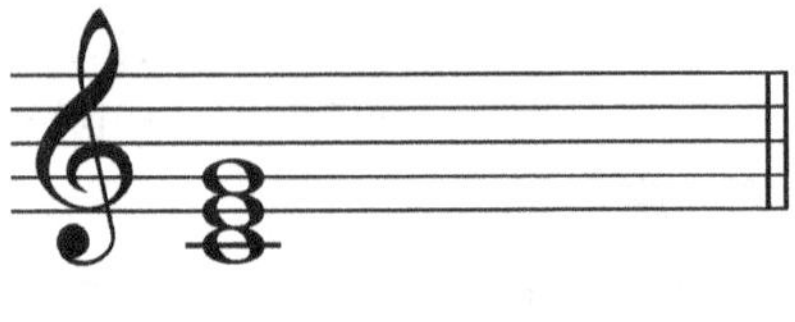

Figure 11.3
Broken

Ascending   Descending

©San Marco Publications 2022   161   Chords

Triads in Major Keys

In a major key, there are three major triads. They occur when you build triads on $\hat{1}$, $\hat{4}$, and $\hat{5}$ of the major scale. They are considered the tonic, subdominant and dominant triads in a key. Figure 11.4 contains the triads built on these scale degrees in C major. All three are major triads because they consist of a major 3rd and perfect fifth above the root.

Figure 11.4

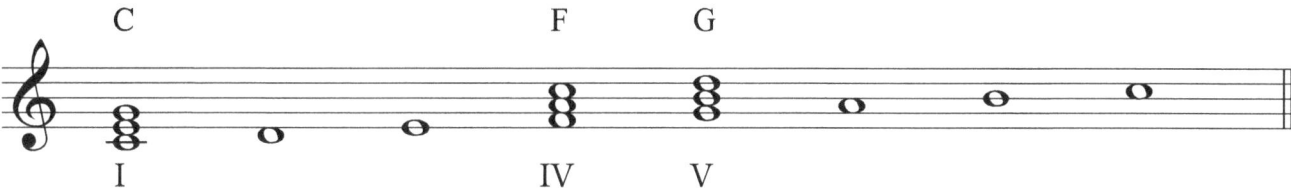

Chord Symbols

We label chords with symbols. A chord can have two symbols. A Roman numeral placed under the chord and a letter name placed above the chord. The Roman numeral is known as a *functional chord symbol* and the letter is known as a *root/quality chord symbol*.

Each Roman numeral corresponds to the scale degree that the chord was built upon. Major triads always receive an uppercase Roman numeral as shown in Figure 11.4.

- The chord built on $\hat{1}$ is the *tonic triad* and it's Roman numeral is **I**.
- The chord built on $\hat{4}$ is the *subdominant triad* and it's Roman numeral is **IV**.
- The chord built on $\hat{5}$ is the *dominant triad* and it's Roman numeral is **V**.

Chords may also have a letter name called the root/quality chord symbol. This name comes from the root of the chord. The letter indicates the root of the chord. The letter written by itself as a capitol letter means that the chord is major.

In C major: The chord built on $\hat{1}$ (C), uses the root/quality chord symbol **C**.
The chord built on $\hat{4}$ (F), uses the root/quality chord symbol **F**.
The chord built on $\hat{5}$ (G), uses the root/quality chord symbol **G**.

1. Write triads on $\hat{1}$, $\hat{4}$, and $\hat{5}$ of the following major scales. Add the functional and the root/quality chord symbols.

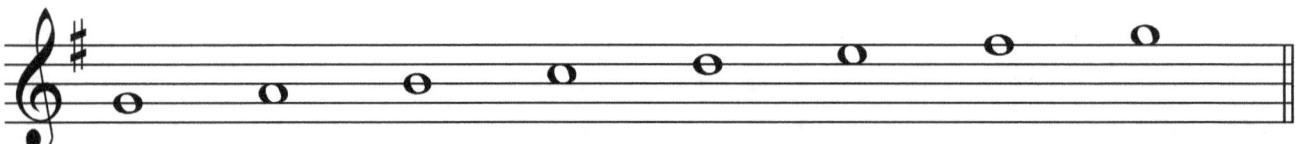

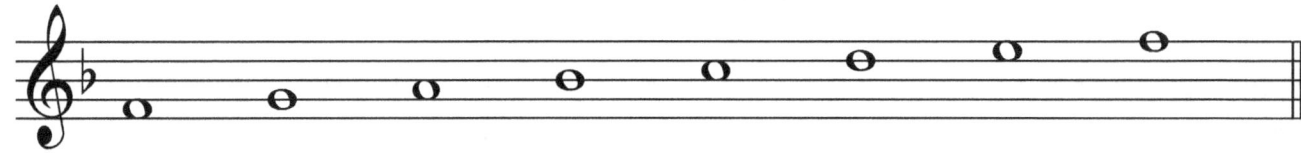

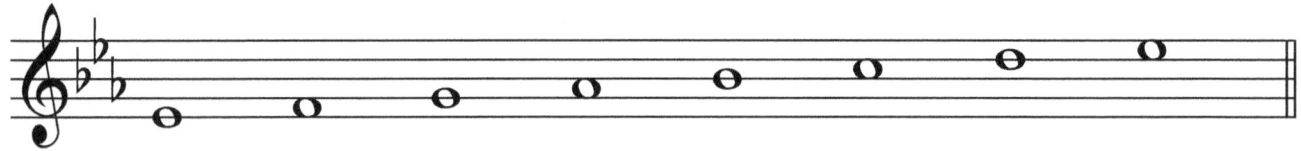

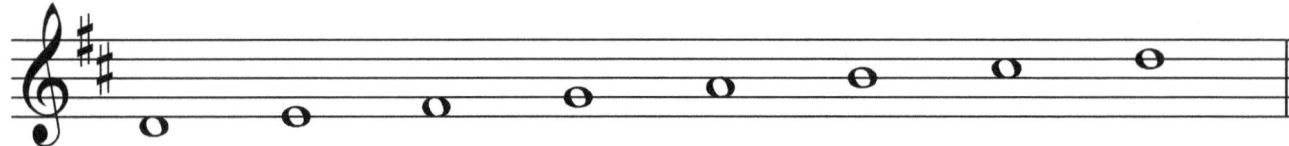

2. Write the following solid triads using key signatures. Add functional and root/quality chord symbols to each.

| The tonic triad of C major | The dominant triad of E♭ major | The subdominant triad of D major | The tonic triad of F major |

| The dominant triad of A major | The tonic triad of B♭ major | The subdominant triad of C major | The dominant triad of G major |

| The tonic triad of G major | The dominant triad of B♭ major | The subdominant triad of F major | The tonic triad of A major |

3. For the following triads: Name the major key. Identify the triad as tonic, subdominant, or dominant. Write the root/quality chord symbols for each.

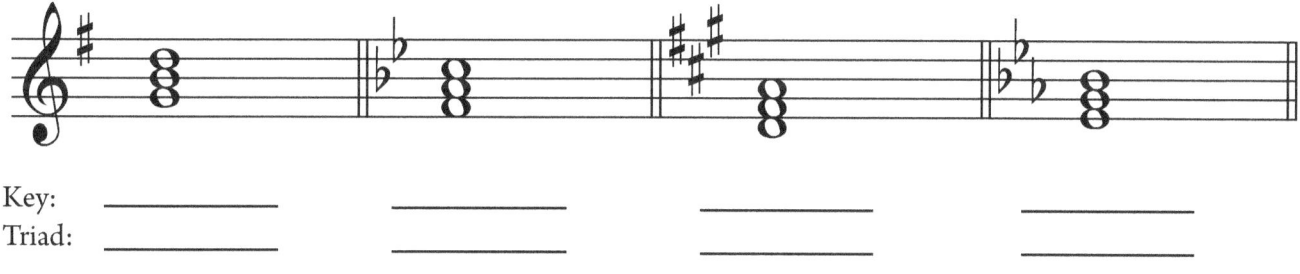

Key: _____ _____ _____ _____
Triad: _____ _____ _____ _____

_____ _____ _____ _____
_____ _____ _____ _____

Minor Triads

Minor triads are considered "minor" because they are made up of specific intervals.

A minor triad consists of a minor third and a perfect fifth above the root.

Figure 11.5 contains a minor triad built on the root D. There is a minor third between D and F and a perfect fifth between D and A. All minor triads contain these intervals between the root and third and the root and fifth.

Figure 11.5

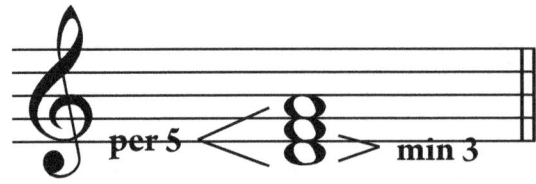

D - F = minor 3rd
D - A = perfect 5th

Triads in Minor Keys

Triads built on $\hat{1}$, $\hat{4}$, and $\hat{5}$ of the harmonic minor scale result in two minor triads (tonic and subdominant) and one major triad (dominant). The dominant triad contains raised $\hat{7}$ and is a major triad. For now, we will always use the harmonic form of the minor scale with raised $\hat{7}$ when building the dominant triad in the minor key.

Figure 11.6 contains the triads built on $\hat{1}$, $\hat{4}$, and $\hat{5}$ in D minor. Functional chord symbols for minor chords use lower case Roman numerals (i, iv). Root/quality symbols for minor chords use the letter name of the root with an "m" beside it to indicate minor (Dm, Gm). Some books use 'min' for minor chords (Dmin, Gmin)

Figure 11.6

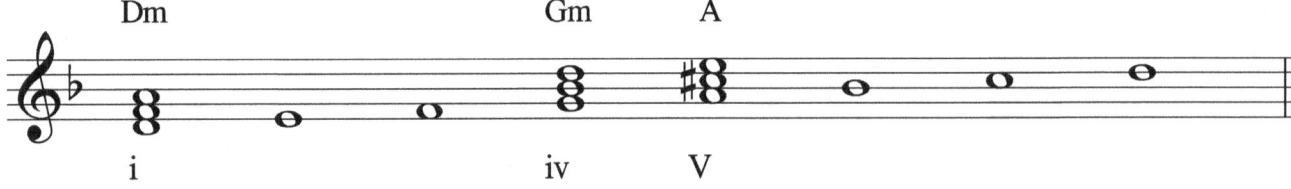

1. Write triads on $\hat{1}$, $\hat{4}$, and $\hat{5}$ of the following harmonic minor scales. Add the functional and the root/quality chord symbols.

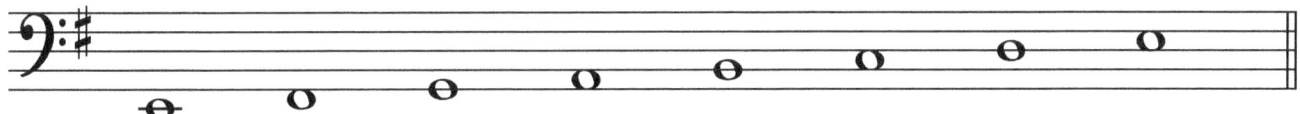

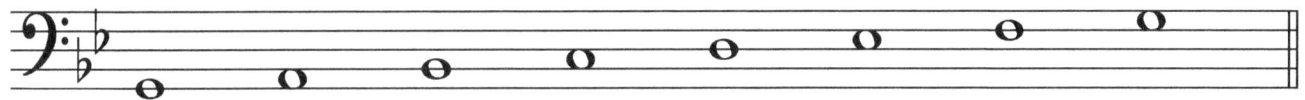

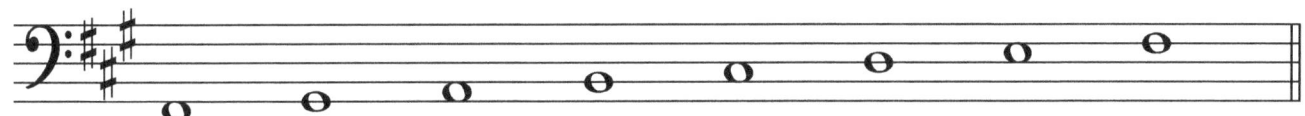

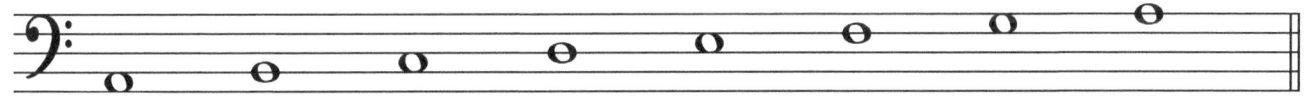

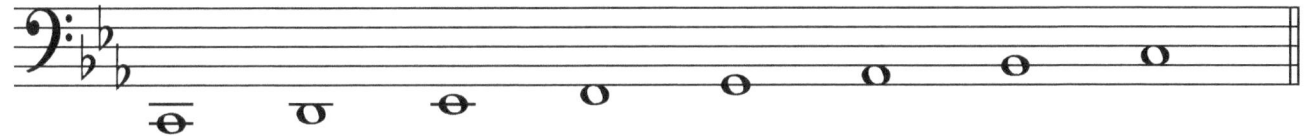

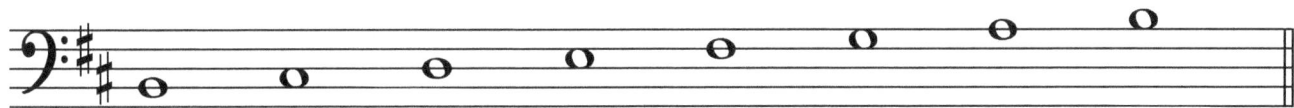

2. Write the following solid triads using key signatures. Add functional and root/quality chord symbols to each.

| The tonic triad of D minor | The dominant triad of G minor | The subdominant triad of C minor | The tonic triad of A minor |

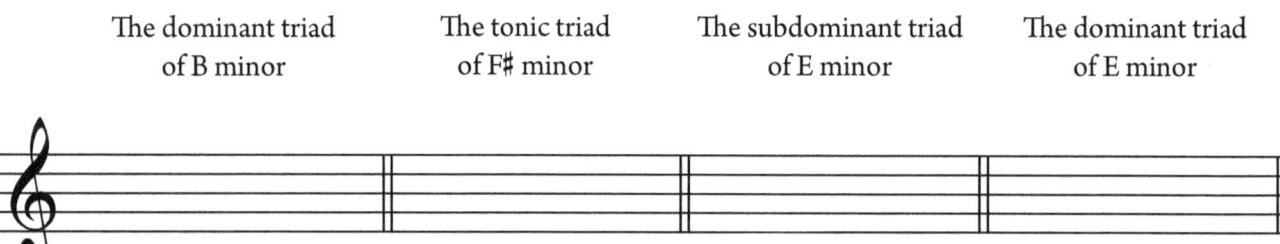

| The dominant triad of B minor | The tonic triad of F# minor | The subdominant triad of E minor | The dominant triad of E minor |

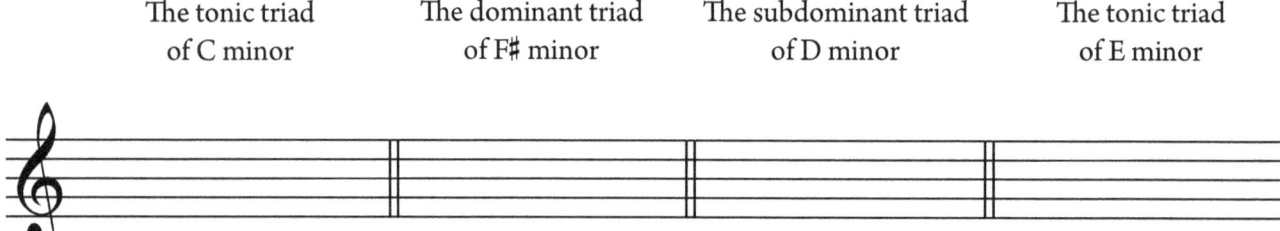

| The tonic triad of C minor | The dominant triad of F# minor | The subdominant triad of D minor | The tonic triad of E minor |

3. For the following triads: Name the minor key. Identify the triad as tonic, subdominant, or dominant. Write the functional chord symbols for each.

Key: _____   _____   _____   _____
Triad: _____   _____   _____   _____

Triad Inversions

Root Position

The three notes of a triad can be placed in a different order within the chord. The lowest note of a triad is very important because it determines its position. If the lowest note is the root, the triad is in *root position*. This is the most common triad. The triads that we have studied so far have been in root position. The triads in Figure 11.7 are in root position because the root C is the lowest note in each case.

Figure 11.7

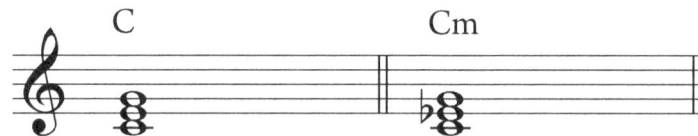

First Inversion

Whenever another note of the triad is the lowest note, the triad is in *inversion*. A *first inversion triad* has the third as the lowest note. The order of the notes of the rest of the chord makes no difference. The bottom note determines the position.

Figure 11.8 contains the E♭ major triad in root positon and first inversion. When the 3rd of the triad (G) is the lowest note, the triad in in first inversion.

The chords have been named in two ways. The root/quality symbol for first inversion is **E♭/G**. This means that it is the E♭ major triad with G on the bottom. This method of naming chords is typical in popular music. The formula for this is triad/bass note.

The functional chord symbol is **I⁶**. "I" indicates that it is a major triad built on $\hat{1}$ in E♭ major and the "6" indicates that it is in first inversion. The origin of the 6 comes from the interval of a 6th between the lowest note G and the highest note E♭ in the triad.

Figure 11.8

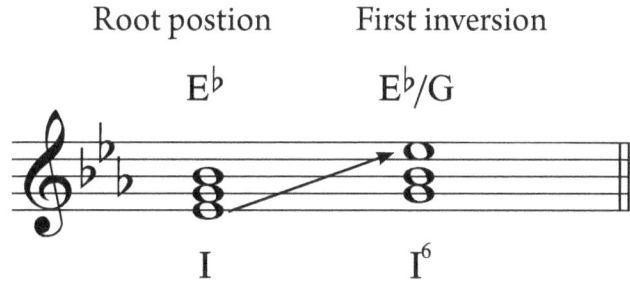

Second Inversion

When the fifth is the lowest note of a triad, it is in ***second inversion.*** Figure 11.9 contains the E♭ major triad in second inversion. The order of the remaining notes does not matter. The lowest note determines the position. Here, B♭, the fifth of the E♭ major triad is the bottom note making this triad second inversion.

The root/quality chord symbol is **E♭/B♭** indicating the E♭ major triad with B♭ as the lowest note. The functional chord symbol is **I**because the intervals above the lowest note are a 6th and a 4th.

Figure 11.9

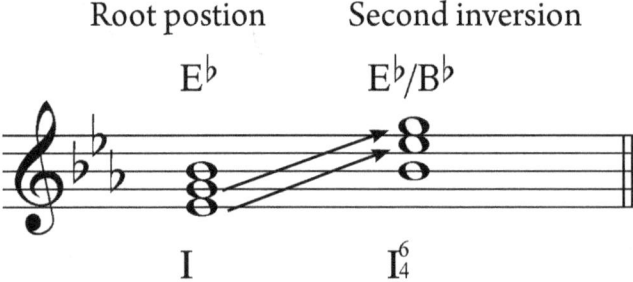

Minor Chord Symbols

The chord symbols for minor triads function in the same way as those for major triads with a few small differences. Figure 11.10 shows the chord symbols for minor triads. In root/quality chord symbols, minor triads are indicated with an "m" beside the uppercase letter. In functional chord symbols, minor triads are shown with a lower case Roman numeral.

Figure 11.10

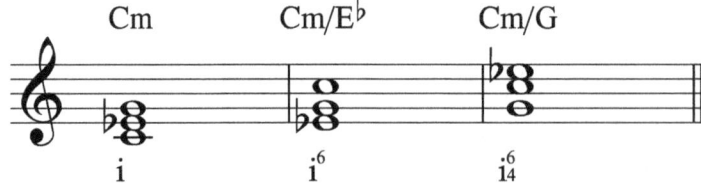

1. Identify the following triads as major or minor. Write the root/quality chord symbols for each.

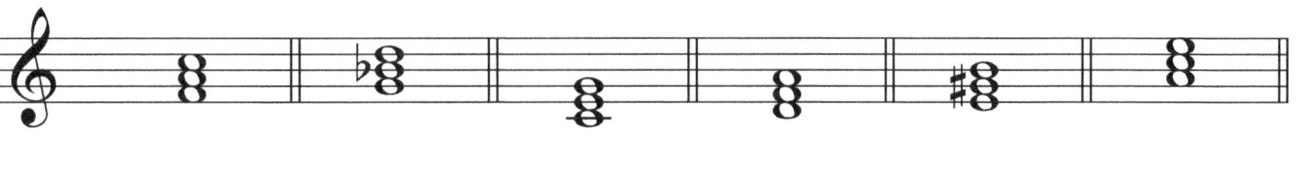

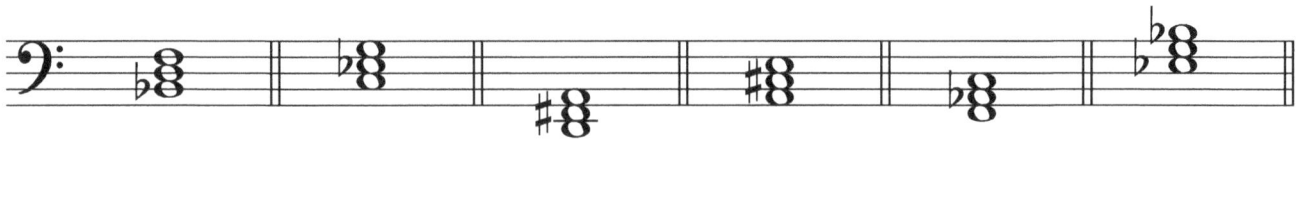

2. Write a major triad and its inversions using the following notes as the root.
   Write the root/quality chord symbols for each.

3. Write a minor triad and its inversions using the following notes as the root. Write the root/quality chord symbols for each.

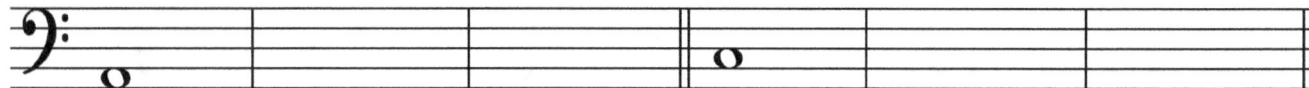

Solving Triads

Solving a triad involves stating its root, quality and position. To solve a triad:

1. If it is not in root position, put it into root position. For Figure 11.11 the root is: **E♭**.

Figure 11.11

2. Determine the intervals between the root and 3rd and the root and 5th. In Figure 11.12 E♭ to G is a major 3rd and E♭ to B♭ is a perfect 5th making its quality **major**.

Figure 11.12

E♭ - G = maj 3   E♭ - B♭ = per 5

3. Examine the lowest note of the given triad. In Figure 11.11 it is the 3rd, G. When the 3rd is the lowest note, the position of the triad is **first inversion**. This triad is solved as follows:

Root: E♭
Quality: major
Position: 1st inversion

1. Name the root of the following triads.

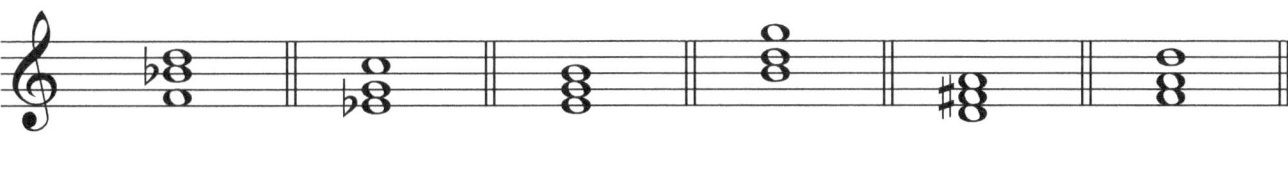

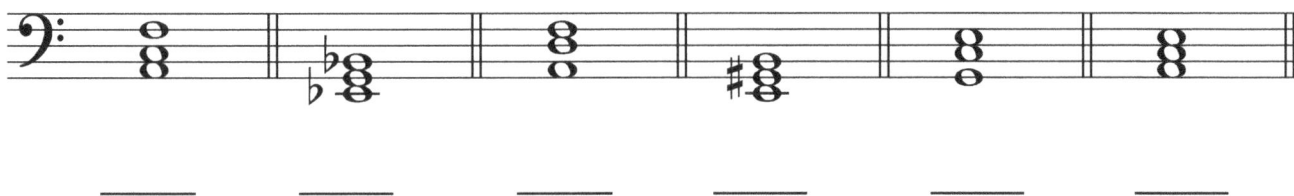

2. Solve the following triads by stating the root, quality, and position.

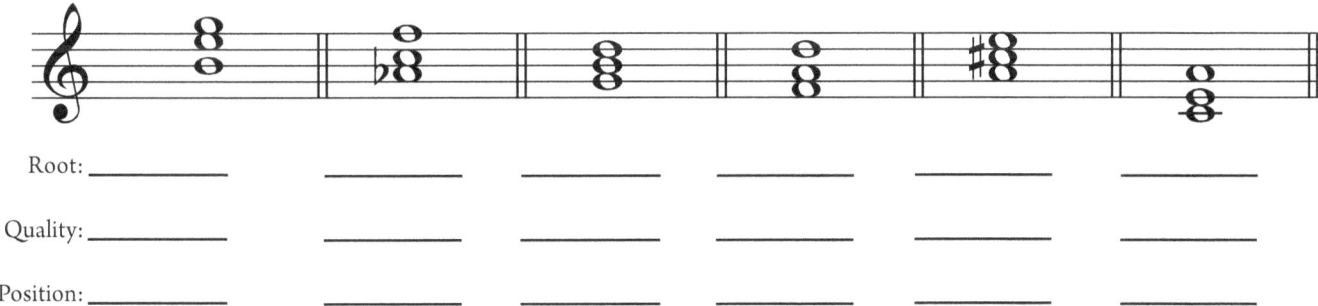

Root: _____   _____   _____   _____   _____   _____

Quality: _____   _____   _____   _____   _____   _____

Position: _____   _____   _____   _____   _____   _____

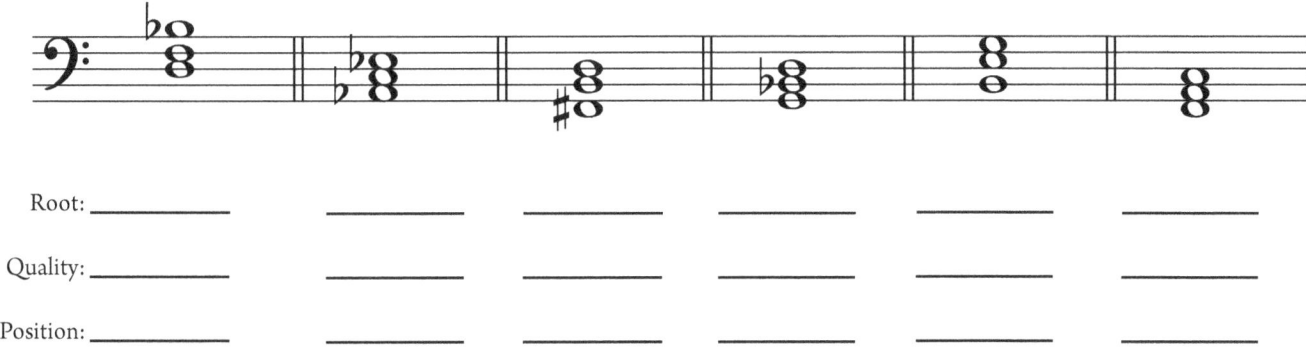

Root: _____   _____   _____   _____   _____   _____

Quality: _____   _____   _____   _____   _____   _____

Position: _____   _____   _____   _____   _____   _____

3. Write the following triads using a key signature for each. Write the functional chord symbol.

| The tonic triad in F major | The dominant triad in C minor | The subdominant triad in B♭ major | The dominant triad in D minor |

| The subdominant triad in F minor | The tonic triad in E major | The dominant triad in B minor | The subdominant triad in A♭ major |

4. Write the following triads using accidentals instead of a key signature.

   a) the tonic triad of G minor in second inversion
   b) the dominant triad of D major in root position
   c) the subdominant triad of E minor in first inversion
   d) the dominant triad of C♯ minor in root position
   e) the tonic triad of E♭ major in first inversion
   f) the subdominant triad of F♯ minor in second inversion

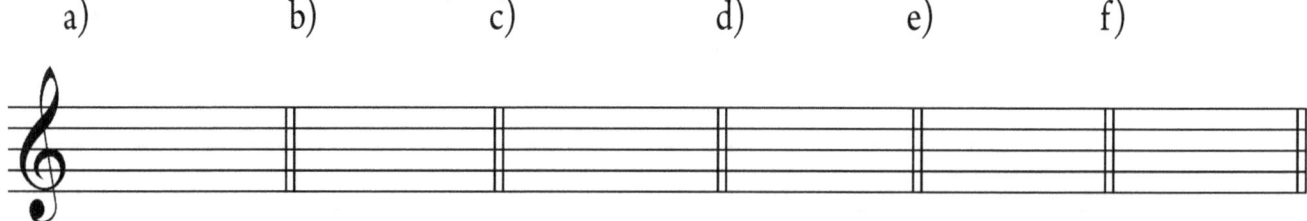

Triads in Open Position

So far, we have studied triads in *close position*. Close position occurs when the notes of the triad are as close together as possible. Triads may also be written in *open position*. In open position, the notes of the triad are spaced out over more than one octave. Often one of the notes of the triad is written more than once or *doubled*. The most common note to double is the root. The lowest note of the triad determines the position of the triad no matter in what order the other notes appear. Figure 11.13 shows different positions of the D minor triad in open position.

Figure 11.13

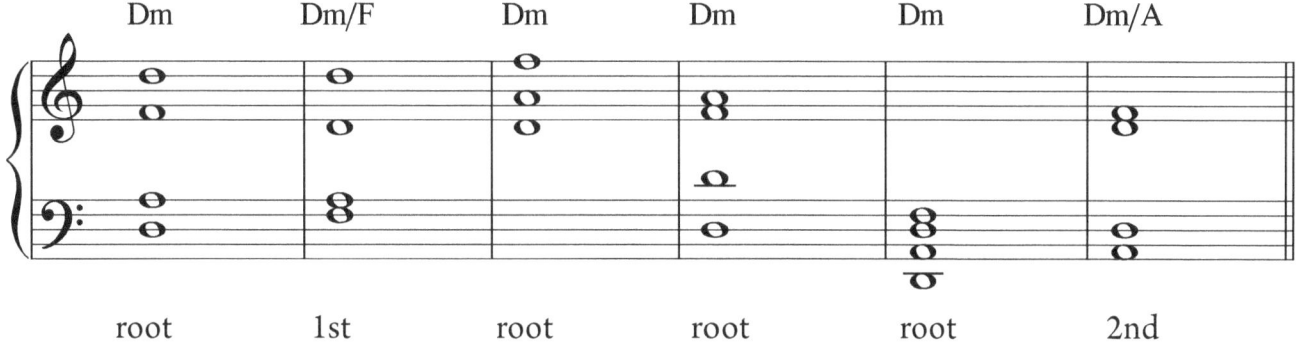

1. State the root, quality and position of the following triads.

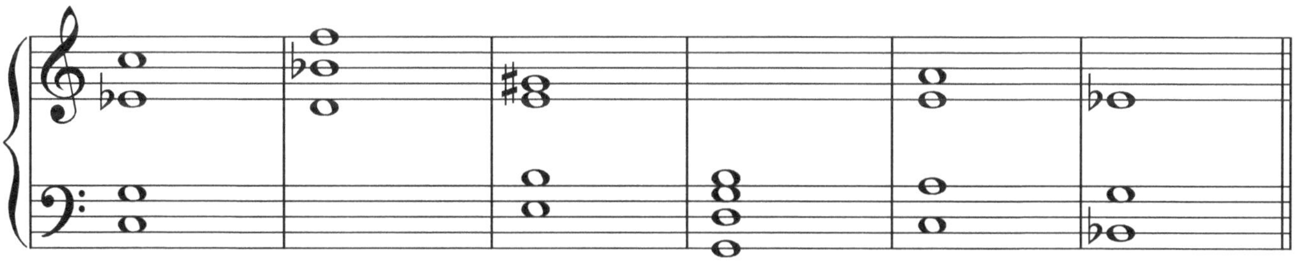

root: _____ _____ _____ _____ _____ _____
quality: _____ _____ _____ _____ _____ _____
position: _____ _____ _____ _____ _____ _____

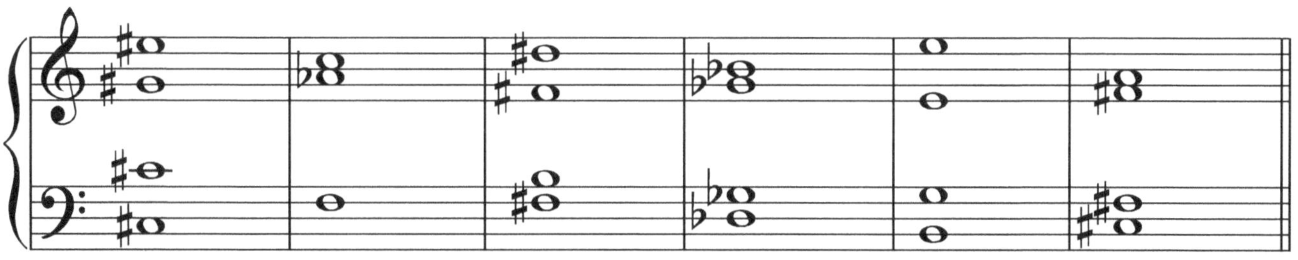

root: _____ _____ _____ _____ _____ _____
quality: _____ _____ _____ _____ _____ _____
position: _____ _____ _____ _____ _____ _____

The Augmented Triad

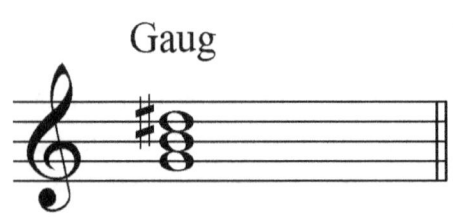

An **augmented triad** consist of the intervals of a major 3rd and an augmented 5th above the root.

   G to B is a major 3rd
   G to D♯ is an augmented 5th

The root/quality chor symbol for an augmented triad is a capital letter followed by "aug." e.g. Daug, Faug.

The Diminished Triad

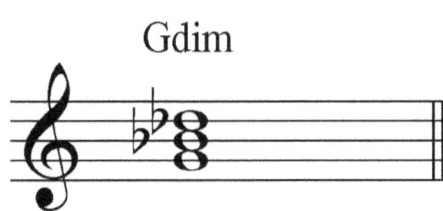

A **diminished triad** consist of the intervals of a minor 3rd and a diminished 5th above the root.

   G to B♭ is a minor 3rd
   G to D♭ is a diminished 5th

The root/quality chord symbol for a diminished triad is a capitol letter followed by "dim." e.g. Fdim Edim.

1. Write diminished triads above the following notes.

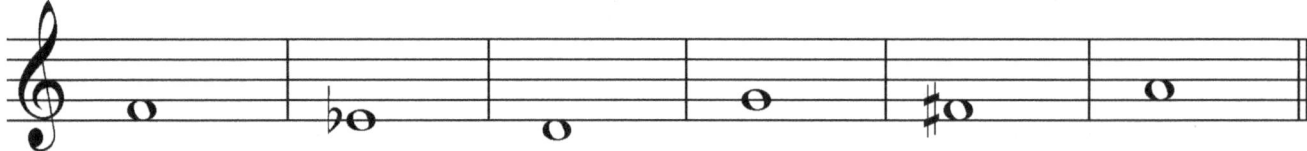

2. Write augmented triads above the following notes.

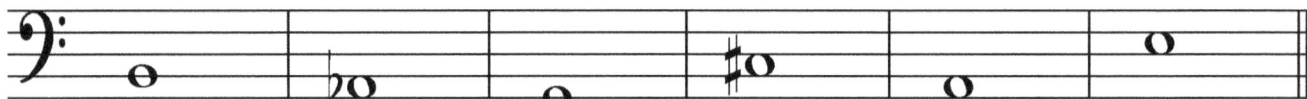

3. Identify the following triads as major, minor, augmented or diminished.

©San Marco Publications 2022

4. Provide the root/quality chord symbols for the following triads.

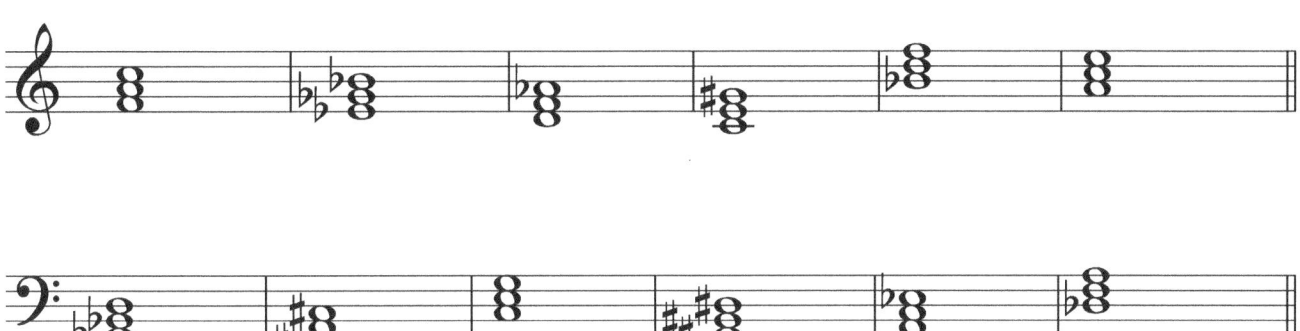

5. State the root, quality and position of the following triads. Add the root/quality chord symbol for each.

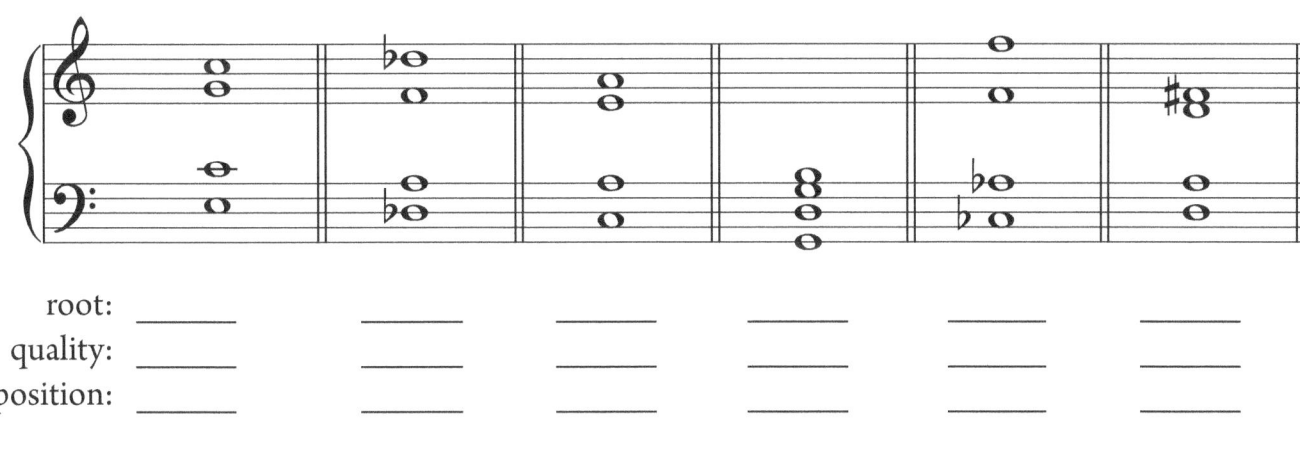

root: _____ _____ _____ _____ _____ _____
quality: _____ _____ _____ _____ _____ _____
position: _____ _____ _____ _____ _____ _____

6. State the root, quality, and position for the following triads.

root: ____ ____ ____ ____ ____ ____
quality: ____ ____ ____ ____ ____ ____
position: ____ ____ ____ ____ ____ ____

root: ____ ____ ____ ____ ____ ____
quality: ____ ____ ____ ____ ____ ____
position: ____ ____ ____ ____ ____ ____

root: ____ ____ ____ ____ ____ ____
quality: ____ ____ ____ ____ ____ ____
position: ____ ____ ____ ____ ____ ____

7. Write the following triads.

F major in root position | G diminished in 1st inversion | D minor in 2nd inversion | C augmented in root position | B♭ minor in 2nd inversion

E major in root position | A diminished in 1st inversion | F♯ diminished in 2nd inversion | B minor in root position | B diminished in 1st inversion

Triads Built on the Major and Minor Scale

Figure 11.14 illustrates the major, minor, and diminished triads that occur in the scale of C major. Each triad can be named for the scale degree on which it is built. The triad built on $\hat{1}$, the tonic, is considered the ***tonic triad*** in C major. The triad formed on $\hat{2}$, the supertonic, is considered the ***supertonic triad*** in C major. The triad built on $\hat{3}$ is the ***mediant triad***, etc.

- The root/quality chord symbol for a major triad is an uppercase letter (C, G, etc.).
- The root/quality chord symbol for a minor triad is an uppercase letter and the letter m (Dm, Em, etc.).
- The root quality chord symbol for a diminished triad is the letter and "dim" (Bdim).
- The functional chord symbol a major triad is an uppercase Roman numeral (I, IV).
- The functional chord symbol for a minor triad is a lowercase Roman numeral (ii, iii).
- The functional chord symbol for a diminished triad is a lowercase case Roman numeral with the " ° " symbol (vii°).

Figure 11.14

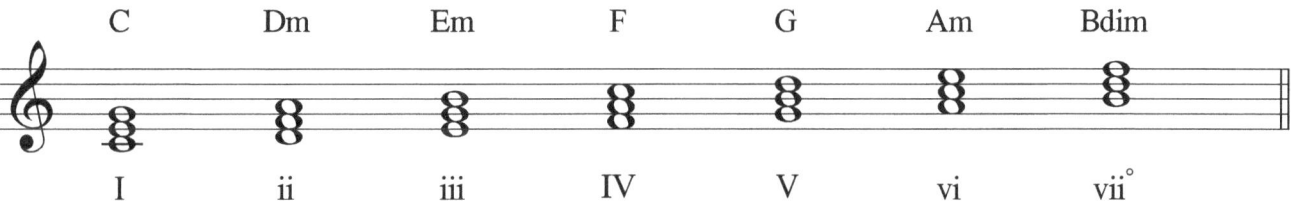

Major, minor, augmented and diminished triads occur in the harmonic minor scale. Figure 11.15 shows the triads on the A harmonic minor scale. Major triads occur on the dominant ($\hat{5}$) and the submediant ($\hat{6}$). Minor triads occur on the tonic ($\hat{1}$) and subdominant ($\hat{4}$). An augmented triad occurs on the mediant ($\hat{3}$). Diminished triads occur on the super tonic ($\hat{2}$) and the leading tone ($\hat{7}$). The raised leading tone is found in III⁺ and vii°.

- The root/quality chord symbol for an augmented triad is an uppercase letter and "aug' (Caug).
- The functional chord symbol for an augmented triad is an uppercase Roman numeral with the " ⁺ " symbol (III⁺).

Figure 11.15

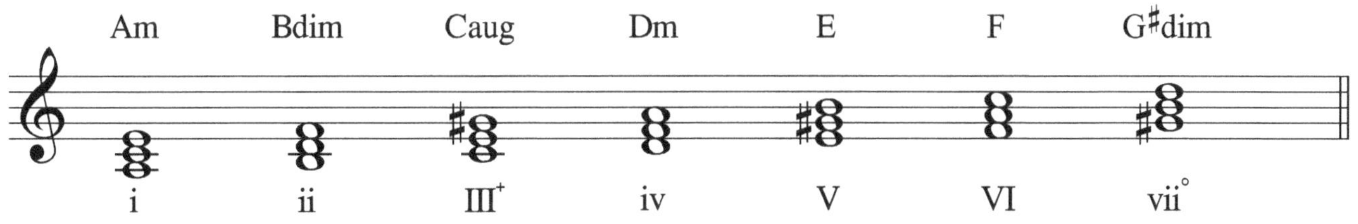

The following table summarizes the triads built on the scale degrees of the major and harmonic minor scales.

Triad	Major Scales	Harmonic Minor Scales
major	$\hat{1}$, $\hat{4}$, $\hat{5}$	$\hat{5}$, $\hat{6}$
minor	$\hat{2}$, $\hat{3}$, $\hat{6}$	$\hat{1}$, $\hat{4}$
diminished	$\hat{7}$	$\hat{2}$, $\hat{7}$
augmented	none	$\hat{3}$

Chord Symbols

Figure 11.16 contains two chords: the leading tone chord and its inversions in A minor, and the subdominant chord and its inversions in G major. Study the notation of the root/quality and functional chord symbols.

Figure 11.16

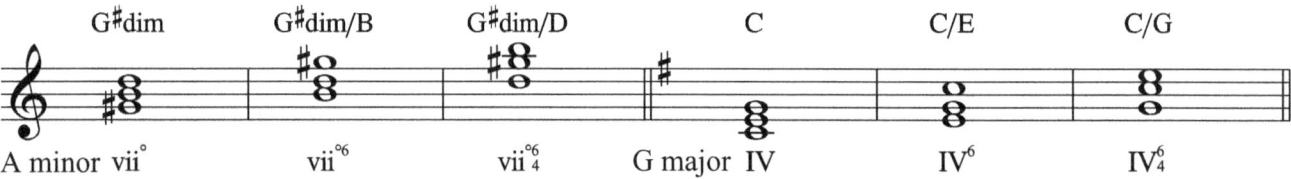

1. Write all the triads found on the F major scale. Add the functional and root/quality chord symbols for each.

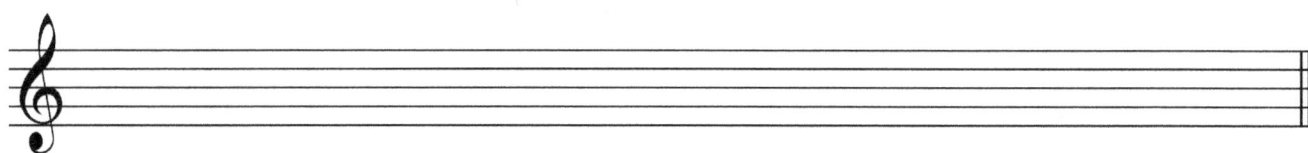

2. Write all the triads found on the D harmonic minor scale. Add the functional and root/quality chord symbols for each.

3. Name the major key for each triad. Write the scale degree name (tonic, mediant, etc.). Label each triad with functional and root/quality chord symbols.

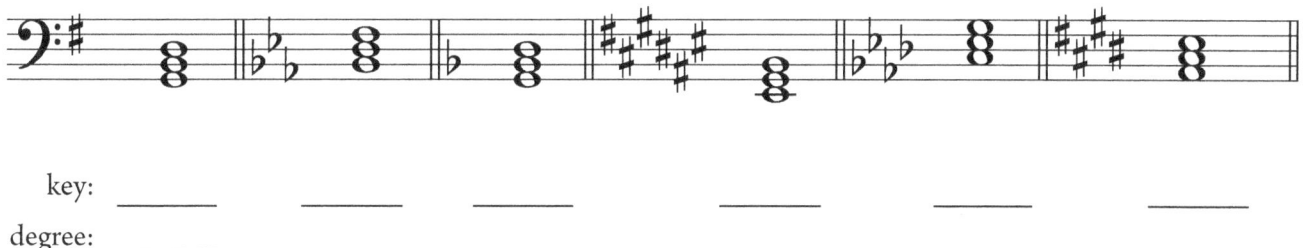

key: _____   _____   _____   _____   _____   _____
degree: _____   _____   _____   _____   _____   _____

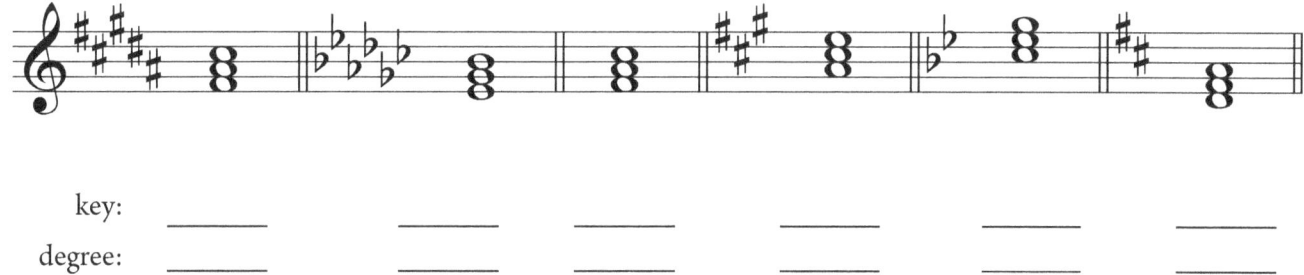

key: _____   _____   _____   _____   _____   _____
degree: _____   _____   _____   _____   _____   _____

4. Name the minor key for each triad. Write the scale degree name (tonic, mediant, etc.). Label each triad with functional and root/quality chord symbols.

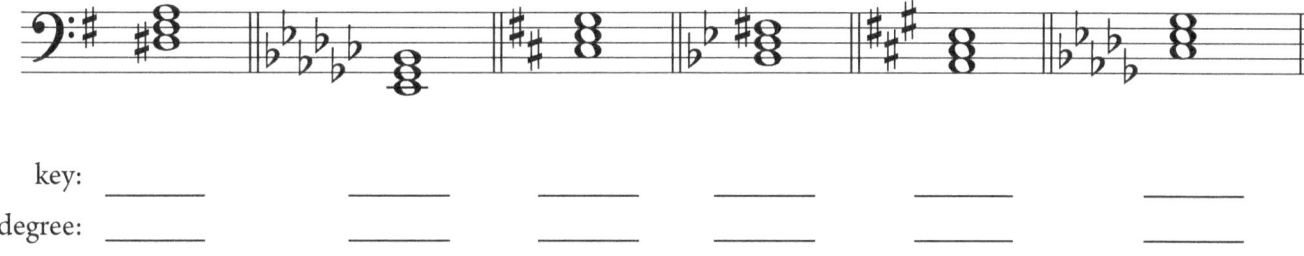

key: _____   _____   _____   _____   _____   _____
degree: _____   _____   _____   _____   _____   _____

key: _____   _____   _____   _____   _____   _____
degree: _____   _____   _____   _____   _____   _____

5. Write the following triads in close position using a key signature for each.

   i. The dominant triad of E harmonic minor in root position.
   ii. The mediant triad of E♭ major in first inversion.
   iii. The supertonic triad of F♯ harmonic minor in second inversion.
   iv. The subdominant triad of B major in root position.
   v. The dominant triad of G harmonic minor in first inversion.
   vi. The submediant triad of F major in root position.

   i.   ii.   iii.   iv.   v.   vi.

6. Write the following triads in close position using accidentals for each. Add the root/quality and functional chord symbols for each chord.

   i. The leading tone triad of B♭ harmonic minor in root position.
   ii. The submediant triad of F♯ major in second inversion.
   iii. The tonic triad of E♭ harmonic minor in first inversion.
   iv. The dominant triad of F harmonic minor in root position.
   v. The supertonic triad of E harmonic minor is first inversion.
   vi. The subdominant triad of D major in root position.

   i.   ii.   iii.   iv.   v.   vi.

7. Write a diminished triad in root position that can be found in the following scales. Use key signatures. Add the root/quality chord symbol to each chord.

   i. C major   ii. G major   iii. E harmonic minor   iv. A♭ major   v. A harmonic minor   vi. E major

   i.   ii.   iii.   iv.   v.   vi.

The Dominant Seventh Chord

Seventh chords are very common in Western music and we are used to hearing them all the time.

One of the most common seventh chords is the ***dominant seventh***. The functional chord symbol for the dominant seventh is V^7. This means that the chord is built on scale degree $\hat{5}$ (the dominant) and there is the interval of a seventh above the root of the chord. It contains four notes: the root, the 3rd, the 5th and the 7th. V^7 is a major triad with a minor 7th above the root. In other words, the intervals above the root are a major 3rd, perfect 5th and a minor 7th.

Figure 11.17 contains the dominant triad and the dominant seventh chord in C major. The root/quality chord symbol for V^7 is G^7.

Figure 11.17

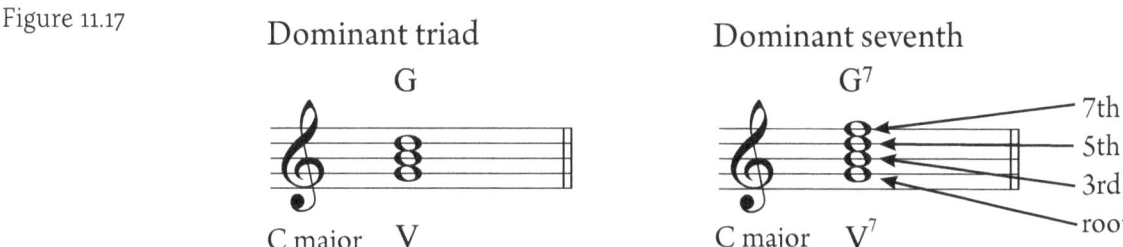

V^7 contains certain notes, like the leading tone, which pull our ear toward the tonic chord.

Figure 11.18 shows V^7 chords in C and G major and D and E minor. When we use a key signature for these chords, the seventh of V^7 is automatically a minor seventh. In minor keys V^7, like V needs a raised $\hat{7}$.

Figure 11.18

The dominant seventh sounds the same in tonic major and minor keys.

Figure 11.19 show the dominant seventh chords in F major and F minor. Even though the notation is different they sound the same and are made up of the same notes.

Figure 11.19

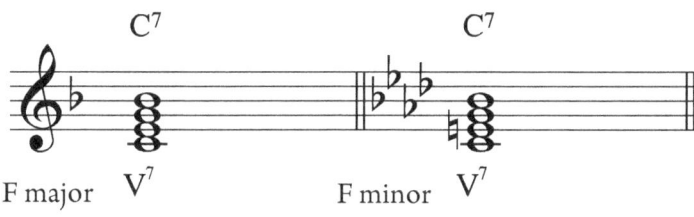

1. Name the key and write the functional and root/quality chord symbols for the following dominant seventh chords.

2. The following dominant 7ths are written in open position. Name the two keys where each one may be found.

key: _____ _____ _____ _____ _____ _____
key: _____ _____ _____ _____ _____ _____

A Note About Terminology

The leading tone is the seventh degree of the scale. It may also be referred to as scale degree 7 ($\hat{7}$). We don't call the leading tone the "seventh." It is considered the *leading tone* or *scale degree seven* ($\hat{7}$). The word "seventh" is the term reserved to indicate the seventh of a seventh chord. In this case the word seventh may also be abbreviated to "7th."

The dominant 7th chord in C major is GBDF. F is the 7th of this chord. B, the 3rd of this chord, is the leading tone or scale degree $\hat{7}$ in C major. B is not called the *7th of C major*. The word "*seventh*" is reserved to indicate the 7th of a 7th chord.

1. Name the major key of the following dominant 7th chords.

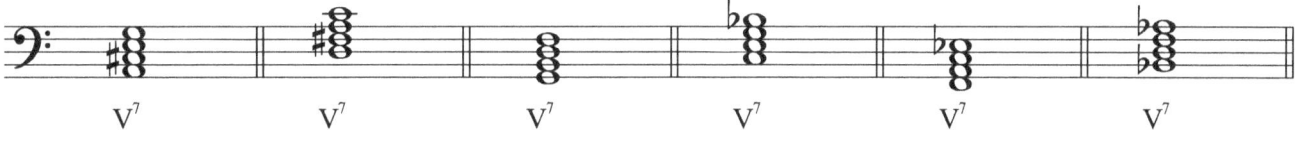

2. Each note below is the root of a dominant 7th chord. Build a dominant 7th chord above each by writing a major 3rd, perfect 5th and minor 7th above the root. Add the root/quality chord symbols above each chord.

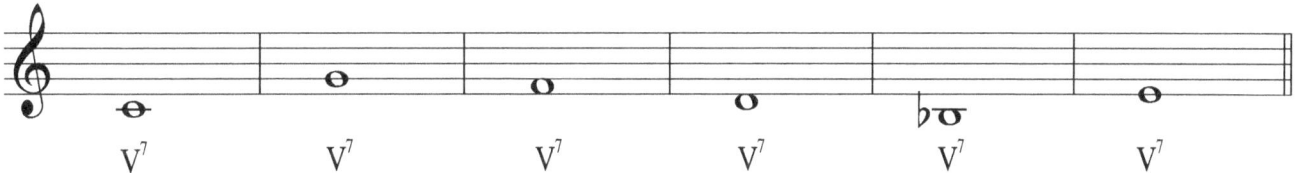

3. Write dominant 7th chords for the following keys. Use a key signature for each.

D minor   G major   A♭ major   C minor   E major   E minor

4. Write dominant 7th chords using a key signature according to the root/quality chord symbols. Name the **major key** for each.

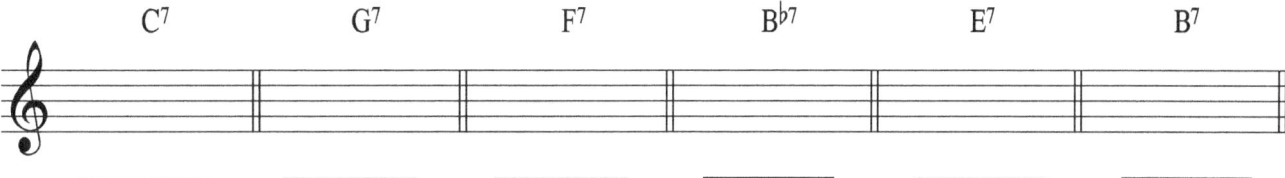

Inversions of the Dominant Seventh

V^7 occurs in root position and three inversions. These are shown in Figure 11.20. Study the root/quality chord symbols.

- If the root is the lowest note, V^7 is in **root position**.
- If the 3rd is the lowest note, V^7 is in **1st inversion**.
- If the 5th is the lowest note, V^7 is is **2nd inversion**.
- If the 7th is the lowest note, V^7 is in **3rd inversion**.

Figure 11.20

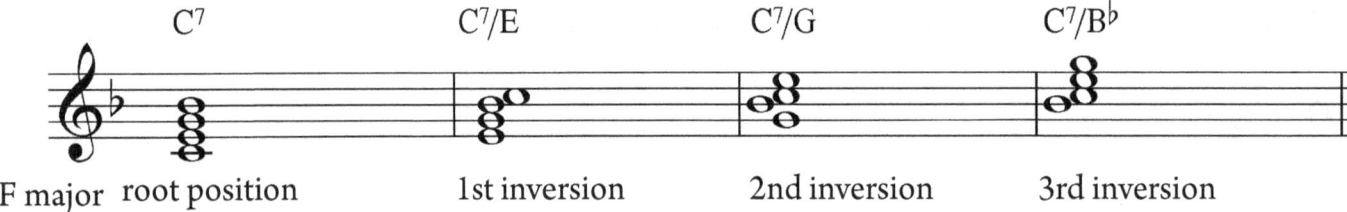

When writing the functional chord symbols for inversions of V^7, some of the numbers are omitted.

Figure 11.21 shows the numbers that indicate the intervals that occur above the lowest note. The lower chord symbols are the actual chord symbols that are used for V^7 and its inversions.

Figure 11.21

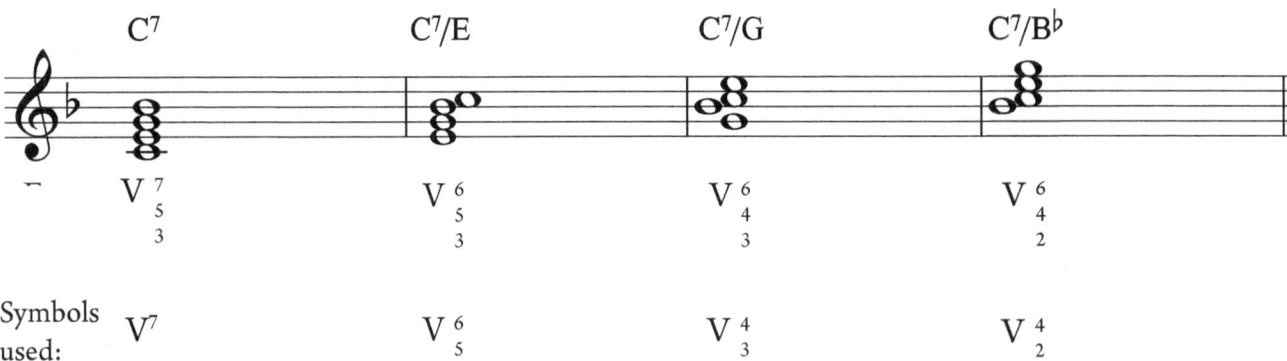

Chords

1. Write dominant seventh chords and their inversion in the following keys using a key signature for each.

G major

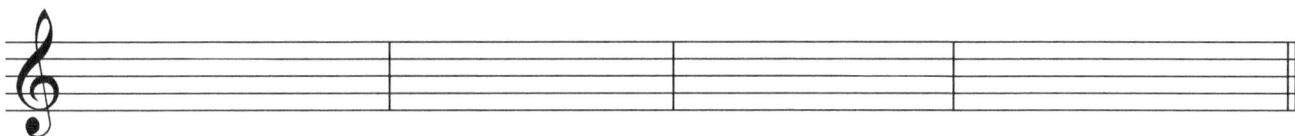

C minor

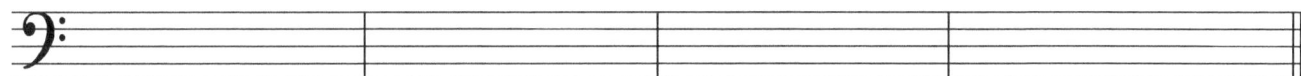

B major

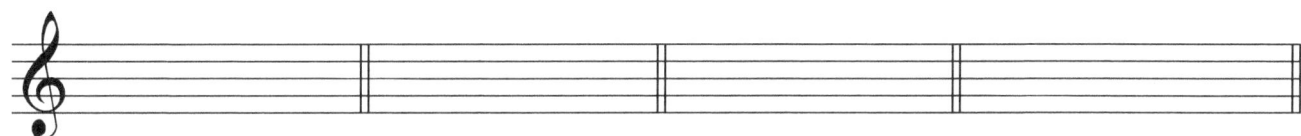

E minor

2. Solve the following dominant chords by stating the two keys, root and position for each.

root: _____ _____ _____ _____ _____ _____
key: _____ _____ _____ _____ _____ _____
key: _____ _____ _____ _____ _____ _____
position: _____ _____ _____ _____ _____ _____

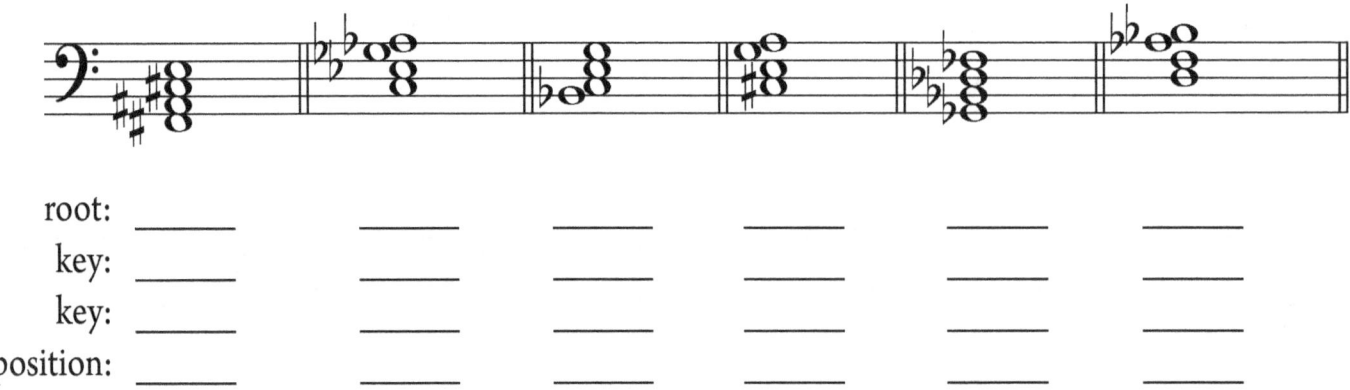

root: _____ _____ _____ _____ _____ _____
key: _____ _____ _____ _____ _____ _____
key: _____ _____ _____ _____ _____ _____
position: _____ _____ _____ _____ _____ _____

3. Add accidentals to the following to make dominant seventh chords. Name the major key for each.

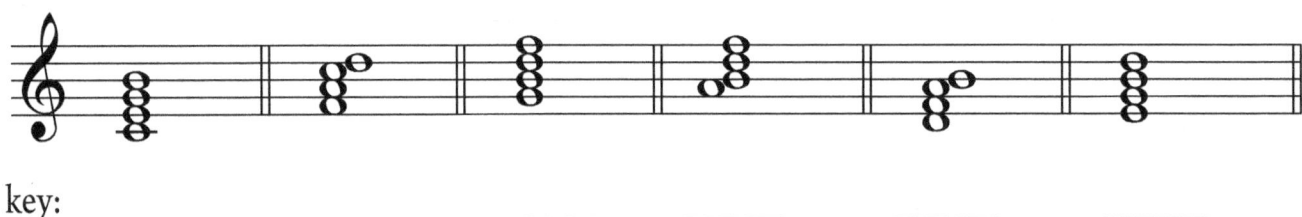

key: _____ _____ _____ _____ _____ _____

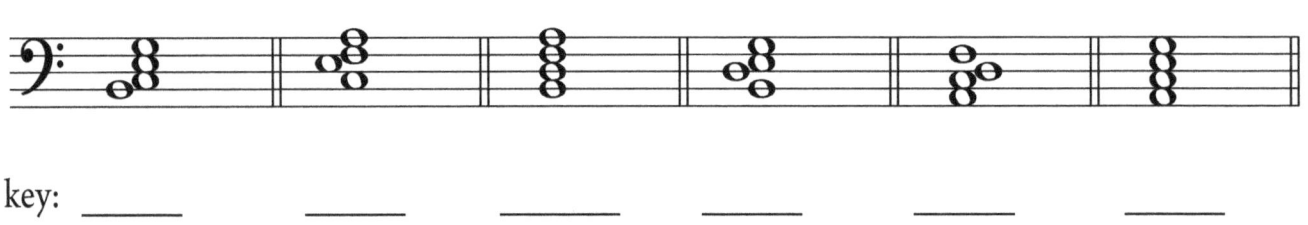

key: _____ _____ _____ _____ _____ _____

4. State the root, key, and position of the following dominant seventh chords.

root: _____ _____ _____ _____ _____ _____
key: _____ _____ _____ _____ _____ _____
position: _____ _____ _____ _____ _____ _____

root: _____ _____ _____ _____ _____ _____

key: _____ _____ _____ _____ _____ _____

position: _____ _____ _____ _____ _____ _____

The Diminished Seventh Chord

The ***diminished seventh chord*** is built on raised $\hat{7}$ in the minor key.

Figure 11.22 contains the diminished seventh built on raised $\hat{7}$ in A minor. The functional chord symbol is vii°⁷.

Figure 11.22

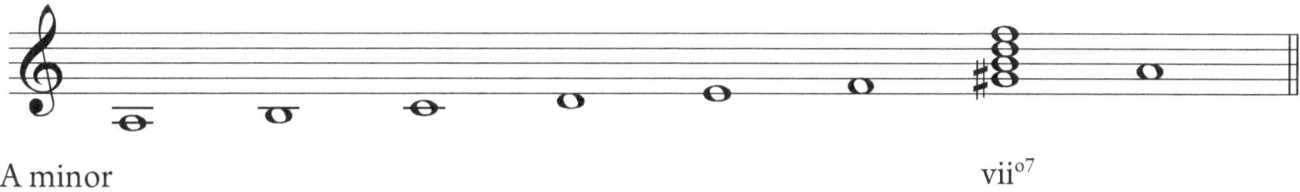

A minor   vii°⁷

Figure 11.23 shows that this chord consists of a diminished triad with a diminished 7th above the root of the chord. The root/quality symbol is G♯dim⁷ or G♯°⁷.

Figure 11.23

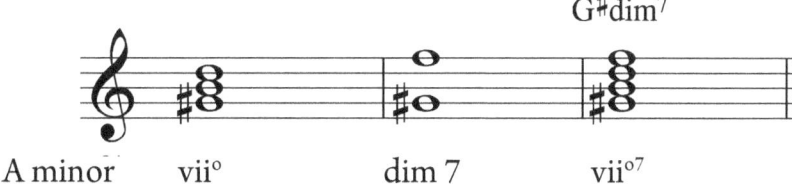

A minor   vii°   dim 7   vii°⁷

1. Name the key and write the functional and root/quality chord symbols for the following diminished 7th chords.

Symbol:

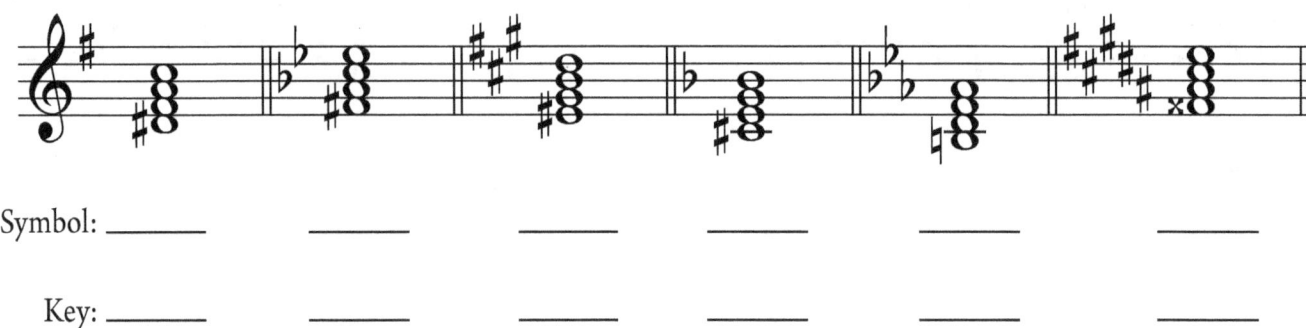

Symbol: _____   _____   _____   _____   _____   _____

Key: _____   _____   _____   _____   _____   _____

2. Write diminished 7th chords in the following keys using a key signature for each.

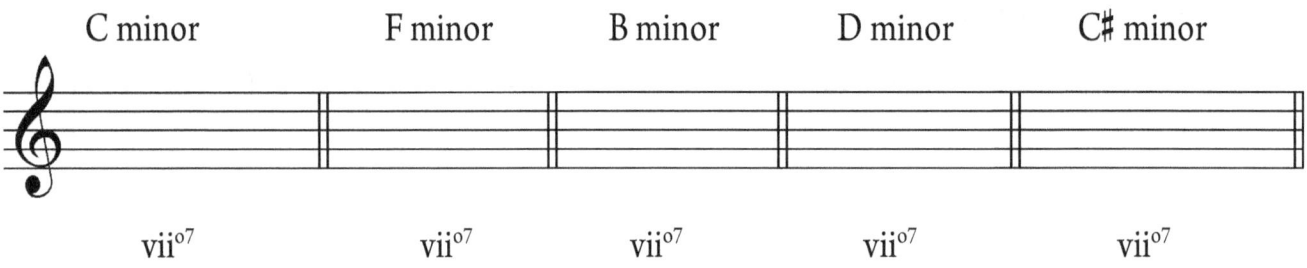

3. Write the following chords using accidentals.

4. Write the following chords according to the functional chord symbols.

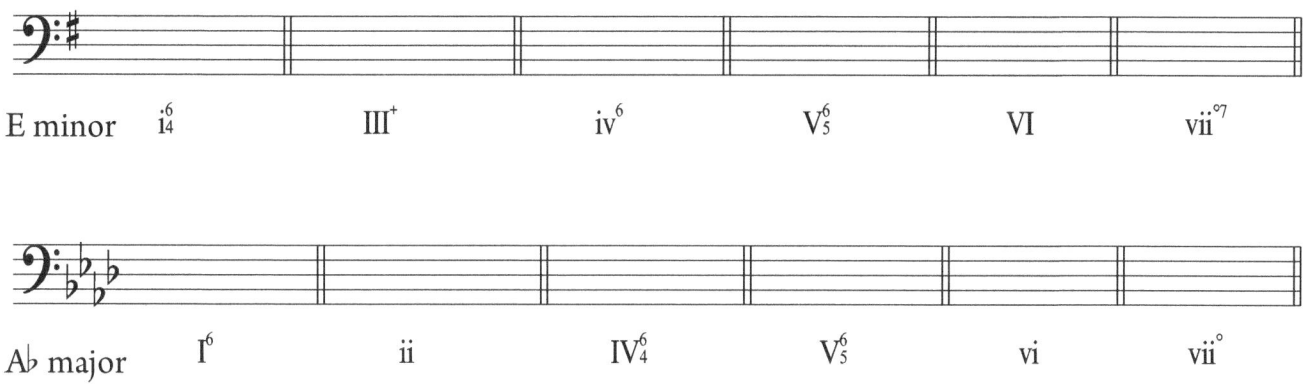

E minor   i$^6_4$ III$^+$ iv^6 V$^6_5$ VI   vii$^{°7}$

A♭ major   I^6 ii   IV$^6_4$ V$^6_5$ vi   vii$^°$

Other Chords

Composers of the late 19th, 20th, and 21st centuries expanded harmonic language and chord structure. The following chords added variety, interest, and dissonant tension to their works.

Chords called **tone clusters**, or *cluster chords* are shown in Figure 11.24. A tone cluster is a chord made up of at least three consecutive tones in a scale. Sometimes they are based on the chromatic scale and are separated by semitones. For example, three adjacent piano keys (such as F, F♯, and G) played simultaneously produce a tone cluster. Tone clusters may also be made up of adjacent diatonic tones. The first clusters were written for the piano, but soon they were being used in music for other mediums. Some modern composers use large keyboard tone clusters called ***forearm clusters***. These are performed by slamming the forearm onto the keys. Examples c) and d) show different ways that forearm clusters can be notated.

Figure 11.24

Polychords are formed by combining two or more different chords. Only triads and 7th chords are combined to form polychords. Most polychords combine elements of two different keys or modes. Figure 11.25 shows how Ravel used two different chords at the same time to produce a polychord. Here, the right plays a G major triad, and the left hand plays a D♯ minor 7th chord.

Figure 11.25

Maurice Ravel
Piano Concerto in G (1931)

Quartal chords are chords made up of a series of fourths. This is in contrast to more familiar chords (like major, minor, dominant, diminished, augmented) that are built on thirds, (tertian chords). Composers sometimes use these chords in intermittant or brief passages in a composition for their unique effect. Figure 11.26 contains a famous quartal chord used by the composer Alexander Scriabin (1871 - 1915). This chord is known as the **mystic chord**. Scriabin based some of his later works on this quartal chord including his Sonata No. 5, Op. 53. In jazz music quartal chords were made popular by McCoy Tyner (John Coltrane's piano player). They have a jazzy sound and work well in modal music.

Figure 11.26

Alexander Scriabin
Sonata No.5, Op.53

1. Match each chord with its description.

_____ a tone cluster or cluster chord

a.

_____ viiº7 of A harmonic minor

b.

_____ a quartal chord

c.

_____ V7 of E minor

d.

_____ a polychord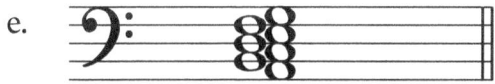

e.

_____ V$^4_2$ of G major

f.

_____ C augmented triad in 1st inversion

g.

_____ V$^4_3$ of F major

h.

192

©San Marco Publications 2022   Chords

Chordal Texture in a Musical Score

Composers use chords in many different textures when writing a musical score. This depends on the style, type of composition, instruments, or performers needed to bring the score to life.

Figure 11.27 is the opening of "Hallelujah Chorus" from Handel's Messiah. This work is written for a 4 voice choir. The four voices work together and create chords as they sing. The staff under the score is added here to show the chords that are formed when the choir sings together. On this staff, the chords are reduced to their simplest form. The bass voice, which is the lowest note, determines the inversion of the chord.

Figure 11.27

Figure 11.28 contains a left hand accompaniment of broken triads. The first 2 measures contain the tonic triad in G major in root position. Measure 3 is the subdominant triad in 2nd inversion.

Figure 11.28

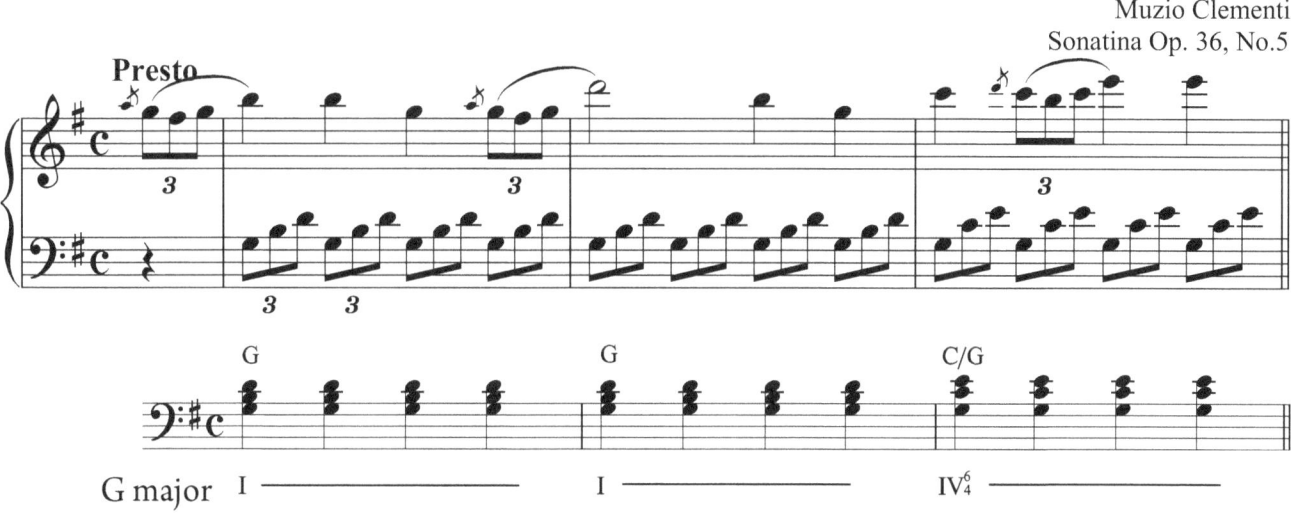

In Figure 11.29 the left hand is made up of extended broken D♭ major chords.

Figure 11.29

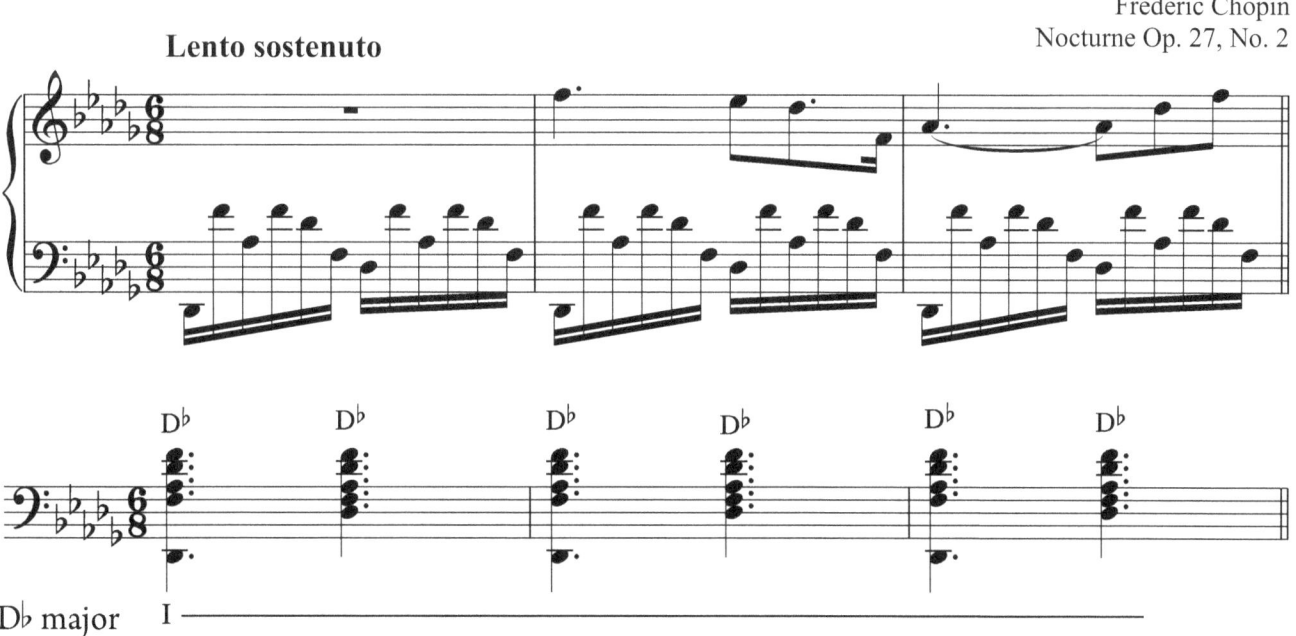

1. For the following musical examples: Name the key. State the root, type, position and scale degree of each outlined chord.

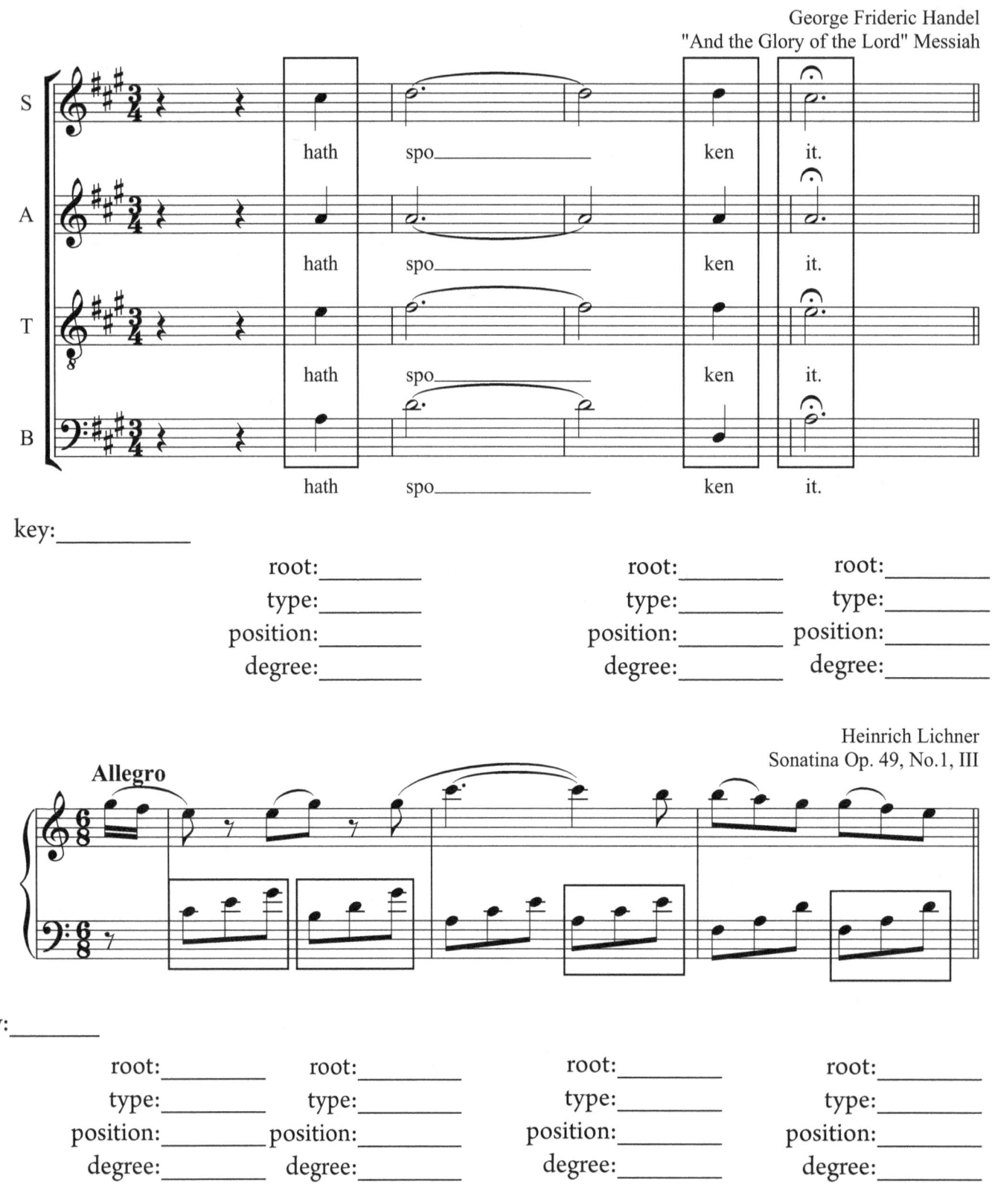

key:_____

root:_____ root:_____ root:_____
type:_____ type:_____ type:_____
position:_____ position:_____ position:_____
degree:_____ degree:_____ degree:_____

key:_____

root:_____ root:_____ root:_____ root:_____
type:_____ type:_____ type:_____ type:_____
position:_____ position:_____ position:_____ position:_____
degree:_____ degree:_____ degree:_____ degree:_____

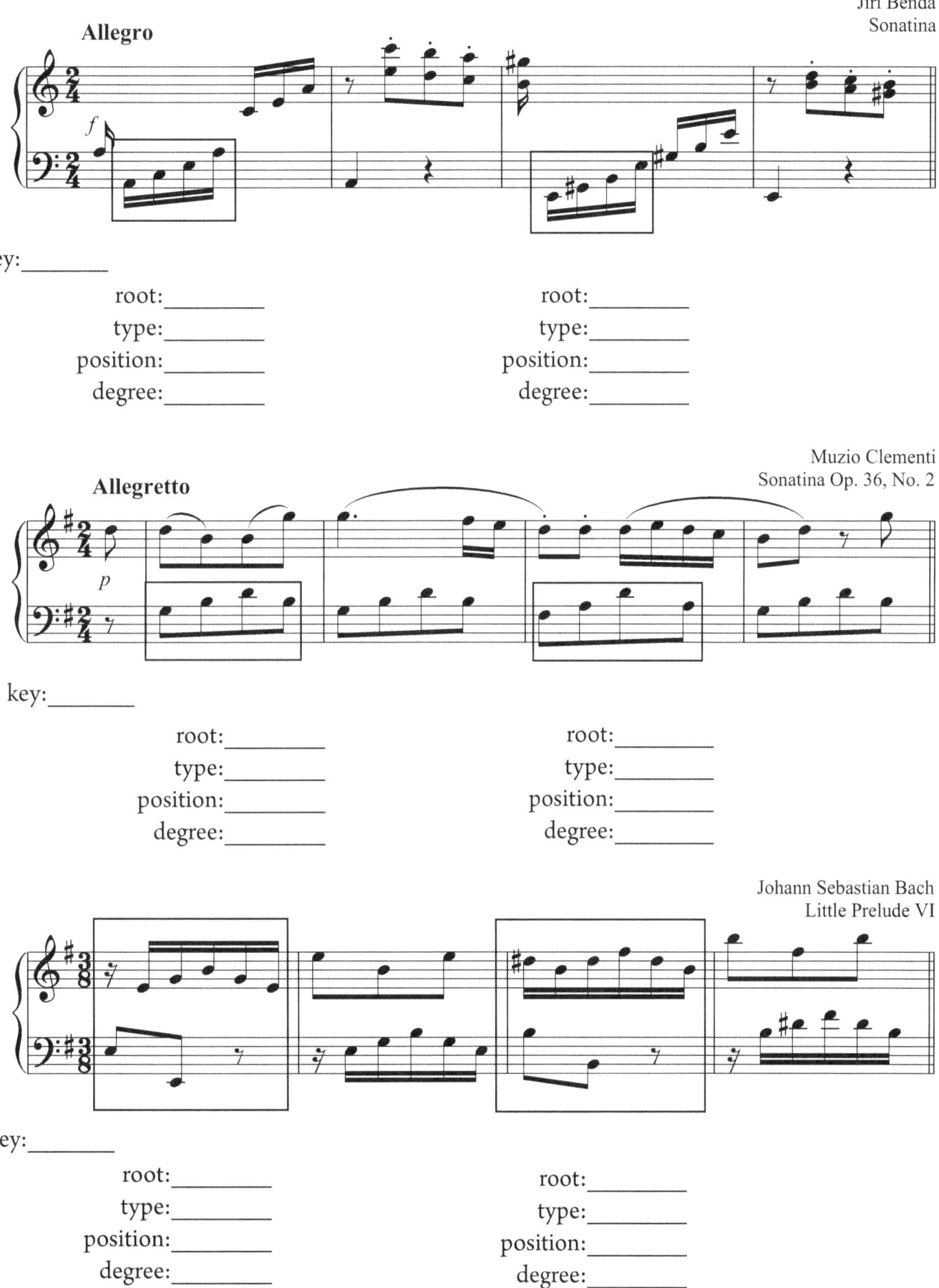

12
Cadences

Music is divided into sections or units of various lengths called *phrases*. A phrase is a musical idea, like a sentence in a story. Most phrases in traditional music are four measures long. A phrase ends with a *cadence*, which is a place of rest in music. A cadence is like the period at the end of a sentence. Cadences consist of two chords which bring a phrase to a close.

There are two types of cadences: *final* and *non-final*. Final cadences bring a phrase to a complete ending. Non-final cadences look forward and do not complete a musical idea. Another phrase is required to complete their non-final character.

Study Figure 12.1. Each line presents a pair of phrases. The phrases move in continuous quarter notes until they pause on a half-note. Harmonically, the most important chord in a phrase is the last one. This is the target or goal of the phrase. It acts in the same way that a comma, question mark or period acts in a sentence. This harmonic event at the end of a phrase is called a cadence.

Figure 12.1

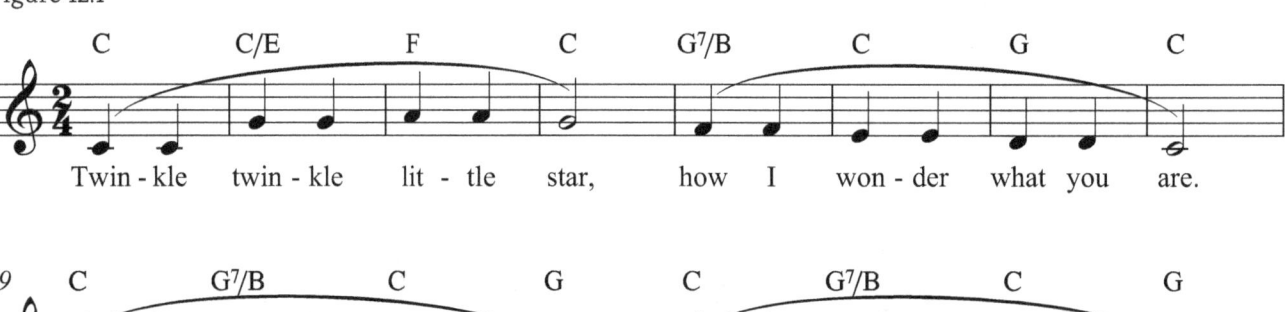
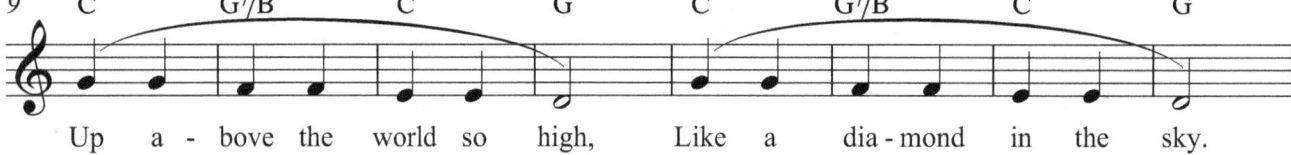
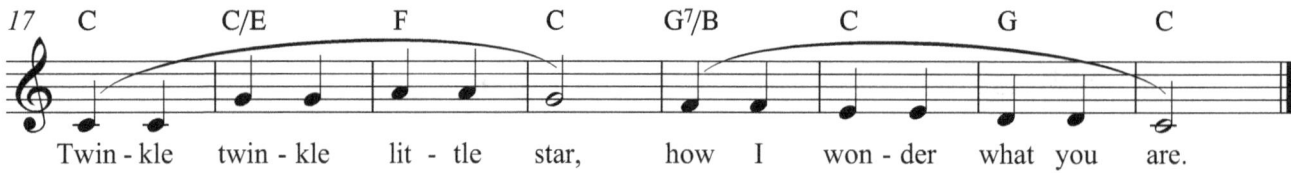

The Authentic Cadence

The most frequently used final cadence is the *authentic cadence*. It is the strongest and most conclusive cadence. It consists of the chords V - I or V - i (in minor keys). Figure 12.2 contains two authentic cadences in keyboard style. Notice the following common features of these cadences.

- They occur on the last two notes of the phrase.
- The first chord is on a weaker beat than the second chord.
- The V chord in a minor key contains raised $\hat{7}$.
- In keyboard style, three notes of the chord are placed in the treble staff, and the bass staff has the root of each chord.
- These cadences are considered *perfect authentic cadences* because they end with the tonic as the top note of the I chord. In the D major cadence, D is the final and top note. In the E minor cadence, E is the final and top note. Ending on the tonic confirms the key and gives the cadence a strong final sound.

Figure 12.2

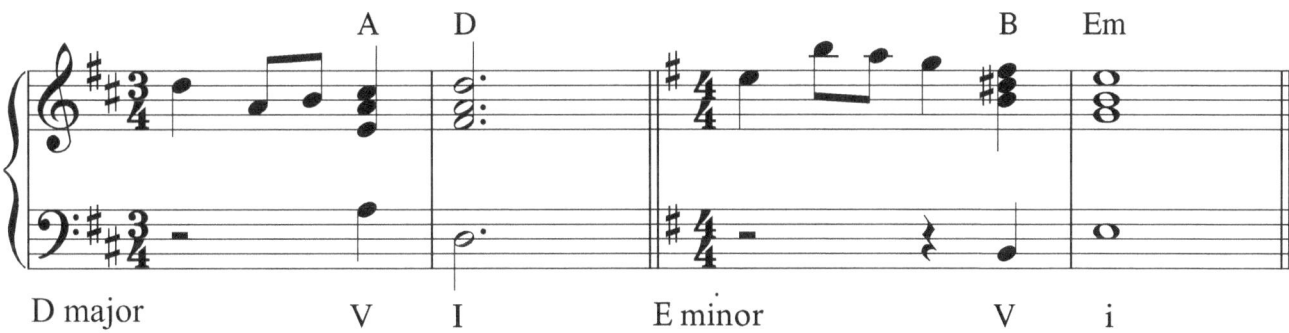

The cadences in Figure 12.3 are considered *imperfect authentic cadences* because they end on a note other than the tonic. The D major cadence ends with the 5th (A) as the final and top note. The E minor cadence ends with the 3rd (G) as the final and top note. These are still final cadences but do not sound as strong and final as a perfect authentic cadence which ends with tonic as the top note.

Figure 12.3

V⁷ - I is also an authentic cadence. Figure 12.4 shows two authentic cadences using V⁷. In the first example in G major, the V⁷ chord is complete using all four notes, D F♯ A C. In the D minor example the V⁷ chord is considered incomplete. Here, the root is doubled, and the 5th of the chord is left out, A C♯ G A. Both of these examples are correct. The root of each chord must be in the bass. The cadence in G major is a *perfect authentic cadence* and the cadence in D minor in an *imperfect authentic cadence*.

Figure 12.4

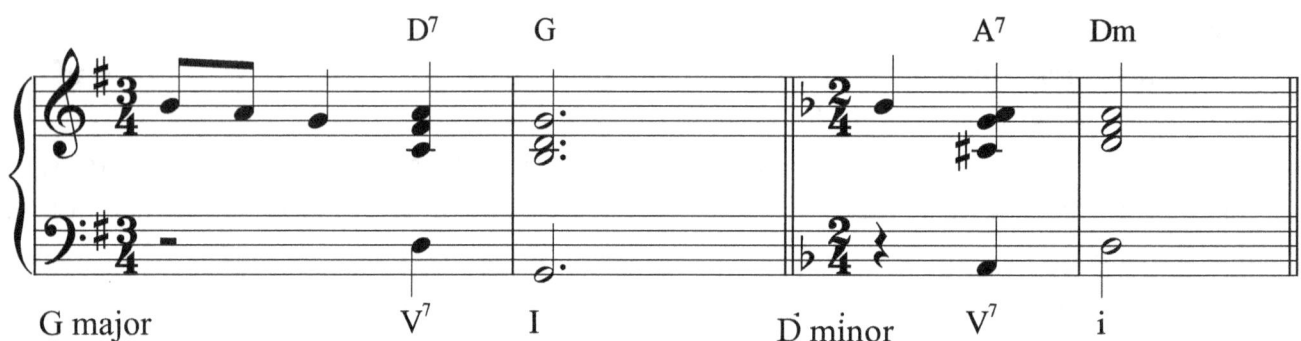

1. For the following authentic cadences: Name the key, write the functional and root/quality chord symbols and name them as perfect authentic or imperfect authentic.

key: _____

cadence: _____

key: _____

cadence: _____

key: _____

cadence: _____

key: _____

cadence: _____

key: _____

cadence: _____

key: _____

cadence: _____

key: _____

cadence: _____

key: _____

cadence: _____

Cadences

The Half Cadence

The *half cadence* is a non-final cadence. It ends on the V chord. Ending a phrase on the V chord leaves the music with an open or unfinished sound. For this reason a piece of music does not end with a half cadence. Half cadences never end on the dominant seventh (V^7). V^7 contains too many strong tones that do not allow a feeling of rest. We will study two half cadences, I - V and IV - V.

Study the half cadences in keyboard style in Figure 12.5.

Figure 12.5

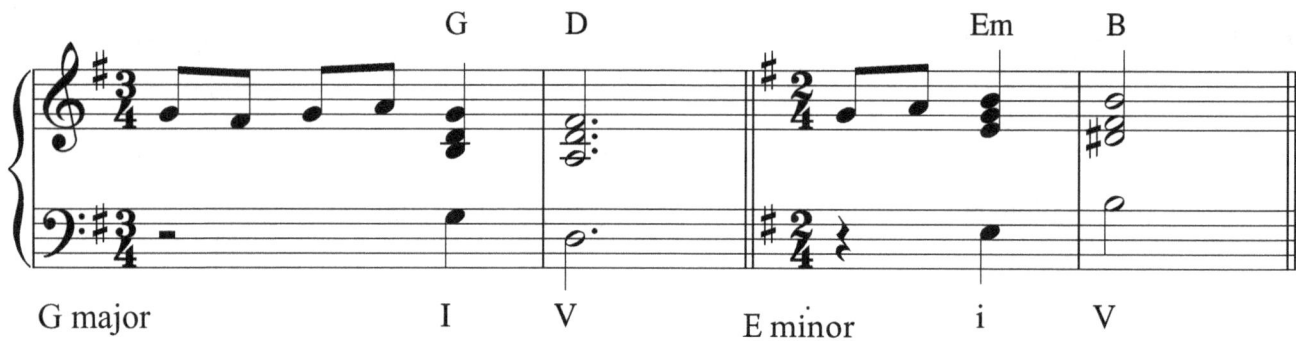

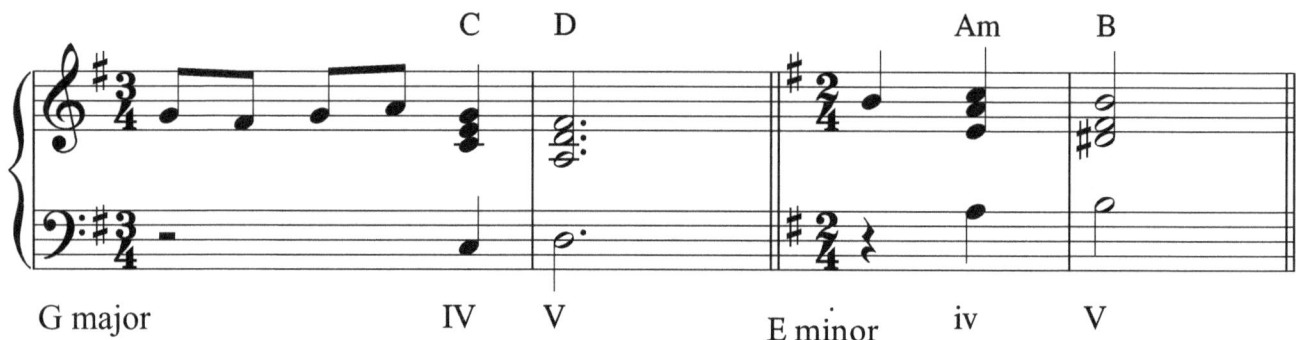

1. For the following cadences: Name the key, write the functional and root/quality chord symbols and name them as half, perfect authentic, or imperfect authentic.

Writing Cadences

Certain guidelines should be followed when writing cadences. Study the following steps for writing an authentic cadence in E minor.

1. Add the key signature and rests at the beginning of the first measure. Cadences often occur over the bar line with the second chord of the cadence on a stronger beat than the first. The first chord usually occurs in the second half or second part of the first measure on a weaker beat. In Figure 12.6 the key signature of E minor is F sharp. It is placed *before* the time signature. Roman numerals indicating the functional chord symbols of the authentic cadence are placed under the staff (V - i). Since this is 3/4 time a half rest is used at the beginning of the measure and the V chord will be placed on beat 3 of the first measure. There are other options that could be used for rhythm here, but this is effective.

Figure 12.6

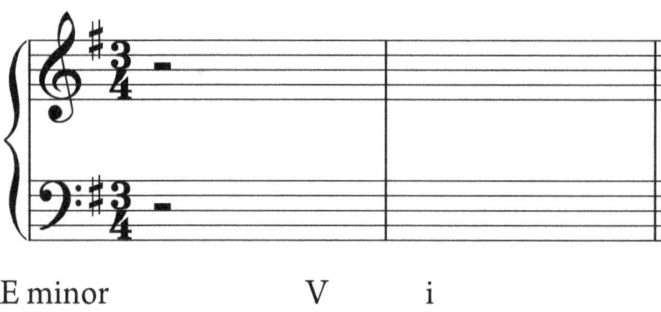

2. Write the bass notes for the V and the i chords. In E minor the root of V is B, and the root of i is E. In Figure 12.7 they are written as a quarter note (B) to complete the first measure, and a dotted half note (E) to complete the second measure.

Figure 12.7

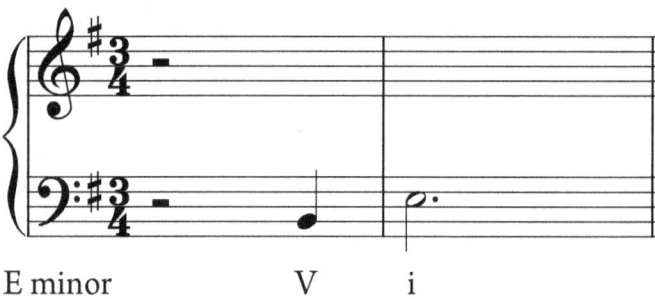

3. Write the notes of the V chord in close position on the treble staff. Close position occurs when the notes of the triad are as close together as possible. In E minor V is B-D♯-F♯. These notes can be in any order as long as they stay in close position. Figure 12.8 uses quarter notes on beat 3 of the first measure for this chord.

Figure 12.8

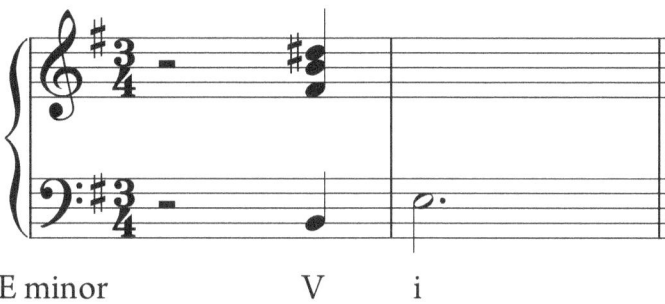

4. Write the notes of the i chord in the second measure. i in E minor is E-G-B. Keep these notes as close as possible to the notes of the V chord. In Figure 12.9 there is one note that is common to both chords (B). This B is kept in the same place in both chords (here it is the middle note). This note is called the **common tone**. Repeating the common tone in the same place creates smooth movement. This movement of notes from chord to chord is called **voice leading**. The leading tone (D♯) rises to the tonic (E). If the leading tone is at the top of the chord, it should rise to the tonic. The F♯ steps up to G.

Figure 12.9

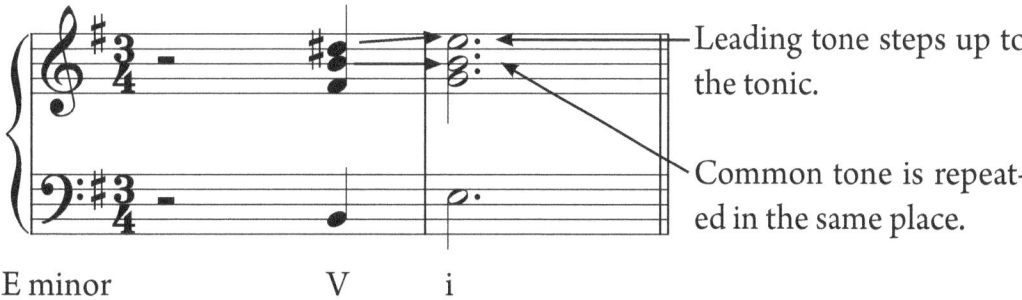

Writing the half cadence I to V is similar to writing the authentic cadence. There is a common tone between I and V. Try to repeat it in the same place and move the other voices down a step. In Figure 12.10 the common tone D is the top note of the chords.

Figure 12.10

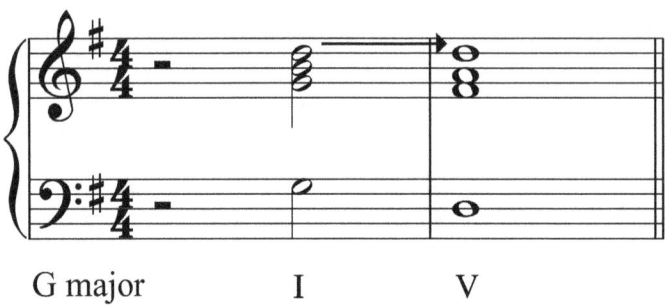

G major   I   V

The chords of the half cadence IV to V have no common tones. This cadence requires special voice leading. When writing this cadence, it is best to move the 3 upper notes in contrary (opposite) motion to the bass. The bass will rise a step, and the upper voices will fall from the notes of the IV chord to the notes of the V chord. In Figure 12.11, 2 voices step and one voice skips down to the notes of the V chord.

In this cadence, the bass steps up from iv to V (G to A). Do not write this cadence with bass falling a 7th from G down to A. This large melodic interval, a 7th, is not allowed here.

Figure 12.11

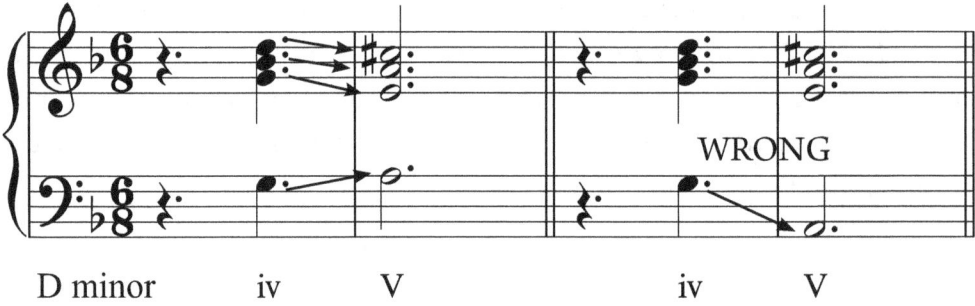

D minor   iv   V   iv   V

When writing this cadence, avoid writing two root position chords consecutively as shown in Figure 12.12. This is considered a mistake in voice leading.

Figure 12.12

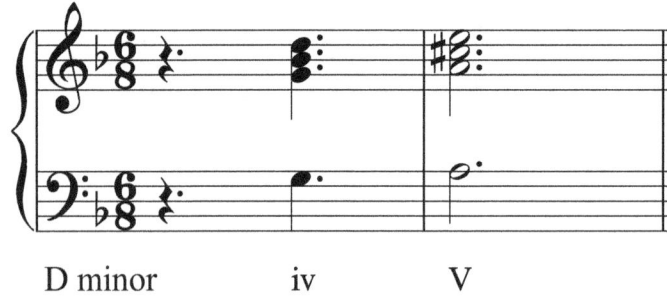

D minor   iv   V

1. Write authentic cadences in the following keys. Add functional chord symbols.

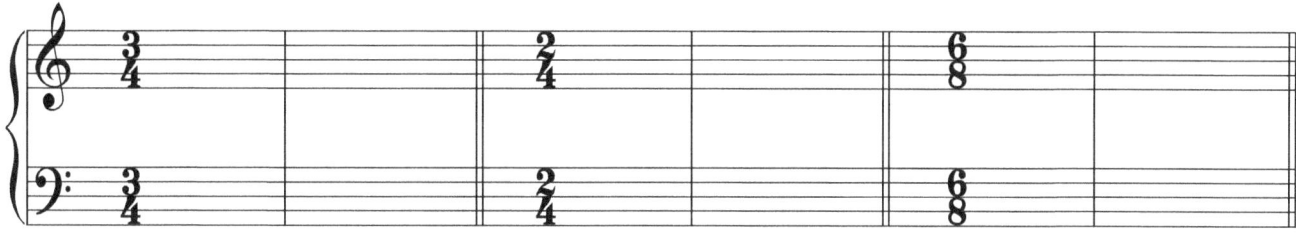

A major   C minor   D major

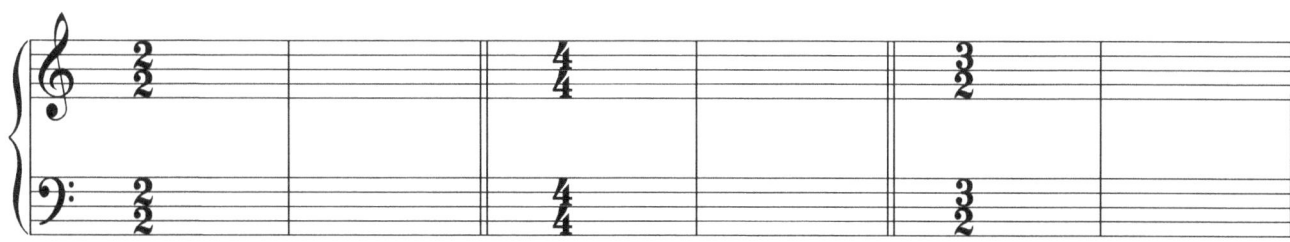

B minor   B♭ major   F major

2. Write half cadences using I (i) - V in the following keys. Add functional chord symbols.

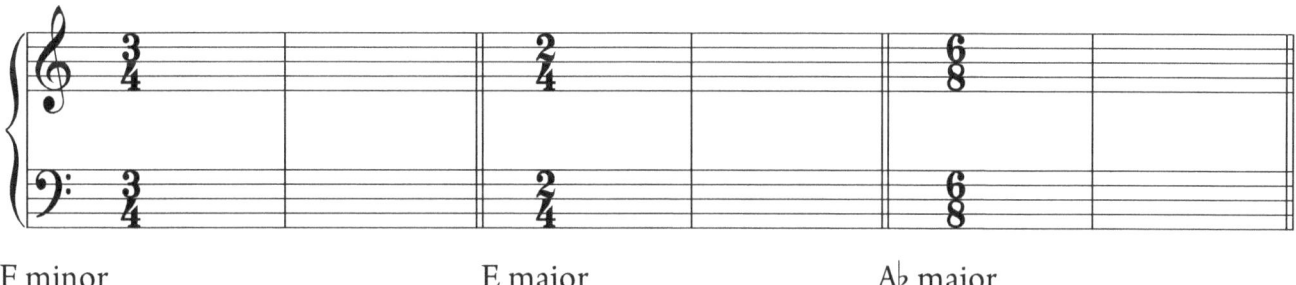

F minor   E major   A♭ major

3. Write half cadences using IV (iv) - V in the following keys. Add functional chord symbols.

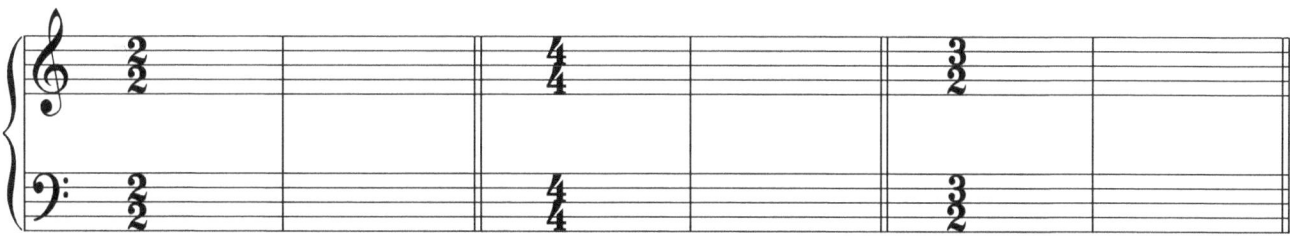

F♯ minor   C major   D minor

Writing Cadence at the End of a Melody

In this lesson, we will learn to write cadences in keyboard style below a given melody. It is important to remember that this is the melody and you should write the notes of the cadence **under** this melody. If you write above the given part, it will change the melody, and that is wrong!
Follow these steps for writing cadences:

1. Name the key of the melody (the melody below is in G major).
2. Write out the letter names of chords I, IV and V in that key (G major).
   - I   G B D G
   - IV   C E G C
   - V   D F♯ A D
3. Choose the two chords that will harmonize the last two notes of the phrase and create a logical cadence (authentic V - I, plagal IV - I, half I - V, or half IV - V). Here, an authentic cadence, V - I, is the only logical choice for the final melody notes A - G.
4. Write the functional chord symbols (V - I).

Figure 12.13

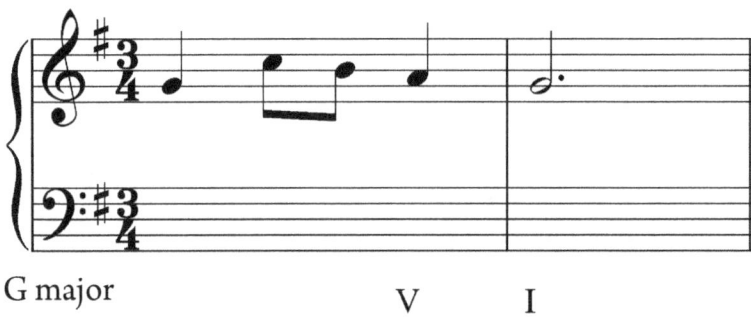

5. Write the roots of the two chords in the bass staff under the final two melody notes. Here, the bass notes for a V - I cadence are D and G.
6. Complete any empty beats in the measure with rests. In this example, the first two beats of measure 1 need a rest.

Figure 12.14

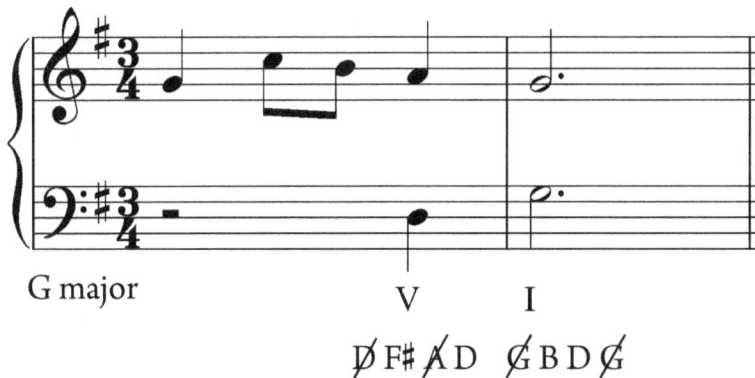

©San Marco Publications 2022

7. In the treble clef, add the remaining notes of the chords under each melody note to create a complete chord. Remember that in minor keys V will have raised $\hat{7}$. In Figure 12.15, it is not possible to keep the common tone (D) in the same place, and it is not possible to have the leading tone (F♯) step up to the tonic. This is common when the melody moves from $\hat{2}$ to $\hat{1}$.

Figure 12.15

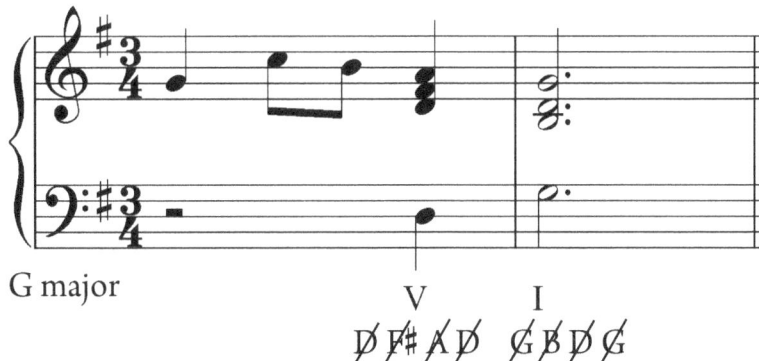

Examine the melody in Figure 12.16 a). We have to determine if this melodic fragment is in E♭ major or C minor. It starts on C, but that doesn't mean it is in C minor. If we look at the three primary chords in each key, it will give us an idea.

	E♭ major			**C minor**
I	E♭ G B♭ E♭		i	C E♭ G C
IV	A♭ C E♭ A♭		iv	F A♭ C F
V	B♭ D F B♭		V	G B♮ D G

When we examine the chords in these two keys, there is only one cadence that fits with the last two melody notes (F - D). That is the half cadence iv - V in C minor. In E♭ major, F - D supports two V chords, and this does not make a cadence. This fragment is in C minor. Figure 11.16 b) shows the half cadence in C minor. Note that there are no common tones and the 3 notes of the iv chord go down to the 3 notes of the V chord. This is in contrary motion to the bass.

Figure 12.16

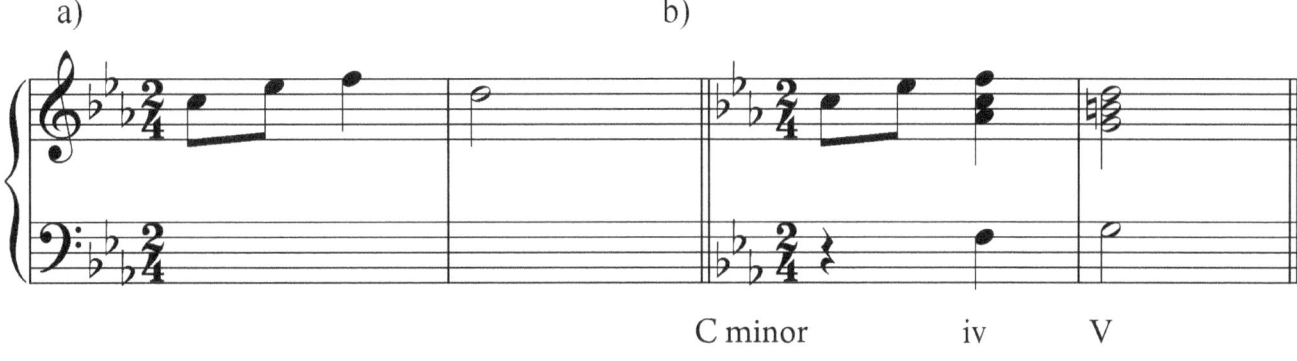

1. For the following melodic fragments: Name the key. Write a cadence at the end in keyboard style. Label the chords with functional chord symbols. Name the cadence as perfect authentic, imperfect authentic, or half.

Cadences

2. For the following phrases: Name the key. Write a cadence in keyboard style at the end of each phrase. Add functional chord symbols. Name the cadence as perfect authentic, imperfect authentic, or half.

Key:_____   Cadence:_____

Key:_____   Cadence:_____

Key:_____   Cadence:_____

Key:_____   Cadence:_____

Key:_____   Cadence:_____

The Plagal Cadence

The *plagal cadence* is a final cadence. In major keys it is IV - I. In minor keys it is iv - i. Like most cadences, it moves from IV on a weak beat to I on a strong beat. Since this cadence does not contain the leading tone, it is not as final sounding as the authentic cadence. The plagal cadence is often heard at the end of church hymns harmonizing the word "Amen." This cadence has its origins in church music but is heard today in music from country to rock.

Figure 12.17 contains plagal cadences in major and minor keys.

Figure 12.17

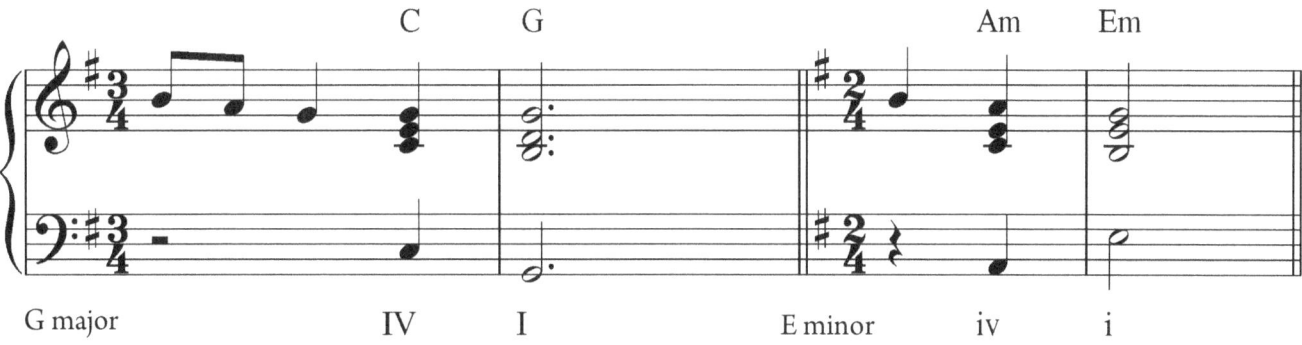

1. For the following cadences: Name the key, write the functional and root/quality chord symbols and name them as plagal, perfect authentic, imperfect authentic or half.

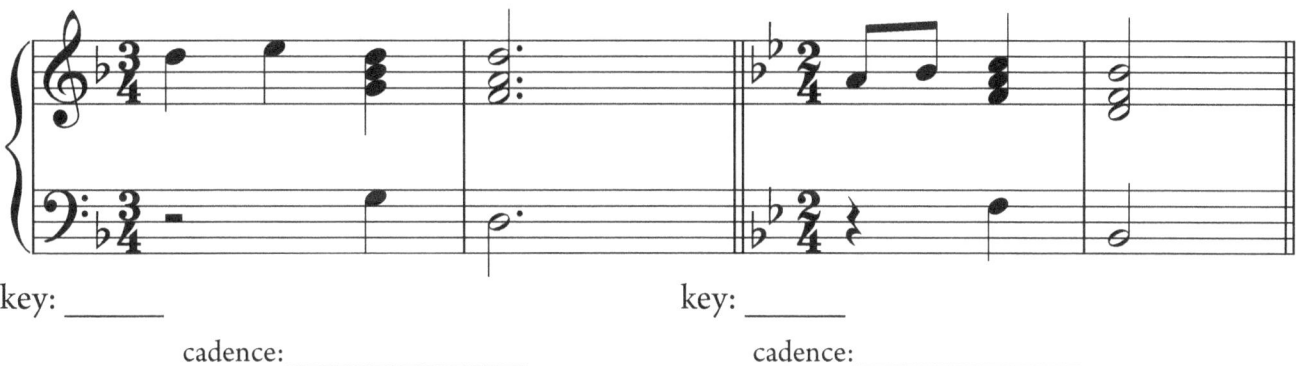

key: _____   key: _____
   cadence: _____   cadence: _____

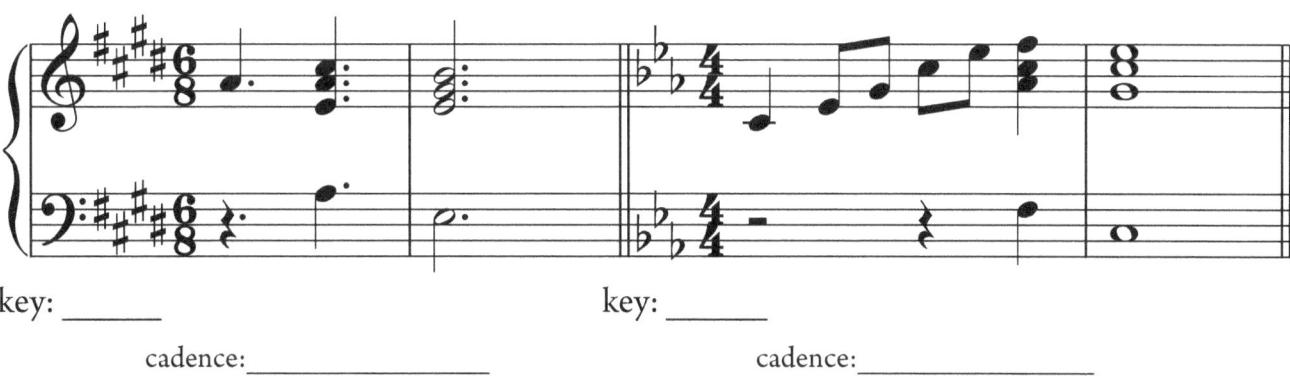

key: _____   key: _____
   cadence: _____   cadence: _____

Cadences

Writing The Plagal Cadence

Certain guidelines should be followed when writing a plagal cadence. Study the following steps for writing an plagal cadence in F major.

1. Add the key signature and rests at the beginning of the first measure. Cadences often occur over the bar line with the second chord of the cadence on a stronger beat than the first. The first chord occurs in the second half or second part of the first measure on a weaker beat. In Figure 12.18 the key signature of F major is B flat. It is placed *before* the time signature. Roman numerals indicating the functional chord symbols of the plagal cadence are placed under the staff (IV - I). Since this is 2/4 time a quarter rest is used at the beginning of the measure and the IV chord will be placed on beat 2 of the first measure. There are other options that could be used rhythmically, but this is effective. Write the bass notes for the IV and I chord in F major.

Figure 12.18

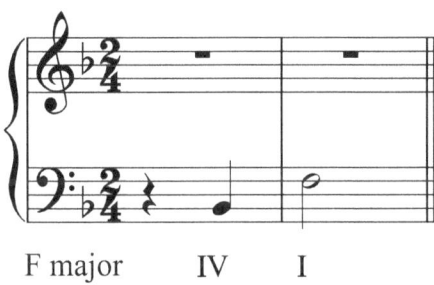

2. Write the notes of the IV chord in close position on the treble staff. Close position occurs when the notes of the triad are as close together as possible. In F major IV is B♭-D-F. These notes can be in any order as long as they stay in close position. Figure 12.19 uses quarter notes on beat 2 of the first measure for this chord.

Figure 12.19

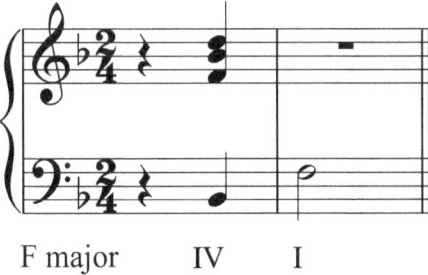

3. Write the notes of the I chord in the second measure. I in F major is F-A-C. Keep these notes as close as possible to the notes of the IV chord. In Figure 12.20 there is one note that is common to both chords (F). This F is kept in the same place in both chords (here it is the bottom note). This note is called the ***common tone***. Repeating the common tone in the same place creates smooth movement and good voice leading.

Figure 12.20

The common tone is repeated in the same place.

F major   IV   I

1. Add key signatures and write plagal cadences in keyboard style in the following keys. Write the functional chord symbols for each cadence.

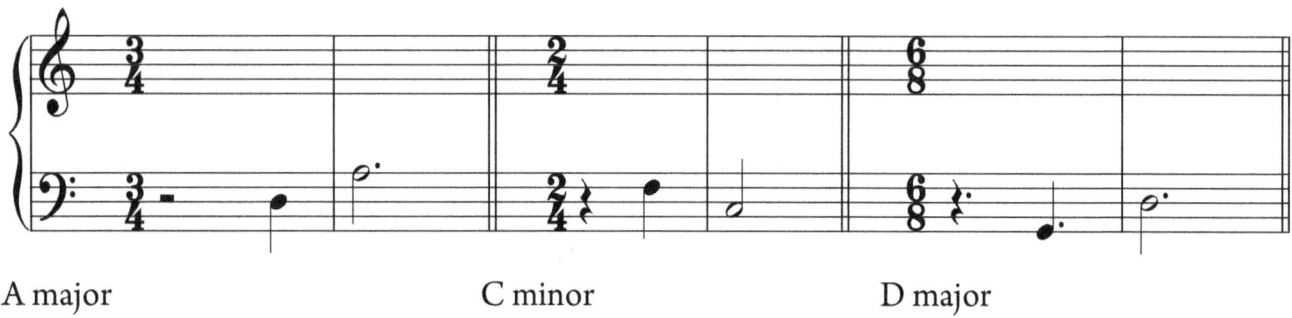

A major   C minor   D major

G minor   B♭ major   E major

Voice Leading

Voice leading was mentioned earlier in relation to writing cadences. Voice leading can be defined in a couple of ways.

1. It can be defined as the way we connect chords, preferably, in the smoothest possible way.
2. It can also be defined as a specific set of rules for how individual voices move from chord to chord. This is most common in four-part writing.

Figure 12.21 contains a chord progression in keyboard style. This progression is clumsy and jumps from one chord to the next.

Figure 12.21

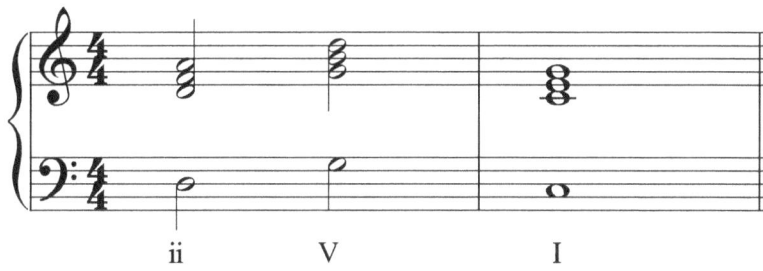

Figure 12.22 contains a much smoother version of the same chord progression. When writing chord progressions, it is best to move to the closest note of the next chord. This progression not only sounds better, but it is easier to play. These chords have common tones that are repeated in the same place between chords. This creates smoother voice leading and a better progression.

Figure 12.22

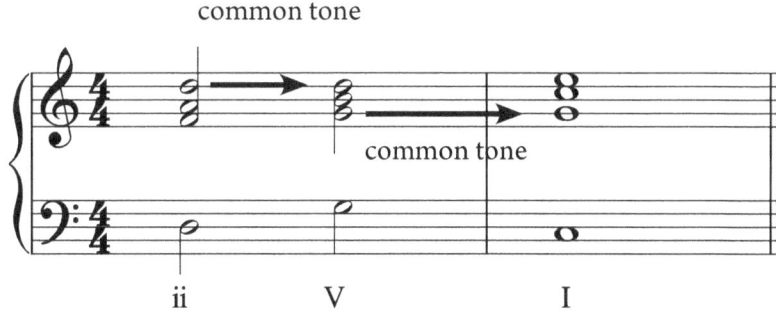

Cadences in Chorale or Four-Part Style

When cadences are written in *chorale* or *four-part style,* the chords are written in four parts. These four parts make up the four voices of a choir. The four voices are the:

Soprano, Alto, Tenor, and **Bass**

In chorale style, the soprano and alto are written on the treble staff and the tenor and bass are written on the bass staff. Figure 12.23 shows the C major chord written in different positions in chorale style. Note the following:

- The music is written on the grand staff.
- The stems of the soprano and tenor go up.
- The stems of the alto and bass go down.
- The root of each chord is doubled (written twice).
- The space between the soprano and alto and between the alto and tenor cannot exceed one octave. The space between the tenor and bass can be larger than an octave as long as it stays within each voice range.

Figure 12.23

Since chorale writing is for the human voice, we need to know the limits and ranges of each part. Voices are as individual as fingerprints. Individual singers vary, and factors like dynamic level can influence a singers range. Figure 12.24 shows the approximate, average ranges for each voice category. You should keep your writing within these voice ranges.

Figure 12.24

Study the following steps for writing an authentic cadence in chorale style in G minor.

1. Add the key signature and rests at the beginning of the first measure. Add functional chord symbols indicating the authentic cadence (V - i). Write the bass notes for the V and i chord in G minor (Figure 12.25).

Figure 12.25

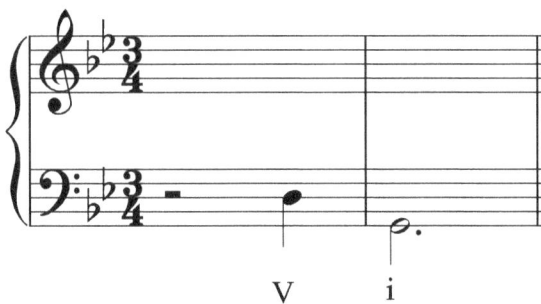

2. Write the notes of the V chord in G minor. V contains the raised leading tone (DF♯AD). It might help to write the letter names of the chord under the staff. Be sure to use the correct stem direction and proper spacing between the voices. The space between the top three voices must not exceed one octave (Figure 12.26).

Figure 12.26

(D F♯ A D)

3. Write the notes of the i chord in G minor. Repeat the common tone (D) in the same voice. Here, it is in the soprano. Move the other voices as smoothly as possible from the V chord to the i chord. In an authentic cadence with a common tone, the remaining two voices step up from the V to the i chord (F♯ to G and A to B) (Figure 12.27).

Figure 12.27

(D F♯ A D) (G B♭ D G)

1. Add the alto and tenor to create authentic cadences in chorale style. (The first one is completed for you).

- It may help to write the letter names of the chord tones under each chord.
- Repeat the common tone in the same voice.
- Move the other voices as closely as possible, preferably by step.
- In minor keys, raise the leading tone in chord V. If the leading tone is in the soprano it must step up to the tonic.
- Be careful of spacing. Do not allow more than one octave space between the top 3 voices.

2. Complete the following authentic cadences by adding the tonic chord.

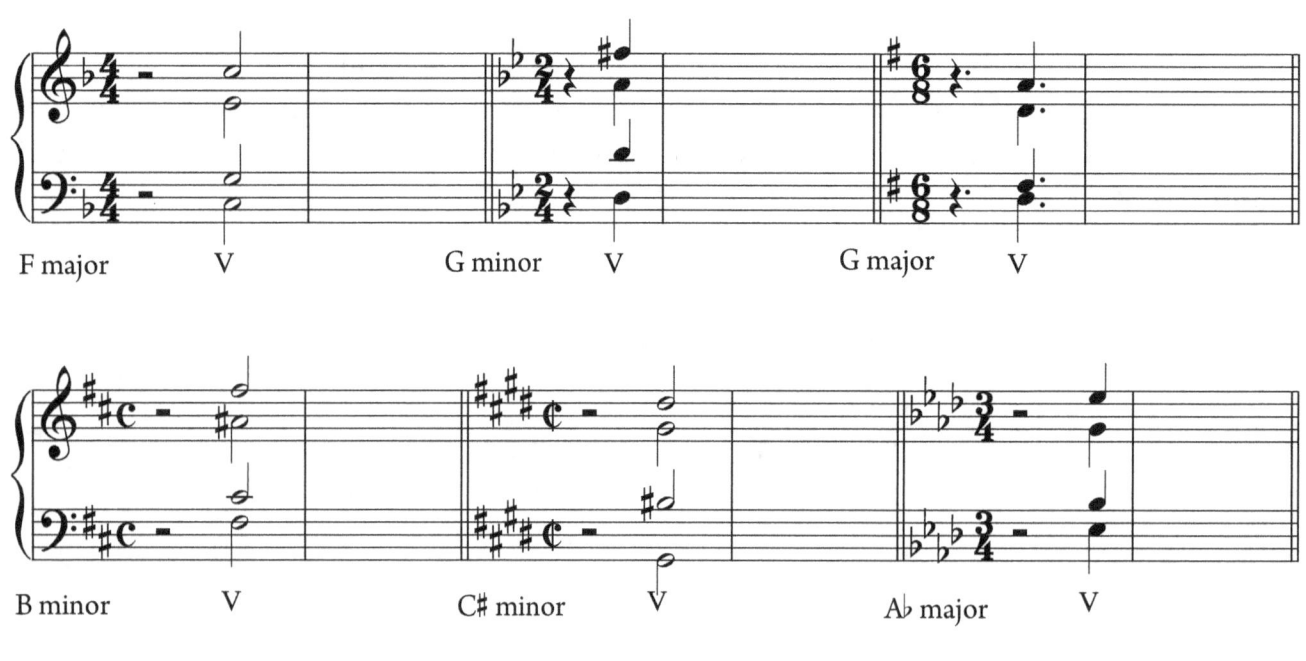

©San Marco Publications 2022

Figure 12.28 is a plagal cadence written in chorale style. Writing this cadence is similar to writing the authentic cadence.

- Repeat the common tone in the same voice.
- Move the remaining voices of the IV chord to the nearest available chord tones of the I chord.

In this example the common tone (C) is repeated in the soprano. The bass moves from the root of IV (F) to the root of I (C). The alto and tenor fall a step.

Figure 12.28

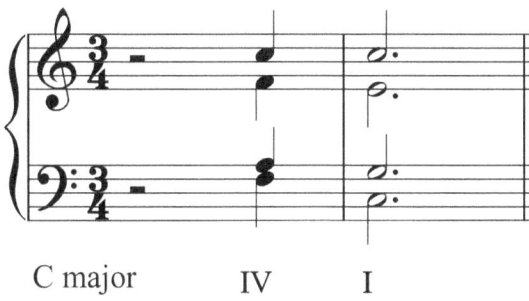

Figure 12.29 is a half cadence written in chorale style. In this example, the bass moves from the root of I (C) to the root of V (G). The common tone (G) is repeated in the tenor. The remaining voices move down by step. Always try to move to the nearest available chord tone and avoid any awkward leaps within a voice part.

Figure 12.29

Figure 12.30 contains the half cadence IV - V written in chorale style. There are no common tones in this cadence. When writing this cadence, it is important to move the three upper voices in contrary motion to the bass. The bass steps up, so the soprano, alto, and tenor all move down. Two voices will step down, and one will skip down. Always write the bass in this cadence moving up a step. The alternative is down a 7th, and this melodic interval is awkward.

Figure 12.30

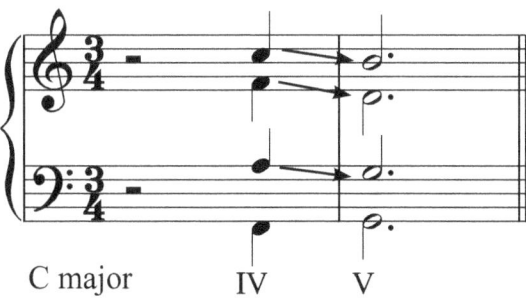

1. Write the following cadences in chorale style.

   a. An authentic cadence in G major
   b. A plagal cadence in C minor
   c. A half cadence (I - V) in B♭ major
   d. An authentic cadence in D minor
   e. A half cadence (iv - V) in A minor
   f. A plagal cadence in E major
   g. A half cadence (i - V) in F♯ minor
   h. An authentic cadence in F minor
   i. A half cadence (IV - V) in D major

2. Name the key. Write an appropriate cadence in chorale style at the end of the following phrases. Add the functional chord symbols and name the cadences.

Key:_____   Cadence:_____

Cadence:_____

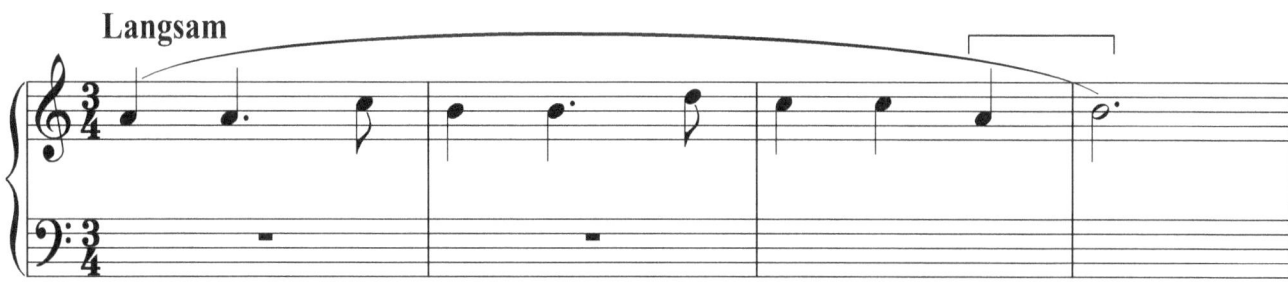

Key:_____   Cadence:_____

Cadence:_____

Cadences

3. Name the key. Write an appropriate cadence in keyboard style at the end of the following phrases. Add the functional chord symbols and name the cadences.

Key:_____   Cadence:_____

                                                  Cadence:_____

Key:_____   Cadence:_____

                                                  Cadence:_____

13
Meter 2

We have studied the time signatures 2/4, 3/4, and 4/4. With these meters, the bottom number tells us that the quarter note receives one beat and the top number tells us how many beats are in each measure. Time signatures with 2, 3, or 4 as the top number are in *simple time*.

Figure 13..1

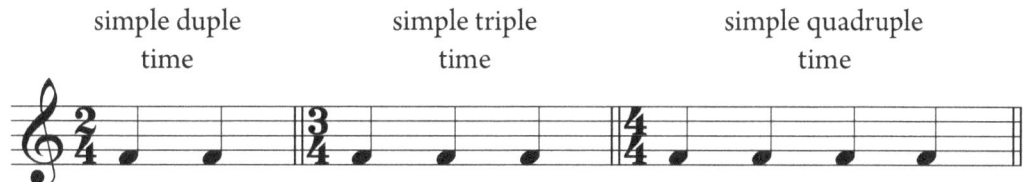

1. Add time signatures at the beginning of each line.

Simple Duple Time

In ***simple duple time*** the top number of the time signature is always 2. The time signature 2/4 is in simple duple time. Every measure is equal to 2 quarter notes.

Another simple duple time signature is 2/2. Here, the half note receives one beat and there are two beats in each measure. In other words, every measure is equal to two half notes. In all simple duple time signatures beat 1 is a *strong* beat and beat 2 is a *weak* beat. Study Figure 13.2.

2/2 two beats in each measure

the half note receives one beat

Figure 13.2

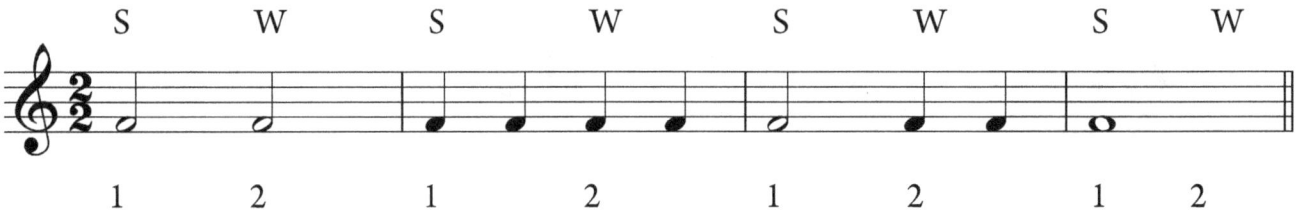

 This is an abbreviation for 2/2 time, sometimes called **cut time** or **alla breve**.

Figure 13.3 is in 2/8 time. Here, there are two beats in each measure and the eighth note receives one beat. Every measure is equal to 2 eighth notes. Beat 1 is strong and beat 2 is weak.

2/8 two beats in each measure

the eighth note receives one beat

Figure 13.3

1. Using 2/4, 2/2 or 2/8 add the correct time signatures to the following melodies.

Simple Triple Time

In *simple triple time* the top number of the time signature is always 3. The time signature 3/4 is in simple triple time. Every measure is equal to 3 quarter notes.

Another simple triple time signature is 3/2. Here, the half note receives one beat and there are three beats in each measure. In other words, every measure is equal to three half notes. In all simple triple time signatures beat 1 is a *strong* beat and beats 2 and 3 are a *weak* beats. Study Figure 11.4.

3/2 three beats in each measure

the half note receives one beat

Figure 13.4

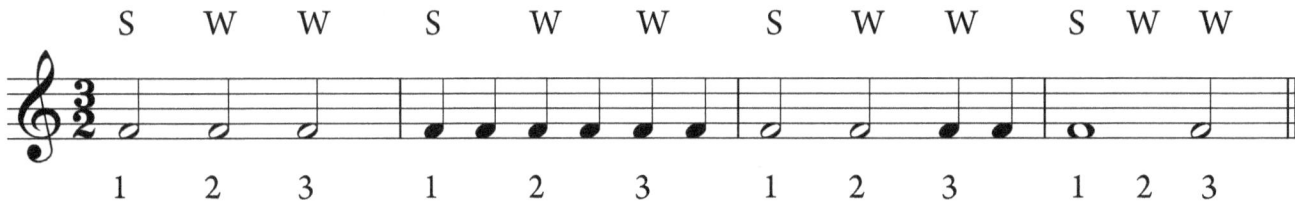

Figure 13.5 is in 3/8 time. Here, there are three beats in each measure and the eighth note receives one beat. Every measure is equal to 3 eighth notes. Beat 1 is strong and beats 2 and 3 are weak. *In 3/8 time all eighth and sixteenth notes are beamed into a complete bar.*

3/8 three beats in each measure

the eighth note receives one beat

Figure 13.5

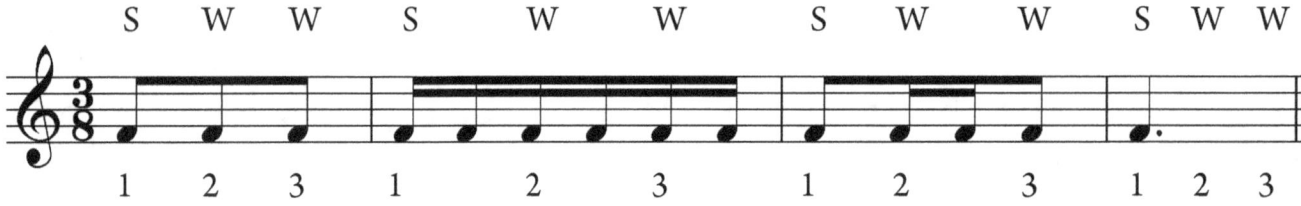

1. Add bar lines according to the time signatures.

Simple Quadruple Time

In **simple quadruple time** the top number of the time signature is always 4. The time signature 4/4 is in simple quadruple time. Every measure is equal to 4 quarter notes.

Another simple quadruple time signature is 4/2. Here, the half note receives one beat and there are four beats in each measure. In other words, every measure is equal to four half notes. In all simple quadruple time signatures beat 1 is a *strong* beat, 2 is a *weak* beat, 3 is a *medium* beat, and beat 4 is a *weak* beat. Study Figure 13.6.

$$\frac{4}{2}$$ four beats in each measure

the half note receives one beat

Figure 13.6

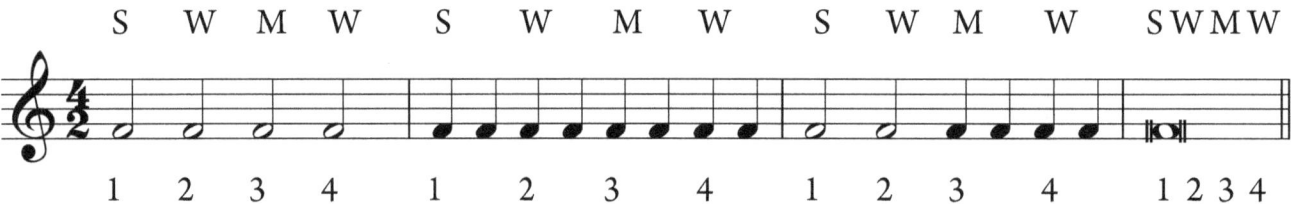

The **double whole note** and **double whole rest** equal 4 half notes. These are also called the **breve** and **breve rest**.

Note*** In 4/2 time a whole rest is not used for one complete measure of silence. Instead, the breve rest represents one complete measure of silence.

Figure 13.7 is in 4/8 time. Here, there are four beats in each measure and the eighth note receives one beat. Every measure is equal to 4 eighth notes.

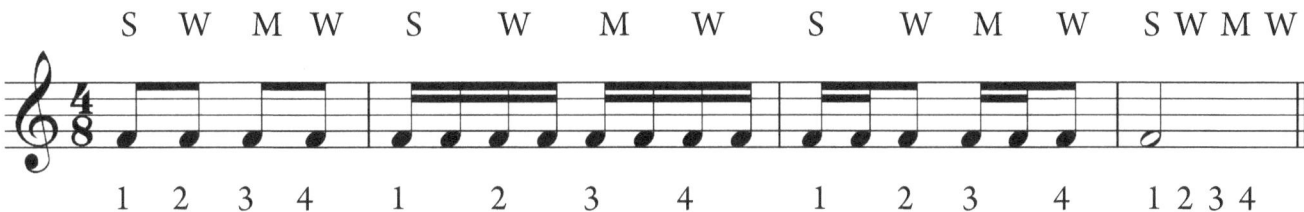

Figure 13.7

1. Add time signatures to the following melodies.

2. Add bar lines according to the time signatures.

3. Add time signatures to the following lines.

The Dotted Whole Note and Rest

A dot after a note or rest increases its value by half. A dotted whole note is worth 1 whole note and 1 half note. This is the equivalent of a full measure in 3/2 time.

Figure 13.8

Rest Review

Figure 13.9 contains all the rests we have studied.

In 4/2 time a breve rest is used to represent one complete measure of silence.

Figure 13.9

1. Add one note to complete each measure according to the time signature.

2. Add one rest to complete each measure according to the time signature.

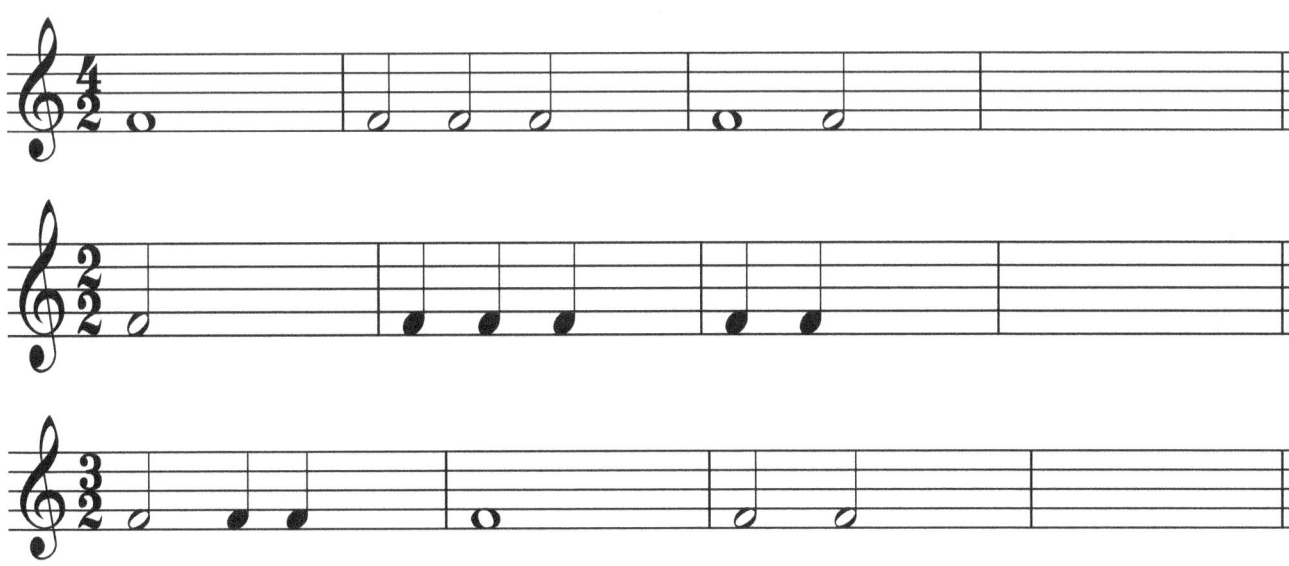

The Sixteenth Note Triplet

To determine the length of a sixteenth note triplet we follow the rule that a triplet's length is the same as two notes of the same value. A sixteenth note triplet is three sixteenth notes in the time of two sixteenth notes. This is equal to one eighth note. In 2/8, 3/8, and 4/8 time this means that triplet sixteenth notes are equal to one beat. Figure 13.10 contains triplet sixteenth notes.

Figure 13.10

1. Add bar lines according to the time signatures.

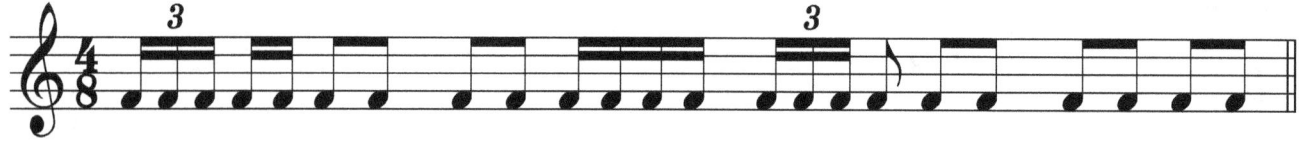

The Quarter Note Triplet

The quarter note triplet follows the triplet rule of three notes in the time of two. In this case one quarter note triplet equals two quarter notes or one half note. This triplet represents one beat in 2/2, 3/2, and 4/2 time.

Figure 13.11 shows quarter note triplets. Quarter note triplets do not have a beam like eighth note triplets. When there is no beam a bracket is added and the number is centered within the bracket. If the notes go up or down sometimes the bracket is angled to match the direction of the notes.

Figure 13.11

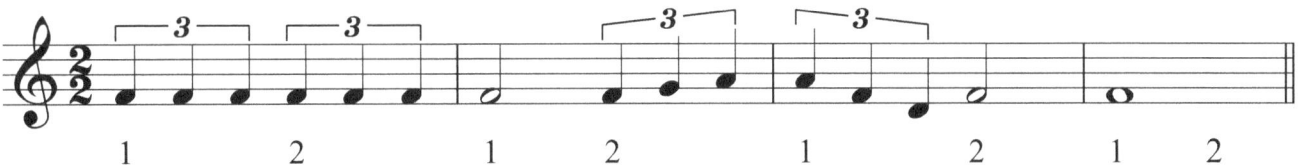

1. Add time signatures to the following lines. Write the beats under each measure.

2. Add bar lines to complete each exampl according to the time signatures

3. Add one rest to complete each measure according to the time signatures.

Syncopation

A lot of music follows a strict 4/4 tempo or four beats to every measure. The first beat of the measure is a strong beat and it is emphasized. Clap the rhythm of Figure 13.12 and count a steady 4 beats. Clap on each beat emphasizing the first beats. These are steady single beats.

Figure 13.12

Figure 13.13 is a syncopated rhythm. Clap the beats, but hold out beat 4 and don't clap on the next, or first, beat which is tied. Instead emphasize the 2nd beats.

Figure 13.13

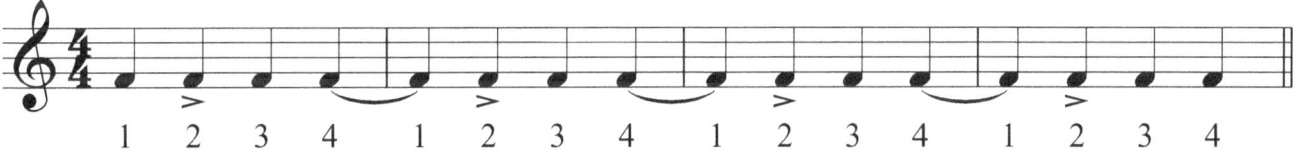

Often, the emphasis is given to the first beat of a measure. Syncopation means to shift the typical accent and emphasize what would normally be a "weak" beat. Not playing on the first beat creates a sense of anticipation and gives the music a jazzy feeling. Syncopation can also be created with longer notes in unexpected places as shown in Figure 13.14. Placing a half note on beat two in measure 2 emphasizes a weak beat by holding it longer. This also occurs with the quarter note on the second half of beat three in measure 3.

Figure 13.14

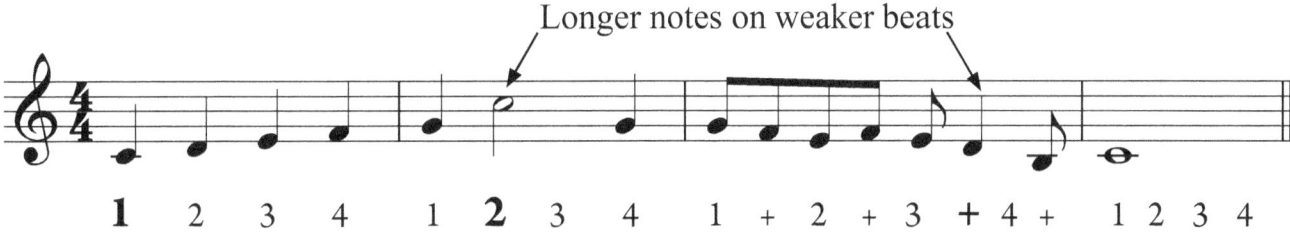

Rests in Simple Time

There are specific rules for adding rests to a measure in simple time. It is important to show each beat as clearly as possible. Each beat or each part of the beat must be completed before beginning the next beat. In Figure 13.15 measure 2, each eighth note beat is finished with an eighth note rest. In measures 3 and 4, the sixteenth note has a sixteenth rest to complete part of the beat and then an eighth rest to finish the remainder of the beat.

Figure 13.15

In Figure 13.16, measure 3, the incomplete sixteenth note beats are completed separately with sixteenth note rests. This shows each beat. Joining these rests into one eighth rest is wrong.

Figure 13.16

In simple triple time each beat or part of the beat should be completed first. Join beats 1 and 2, a strong and weak beat, into one rest. **Do not join beats 2 and 3, two weak beats, into one rest.** Never join two weak beats into one rest.

Figure 13.17

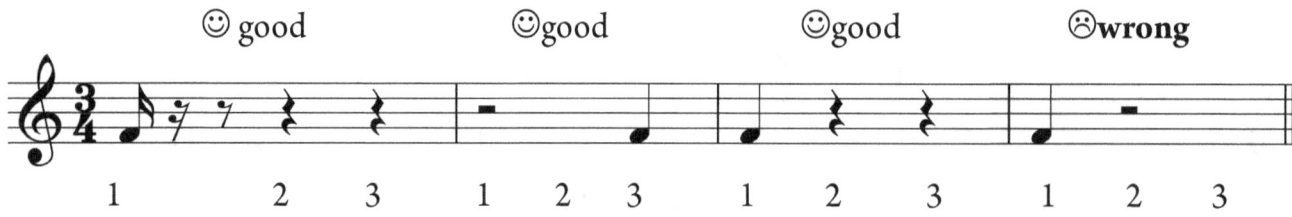

We never use rests larger than one beat unless it is in the first half or last half of a measure in simple quadruple time (4/4, 4/8). Join beats 1 and 2 and beats 3 and 4 into one rest. **Never join beats 2 and 3, a weak beat and a medium beat, into one rest.** As in all simple time signatures, finish any incomplete beats first.

Figure 13.18

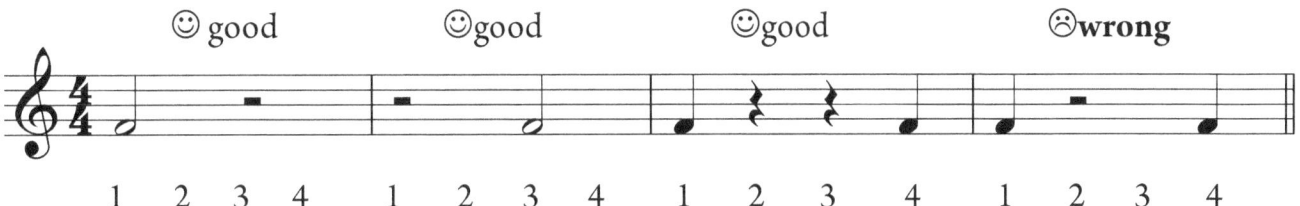

A whole rest represents a complete measure of silence in almost all time signatures. The breve rest is used to show a complete measure of rest in 4/2 time.

Figure 13.19

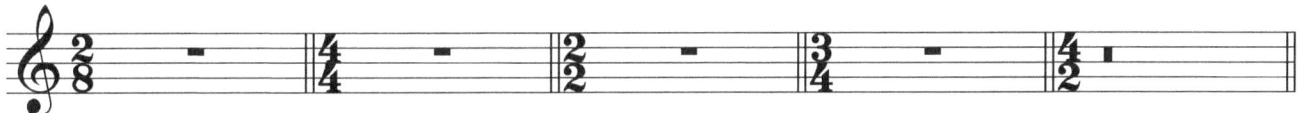

1. Complete the following **single quarter note** beats by adding rests.

2. Add one rest under each bracket to complete the following measures.

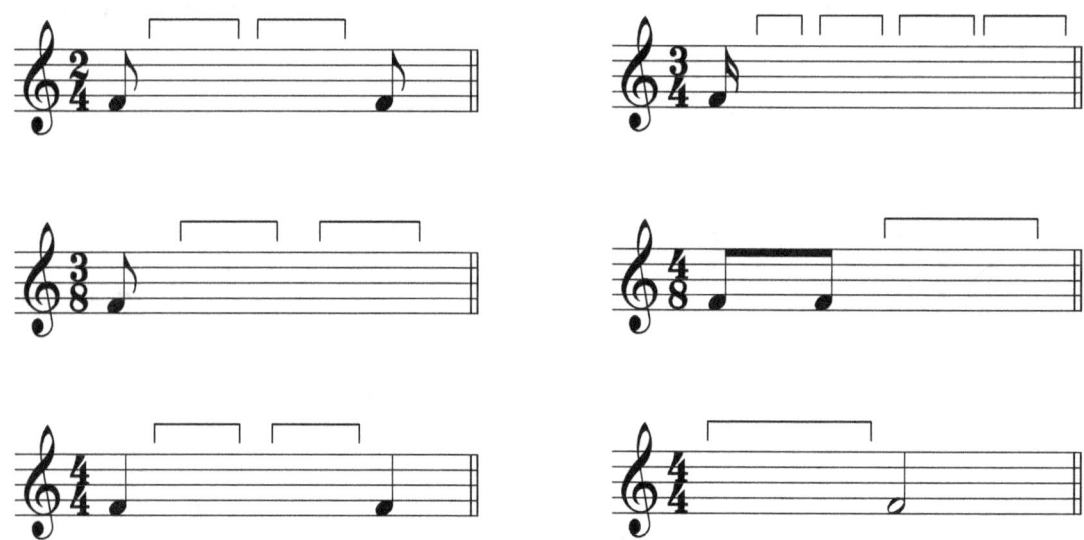

2. Mark each measure in the following examples as ☑ if the rests are correct, or ☒ if the rests are incorrect.

3. Add the correct number of rests under each bracket to complete each measure.

4. Add the correct rests under each bracket to complete the following measures.

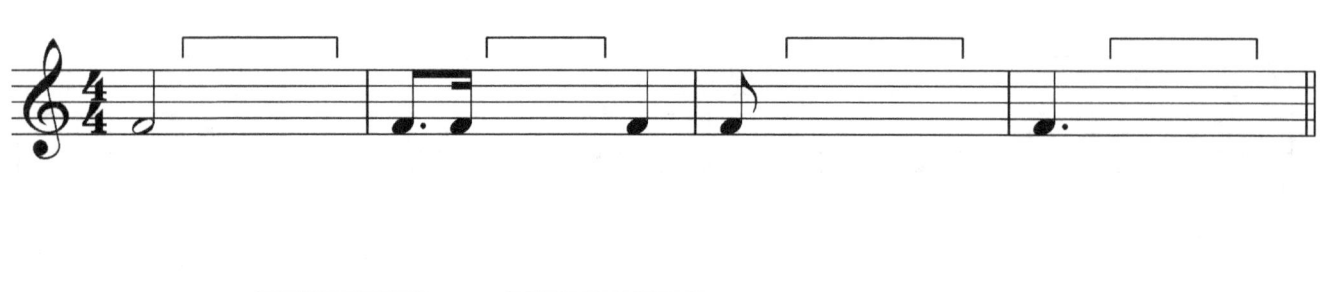

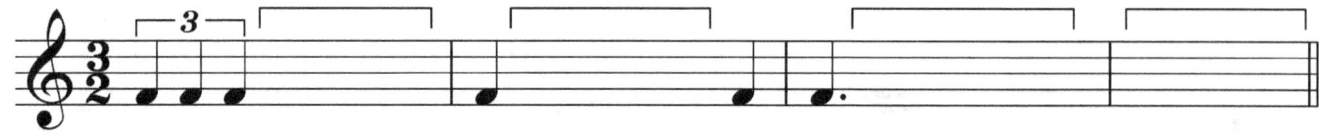

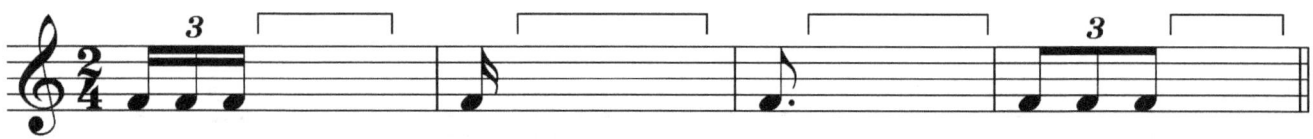

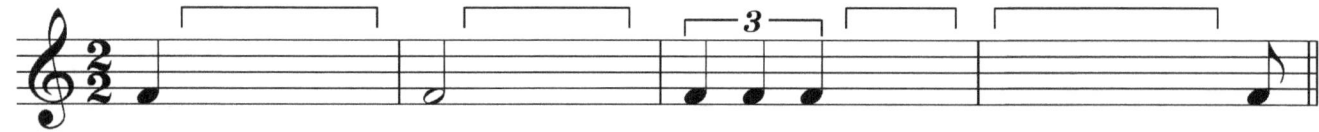

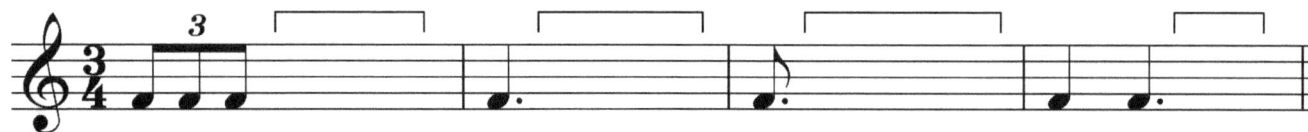

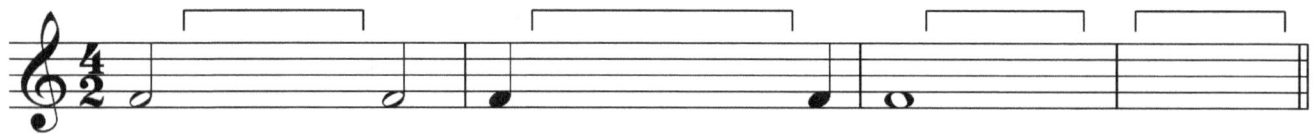

Grouping Notes

In 2/2, 3/2 and 4/2 time.
Use a whole note instead of 2 tied half notes within a measure.

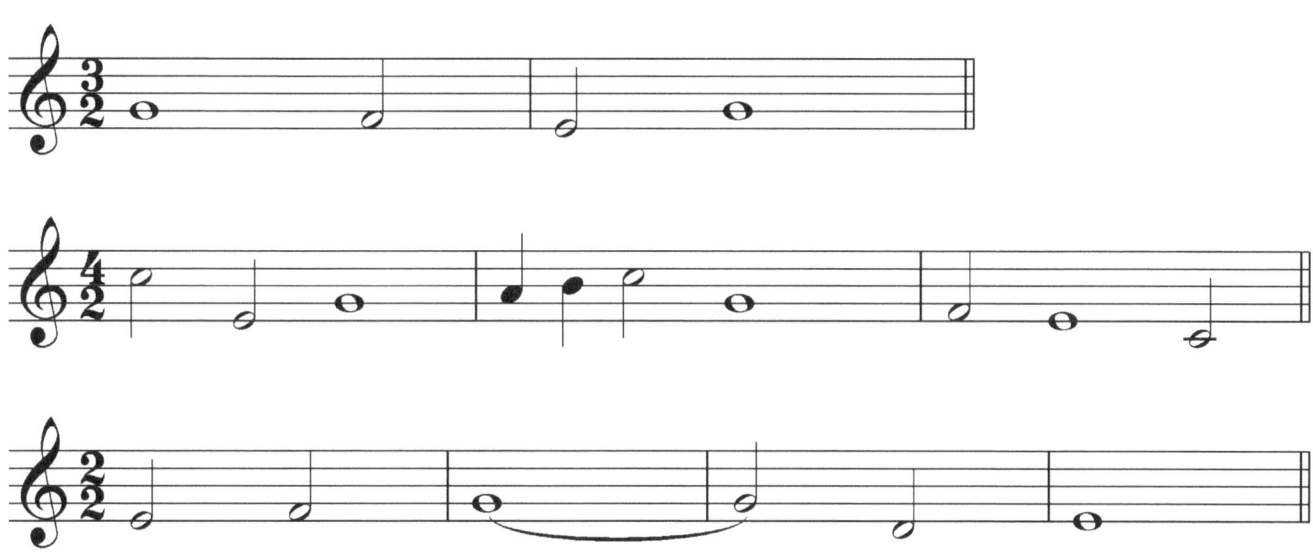

Beam eighth notes by half note beats.

Beam sixteenth notes by quarter note beats.

1. Rewrite the following rhythms grouping them correctly.

2. Rewrite the following melodies correcting any mistakes in the grouping of notes and rests. The first example is done for you.

Edvard Grieg
Norwegian Melody

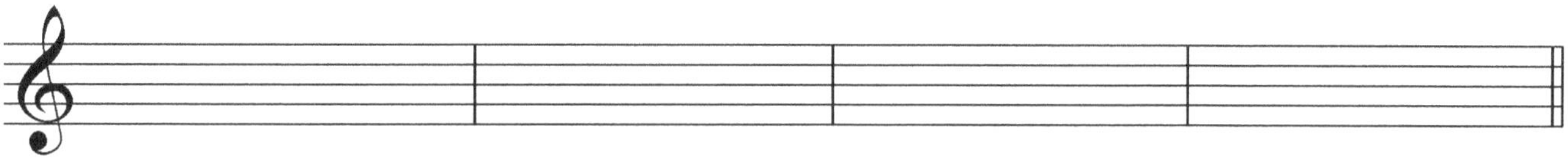

Robert Schumann
Symphony No. 3

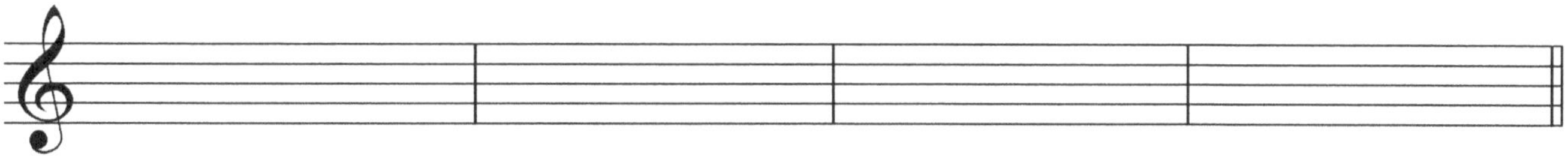

Gustav Mahler
Resurrection Symphony, I

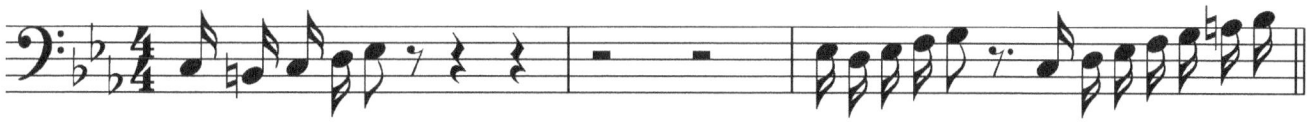

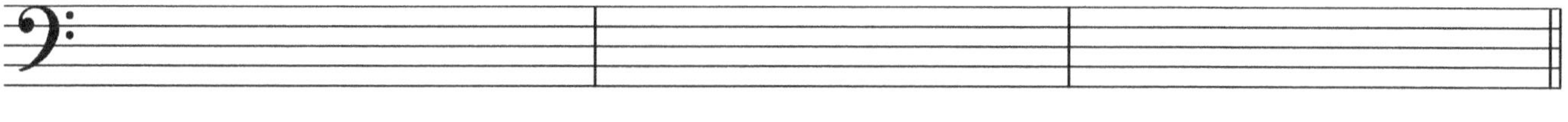

Compound Time

Simple time has 2, 3, or 4 for the top number of the time signature. Compound time has 6, 9, or 12 for the top number of the time signature. Simple and compound time can be duple, triple or quadruple, depending on the number of beats in each measure.

Compound time breaks itself into groups of three. Compound duple time equals two groups of three, and the top number is 6. Compound triple equals three groups of three, and the top number is 9. Compound quadruple equals four groups of three, and the top number is 12. The main beat is a dotted note, since a dotted note can be divided into three equal parts. Let's examine the three types of compound time.

Compound Duple Time

Compound duple time has two beats in each measure. Each beat is equal to three pulses. In compound duple time, the upper number of the time signture is always 6. The lower number may be 8, 4, or 16.

Figure 13.20 shows three different compound duple time signatures. The first measure, in 6/8 time, contains six eighth note pulses. The main beat is a dotted quarter since it represents one group of three pulses.

In 6/4 time, there are six quarter note pulses in each measure. The main beat is a dotted half note since it represents one group of three quarter note pulses.

Figure 13.20

In 6/8 time we do not say there are 6 beats in each measure. We say there are 2 beats in each measure and each measure contains 6 *pulses*. Every beat is a group of 3 pulses. Since there are 2 beats, 3 + 3 = 6 pulses. Therefore, 6/8 time is grouped into 2 groups of 3 pulses. 6/8 time is **compound duple time**. **Compound** refers to each beat grouped in 3 pulses, and **duple** refers to two beats in each measure.

Figure 13.21 shows the difference in the way beats are grouped in 3/4 and 6/8. Both time signatures are equal to 6 eighth notes, but 3/4 is grouped into 3 groups of 2 eighth notes and 6/8 into 2 groups of 3 eighth notes.

The accent structure for 6/8 time is: **Strong** weak weak **Medium** weak weak

Figure 13.21

1. The following pieces are in 6/8 time. Circle the 2 main beats in each clef. Each beat consists of 3 pulses.

Samual Arnold
Gigue

Ludvig Schytte
Etude

2. Add bar lines according to the time signatures. Circle each beat (group of 3 pulses).

Compound Triple Time

Compound triple time has 3 beats (3 groups of 3) in each measure. In 9/8 time there are 9 eighth notes in every measure. These are 9 pulses. There are 3 groups of 3 pulses which are considered 3 beats. Each beat is equal to a dotted note. In compound triple time the upper number of the time signature is always 9. The lower number may be 8, 4, or 16.

Figure 13.22

2. Add time signatures at the beginning of each line. Circle each beat (group of 3 pulses).

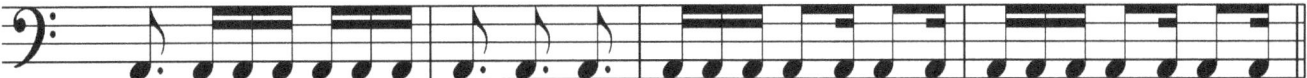

Compound Quadruple Time

Compound quadruple time has 4 beats (4 groups of 3) in each measure. In 12/8 time there are 12 eighth notes in every measure. We consider this 12 pulses. There are 4 groups of 3 pulses which are considered 4 beats. Each beat is equal to a dotted note. In compound quadruple time the upper number of the time signature is always 12. The lower number may be 8, 4, or 16.

Figure 13.23

3. Add bar lines according to the time signatures. Circle each beat (group of 3 pulses).

Grouping Notes in Compound Time

In compound time notes and rests are grouped to show each beat as clearly as possible.

Figure 13.24 contains two measures of 9/8 time. In this time signature, the main beat is equal to a dotted quarter note. The notes in each measure are organized to reflect this. All notes belonging to one beat are placed together.

Figure 13.24

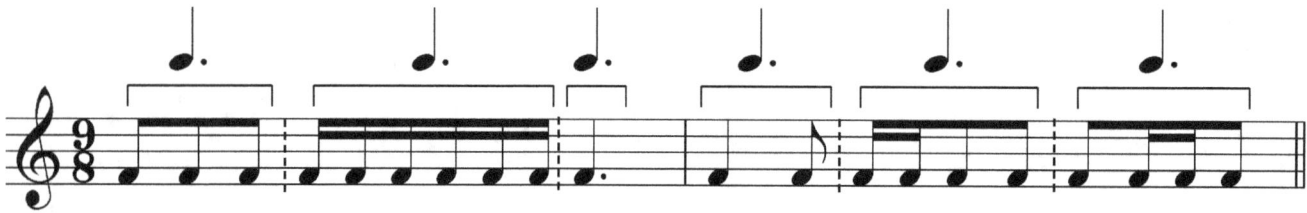

4. Rewrite the following passages grouping them according to the time signature.

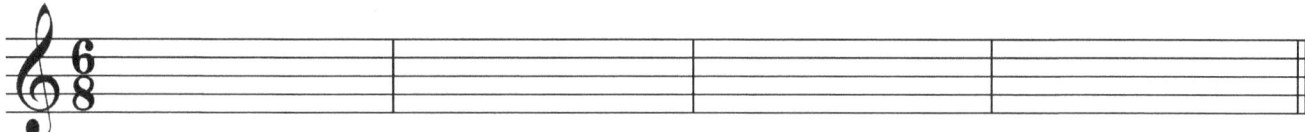

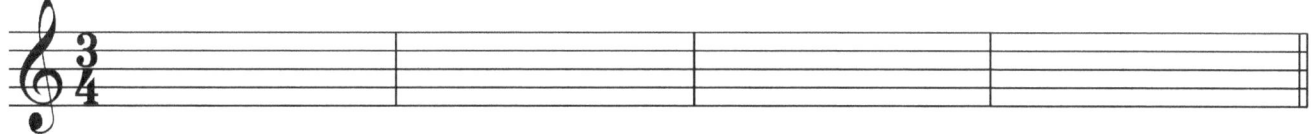

Rests in Compound Time

Dotted rests are not used in simple time. These rests are only used in compound time and represent one beat. Two beats may be joined into one dotted rest to represent the first half or the last half of a measure of compound quadruple time.

Figure 13.25

In compound time, each beat equals 3 pulses. The first 2 pulses of a beat should be joined into one rest as shown in Figure 13.26 a) and b). The last 2 pulses of a beat should use separate rests as shown in Figure 13.26 c) and d). Never join pulse 2 with pulse 3.

Figure 13.26

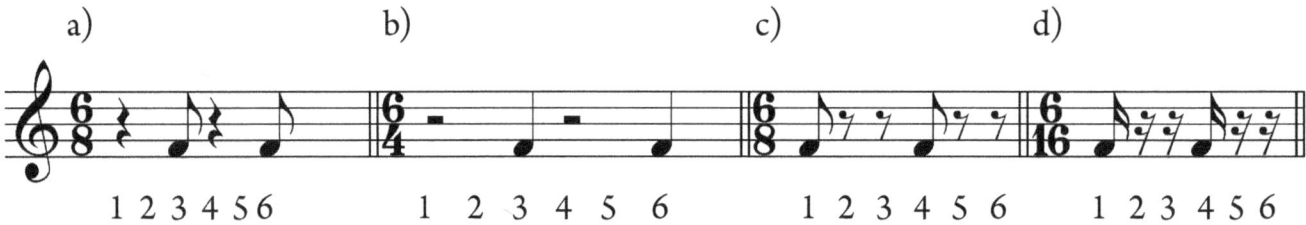

In compound triple time beats 1 and 2 may be joined into one rest. Do not join beats 2 and 3 into one rest.

Figure 13.27

In compound quadruple time beats 1 and 2 should be joined into one rest. Beats 3 and 4 should be joined into one rest. Do not join beats 2 and 3 into one rest.

Figure 13.28

5. Add rests under the brackets to complete each measure.

6. Add the correct time signature to the following.

Ottorino Respighi
Pines of the Giancolo

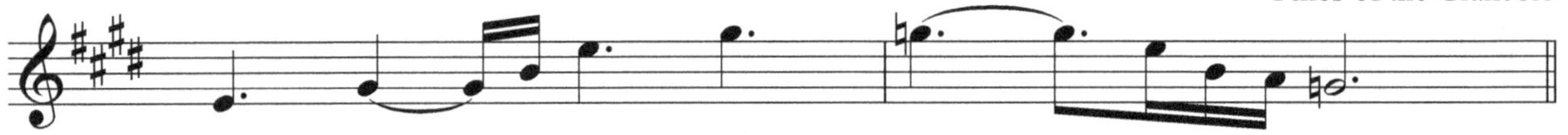

Franz Liszt
Rhapsodie Espagnole

Franz Liszt
Sonata in B minor

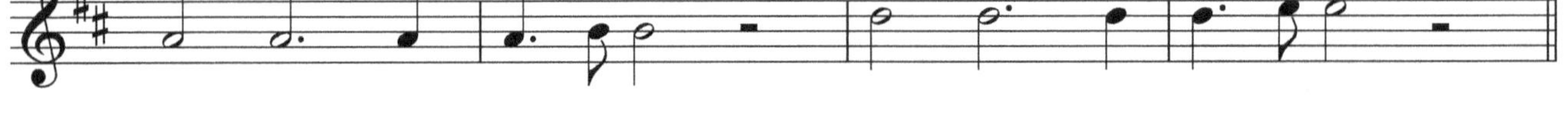

Sergei Prokofiev
Sonata No. 3, V

Girolamo Frescobaldi
La Spagnoletta

Cesar Franck
Symphonic Variations

Joseph Haydn
Symphony in B flat, IV

Muzio Clementi
Sonata for 4 hands

Ludwig van Beethoven
Sonata Op. 31, No. 1

Albert Roussel,
Le Festin de L'Araignee

Double Dotted Notes

An additional dot may be added to an already dotted note or rest. The second dot increases the duration of the note or rest by half the value of the first dot. Figure 13.29 shows double dotted notes and equivalent values. Double dotted rests have the same values.

Figure 13.29

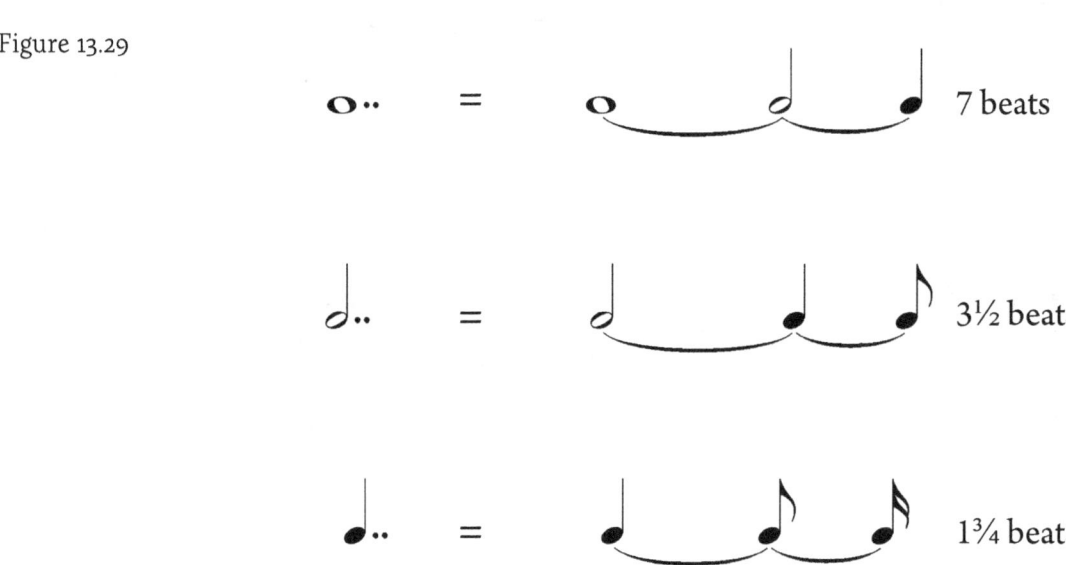

A double dotted note is usually followed by whatever note finishes the measure or the beat. Figure 13.30 illustrates this. Notice the double dotted eighth note in measure 2 which is worth ⅞ of a beat. This is usually joined with a thirty-second note to make one complete beat.

Figure 13.30

1. Complete the following:

   a. 1 eighth note equals _____ sixteenth notes.
   b. 1 dotted half note equals _____ quarter notes.
   c. 1 dotted eighth note equals _____ sixteenth notes.
   d. 1 dotted whole note equals _____ half notes.
   e. 1 dotted whole note equals _____ quarter notes.
   f. 1 double dotted quarter note equals _____ sixteenth notes.
   g. 1 double dotted whole note equals _____ quarter notes.
   h. 1 double dotted half note equals _____ eighth notes.

2. Write a single note which is equal to the the value of the following.

3. Write a single rest which is equal to the the value of the following.

Meter 2

Irregular Divisions of the Beat

A *tuplet* is the general name for a group of notes that do not follow the normal rules of counting. ***Triplets, duplets, quadruplets, quintuplets, sextuplets,*** and ***septuplets*** are all tuplets.

For review, a *triplet* is a group of three notes played in the time of two notes of the same value. Triplets generally occur in simple time Figure 13.31.

Figure 13.31

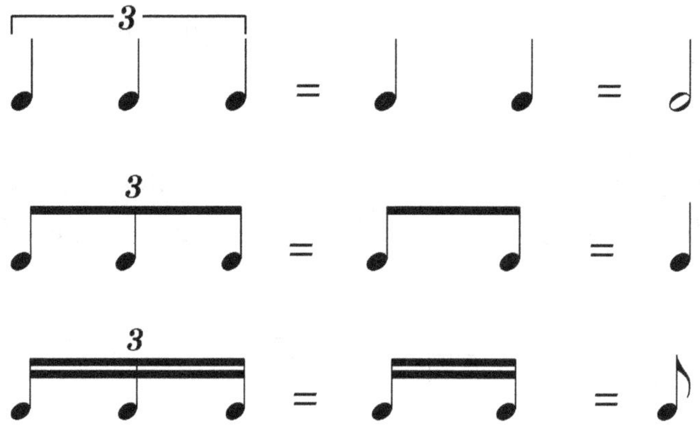

A *duplet* is a group of two notes played in the time of three notes of the same value. Duplets occur in compound time representing a group of three pulses or one beat Figure 13.32.

Figure 13.32

1. Add bar lines to the following according to the time signatures.

In simple time the beat may be divided into irregular groups of three, five, six or seven. A group of 5, 6, or 7 notes is played in the time of a group of 4 of the same kind in simple time.

Figure 13.33

In compound time the beat may be divided into irregular groups of two, four, five, or seven. In compound time the main beat is a dotted note. Each group represents one beat (three pulses). Some of the groups look the same in simple and compound time. To determine the beat in the melody with irregular groupings look at the time signature and the other beats in the bar.

Figure 13.34

Many composers used irregular groupings in their work. Figure 13.35 is an example of irregular groups in a composition by Tchaikowsky. Here, each group represents one beat in simple time.

Figure 13.35

Peter Il'yich Tchaikowsky

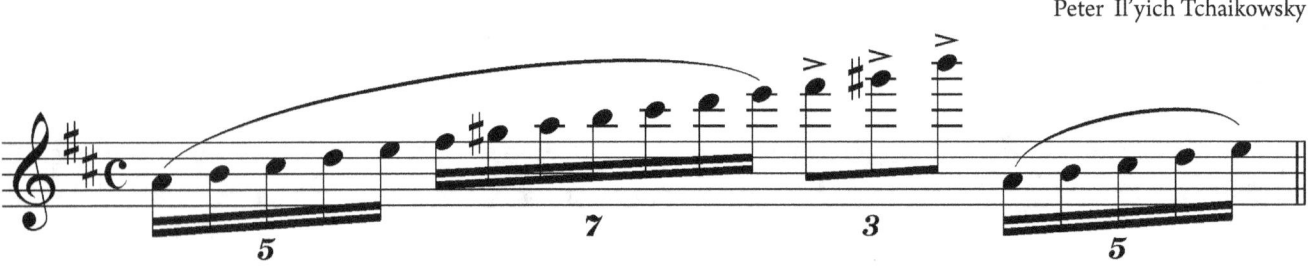

1. Add bar lines to the following excerpts which begin on the first beat of the bar.

Stephen Heller
Prelude, Op. 119, No. 30

Peter Il'yich Tchaikowsky
Nutcracker Suite (Danse Arabe)

Joseph Haydn
Variations Hob. XVII/6

Frédéric Chopin
Etude, Op. 10, No. 9

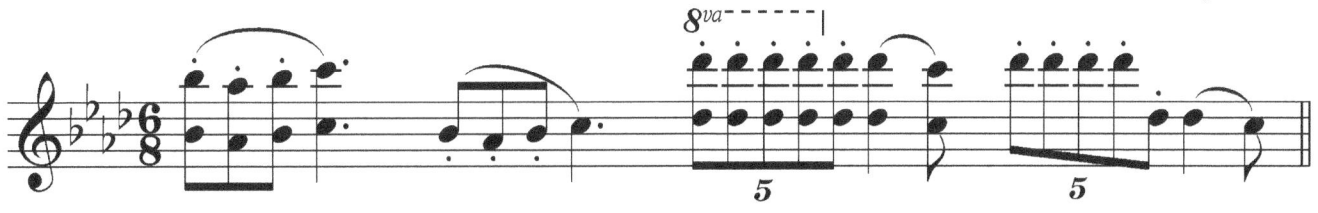

Frédéric Chopin
Waltz, Op. 69, No.1

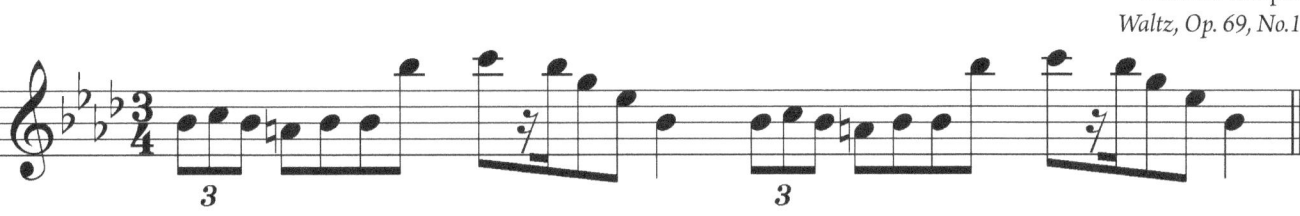

Giacomo Puccini
Madam Butterfly (One Fine Day)

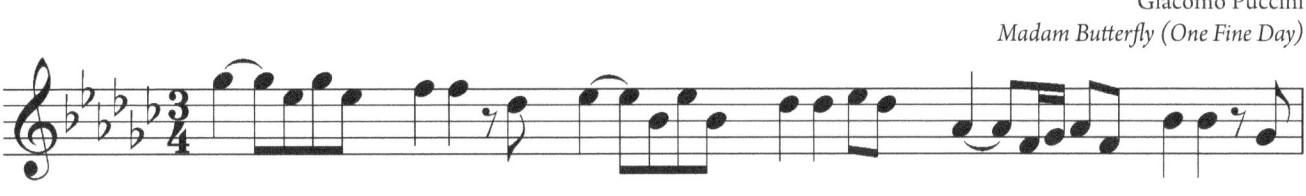

Lili Boulanger
Nocturne

Hybrid Meters

Hybrid meters are a combination of simple and compound time. Each measure is made up of dotted (groups of three) and non-dotted (groups of two) notes. Because of this, some beats are longer than others. The top number of a hybrid time signature shows the number of pulses in a measure and the bottom number shows which note gets the pulse.

Hybrid Duple Time

In *hybrid duple time,* the top number of the time signature is always 5. The bottom number may be 4, 8, or 16. There are two beats and five pulses in each measure. This consists of one beat that is worth three pulses and one beat that is worth two pulses. The beats may be grouped as 3 +2 or 2 + 3 as shown in Figure 13.36.

Figure 13.36

Hybrid Triple Time

In *hybrid triple time,* the top number of the time signature may be 7 or 8. The bottom number may be 4, 8, or 16. In Figure 13.38 there are three beats and seven pulses in each measure. This consists of one beat that is worth three pulses and two beats that are worth two pulses each. The beats may be grouped as 3 +2 +2, 2 + 3 + 2 or 2 + 2 + 3.

Figure13.37

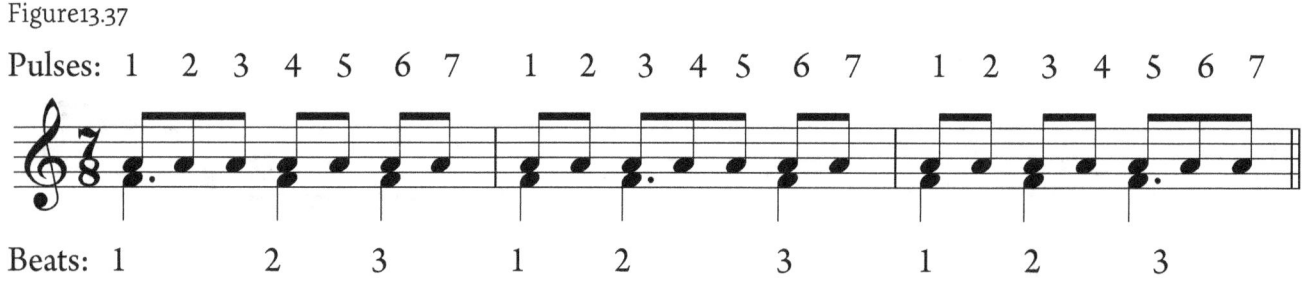

In Figure 13.38 there are three beats and eight pulses in each measure. There are two compound beats and one simple beat. This consists of two beats that are worth three pulses and one beat that is worth two pulses each. The beats may be grouped as 3 +3 +2, 2 + 3 + 3 or 3 + 2 + 3. Do not confuse this with 4/4 which also has 8 eighth notes. 4/4 is grouped into four groups of two eighth notes.

Figure 13.38

Hybrid Quadruple Time

In *hybrid quadruple time,* the top number of the time signature may be 9, 10, or 11. The bottom number may be 4, 8, or 16. There are four beats in each measure. This hybrid meter is less common than the other two. Figure 13.40 shows some of the possibilities for hybrid quadruple time, but many groupings are possible. The following is the beat breakdown for these time signatures:

- One dotted beat and two non-dotted beats equaling 4 beats and 9 pulses.
- Two dotted beats and two non-dotted beats equaling 4 beats and 10 pulses.
- Three dotted beats and one non-dotted beat equaling 4 beats and 11 pulses.

The arrangement of the beats in each time signature can vary.

Figure 13.39

1. Add bar lines according to the time signatures.

2. Add time signatures to the following two measure examples.

3. Add bar lines according to the time signatures.

- *In hybrid time a whole rest indicates a full measure of silence. as shown in* Figure 13.40.

Figure 13.40

- *When adding rests in hybrid time, show each each beat with one rest when possible.*

In Figure 13.41 there are two beats in each bar. Each beat is indicated with one rest. Measure a) completes the second beat with a quarter rest indicating one beat. Measure b) needs a dotted quarter to complete the first beat.

Figure 13.41

- *If a measure has incomplete beats, finish them before moving on to the rest of the measure.*

In Figure 13.42 a) the first beat is completed with a sixteenth rest and two eighth rests. Do not join pulse two and three into one rest.

- *Use dotted rests to show one complete compound beat.*

Figure 13.42 b) is another option for rest placement. Here, the first beat is treated as the simple beat and the second, compound beat is shown as a dotted rest. Both measures are correct.

- *Combine the first two beats into one rest in hydrid triple. Combine the first two beats and last beats into one rest in quadruple time.*

In Figure 13.42 c) the first two beats of 7/8 are joined into one rest. The last two beats of 11/16 are joined into one rest.
There are many correct ways to complete these bars with rests. It depends where the simple and compound beats occur within the measure.

Figure 13.42

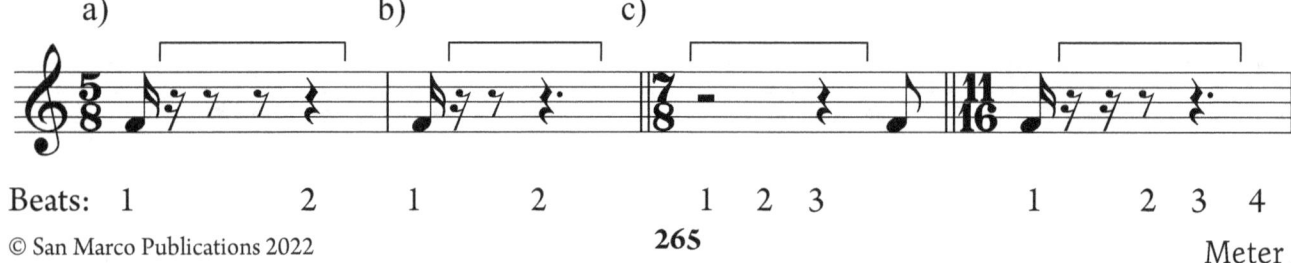

© San Marco Publications 2022

The examples in Figure 13.43 show incorrect and correct rest groupings in a measure. This should help you avoid some common errors when writing rests in hydrid time.

Figure 13.43

1. Add rests complete the following measures.

14

Transposition

Transposition takes place when notes are moved up or down. The intervals between the notes remain the same.

To start, we are going to transpose by writing melodies at a different octave.

Figure 14.1 shows a short melody transposed up one octave from the bass clef into the treble clef.

Figure 14.1

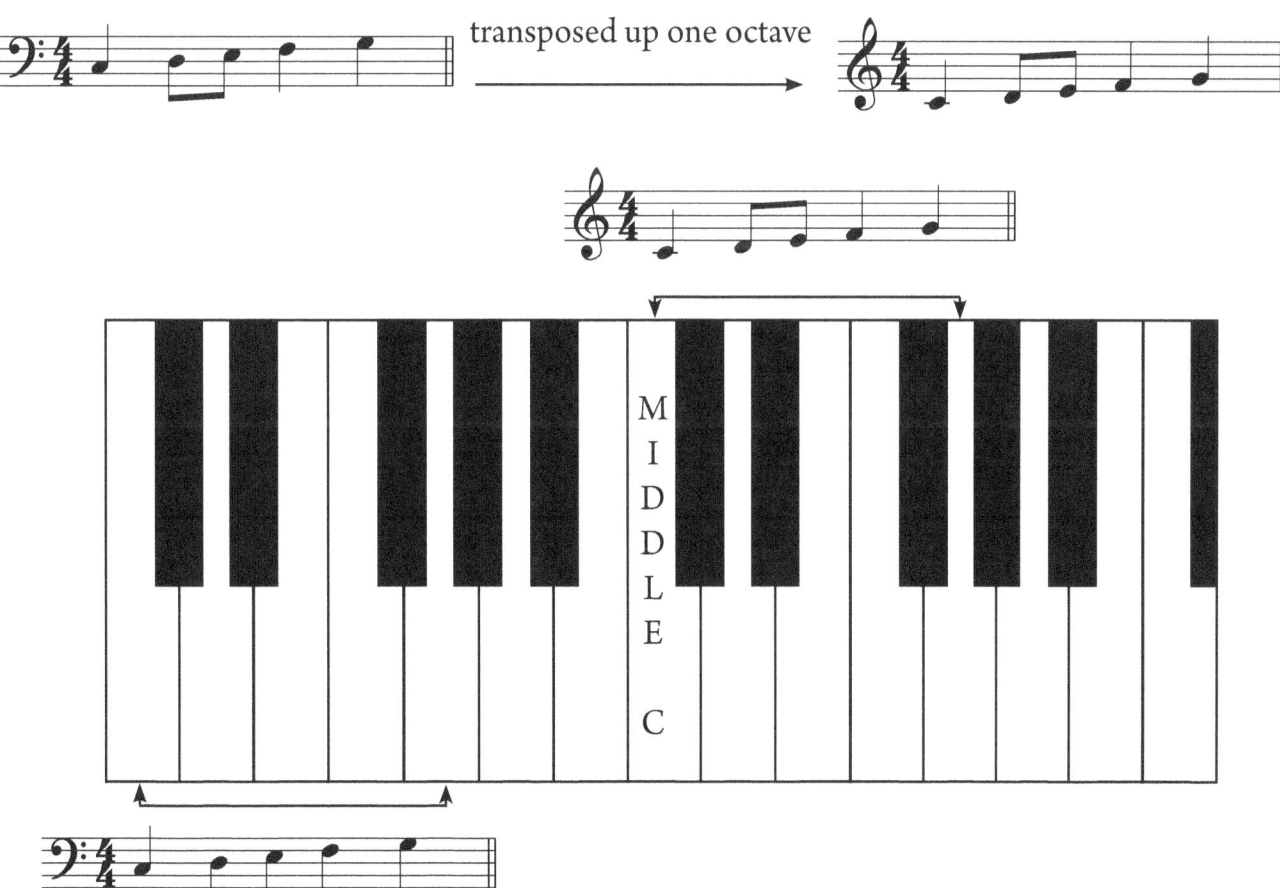

This is not the only way to transpose. Notes on the treble staff may be transposed down onto the bass staff.

The melody in Figure 14.2 is transposed down one octave from the treble staff to the bass staff.

When you transpose by an octave:

1. The key remains the same. The clef changes, but you use the same key signature (written correctly for the new clef).
2. The time signature remains the same.
3. Every note moves the interval of a perfect octave.
4. The normal rules of stem direction are followed.

This melody requires quite a few ledger line notes on the bass staff to obtain the correct pitch.

Figure 14.2

Francois Couperin
Concerto No. 8

1. Transpose the following down one octave using the bass clef.

Felix Mendelssohn
Song Without Words "Faith"

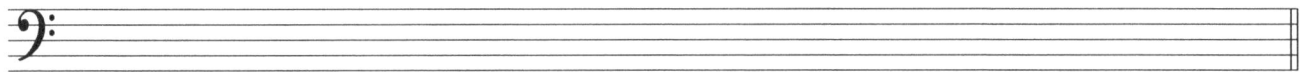

2. Transpose the following up one octave using the treble clef.

3. Rewrite the following melodies at the same pitch in the bass clef.

4. Rewrite the following melodies at the same pitch in the treble clef.

Transposition Up By Interval

Music may be transposed from one key to another. Major key melodies can only be transposed to other major keys and minor keys to other minor keys.

A melody can be transposed up by a specific interval. For example, you can transpose a melody up a perfect 5th, or a minor 3rd, or a major 2nd, or any other interval. Here are the steps for transposing a melody up by the interval of a major 3rd:

1. Determine the key of the original melody. You have to know what key you are starting in before you can determine the key to which you are going. The melody in Figure 14.3 is in F major.

Figure 14.3

2. Determine the interval of a major 3rd above F. Figure 14.4 shows that a major 3rd above F is A. The new key will be A major. The key signature of A major is three sharps. A major key can only be transposed to another major key.

Figure 14.4

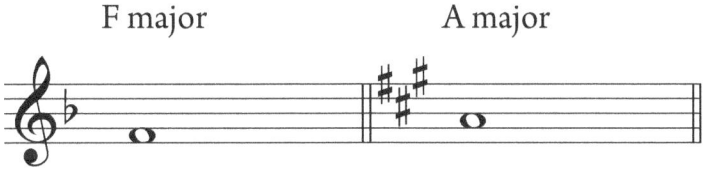

The major 3rd above F is A

3. Write the new key signature. In this case, three sharps for A major. Rewrite the melody moving every note up a 3rd. The key signature takes care of the quality of the intervals in the transposition. Copy everything from the original including the time signature, composer, dynamics, etc. Figure 14.5 contains the original melody transposed into the key of A major.

Figure 14.5

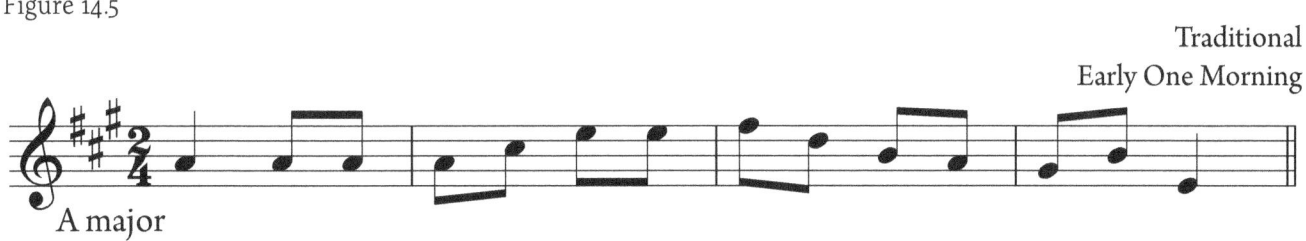

You can only transpose from one major key to another major key. Even if you transpose by a minor interval, the melody still remains major. Figure 14.6 is in F major and contains two accidentals. Let's transpose it up a minor 3rd.

Figure 14.6

F major

A minor 3rd above F is A♭. The new key will be A♭ major. Write the key signature of A♭ major (4 flats), add the time signature, and move every note up a 3rd. There are 2 accidentals that will be part of the transposition. Beat 1 of m.2 is lowered one half step in the original and must be lowered in the transposed version. Beat 2 of m.3 is raised one half step in the original and must be raised in the transposed version.

Figure 14.7

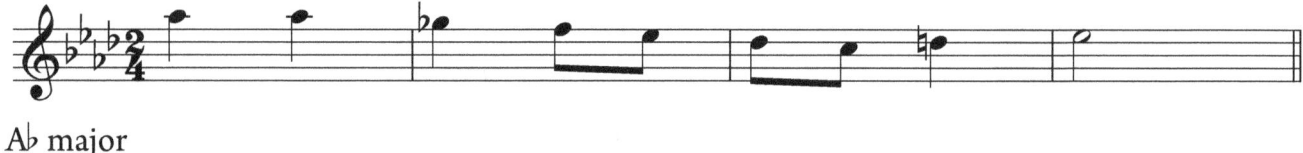

A♭ major

Figure 14.8 is the original F major melody transposed up a minor 2nd to the key of G♭ major.

Figure 14.8

G♭ major

1. In the following examples you are given the original key. Transpose the tonic of these keys by the following intervals. Write the new key signature, the new tonic, and name the key.

2. Name the key of the following melody. Transpose it according to the given intervals. Name the new keys.

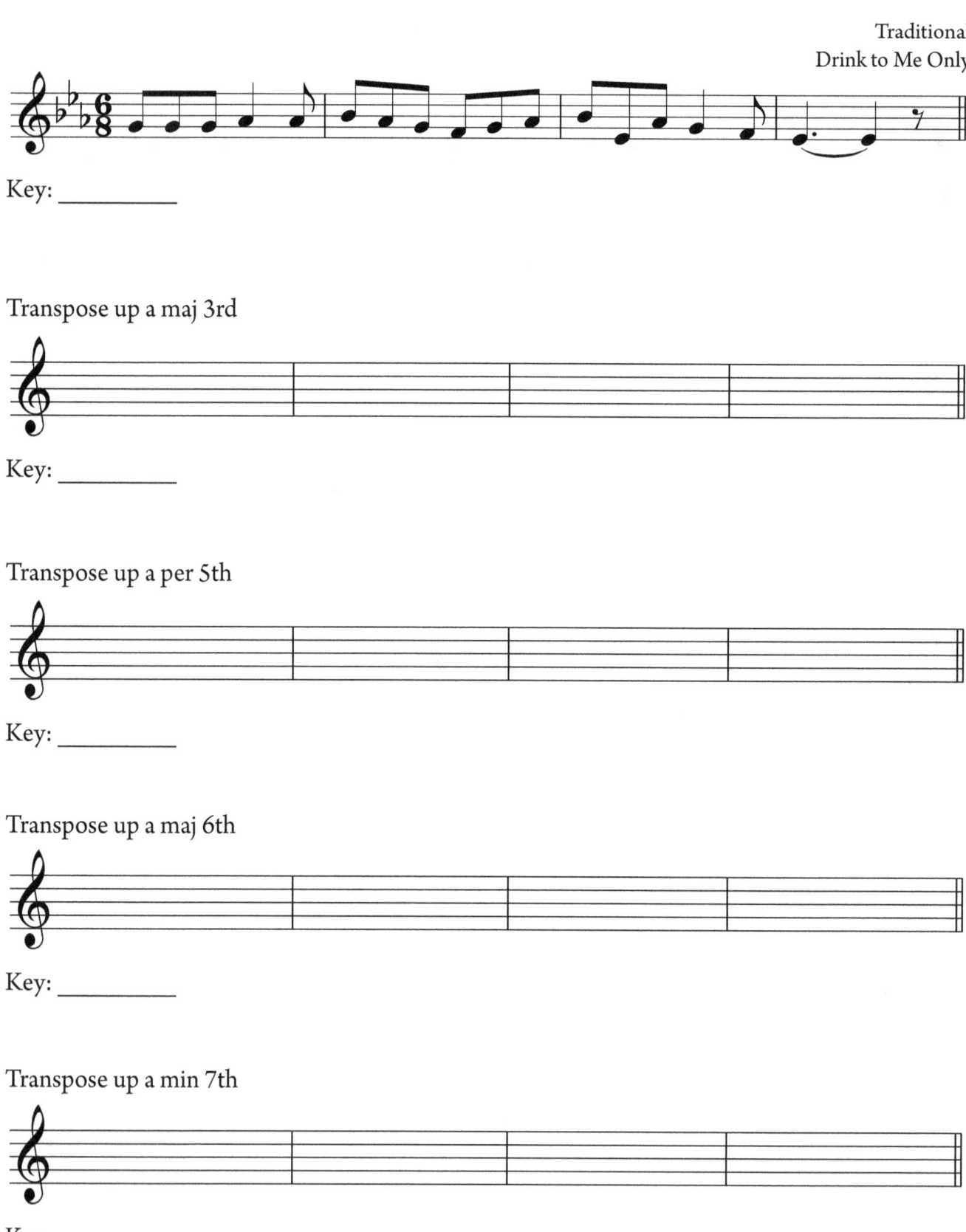

Transpostion By Key

You may be asked to transpose to a specific key. The steps for this are similar to transposing by interval. To transpose a melody into the key of B♭ major:

1. Determine the key of the original melody. The melody in Figure 14.9 is in G major.

Figure 14.9

G major

2. The distance from G to B♭ is up a 3rd. Write the key signature of B♭ major and move every note from the original melody up a 3rd. Copy everything from the original including the time signature, composer, tempo, etc. Figure 14.10 contains the original melody transposed into the key of B♭ major.

Figure 14.10

B♭ major

1. Name the key of the following melody. Transpose it **up** to the indicated keys.

key: _____

D major

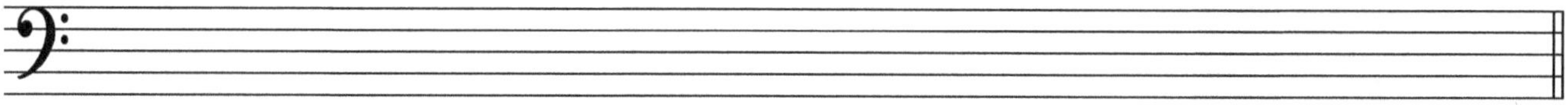

E♭ major

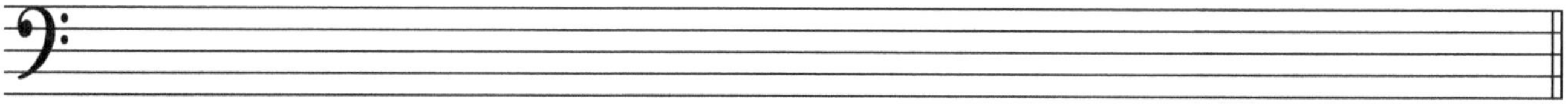

B major

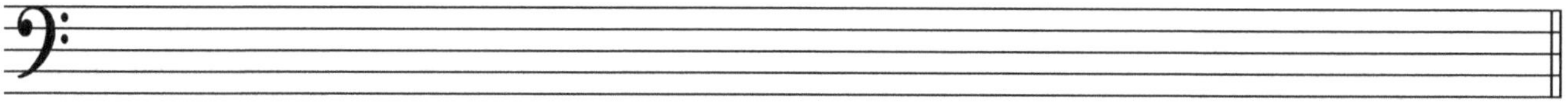

A major

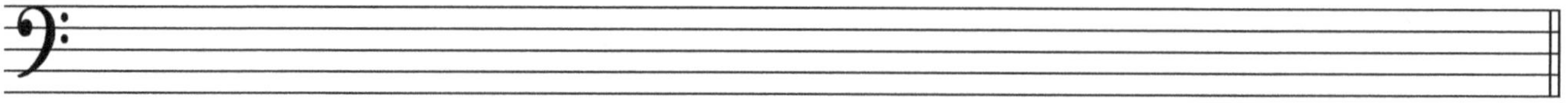

Transposition

Transpostion Down By Interval

A melody can be transposed down by a specific interval. It is similar to transposing up. Here are the steps for transposing a melody down by the interval of a major 3rd:

1. Determine the key of the original melody. The melody in Figure 14.11 is in C major.

Figure 14.11

Johann Wilhelm Hassler
Minuet, Op. 38, No. 4

C major

2. Determine the interval of a major 3rd below C. Figure 14.12 shows that a major 3rd below C is A♭. The new key will be A♭ major. The key signature of A♭ major is four flats.

Figure 14,12

The major 3rd below C is A♭

3. Write the new key signature, four flats for A♭ major. Rewrite the melody moving every note down a 3rd. This melody has accidentals. Insert the accidentals where they occurred in the original. The first is raised a half step; the second lowered a half step. The original melody used a sharp and a natural. Using the new key signature, a natural and a flat are required to raise and lower these notes. Copy everything from the original including the time signature, composer, tempo, etc. Figure 14.13 contains the original melody transposed into the key of A♭ major.

Figure 14.13

Johann Wilhelm Hassler
Minuet, Op. 38, No. 4

A♭ major

1. In the following examples you are given the original key. Transpose the tonic of these keys by the following intervals. Write the new key signature, the new tonic, and name the key.

2. Name the key of the following melody. Transpose it according to the given intervals. Name the new keys.

Anton Diabelli
Sonatina, Op. 168, No. 1

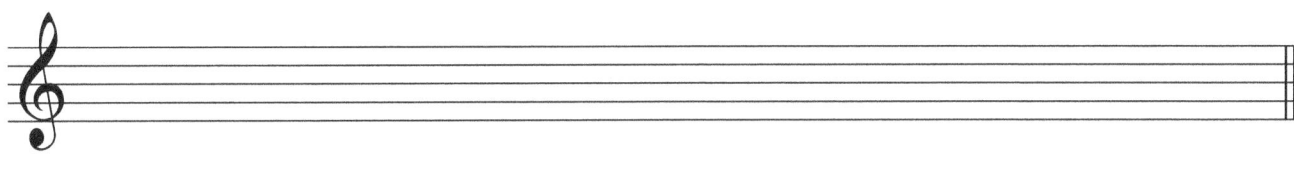

Key: _____

Transpose down a maj 2nd

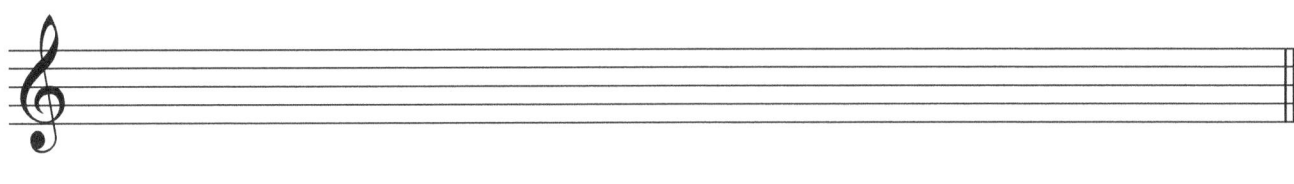

Key: _____

Transpose down a per 4th

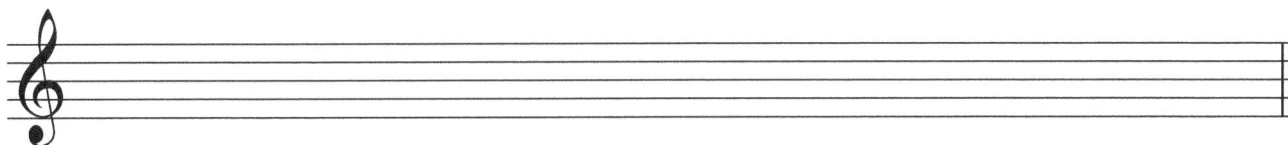

Key: _____

Transpose down a min 3rd

Key: _____

3. Name the key of the following melody. Transpose it to the indicated keys. Name the interval of transposition.

Ludwig van Beethoven
Symphony No. 9, IV

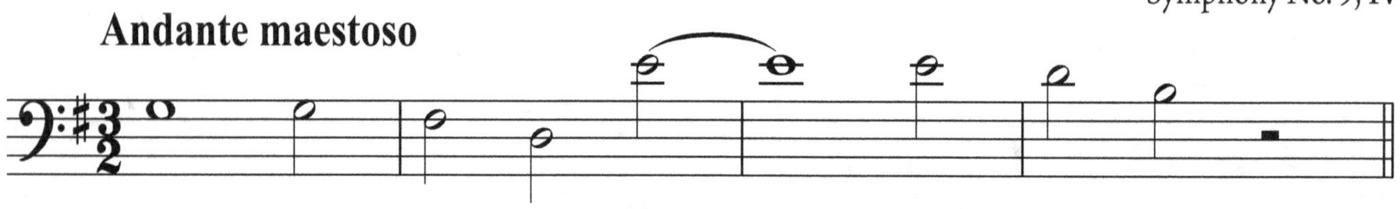

Andante maestoso

Key: _____

Down to D major

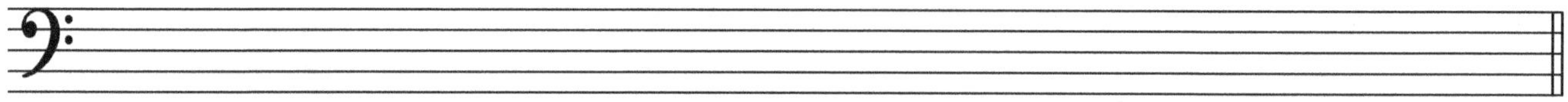

Interval of transposition: _____

Down to E♭ major

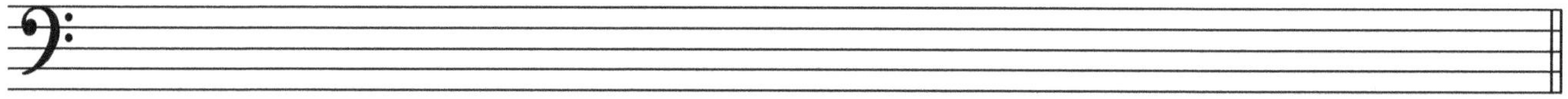

Interval of transposition: _____

Down to B major

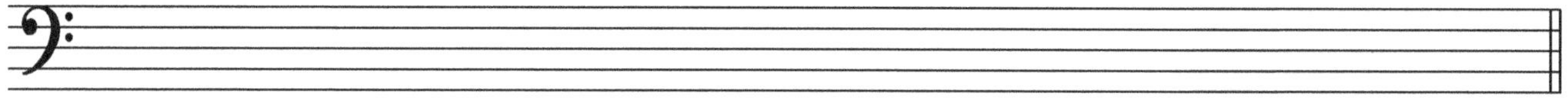

Interval of transposition: _____

Up to A major

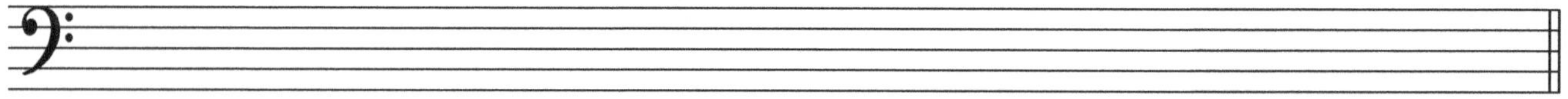

Interval of transposition: _____

©San Marco Publications 2022

Transposition

Transposing Instruments

Some instruments produce a pitch that is different than the one that is written. These instruments are known as ***transposing instruments***. Suppose you write a piece for trumpet and give a copy to your friend who plays piano, to play along with you. You find the resulting sound is horrible. Why? The trumpet is a transposing instrument, and the piano is not. Not every C and D, or every note for that matter, is the same. It depends on the instrument you are playing.

Concert Pitch

The pitch of a note is created by the vibration of air. These vibrations can be measured and given a frequency number called **hertz** (Hz). Many instruments play in **concert pitch**. This means when they play a note they produce a specific frequency. When you play middle C on the piano, you produce a note with the frequency of 261 hz. This is an exact pitch, and it is associated with concert pitch. Here is a list of some of the instruments that play in concert pitch.

- Piano
- Violin, viola, cello , bass
- Guitar
- Flute, piccolo
- Harp
- Oboe
- Bassoon
- Trombone
- Pitched percussion instruments like marimba, xylophone, timpani
- Tuba

Transposing Instruments - Instruments in B flat

Transposing instruments read the same music and use the same staff, clefs and notes as concert pitch instruments. The difference is when a trumpet plays the note C, it does not register as C according to the hertz scale (261 hz) and it does not match the C on the piano. The trumpet is a B♭ instrument and when it plays C, you hear a B♭ in concert pitch, or it matches the B♭ on the piano. This is what is meant by a transposing instrument. Some B♭ instruments are:

- Trumpet
- Clarinet
- Soprano saxophone

Figure 14.14 contains a melody for B♭ trumpet. When it is played, what we hear, concert pitch, is on the second staff. Since we hear B♭ when the trumpet plays C, concert pitch is heard a major 2nd below. In this *Concerto*, a piece for trumpet and orchestra, when the trumpet plays F, we hear E♭. This trumpet concerto is in E♭ major, but the B♭ trumpet plays in F major, a major 2nd higher than concert pitch. The string section, which plays in concert pitch, is playing in E♭ major.

If you have a melody written in concert pitch and want to write it for a B♭ instrument, you have to transpose it up a major 2nd.

If you have a melody written for a B♭ instrument and want to write it in concert pitch, you have to transpose it down a major 2nd.

Figure 14.14

1. The following melody is written for clarinet in B♭. Name the key and transpose it into concert pitch. Name the new key.

Key: _____

Key: _____

2. The following melody is written in concert pitch. Name the key and transpose it for trumpet in
   B♭. Name the new key.

   Johann Nepomuk Hummel
   Trumpet Concerto, III

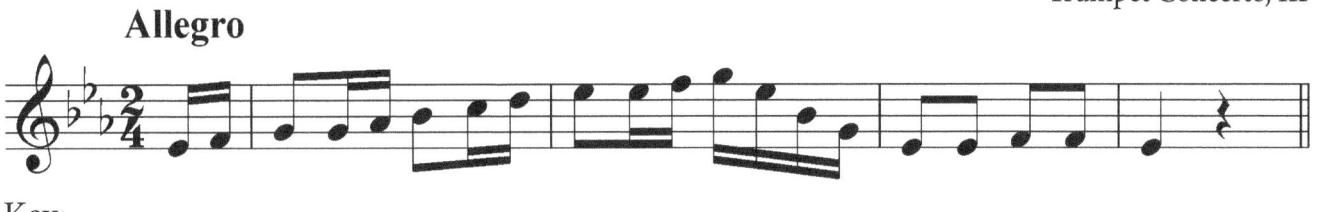

Key: _____

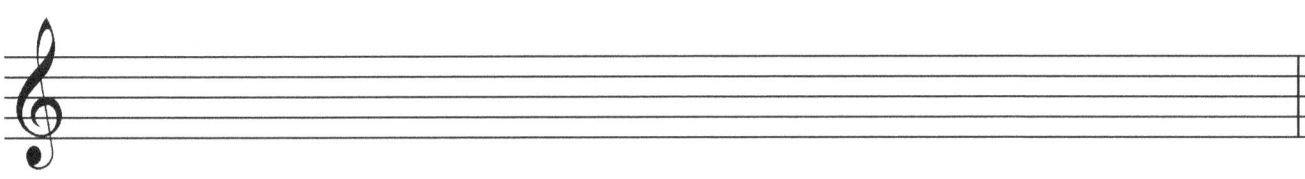

Key: _____

3. The following melody is written for clarinet in B♭. Name the key and transpose it into concert
   pitch. Name the new key.

   Wolfgang Amadeus Mozart
   Symphony No. 40, Minuet

Key: _____

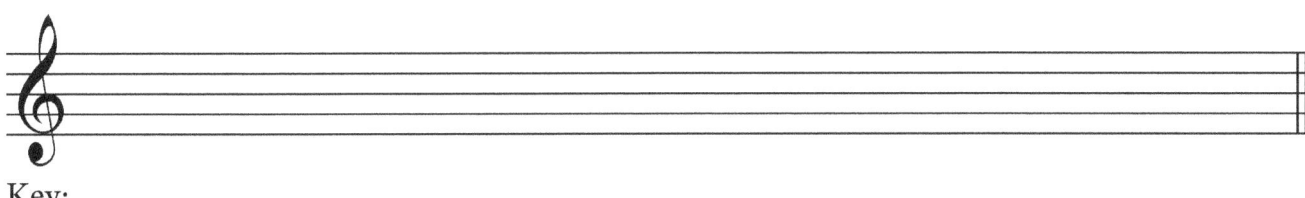

Key: _____

Transposing Instruments - Instruments in F

Two instruments transpose in the key of F:

- French horn
- English horn

They both transpose in the same manner, a fifth away. Music for these instruments must be transposed down a perfect 5th to get to concert pitch. (See Figure 14.15) In other words, a melody in concert pitch must be written up a perfect 5th to sound correct when played by an F instrument. A melody written for an F instrument must be transposed down a perfect 5th to sound correct at concert pitch.

Figure 14.15

French/English horn plays:

We hear at concert pitch:

1. The following melody is written for horn in F. Name the key and transpose it into concert pitch. Name the new key.

Wolfgang Amadeus Mozart
Concerto for Horn K. 447, III

Key: _____

Key: _____

2. The following examples are in concert pitch. Name the keys and rewrite each one for the instrument indicated. Name the new keys.

Wolfgang Amadeus Mozart
Allegro, K.312

Allegro

Key: _____

Clarinet in B♭

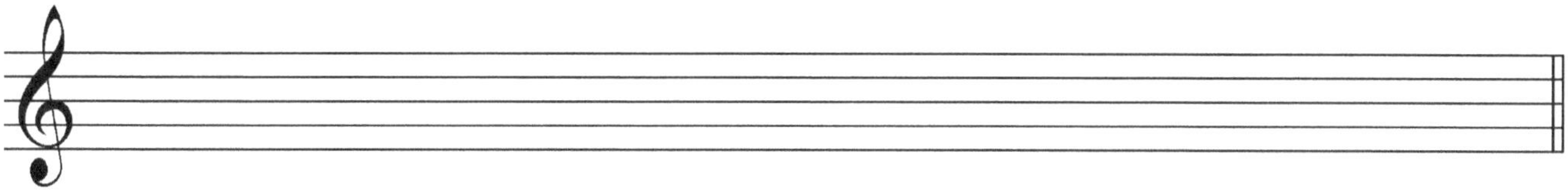

Key: _____

French Horn

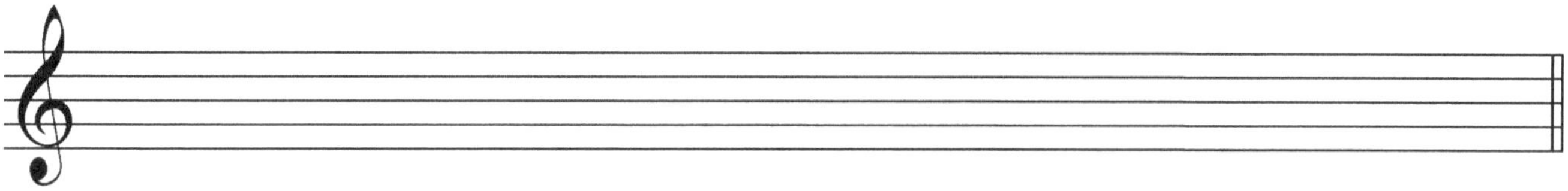

Key: _____

Antono Vivaldi
The Four Seasons, Spring

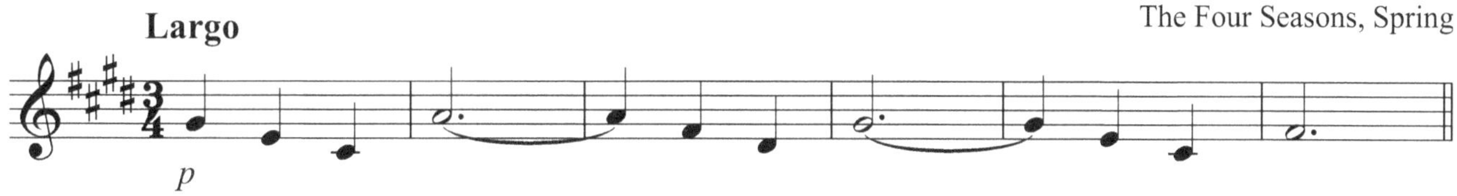

Largo

Key: _____

English Horn

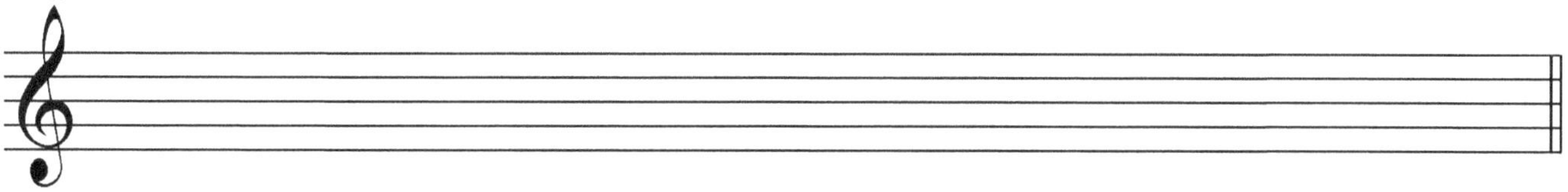

Key: _____

Trumpet in B♭

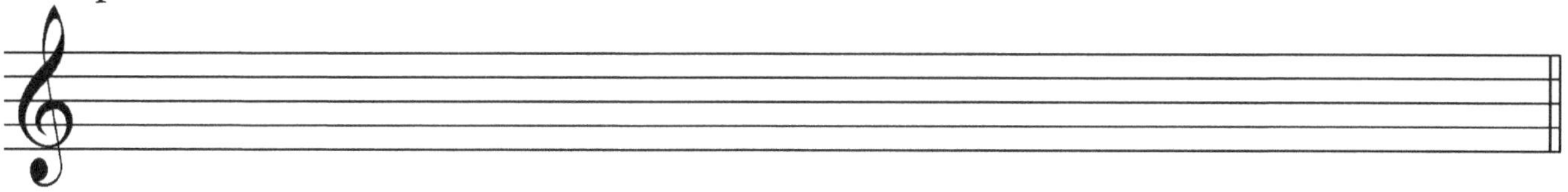

Key: _____

Transposition

15
Score Types

Score is a common term for notated music. There are several types of scores which we will discuss in this lesson.

Piano Score

A piano score is written on the grand staff. It consists of the treble and the bass staff joined by a bracket or brace. The bar lines go through both staves. The tempo indication is placed at the beginning of the staff. The key signature comes after the clef and is followed by the time signature. Dynamics ($f\,p$) are placed between the two staves. Figure 15.1 is a piano score.

Figure 15.1

Sonatina in F major

Ludwig van Beethoven

Allegro assai

Orchestral Score

An orchestral score has staves for all the instruments that are playing. The instruments are placed in the following order: woodwinds, brass, percussion (timpani), strings. Each section is divided with a bracket on the left side. the instruments are placed on the staff from highest to lowest in each family. The instrument names are usually written in Italian. On this score, the English translations are included. There is one tempo mark at the beginning, and each part receives its own dynamic marking.

Figure 15.2

Vocal Scores

Short Score

Short score, which is sometimes called condensed score, looks a little like piano score but there are some differences. This score consists of the treble and bass staves joined at the beginning by a line and a brace. In vocal music, the bar lines do not run through the entire staff.

This score is written for the four voices of a choir: soprano, alto, tenor, and bass. The soprano and alto parts are written on the treble staff, and the tenor and bass parts ware written on the bass staff.

Stem direction rules are different in short score. The soprano stems go up, and the alto stems go down in the treble clef. The tenor stems go up, and the bass stems go down in the bass clef. This separates the parts, and each singer can clearly see their line. The text to be sung is placed between the staves. Figure 15.3 is an example of a short score.

Figure 15.3

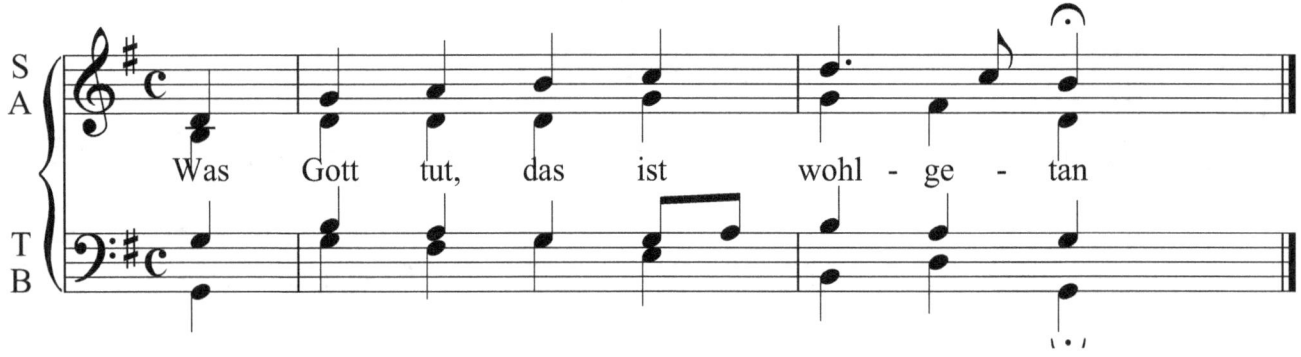

Modern Vocal Score

Modern vocal score is an example of ***open score***. In open score, each part gets its own staff. The three upper parts are written on treble staves. The bass part is written on the bass staff. The tenor part is written one octave higher on the treble staff. Each part receives the text to be sung.

Figure 15.4 is the chorale from Figure 15.3 written in modern vocal score.

Figure 15.4

Chorale No. 293
Was Gott tut, das ist wohlgetan

Johann Sebastian Bach

S: Was Gott tut, das ist wohl - ge tan.
A: Was Gott tut, das ist wohl ge tan.
T: Was Gott tut, das ist___ wohl ge tan.
B: Was Gott tut, das ist wohl ge tan.

String Quartet Score

String quartet score is an open score. The instruments in this score are first violin, second violin, viola, and cello (violoncello). The violin parts are written using two treble staves. The viola is written using the alto staff and the cello is written using the bass staff.

Figure 15.5 is written in string quartet score. The instruments are abbreviated as:

- Vln. I
- Vln. II
- Vla.
- Vlc.

Figure 15.5

Writing in Short and Open Score

There are few things to consider when transcribing a passage from short to open score or vice versa. The example in Figure 15.6 is in short score. The stem direction goes up for soprano and tenor and down for alto and bass. The tempo is written once, the dynamic sign is written once, and the fermata is written above the soprano and below the bass.

Figure 15.6

Figure 15.7 shows the same example written in open score for SATB. Normal rules of stem direction are followed. The tempo is written once at the top, and each part receives a dynamic marking. Each part receives a fermata. All four voices are lined up evenly on the score.

Figure 15.7

In short score, the ties in the soprano and tenor parts curve upwards, and the ties in the alto and bass parts always curve downwards. Figure 15.8 contains ties in the soprano and alto.

Figure 15.8

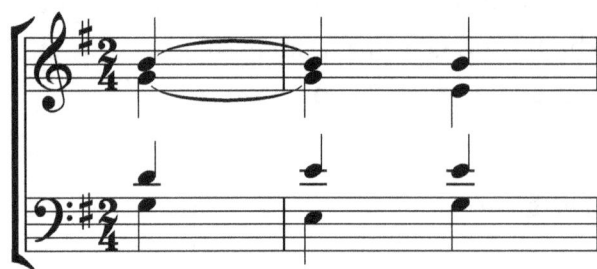

In open score, ties are always written on the opposite side of the note to the stem.

Figure 15.9

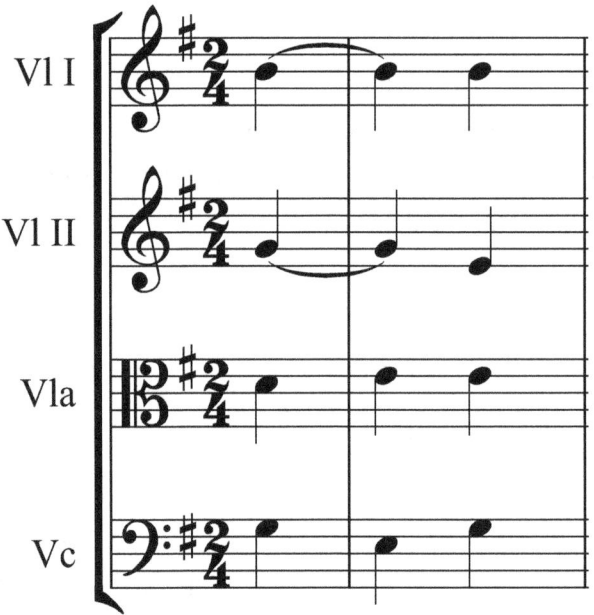

Sometimes, two parts can sing an identical note or a "unison," or they may sing the interval of a second.

Study the soprano and alto parts in figure 15.10. On beat one they are singing the same G. On beat two the soprano has a G, and the alto has the F directly below it.

Figure 15.10

These parts are transcribed into short score in Figure 15.11. In a short score, a unison is shown by writing one note-head with two stems. One stem points up, and the other points down.

For the interval of a major second on beat two, the F in the alto is moved slightly to the right. This allows both notes to be seen.

Figure 15.11

1. Write the following passage in open score for a string quartet.

Johann Sebastian Bach
Chorale no. 67: Freu'dich sehr, o meine Seele

2. Write the following passage in modern vocal score.

Johann Sebastian Bach
Das walt' mein gott

3. Write the following passage in short score.

Ludwig van Beethoven
String Quartet Op 18, No. 1

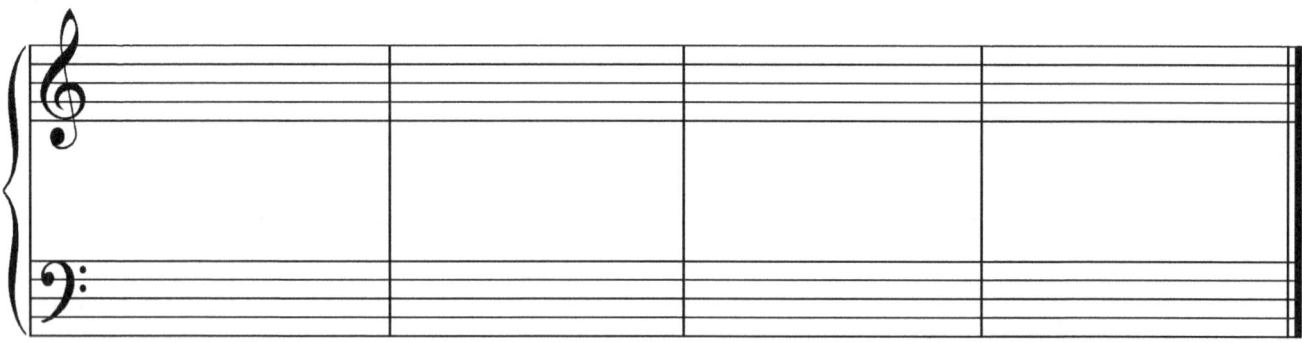

4. Write the following passage in string quartet score.

Franz Joseph Haydn
String Quartet Op 76, No. 3

5. Write the following passage in short score.

Johann Sebastian Bach
O Haupt Voll und Wunden

16

Melody

What is melody?

Most musical compositions have a line of notes that are played one after the other to form a tune. This is called a *melody*. A melody is the main tune of a song. Figure 16.1 is the popular melody 'Mary had a Little Lamb.'

Figure 16.1

The Phrase

Most traditional melodies move in four measure sections called *phrases*. A phrase is like a musical sentence. Like the sentence in a story, a phrase represents one musical idea. A phrase is indicated by a long curved line called a *phrase mark*. A phrase mark looks like a large slur. This line indicates the beginning and end of the phrase. Figure 16.1 contains a phrase mark above the melody. This melody is four measures long, which is the most common length of a musical phrase.

How a Melody Moves

The notes of a melody can move in different ways:

- They can move by **step**.
- They can move by **leap**.
- They can move **repetition**.

Most good melodies use all three types of movement. Figure 16.2 shows the three types of movement working together in the first two phrases of the melody 'Twinkle Twinkle Little Star.' Each phrase is four measures long. A leap is the interval of a 3rd or more. Here, the melody leaps a 5th from the last note of m.1 to the first note of m.2. (m. is an abbreviation for the word measure.)

Figure 16.2

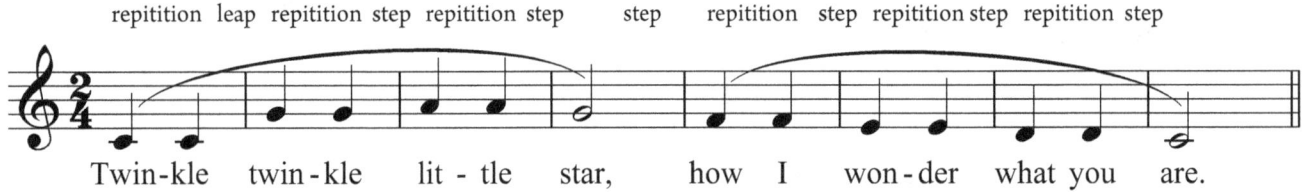

1. Name the key and mark the steps (S), leaps (L), and repetition (R) in the following melodies.

English Folk Song

key:

Norwegian Folk Song

key:

Writing a Stepwise Melody

In this lesson, we are going to learn to write melodies that move by step. The melody in Figure 16.3 moves by step. It is in G major and uses the notes of the G major scale. It is four measures long and begins and ends on the tonic (G). The tonic is like home base for a piece of music. You can expect to see the tonic used frequently. A piece in the key of G major is all about G. Often a piece in G will start and end on G and contain many G's throughout. G, the tonic, is the star of a piece in G major. This melody has a natural arch that peaks at E. E is the *climax* or high point of the melody. Many melodies will have one high note that is the climax and not repeated. The rhythm of the melody is indicated above the staff.

Figure 16.3

G major

The melody in Figure 16.4 moves entirely by step. It is in F major and uses the notes of the F major scale. The motive in m.1 is repeated a step higher in m.2 before the melody steps down to the tonic. This melody begins and ends on the tonic (F). It is the strongest way to begin and end a melody because the tonic is the most prominent note in any key. It clearly establishes F major as the key.

Figure 16.4

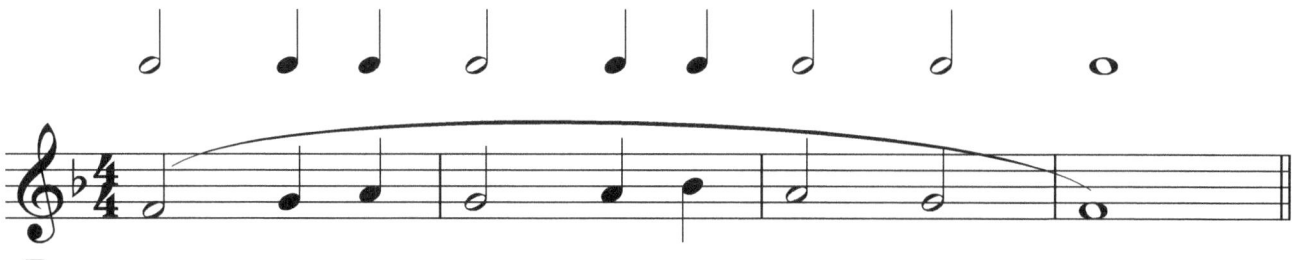

F major

1. Complete this melody using the notes of the C major scale and the given rhythm. Use stepwise motion or repeated notes, ending on the tonic (1̂). Draw a line marking the phrase.

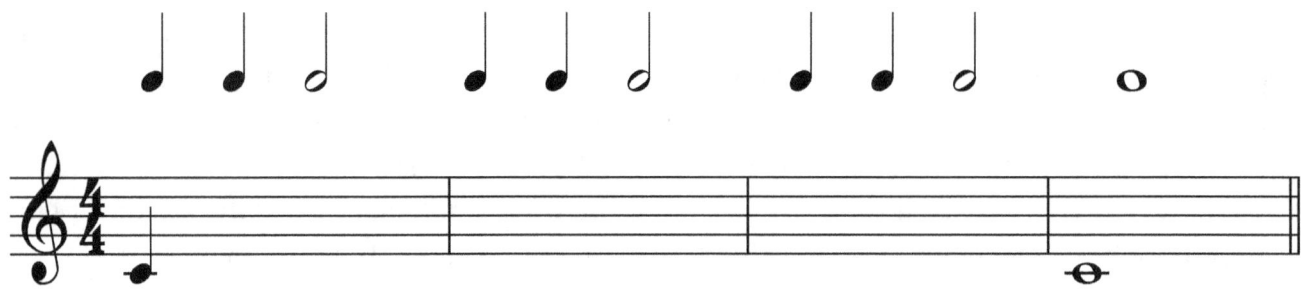

2. Complete this melody using the notes of the F major scale and the given rhythm. Use stepwise motion or repeated notes, ending on the tonic (1̂). Draw a line marking the phrase.

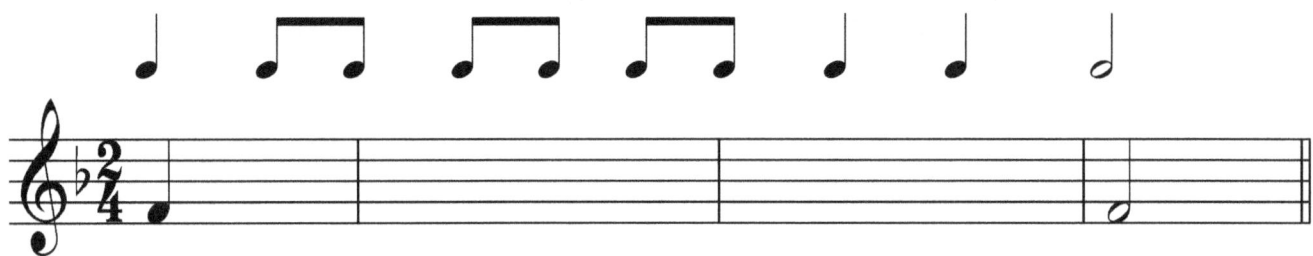

3. Complete this melody using the notes of the G major scale and the given rhythm. Use stepwise motion or repeated notes, ending on the tonic (1̂). Draw a line marking the phrase.

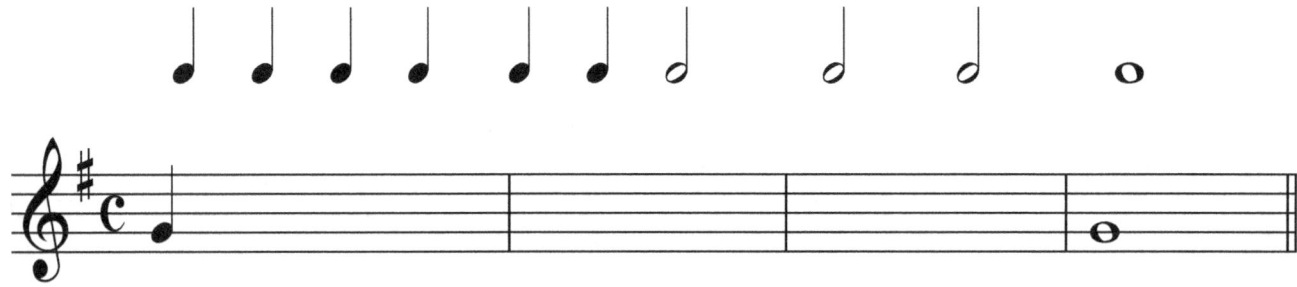

Stable Pitches

The strongest and most **stable pitch** of any key is the tonic. A stable pitch is a note that has strength, finality, and completeness. Many melodies begin and end on the tonic. The melody in Figure 16.5 is in the key of G major and begins and ends on the tonic ($\hat{1}$).

Figure 16.5

G major

Another relatively stable pitch, is scale degree $\hat{3}$. Scale degree $\hat{3}$, is the 3rd of the tonic triad and has a certain amount of strength and stability, although it is not as strong as $\hat{1}$. The melody in Figure 16.6 ends on $\hat{3}$.

Figure 16.6

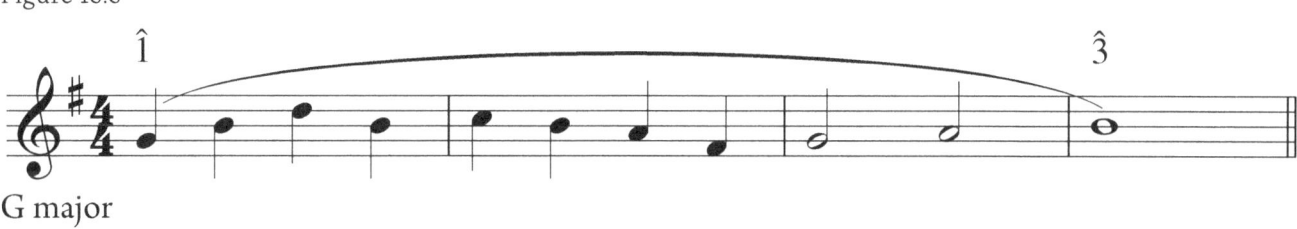

G major

Unstable Pitches

Some pitches within a key are considered **unstable**. An unstable pitch is a note that lacks finality or completeness. A composition would not end on an unstable pitch, but a phrase might. Unstable pitches are found on scale degrees $\hat{2}$ and $\hat{7}$. If scale degree $\hat{1}$ is like a period at the end of a sentence, scale degree $\hat{2}$ or $\hat{7}$ is like a question mark.

The melody in Figure 16.7 ends on scale degree $\hat{2}$.

Figure 16.7

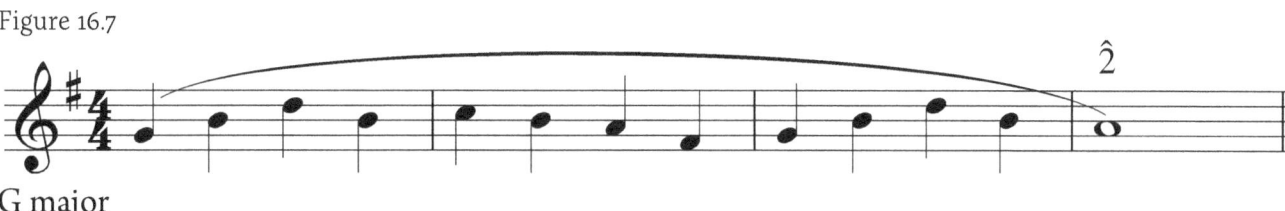

G major

1. Name the major key of each melody. Write the scale degree number for the last note and mark it as stable or unstable.

Conjunct and Disjunct Motion

Melodies move in various ways. When a melody moves by step, the motion is called ***conjunct motion***. When a melody moves by skip or leap, the motion is called ***disjunct motion***. Good melodies are a combination of both of these with some repitition. Let's compare a few melodies. The melody in Figure 16.8 consists only of disjunct motion. Every note leaps and there is no stepwise motion until the last two notes. The result is a fractured melody that would be very hard to sing and to play on some instruments.

Figure 16.8

G major

The melody in Figure 16.9 contains only conjunct or stepwise motion. Although it is not a terrible melody, using only scalewise motion is not very interesting.

Figure 16.9

G major

Figure 16.10 contains a melody that is a combination of conjunct and disjunct motion. The balance of both types of motion produces an interesting melody. It should be noted that this melody is in G major and both the tonic and dominant chords are outlined within it. The tonic chord (G B D) occurs in m.1 and the dominant chord (D F♯ A) can be found in m.3. These are the two most prominent chords in any key. Using these chords creates a strong melody that is clearly based on the key of G major. In this level, we are going to write melodies that use stepwise motion and skips or leaps based on the tonic and dominant triads.

Figure 16.10

G major

Writing a Melody

The tonic and dominant chords are very strong elements to use in a melody. Figure 16.11 shows some of the ways the tonic triad in C major can be incorporated into a melody to add interest and variety with disjunct motion. Study the C major tonic triads used melodically.

    a) The tonic triad (C E G) is written into the melody creating skips of a 3rd.
    b) The skips are softened slightly with stepwise motion beween the 3rd and 5th (E F G).
    c) The stepwise motion may be placed between the root and 3rd (C D E).
    d) The triad may be outlined backwards from the 5th down to the root (G E C).

Figure 16.11

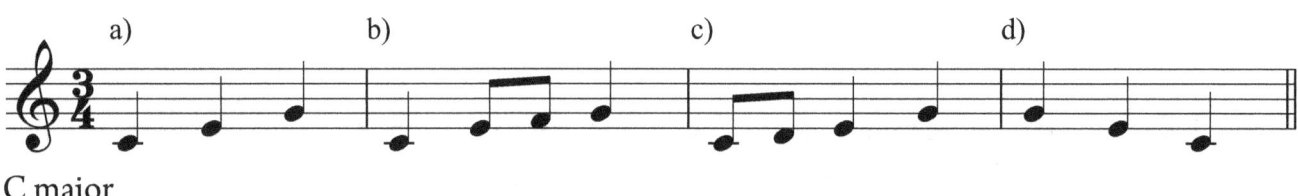

C major

The dominant triad is also effective in a melody. Since the dominant triad contains the leading tone, it is often followed by the tonic. It is very strong to end a melody on $\hat{1}$. This is the most stable tone in any key. When you end a melody on $\hat{1}$ it is often preceded by $\hat{7}$ or $\hat{2}$, both notes of the dominant triad. A strong melodic ending consists of the final two notes $\hat{2}$ - $\hat{1}$ or $\hat{7}$ - $\hat{1}$. Figure 16.12 shows two strong endings for a melody using the notes of the dominant triad. a) outlines the dominant triad in C major (G B D) and ends on the tonic ($\hat{2}$ - $\hat{1}$). b) uses the root and 3rd of the dominant triad and ends on the tonic ($\hat{7}$ - $\hat{1}$).

Figure 16.12

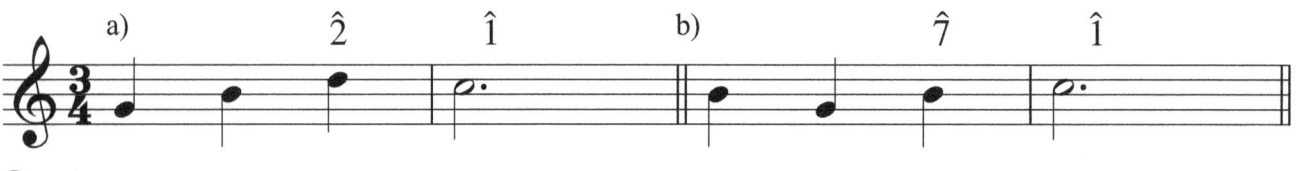

C major

1. Write a melody in F major using a combination of stepwise motion and skips outlining the tonic or dominant triad. Use the rhythm provided and end on a stable pitch ($\hat{1}$ or $\hat{3}$).

2. Write a melody in D major using a combination of stepwise motion and skips outlining the tonic or dominant triad. Use the rhythm provided and end on a stable pitch ($\hat{1}$ or $\hat{3}$).

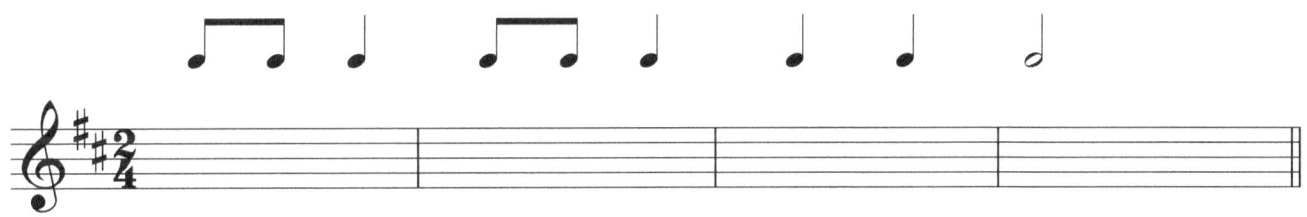

3. Write a melody in B♭ major using a combination of stepwise motion and skips outlining the tonic or dominant triad. Use the rhythm provided and end on a stable pitch ($\hat{1}$ or $\hat{3}$).

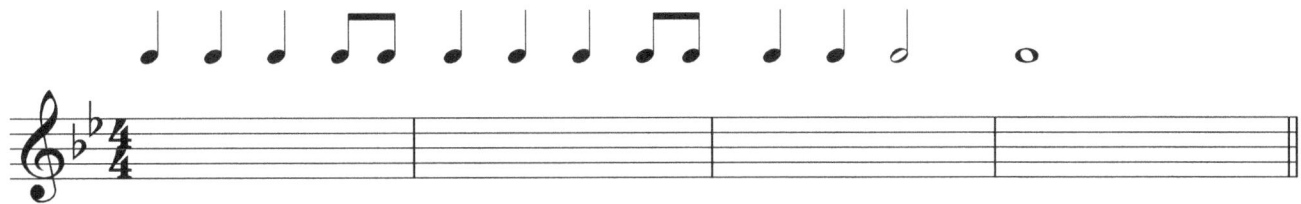

The Motive

Many phrases are built from smaller groups of notes called ***motives***. A motive is a specific pattern of notes and rhythms. Motives can be repeated at a higher or lower pitch.

Figure 16.13 contains a melodic motive in m.1 consisting of a half note, two eighths and a quarter. It skips up a 3rd and then steps down. In the two measures that follow, the motive is repeated a step higher each time.

Figure 16.13

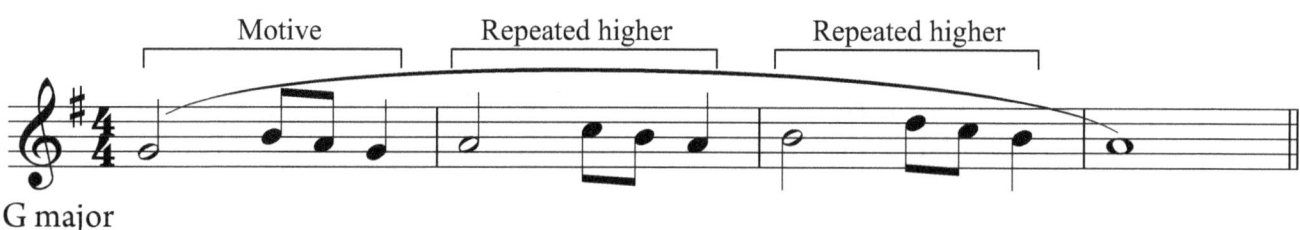

G major

Figure 16.14 contains the famous motive from the first movement of Beethoven's Fifth Symphony (Op. 67). The opening four note motive in mm.1 and 2 is repeated down a step in mm.3 and 4. This motive consists of an eighth rest followed by 3 eighth notes and a half note the interval of a 3rd lower. Beethoven based this large composition on this 4 note motive.

Figure 16.14

1. Name the major key of each of the following melodies. Circle the melodic motive each time it occurs in each melody.

key:

key:

key:

2. Name the key and find and circle the motives in the following melodies.

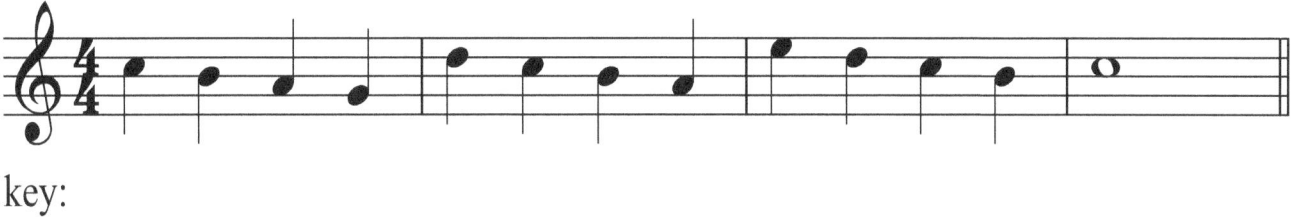

key:

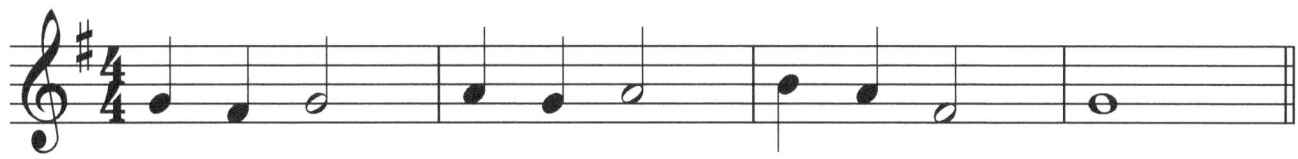

key:

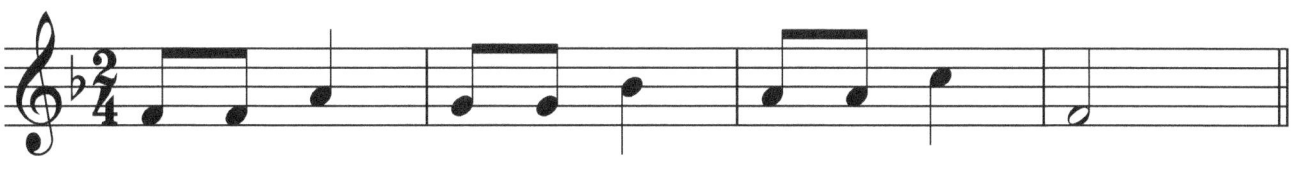

key:

Antecedent and Consequent Phrases

Every piece of music has an overall plan or structure, this is the "big picture". This is called the *form* of the music.

Antecedent and *consequent* (question and answer) phrases are common in music. The antecedent phrase acts as a question, often ending on an unstable tone ($\hat{2}$ or $\hat{7}$), which requires an answer. The consequent phrase provides the answer to the antecedent phrase and usually ends on a stable tone ($\hat{1}$ or $\hat{3}$).

We can label music with letters to distinguish the differences within a piece. In this lesson we are going to look at melodies consisting of two phrases, and learn to identify their form and label them with letters.

The melody in Figure 16.15 consists of two phrases that are almost identical. The difference between the first and second phrase is the ending. The first phrase, the antecedent, ends on an unstable tone ($\hat{2}$). The second phrase, the consequent, is a repetition of the first phrase but changes slightly near the end and concludes on a stable tone ($\hat{1}$). Both phrases are nearly the same. We label the first phrase with the letter "**a**." The second phrase is very similar but not exactly the same, so we label it "**a¹**."

Since both phrases are very similar, they form a melodic idea called a *parallel period*.

Figure 16.15

The two phrases in the melody in Figure 16.16 are different. Unlike the previous example the second phrase is not a repeat of the first with a different ending, but a completely new musical idea. In this case, we label phrase one "**a**" and phrase two "**b**". The two phrases work together to create a complete section. However, they are different melodically and the labels indicate the difference.

Since the two phrases use melodies that are different they form an idea called a ***contrasting period***.

Figure 16.16

1. Name the key of the following melody. Mark the phrases. Label the first phrase with the letter **a**. Label the second phrase with the letter **a¹** or **b** to show whether it is similar or different. Circle melodic motive 1 each time it occurs in the melody.

key:

The first phrase ends on: ❏ a stable scale degree   ❏ an unstable scale degree

The second phrase ends on: ❏ a stable scale degree   ❏ an unstable scale degree

This is a: ❏ parallel period   ❏ contrasting period

2. Name the key of the following melody. Mark the phrases. Label the first phrase with the letter **a**. Label the second phrase with the letter **a¹** or **b** to show whether it is the same or different.

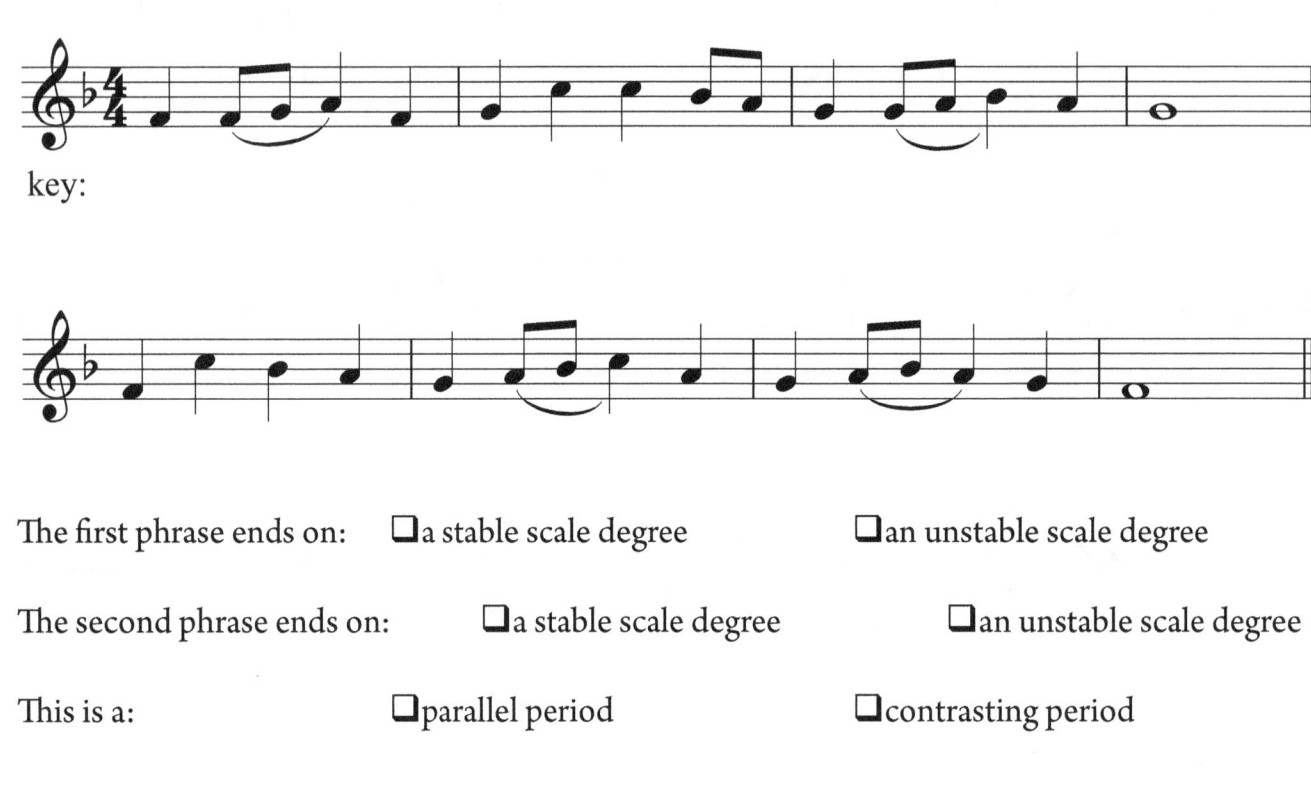

key:

The first phrase ends on: ❏ a stable scale degree   ❏ an unstable scale degree

The second phrase ends on: ❏ a stable scale degree   ❏ an unstable scale degree

This is a: ❏ parallel period   ❏ contrasting period

Composing a Consequent Phrase to a Given Melody

You may be asked to create a parallel period by composing a 4 measure consequent or answer phrase to a given melody. Here are the steps for writing this melody.

1. Examine the given melody and decide the key. The melody in Figure 16.17 is in F major.
2. Look at the last note of the phrase. Is it an stable or unstable scale degree? Here, it is $\hat{2}$, an unstable degree.

Figure 16.17

3. Since we are writing a parallel period we want the new phrase to begin the same way as the original phrase. Rewrite the opening phrase and change the ending so it ends on a stable scale degree ($\hat{1}$ or $\hat{3}$). Scale degree $\hat{1}$ is the strongest choice and is especially good if it is approached from a step below ($\hat{7}$-$\hat{1}$), or from a step above ($\hat{2}$-$\hat{1}$). Measure 3 of Figure 16.18 uses the same rhythm as the first two measures. This is good because it provides rhythmic unity. Try not to introduce a new or unusual rhythm when writing these phrases. This phrase concludes by stepping down to scale degree $\hat{1}$.

Figure 16.18

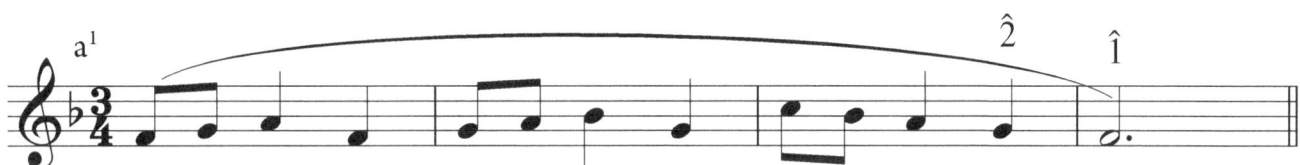

1. Create a parallel period by writing a 4 measure answer to the given question phrase. End your melody on a stable tone ($\hat{1}$ or $\hat{3}$). Mark the phrases.

key:

key:

key:

key:

key:

key:

Implied Harmony

The notes of a melody can imply or suggest certain chords that could go along with it. This is called the ***implied harmony***. Figure 16.19 contains the I, IV, and V chords in G major.

Figure 16.19

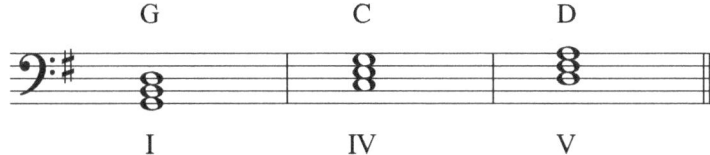

Chords can be used with a melody if they contain the same notes as those found in the melody. Study the implied harmony for the melody in Figure 16.20.

The G and the B in m.1 suggest chord I in G major. It is the opening measure. Most pieces begin with the tonic chord. This helps to establish the key or tonality. The eighth note A in m.1 is not part of the G chord (GBD). This note provides movement to the melody and connects the two chord tones G and B. It is called a ***passing tone***. Passing tones are called ***non-chord tones***. These are notes that are not part of the underlying chord.

The two C's in m.2 imply the IV chord (CEG) in G major.

The D and G in m.3 imply the I chord, and the A in m.4 implies the V chord.
It is important that the notes at the end of a melodic phrase imply a logical cadence.
Here I - V implies a half cadence. The end of a phrase must have a logical cadence.

The D and the F♯ in m.7 imply V (DF♯A), and the final note in m.8, G, implies I. This implies a perfect authentic cadence in G major.

Ending a phrase on the tonic and approaching it from a step below ($\hat{7}$ - $\hat{1}$) or from a step above ($\hat{2}$ - $\hat{1}$) is extremely strong melodically and tonally. It suggests a perfect authentic cadence and effectively reinforces the key.

Figure 16.20

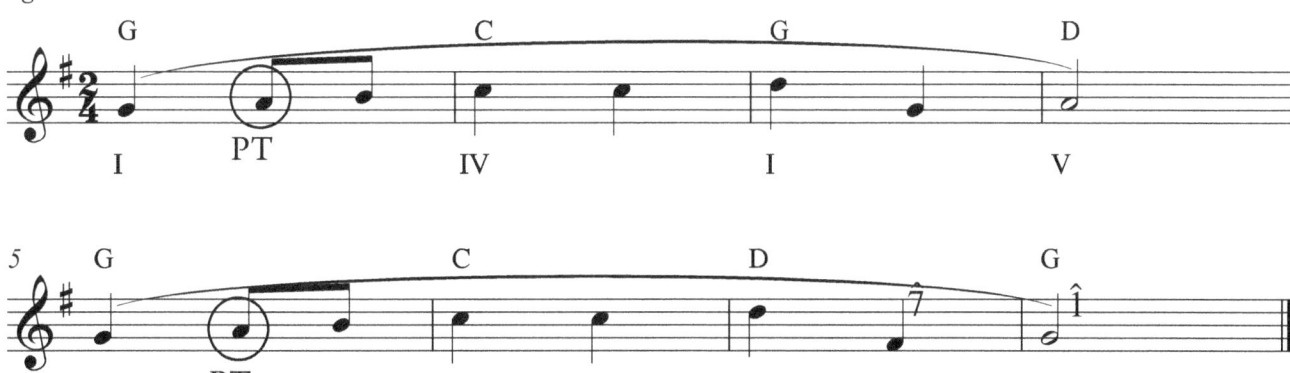

For Figure 16.21, The D, F and A in m.1 suggest the i chord in D minor. This is the opening measure. Most pieces begin with the tonic chord. This helps to establish the key or tonality.

The G and B flat in m.2 imply the iv chord in D minor.

The A and C sharp in m.3 imply the V chord in D minor.

The final measure contains a D implying i and forming an authentic cadence with V in the previous measure.

Musical phrases must make harmonic sense and this includes implying a logical cadence at the end of the phrase.

Figure 16.21

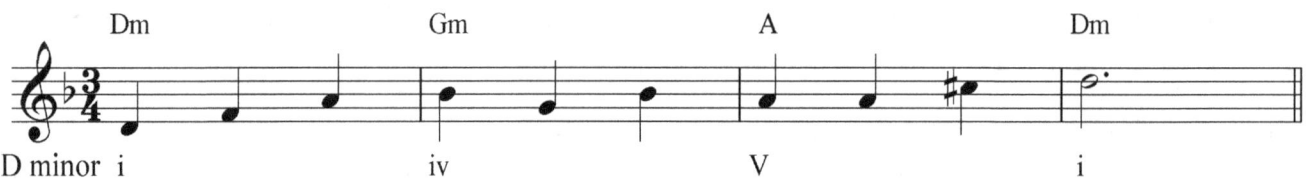

1. Name the key of each of the following melodies. Using Roman numerals I, IV, and V, or i, iv, and V, write the implied harmony under each. Circle and mark any passing tones PT.

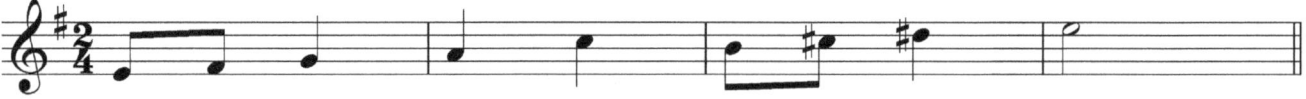

key:

key:

key:

1. Name the key of each of the following parallel periods. Using Roman numerals I, IV, and V, write the implied harmony under each. Circle and mark any passing tones PT.

key:_____

key:_____

key:_____

Melody

Writing a Melody

We are going to write a two phrase melody based on two given measures.

Figure 16.22 contains two measures of a melody. Study the steps for writing a two phrase melody based on these measures.

Figure 16.22

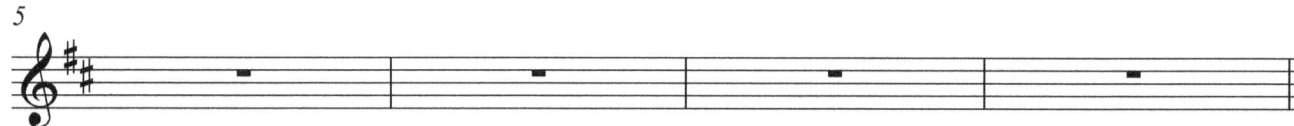

1. Name the key. This melody is in D major.

2. Make a structural plan and label the sections "a" and "a¹" to show the question and answer phrases.

3. Decide on the implied harmony for the existing measures.

4. Sketch in the implied harmony for the remaining measures. In this example, I and V are used for mm.3 and 4, implying a half cadence at the end of the first phrase. Since this is a parallel period, the second phrase (a¹) begins with a repeat of mm.1 and 2. The implied harmony for mm.7 and 8 is V - I suggesting an authentic cadence.

5. Add the root/quality chord symbols above the staff.

6. Complete the opening measures of "a¹" by copying mm.1 and 2 into mm. 5 and 6.

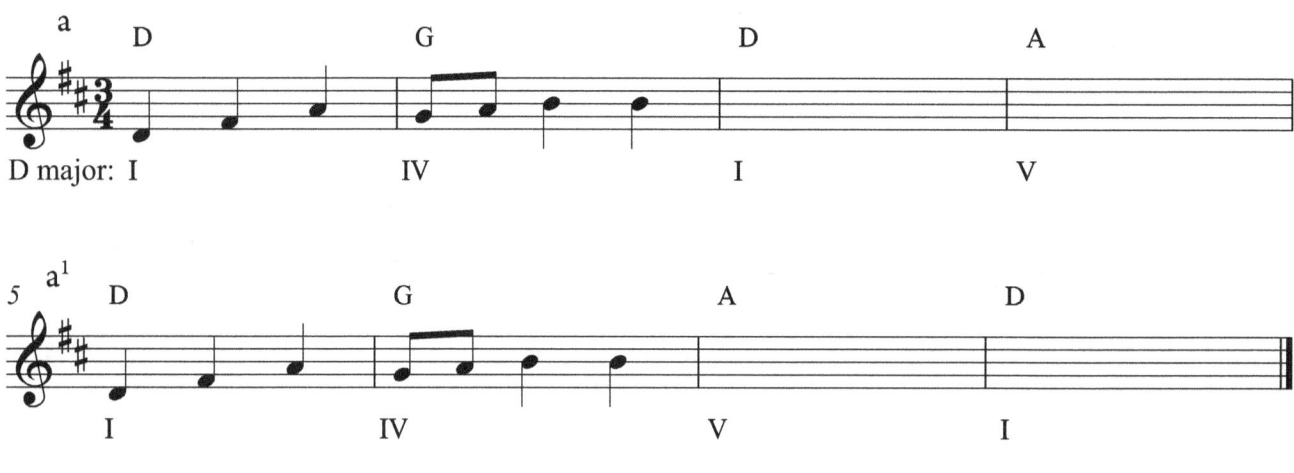

6. Complete the first phrase by writing the melody in mm. 3 and 4. This phrase should end on an unstable degree like $\hat{2}$ or $\hat{7}$. Here, it ends on $\hat{2}$. This supports a half cadence which is ideal for the question portion of this melody.

7. This two measure response uses similar rhythmic values to those found in the opening measures. Try to stick to a similar rhythm to maintain rhythmic unity in your writing. The use of an unrelated rhythm may not make sense or seem out of place.

8. The first phrase ends on a dotted half note. This works well since a cadence is a place of rest and requires a slowing of the rhythm. The cadence occurs over the bar with I on a weak beat and V on a strong beat. This is the typical rhythm of a cadence. The second chord of a cadence usually ends on a stronger beat than the first chord.

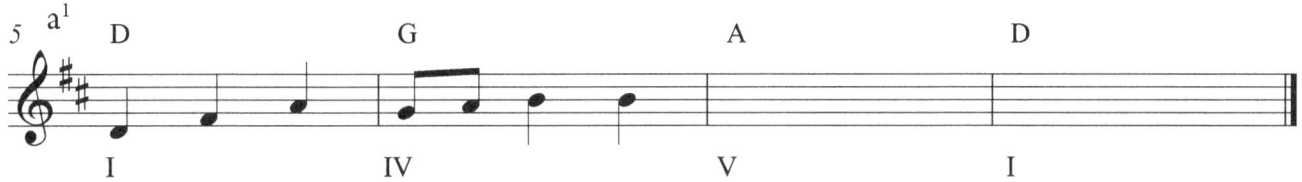

9. Complete the final two measures of the second phrase. This phrase should end on a stable chord tone. Here, it ends on $\hat{1}$ and is approached by $\hat{7}$. Concluding a phrase with $\hat{7}$ - $\hat{1}$ or $\hat{2}$ - $\hat{1}$ in the melody is extremely strong and supports a perfect authentic cadence.

10. The rhythm of the final two measures matches the rhythm of mm. 3 and 4. Although this is not necessary, it provides rhythmic unity.

11. Indicate each phrase by adding phrase marks.

1. For the following melodic fragments:

   i. Name the key.
   ii. Label the formal structure using "a" and "a¹."
   iii. Complete the first phrase according to the given implied harmony.
   iv. If not already given, indicate the implied harmony for the second phrase.
   v. Write the second phrase creating a *parallel period*.
   vi. Add root/quality chord symbols to both phrases.
   vii. Mark each phrase.

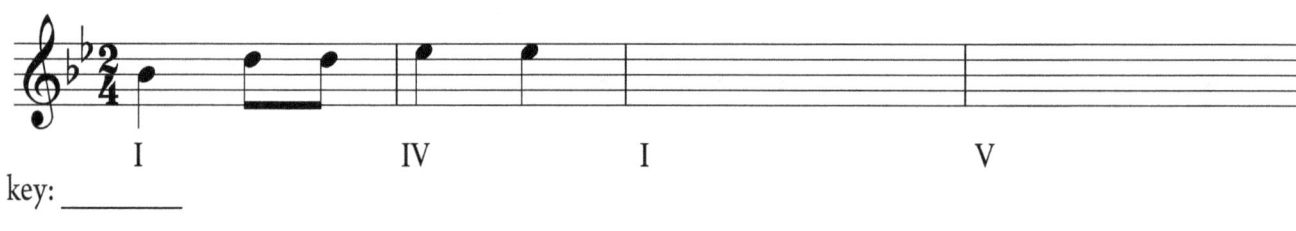

       I   IV   I   V

key: _____

       I   IV   I   V

key: _____

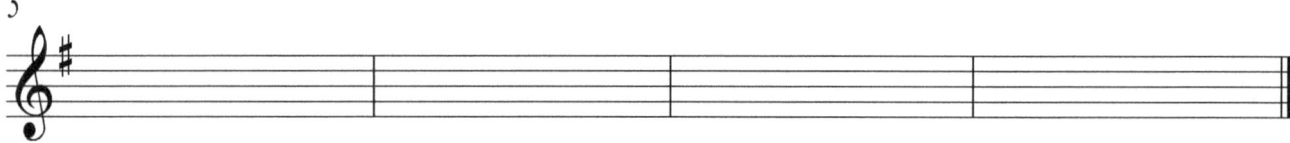

I   V   IV   V

key: _____

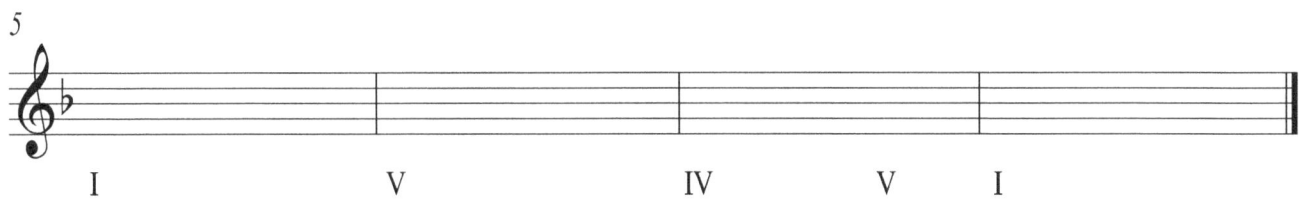

I   V   IV   V   I

I   V   IV   V

key: _____

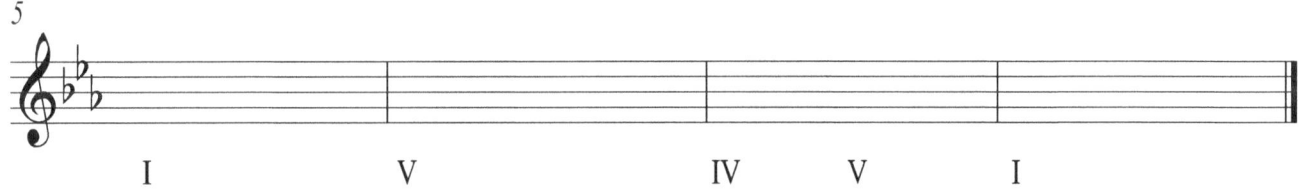

I   V   IV   V   I

I   V   I   V

key: _____

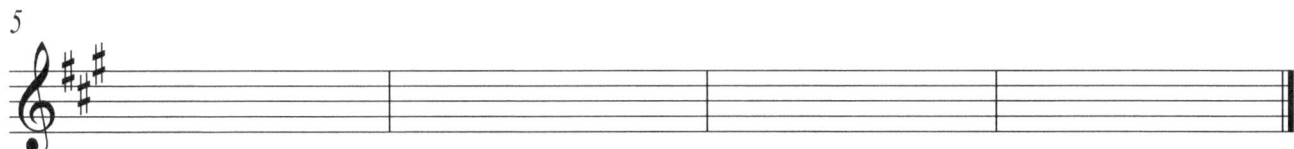

Non-Chord Tones

A melody may have notes that are not part of the implied harmony. These are called **non-chord tones**. Non-chord tones always have a function or a reason for being. We do not write a note that is not part of the underlying harmony unless we can explain its function. In this level, we will study two different non-chord tones.

The Passing Tone (PT)

Non-chord tones are classified according to how they are approached and left. A **passing tone** is a non-chord tone that is approached and left by step. It fills in the interval of a 3rd. In Figure 16.23(a), all of the notes are part of the implied harmony (I). They are chord tones. In (b), there are two notes that are not part of the I chord. These are non-chord tones. The notes D and F are not part of the I chord in C major (C-E-G). These two notes fill in the interval of a 3rd between C and E and E and G. Each non-chord tone is approached and left by step. The D is approached by step from C and is left by step to E. The F is approached by step from E and left by step to G.

When we analyze music, non-chord tones are circled and marked with an abbreviation to indicate their function. Here, PT is used for passing tone.

Figure 16.23

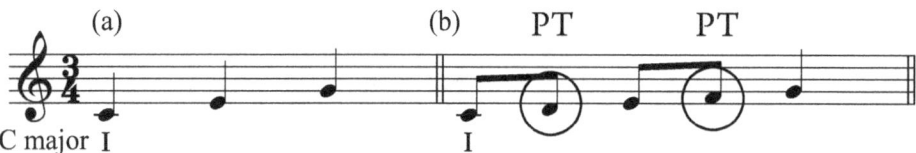

The Neighbor or Auxilliary Tone (NT)

A **neighbor tone** sometimes called an **auxiliary tone**, is a non-chord tone that moves a step above or a step below two common tones. It is approached and left by step. Figure 16.24 contains two neighbor tones. In this measure, the harmony could imply IV in C major (F-A-C). Anything that is not an F, A, or C is a non-chord tone. The two G's are not part of this chord. The first is an upper neighbor to the note F. The second is a lower neighbor to the A. They are circled and labeled NT to indicate their function.

Figure 16.24

Figure 16.25 is based on the melody from Figure 16.21. Here, the addition of passing tones and a neighbor tone add movement and interest to the original melody. Play and compare both.

Figure 16.25

D minor i   iv   V   i

1. For the following melodies: Name the key. Add functional chord symbols stating the implied harmony. Circle and label any non-chord tones.

Key:_____

Key:_____

Key:_____

Key:_____

Key:_____

2. Name the keys of the following melodies. Rewrite them adding passing and neighbor tones where appropriate. Add functional chord symbols stating the implied harmony.

Writing a Contrasting Period

The parallel period consists of two similar four measure phrases labeled: **a** and **a¹**. The labels **a** and **a¹** indicate the similarity between the two phrases.

The ***contrasting period*** consists of two differing four measure phrases labeled: **a** and **b**.
The melodic material in the second (consequent) phrase is different than **a**. For this reason, it is labeled "**b**".

Study and play the melody in Figure 15.8. There are two phrases: an antecedent and a consequent. Each phrase begins with an anacrusis. However, section **a** and section **b** differ. Section **b** uses the same rhythm as section **a**, but it contains new melodic material. This type of melody, with two differing phrases, is a contrasting period.

Figure 15.8

In Figure 15.9, the consequent phrase **b**, contains a contrasting melody based on a descending melodic sequence using rhythm from m.1. A ***melodic sequence*** is the repetition of a melodic idea at a higher or lower pitch.

Figure 15.9

You will be asked to compose the consequent or "**b**" phrase of a contrasting period. There are many ways to do this. The most important point is to try and hear in your mind what you have written. When you write an exam, you will not have access to an instrument. However, in the early stages, when you are practicing writing melodies, it may be a good idea to play them on your instrument to see whether you have written the sounds that you intended.

Writing a melody is more than creating patterns of notes on paper. It is about your creativeness and imagination. The most important features of a good melody are its rhythmic organization and the shapes produced by the pitches of the notes.

Here are some ideas to help you create good melodies.

1. When planning the rhythm of a consequent phrase look at the rhythm of the given (antecedent) phrase. Try to base your melody on related rhythms. The rhythm of the consequent phrase in Figure 13.28 is based on one measure of rhythm found in the antecedent phrase. Introducing an unusual or foreign rhythmic figure in the consequent phrase may make it sound like it does not belong to the complete period.

2. In Figure 13.28, the antecedent phrase begins with an anacrusis. The consequent phrase also begins with an anacrusis. This is very common and creates rhythmic unity.

3. A melody should have a sense of direction or shape. It may move to a high point or climax and then down again. Try not to circle around the same few notes.

4. Scalewise motion is good. A leap is the interval of a 3rd or more. Leaps are good for contrast, but try to avoid too many of them because the melody could lose its shape.

5. Avoid dissonant intervals. In major keys, an augmented 4th occurs between $\hat{4}$ and $\hat{7}$ and should be avoided. You can write a diminished 5th, but try to leave this interval to a melody note that is within its compass. Figure 13.29 illustrates a melody using these intervals.

Figure 13.29

6. The final note of the first or antecedent phrase is often an unstable scale degree like $\hat{2}$ or $\hat{7}$. This implies a half cadence. A logical cadence must be implied at the end of a phrase. End the consequent phrase on a stable tone, preferably the tonic. This implies an authentic cadence. A melody that ends on the tonic is very strong and reinforces the tonality or key. This final tonic note is often approached from below by scale degree $\hat{7}$, or from above, by scale degree $\hat{2}$. Study and play the phrase endings in Figure 13.30.

Figure 13.30

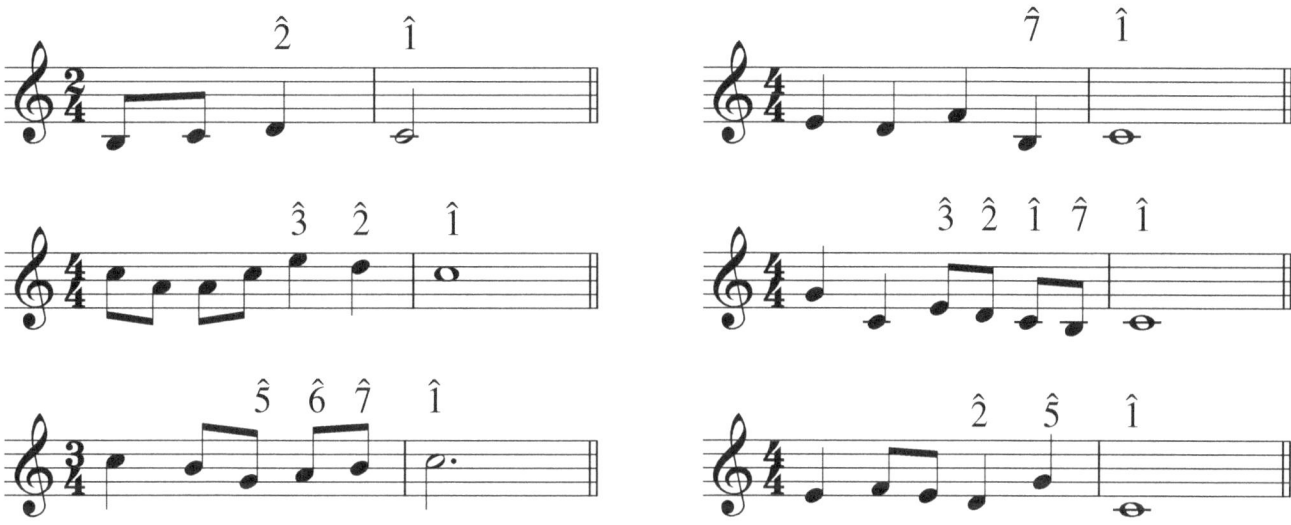

1. For following antecedent phrases: Name the key. Write a consequent phrase creating a **contrasting parallel period**. End on a stable scale degree. Mark the phrases. Name the implied cadences at the end of each phrase. Label each phrase **a** and **b**.

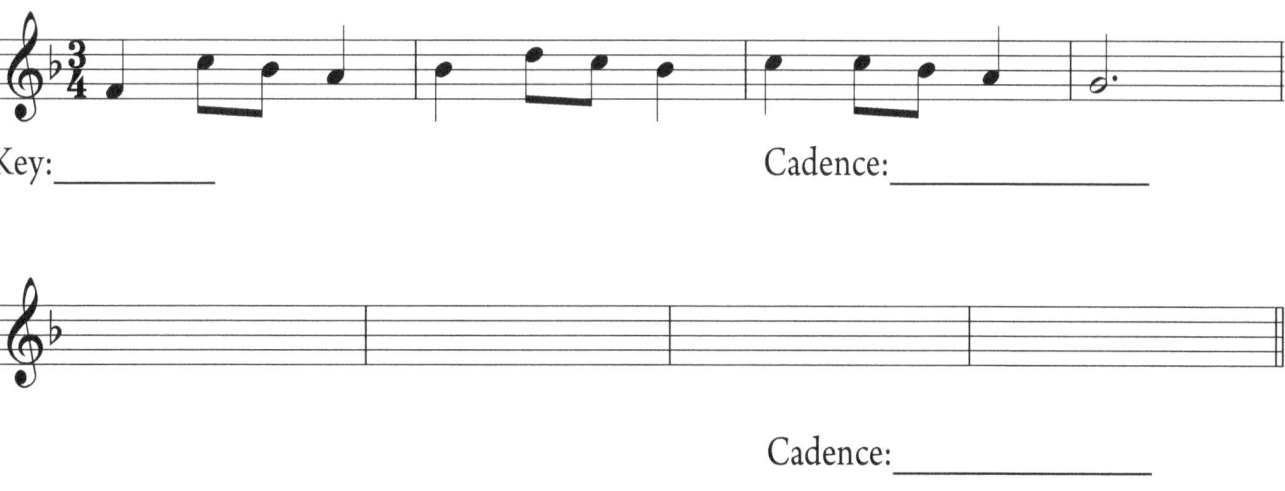

Key:_____   Cadence:_____

                                Cadence:_____

Melodic Contour

The motion between individual notes gives a melody *contour*. Contour determines what makes a melody memorable and expressive. When one note moves to another, it can repeat, move up or down, or it can move by step or by leap.

There are five possible combinations of these movements, so there are five basic types of melodic motion. A melody can move up by step, down by step, up by leap, down by leap, or repeat.

It's the combination of these five types of motion that give a melody its contour. We can visualize the contour of a melody as a long line or ribbon. This line gives us information about the melody's balance between up, down, step, leap, and repeat.

The example in Figure 16.31 a) has a wavy line that is created by leaps, steps, and directional changes. Figure 16.31 b) is a classic arched melody that moves to a high point in the phrase (climax), and then returns downward. Both are effective.

Figure 16.31

Extreme melodic shapes are not always suitable. A spiky, harsh shape occurs when a melody has too many large leaps. Figure 16.32 contains a melody with too many large leaps, resulting in a disjunct, unmusical melody.

Figure 16.32

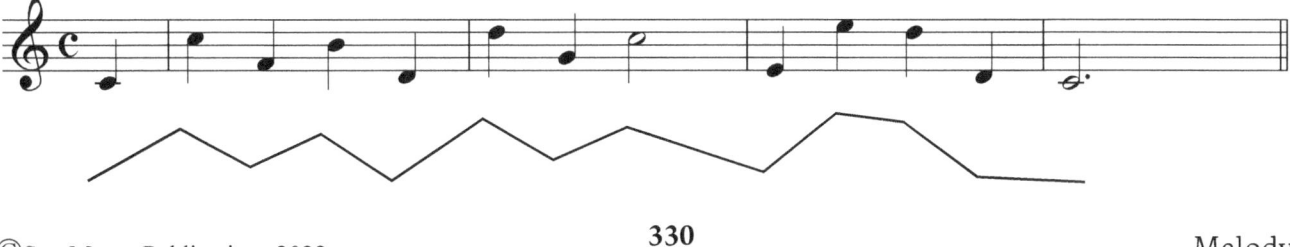

The melody in Figure 16.33 circles around the same few notes. This results in an uninteresting, flat shape. Try to avoid this type of melody.

Figure 16.33

Understanding contour helps us understand what makes melodies memorable and expressive. Good melodies tend to have diverse contours; that is, they tend to make balanced use of all different types of melodic motion. These types of melodies may use all five types of melodic motion in each phrase. An effective melody will often contain opposite pairs of motion such as a leap followed by a step, ascending notes followed by descending notes, or both.

Writing Melodic Leaps

Stepwise motion in a melody is good, but like anything, too much can make a melody boring. Leaps within a melody can add drama and interest, but they must be treated carefully. The following information is a general guideline to help you create effective melodies. However, occasional exceptions may be found in musical literature.

- Don't write more than three leaps in the same direction. Too many leaps may create an excessively large range and affect the shape of a melody. The melody in Figure 16.34 contains three ascending leaps and then it changes direction.

Figure 16.34

Anonymous
Minuet BWV 116

The melody in Figure 16.35 has six leaps in a row covering two octaves. This is a considerable range and not very effective especially if you have to sing it.

Figure 16.35

- More than one leap in a row in the same direction sounds like a broken chord. When writing more than one leap up or down, be sure that they combine to outline a recognizable chord or harmony. Study the melody in Figure 16.36 which contains efficient leaps outlining specific chords within the key.

Figure 16.36

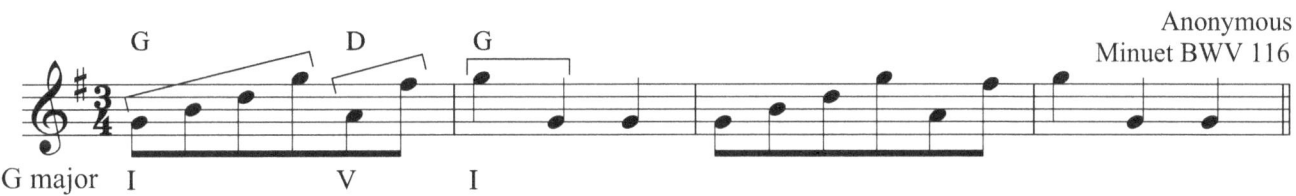

The melody in Figure 16.37 contains leaps that are poor. The leaps in m.1 are good because they outline the tonic triad. The leaps in m.3 do not outline a recognizable chord in G major. Not only are they bad, but they sound bad as well. This type of consecutive leap should be avoided.

Figure 16.37

1. Name the keys and put brackets on the consecutive leaps in the following melodies. Add a √ on the correct leaps, and an × on the incorrect leaps.

- It is best to approach a large leap (a 6th or more) with a note from within the leap. This is a note that occurs between the two notes of the leap. The leap in Figure 16.38 a) works well because it is approached by a note that is found within it. Figure 16.38 b) is poor because the note of approach is not within the notes of the leap.

Figure 16.38

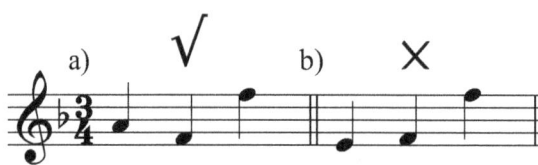

The two downward leaps in Figure 16.39 work well because they are approached from a note within the leap.

Figure 16.39

Christian Petzold
Minuet BWV 115

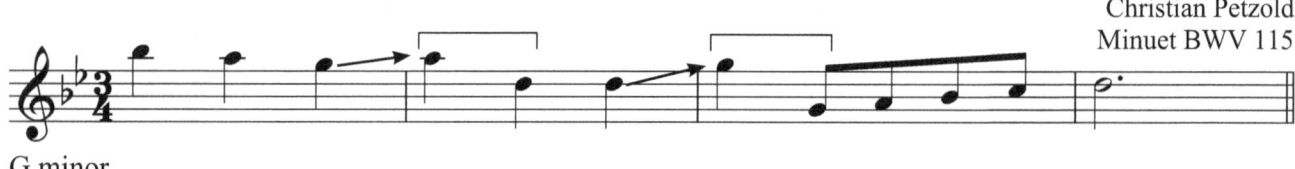

G minor

1. Mark the correctly approached leaps with a √ and the incorrectly approached leaps with an × in the following melodies.

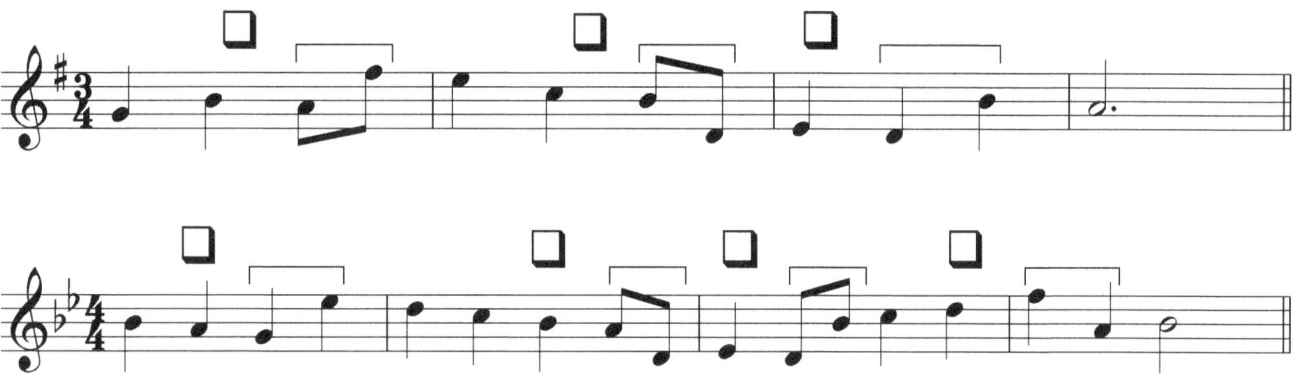

- As a general guideline, it is best to leave a large leap (a 6th or more) by movement in the opposite direction to a note within the leap. There may be occasional exceptions to this when the leap is being followed by a repeated note. In Figure 16.40 each leap is followed by a note found between the two notes of the leap.

Figure 16.40

Anonymous
Aria BWV 131

- Avoid a leap of a major 7th (Figure 16.41 a.). This is an awkward dissonant interval.
- A leap of a minor 7th is fine because it implies a 7th chord (Figure 16.41 b.). If you write a minor 7th, it is important to approach it as you approach all large intervals, from a note within the interval. 7ths should be left by step in the opposite direction. A 7th is an interval that requires resolution. This resolution is downward by step.
- When a melody moves in the same direction for more than one note, we hear the interval formed by the first and last notes. Try not to outline an augmented interval or a major 7th (Figure 16.41c.)

Figure 16.41

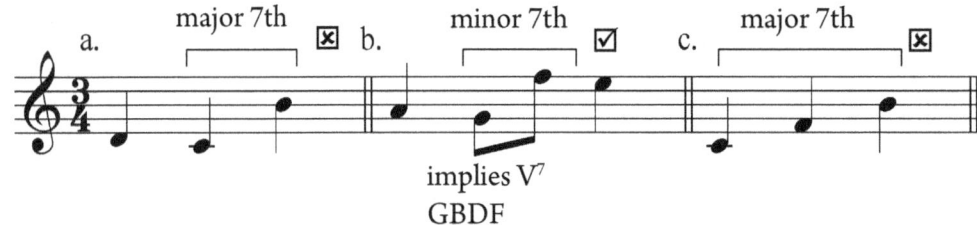

1. Complete the following melodic fragments to create four bar melodies in major keys. End each melody on a stable tone ($\hat{1}$ or $\hat{3}$).

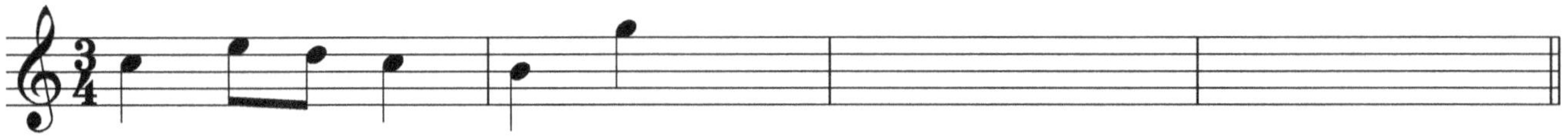

key:_____

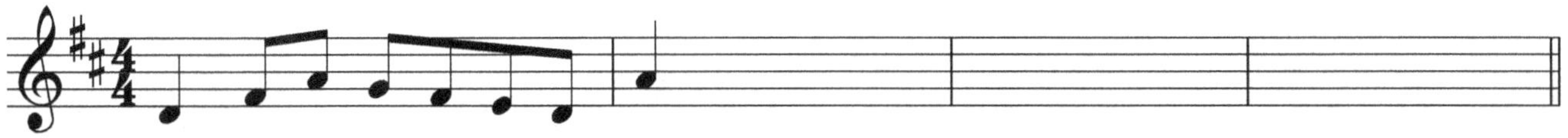

key:_____

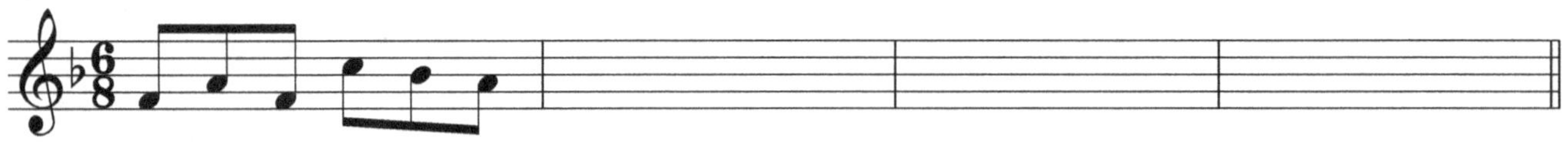

key:_____

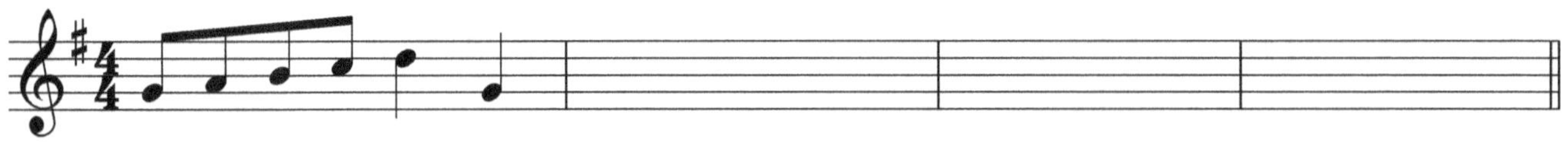

key:_____

©San Marco Publications 2022

Minor Key Melodies

Avoid writing augmented intervals melodically. They are dissonant intervals and do not sound good in a melody. Two augmented intervals to be aware of are shown in Figure 16.42.

1. An augmented 2nd occurs between $\hat{6}$ and raised $\hat{7}$ in minor keys when using the harmonic minor scale.
2. An augmented 4th occurs in both major and minor keys between $\hat{4}$ and $\hat{7}$.

Figure 16.42

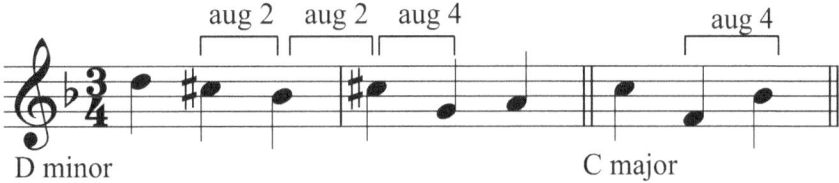

The D minor melody in Figure 16.43 contains two augmented 2nds between the submediant ($\hat{6}$) and the leading tone ($\sharp\hat{7}$). These should be avoided.

Figure 16.43

Figure 16.44 is a better version of the same melody using the melodic form of the minor scale. In m.2 the descending form of D melodic minor is used with the subtonic ($\hat{7}$) and submediant ($\hat{6}$). In m.3 the ascending form of D melodic minor is used with the raised submediant ($\natural\hat{6}$) and leading tone ($\sharp\hat{7}$). This eliminates the augmented 2nds.

Here, the descending version of the melodic minor scale was used for notes that were going down, and the ascending version was used for notes going up. However, it is fine to use the descending version for notes going up and vice versa. In either case, the augmented 2nd is avoided.

Figure 16.44

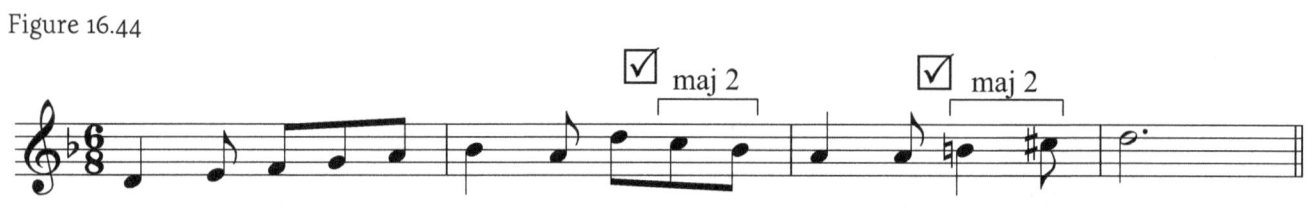

D minor

Study the two phrase melody in Figure 16.45. The implied harmony is stated using functional chord symbols. It is crucial that your melodies make harmonic sense. The first phrase ends on an unstable scale degree ($\hat{2}$), supporting a half cadence. The second phrase ends on a stable scale degree ($\hat{1}$) supporting an authentic cadence. The non-chord tones are passing tones and neighbor tones. Circle and label the non-chord tones in these phrases.

Figure 16.45

1. Complete the following melodic fragments using the given implied harmony to create four bar melodies in minor keys. End each melody on a stable tone. Name the key of each.

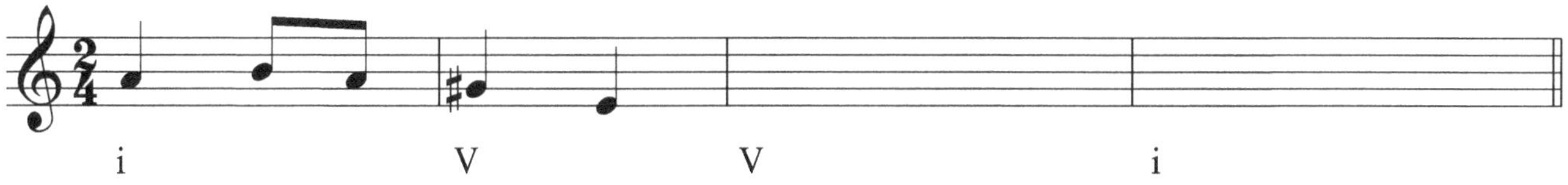

    i   V   V   i

Key:_____

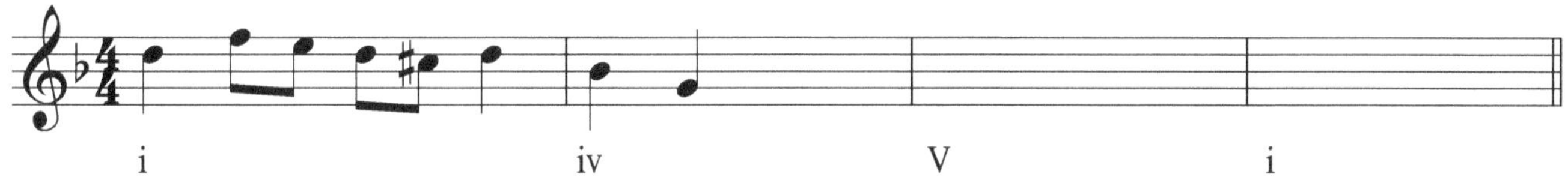

    i   iv   V   i

Key:_____

    i   V   iv   i   iv   V   i

Key:_____

    i   iv   V   i

Key:_____

2. Complete the following melodic fragments using the given implied harmony to create four bar melodies in minor keys. End each melody on an unstable scale degree implying a half cadence. Name the key of each.

    i   V   iv   V

Key:_____

    i   iv   i   V

Key:_____

3. For the following melodic fragments:

   - Name the key.
   - Complete the consequent (a) phrase, ending on an unstable scale degree ($\hat{2}$, $\hat{7}$, $\hat{5}$).
   - Write an antecedent (b) phrase creating a contrasting period ending on a stable scale degree ($\hat{1}$).
   - State the implied harmony using functional chord symbols.

Key:_____

Key:_____

Key:_____

17
Music Analysis

All of the concepts we have studied in theory can be put to good use when we look at a piece of music. *Music analysis* is studying a composition and figuring out its features. In this lesson, we are going to look at music and answer questions using the information we have learned.

1. Answer questions relating to the following musical example.

a. Add the correct time signature directly on the music.

b. Name the key of this piece._____

c. Circle a complete F major scale in this piece.

d. Draw a phrase mark over the phrase.

e. On which scale degree does this phrase end?_____

f. Is this a stable degree? _____

g. Define *Allegro*._____

h. Explain the sign at letter A._____

i. Explain the sign at letter B._____

j. Label all the leading tones LT.

©San Marco Publications 2022   340   Music Analysis

Form in Melody - Review

The overall plan or structure of a piece of music is known as *form*. We label music with letters to distinguish the differences within a composition.

Let's examine the two phrase melody in Figure 17.1. This melody is in the key of D major and begins on the stable scale degree $\hat{3}$ (F♯). The first phrase ends on the unstable degree $\hat{2}$ (E). The second phrase begins like the first and continues until the end where the last bar is slightly different, ending on the stable scale degree $\hat{1}$ (D).

We can label each phrase with a letter to indicate the form. The first phrase is labeled '**a**.' The second phrase being the same, except for the ending, is labeled '**a¹**.' This shows that the phrases are related, but there is a slight variation. If the phrases were exactly the same, they would be labeled with two '**a**'s. It should be noted that each phrase is four measures long. This is a common length for a phrase.

These two phrases together for a section called a *parallel period*.

Figure 17.1

Ludwig van Beethoven
Symphony No. 9, IV

D major

Figure 17.2 contains a melody that is made up of two distinctly different phrases. Each phrase begins with a quarter note upbeat. This, along with the rhythm, which is the same between the two phrases, is a unifying feature. However, the phrases are still very different. The first phrase contains a melody that ascends, and the second phrase contains a melody that descends. They work well together, but are not the same. To show this difference, the first phrase is labeled '**a**' and the second phrase is labeled '**b**.'

These two phrases together form a section called a ***contrasting period***.

Figure 17.2

1. For the following melodies: name the key, mark the phrases, and label them with letters (a, a¹, b) indicating their form.

key:

Irish Air

key:

American Folk Tune

key:

Carol based on Chant
"O Come, O Come Emmanuel"

key:

Allegro

Alexander Reinagle
(1756 - 1809)

a. Add the correct time signature directly on the music.

b. Name the key of this piece._____

c. Name the composer of this piece. _____

d. Draw a phrase mark over each phrase.

e. Label the phrases according to the form (a, a^1, b)

f. These two phrases for a: ☐ contrasting period   ☐ parallel period

g. Does the second phrase end on a stable or unstable degree? _____

h. Define **Allegro**._____

i. How are measure 1 and 2 similar to 5 and 6? _____

j. Locate and circle a half step in this piece.

Music Analysis

Carefree

Daniel Gottlob Turk
((1756 - 1813)

a. Add the correct time signature directly on the music.

b. Name the key of this piece._____

c. Name the composer of this piece. _____

d. Draw a phrase mark over each phrase.

e. Label the phrases according to the form (a, a¹, b)

f. These two phrases for a: ☐ contrasting period   ☐ parallel period

g. Does the second phrase end on a stable or unstable degree? _____

h. Define **Moderato**._____

i. Find and circle one accidental in this piece.

j. Name the interval at letter A. _____

k. Name the interval at letter B. _____

More About Form

Study the piano piece in Figure 17.3 This piece is made up of four phrases.

Phrase 1:

The letter '*a*' is used to identify the first phrase (mm.1 - 4) and any other phrases that are exactly the same. This phrase ends on scale degree $\hat{5}$, making it feel unfinished. It is four measures long and ends on a half note, giving pause before the next phrase begins.

Phrase 2:

The second phrase (mm.5 - 8) acts as a resolution or answer to the first phrase. It is labeled 'a^1.' 'a^1' is used to label phrases that are very similar to '*a*' but may contain some slight differences. This phrase is the same as '*a*' except for the last note. It is four measures long and ends on a stable pitch ($\hat{1}$). It also ends with a rest, giving pause before the next section starts.

Phrase 3:

The third phrase (mm. 9 - 12) is labeled '*b*' because the melody is different than phrase '*a*.' Music needs **repetition** so the listener has something familiar to hear, but it also needs **contrast** so it does not become boring. The two elements work together to make great compositions. If '*a*' was stated three times in a row, it might become too repetitive. This new material provides diversity and contrast. Phrase 3 is four measures long and ends on an unstable pitch ($\hat{5}$).

Phrase 4:

The fourth phrase (mm.13 - 16) is the same as phrase two, and like phrase two, it is labelled 'a^1.' This phrase rounds out the piece and it ends on a stable pitch.

Figure 17.3

1. Answer the questions dealing with the following compositions.

a. Add the time signature directly on the music.

b. Name the key of this piece. _____

c. Mark the phrases with slurs.

d. Label the phrases with *a*, *a¹*, and *b*.

e. Name the chord formed by the notes at A: _____ B: _____

1. Who composed the music shown above? _____

2. What is the name of the composition? _____

3. What key is it in? _____

4. What four voices are used to sing this piece?

   _____ _____ _____ _____

5. Name the triad formed by the notes at A _____

6. Name the interval at B. _____

7. Name the interval at C. _____

8. Name the interval at D. _____

Sonatina

Cornelius Gurlitt
1820 -1901

1. Name the composer of this piece? _____

2. Name the key of this piece. _____

3. Write the time signature on the score.

4. Define "moderato" _____

5. How many phrases are in this example? _____

6. Does the first phrase end on a stable or unstable degree? _____

7. Does the second phrase end on a stable or unstable degree? _____

8. Label the phrases either: (a - a[1)]) or (a - b) depending on the form.

9. What triad is formed by the notes in the box at letter A: _____

10. What triad is formed by the notes in the box at letter B: _____

11. Find the interval of a melodic minor 3rd, circle it, and label it min 3.

12. Find the interval of a melodic perfect 5th, circle it, and label it per 5.

13. Find two different diatonic semitones, circle them, and label them DS.

14. How many slurs occur in this piece? _____

Muzio Clementi
1752 -1832

1. Name the composer of this piece? _____

2. When did he live? _____

3. Write the time signature on the score.

4. Name the key of this piece. _____

5. Define "allegro." _____

6. Define "dolce." _____

7. For the triad at letter A, name the: Root _____ Quality _____ Inversion _____

8. For the triad at letter B, name the: Root _____ Quality _____ Inversion _____

9. How many times does the broken tonic triad occur in the bass clef. _____

10. Find a melodic major 2nd, circle it and label it maj 2.

11. Find a melodic major 3rd, circle it and label it maj 3.

12. Find a diatonic half step, put a box around it and label is DHS.

1. Name the key of this piece? _____

2. Write the time signature on the score.

3. Check the terms that apply to this time signature. ❑compound ❑triple ❑simple ❑duple

4. Mark the phrases with a slur.

5. Label each phrase using the letters *a, a¹* or *b*.

6. Define "andantino."_____

7. Name the triad at letter A.   root: _____   quality: _____

Music Analysis

Binary Form

Periods can be combined to create larger musical forms. One of the most simple forms is ***binary form.*** The prefix 'bi" means 'two.' A piece in binary form consists of two different or contrasting sections that are labelled **A** and **B**. Lowercase letters are used to label the single phrases of the parallel and contrasting period. Uppercase letters are used to label the sections in binary form because they are larger.

Figure 17.4 contains the folk song *Greensleeves*. This is an example of a 16 measure piece in binary form. It consists of two parallel periods. The first 8 measure section is given the label **A**. The second, 8 measure section is contrasting to the A section, and given the label **B**. The phrases of the A section could be labelled ***a*** and ***a¹*** and the phrases of the B section could be labelled ***b*** and ***b¹***. However, when analyzing binary form, the phrases are not always so cut and dry. Binary form is just labelled with A and B to reflect the two larger contrasting sections.

Figure 17.4

Ternary Form

Study Figure 17.5. This piece is in a three-part form called **ternary form** (ABA). The prefix 'ter' means 'three.' This form has three parts labelled A - B - A. In ternary form, the A section always returns after a contrasting B section.

In Figure 17.5 the first section (mm.1 - 8) is labelled A. The second contrasting section (mm. 9 - 16) is labelled B. The final section (mm. 17 - 24) is an exact repitition of the first section, and is labelled A. Sometimes the final A section is not an exact repitition of the first section. The composer may shorten, lengthen, alter the melody slightly, or vary the accompaniment of the final A section. In this case the form would be analyzed as ABA[1] to reflect this variation.

Figure 17.5

Binary and ternary forms are fairly simple, but they act as a basis for more complex forms in music. Phrases are used to organize a piece. Antecedent and consequent phrases are grouped to form periods. The periods come together to make sections, and the sections come together to make a composition. The sections vary by musical idea and are identified and labeled by their contrast or difference from one another. Compositions with the AB structure are in binary form, and compositions with ABA or ABA[1] are in ternary form.

Anton Diabelli
Op. 125. no. 3

1. Name the key of this piece. _____

2. Write the time signature directly on the score.

3. The form of this piece is: ❑ binary   ❑ ternary

4. Label the score by using A, A¹, and B to define the form.

5. Define *Allegretto*. _____

6. Check all statements below that apply to the chord at A:

    ❑ tonic triad   ❑ subdominant triad   ❑ C major triad   ❑ root position   ❑ broken chord

7. Check all statements below that apply to the chord at B:

    ❑ tonic triad   ❑ dominant triad   ❑ G major triad   ❑ 1st inversion   ❑ solid or blocked chord

8. Name the cadence at C:

    ❑ perfect authentic cadence   ❑ half cadence   ❑ imperfect authentic cadence

9. Symbolize the chords of this cadence on the score using functional chord symbols.

©San Marco Publications 2022

Music Analysis

Anton Diabelli
Op. 125 No. 4

1. Name the key of this piece. _____

2. Write the time signature directly on the score.

3. Check the words below that apply to this time signature.

    ❏triple   ❏compound   ❏duple   ❏simple   ❏quadruple

4. Mark the phrases using a slur.

5. The form of this piece is: ❏binary   ❏ternary

6. Label the score by using A, A¹, and B to define the form.

7. Define **Moderato**. _____

8. Name the chord at letter A: _____

9. For the chord at letter B name the: root_____ quality _____ position _____

10. For the chord at letter C name the: root_____ quality _____ position _____

11. The cadence at D is: ❏half   ❏perfect authentic   ❏imperfect authentic

12. Write the functional chord symbols for this cadence directly on the score.

13. Find and circle a broken dominant triad on the score. Label it DT.

14. Find and circle a broken tonic triad on the score. Label it TT.

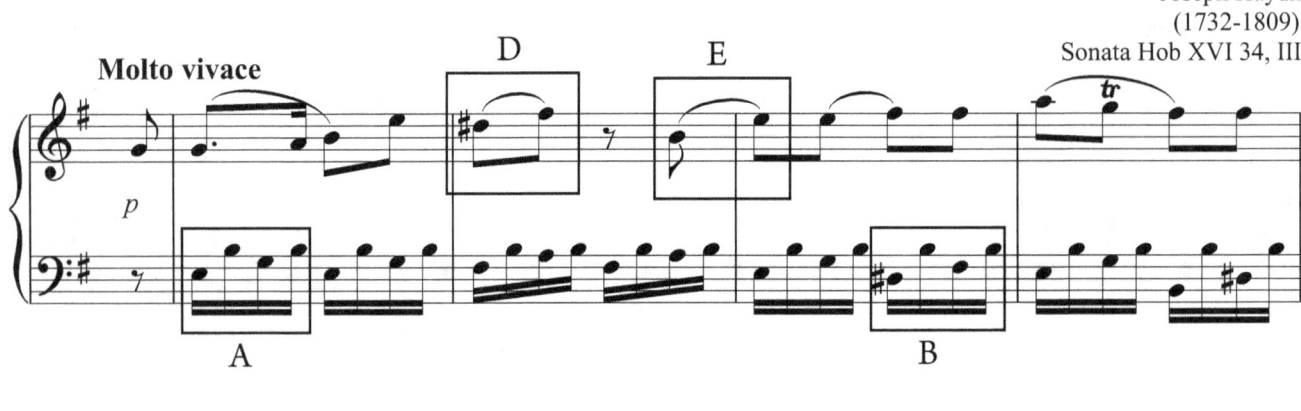

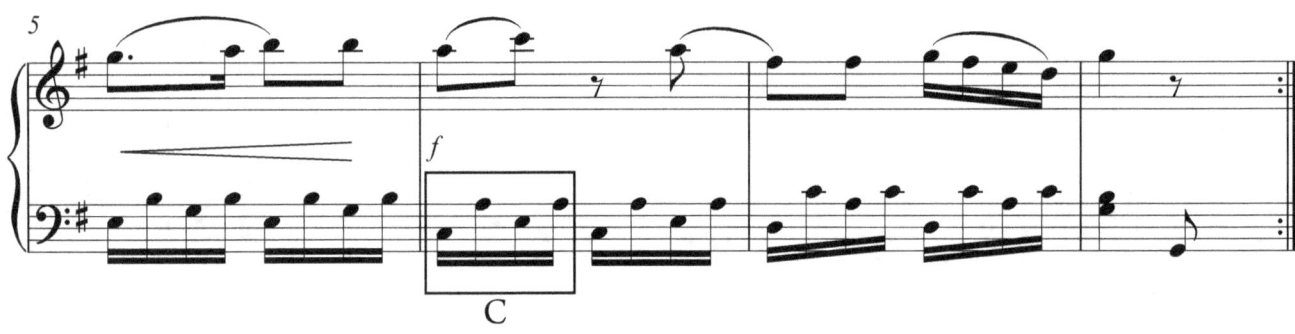

1. Name the key of this piece. _____

2. Write the time signature directly on the score.

3. This excerpt is written for a right hand melody with left hand accompaniment. This is and example of:

   ❑polyphonic music   ❑homophonic music   ❑contrapuntal music   ❑absolute music

4. What musical era was this piece composed? _____

5. Name the chord at A: root_____   quality_____   position_____

6. Name the chord at B: root_____   quality_____   position_____

7. Name the chord at C: root_____   quality_____   position_____

8. In this piece, chord A is the: ❑tonic triad   ❑subdominant triad   ❑dominant triad

9. In this piece, chord B is the: ❑tonic triad   ❑subdominant triad   ❑dominant triad

10. In this piece, chord C is the: ❑tonic triad   ❑subdominant triad   ❑dominant triad

11. Define **Molto vivace**: _____

12. This excerpt is an example of a: ❑parallel period   ❑contrasting period

13. Name the interval at D: _____

14. Name the interval at E: _____

The Primary Triads

The three most important triads in any key are built on the tonic (I, i), subdominant (IV, iv) and dominant (V). These are known as **primary triads**. Most folk music, sacred music, all of the blues, and a lot of rock are based on primary triads.

Figure 17.6 contains the well-known hymn "Amazing Grace." The entire hymn is based on I - IV and V.

Figure 17.6

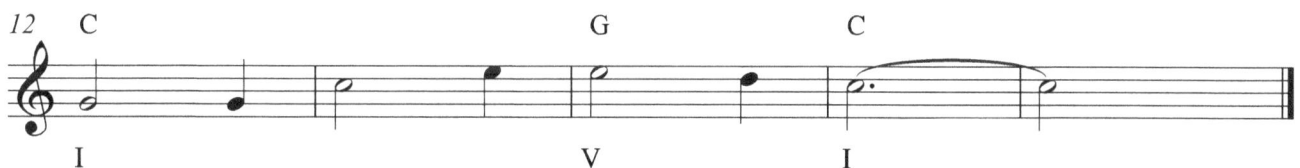

Primary Triad Functions

The Tonic (I or i)

The tonic triad in root position is the strongest chord in tonal music. It is important as a point of departure. Most music begins with the tonic and departs to other chords from it. The tonic might even be more important as a point of arrival. Almost all compositions end on the tonic chord. It acts like the home base for a piece of music. Like gravity, other chords pull towards the tonic.

The Dominant (V)

Some may argue that the dominant chord is the most important chord because of its pull to the tonic. The dominant actually helps us locate the tonic. The presence of the leading tone in the dominant chord creates an anticipation of the tonic chord. The leading tone has a natural tendency to pull to the tonic. Certain chords that contain the leading tone are referred to as **dominant function chords**. V is called the **dominant** because it is the most active dominant function chord.

The Subdominant (IV or iv)

The subdominant chord often leads to the dominant. For this reason, it can be called a **pre-dominant chord**. A pre-dominant chord is a chord that comes before a dominant functioning chord. Movement from chord to chord is called a **harmonic progression**. Movement from the pre-dominant to the dominant to the tonic is one of the strongest progressions in tonal music (IV - V - I).

1. Identify the following chords by writing the functional (Roman numeral) chord symbols under each. (I, IV and V or i, iv and V)

E minor

B minor

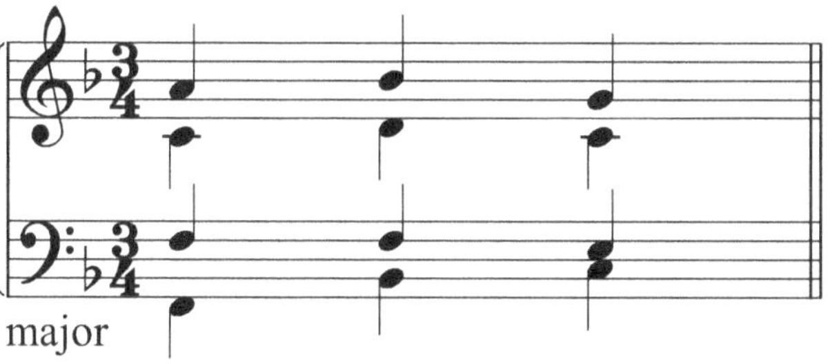

F major

A minor

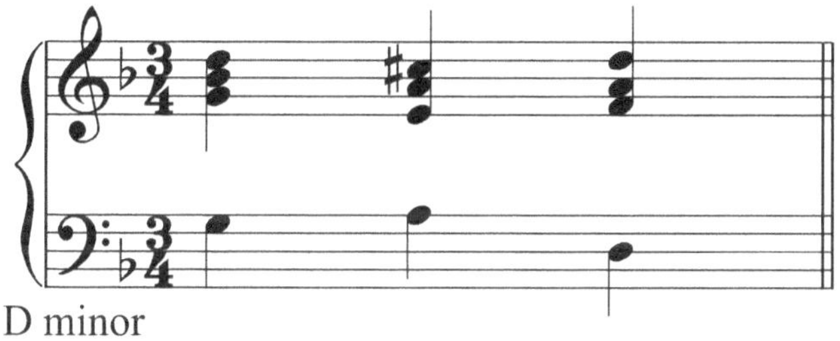

D minor

E major

G flat major

G sharp minor

2. Name the numbered chords as tonic, subdominant or dominant.

Wolfgang Amadeus Mozart

E flat major

1. _____

2. _____

3. _____

4. _____

Harmonic Progression

A ***harmonic progression*** is a succession of two or more chords. In tonal music, a progression is not just any two or more chords. Some progressions are better than others.

The most basic progression in tonal music is I - V - I. We call this the ***fundamental progression***. All that is needed to determine the key of the piece are the V and I (or i) chords. In tonal music, the relationship between the tonic and dominant define the key.

The first phrase of the Sonatina in Figure 17.7 consists of the progression I - V - I - V in D major. This phrase ends on a half cadence (I - V).
The non-chords tones are ***double passing tones***. These passing tones are written in 3rds. Double passing tones are usually written in intervals of 3rds or 6ths.

Figure 17.7

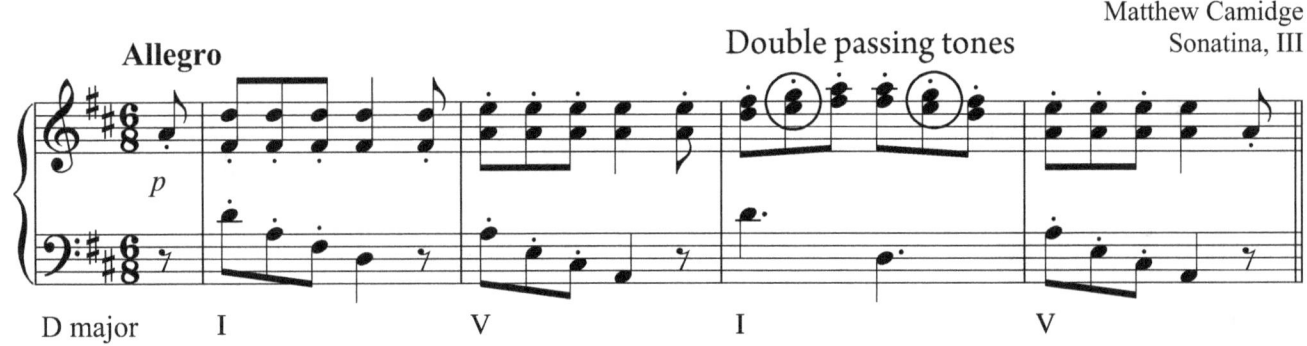

1. Write the functional chord symbol under each chord marked with ★.

1. In what musical era was this composed? _____

2. What is the key of this piece? _____

3. Write the time signature on the score.

4. Name the chord at A: _____

5. In this key, the chord at A is the: ❏tonic chord   ❏subdominant chord   ❏dominant chord

6. Name the chord at B: _____

7. In this key, B is the: ❏tonic chord   ❏subdominant chord   ❏dominant chord

8. Name the non-chord tones at C: _____ D: _____

9. Define **Allegretto**: _____

10. Define *fp*: _____

11. Does the melody end on a stable or unstable chord tone? _____

George Frideric Handel
(1685 - 1759)

1. Name the composer of this piece. _____

2. Name another composition by this composer. _____

3. What musical period was this piece composed? _____

4. Name the key of this piece. _____

5. Write the time signature on the score.

6. This is an example of: ❏ simple triple time   ❏ compound triple time

6. The chord at A is the: ❏ tonic chord   ❏ subdominant chord   ❏ dominant chord

7. The chord at B is the: ❏ tonic chord   ❏ subdominant chord   ❏ dominant chord

8. The chord at C is the: ❏ tonic chord   ❏ subdominant chord   ❏ dominant chord

9. How many times does the tonic chord appear in this excerpt? _____

10. Name the intervals at D: _____   E: _____   F: _____

11. How many times does the leading tone appear in this piece? _____

12. How many times does the subtonic appear in this piece? _____

©San Marco Publications 2022

Music Analysis

1. Name the key of this piece. _____

2. Write the time signature directly on the score.

3. This piece is written for a melody with piano accompaniment. This is and example of:

    ❏ polyphonic texture   ❏ homophonic texture   ❏ counterpoint   ❏ monophonic texture

4. In what musical era was this piece composed? _____

5. Name another composer from the same era. _____

6. Add the correct rest or rests to the voice part in m.1.

7. Name the interval at A: _____

8. Name the interval at B: _____

9. Name the interval at C: _____

10. Find and circle one leading tone in the voice part. Label it LT.

©San Marco Publications 2022   364   Music Analysis

Voice Leading

Voice leading is concerned with the horizontal or linear aspect of music and is as important as the vertical or chordal aspect. Voice leading is very important in polyphonic music since it consists of the performance of more than one melody at the same time. Examples of this can be found in the

There are four types of motion that can occur between two voices horizontally.

1. ***Contrary motion*** occurs when two voices move in the opposite direction. Figure 17.8 shows voices moving in contrary motion.

Figure 17.8

2. ***Oblique motion*** occurs when one voice is stationary, while the second voice moves to another pitch (up or down). Figure 17.9 shows voices moving in oblique motion.

Figure 17.9

3. ***Similar motion*** occurs when two voices move in the same direction (up or down), but not by the same interval. Figure 17.10 shows voices moving in similar motion.

Figure 17.10

4. ***Parallel motion*** occurs when two voices move in the same direction (up or down), by the same basic interval. Figure 17.11 shows voices moving in parallel motion.

Figure 17.11

1. List the type of motion in each example. Contrary, oblique, similar, or parallel.

Study the voice leading in Figure 17.12. Both (a) and (b) are examples of parallel motion. However, there is a difference. The intervals in (a) are a major 6th and a minor 6th, while the intervals in (b) are both major 6ths. The term parallel motion does not always mean the intervals are exactly the same. The *number* is the same, but the *quality* can be different. Both intervals move in parallel motion but technically (b) is more parallel than (a). The term parallel motion does not take into account the quality of the interval.

Figure 17.12

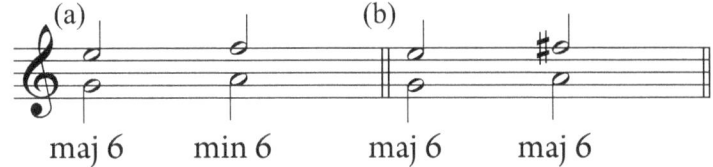

In traditional harmony and counterpoint, certain parallel perfect intervals are forbidden. These intervals are parallel perfect 5ths, parallel perfect octaves, and parallel perfect unisons. These intervals are very consonant, and when they move in parallel motion, they can lose their individual identity. The first three examples of parallel motion in Figure 17.13 should be avoided. However, a diminished 5th followed by a perfect 5th is fine.

Figure 17.13

©San Marco Publications 2022

1. The following voices move in parallel motion. Mark the correct examples with ✓ and the incorrect examples with ✗.

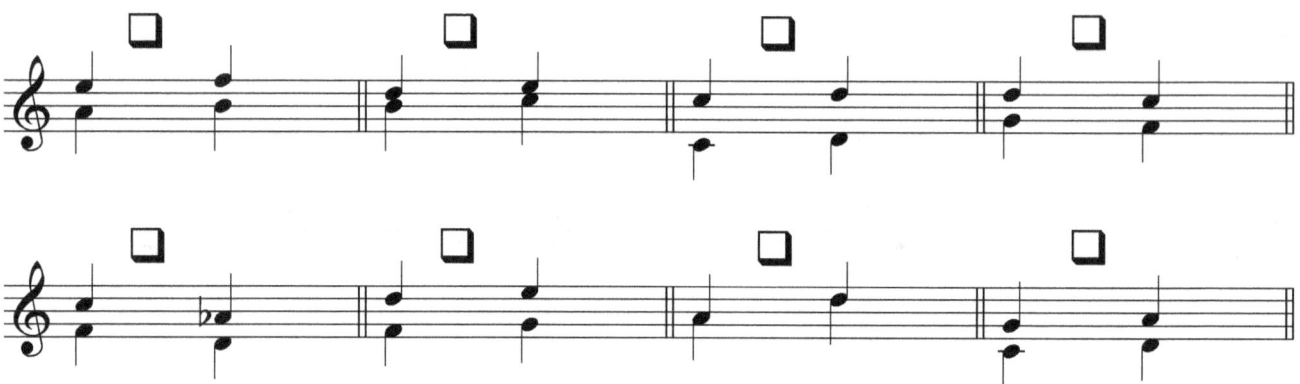

2. Answer the questions that deal with the following musical examples.

a. Name the key of this phrase. _____

b. Write the time signature directly on the score.

c. In what musical period was this piece composed? _____

d. What open score is this written for? _____

e. State the implied harmony using functional and root/quality chord symbols on the score.

f. Find and circle a melodic sequence.

g. Name the cadence at the end of this phrase. _____

Passepied

George Frideric Handel
(1685-1759)

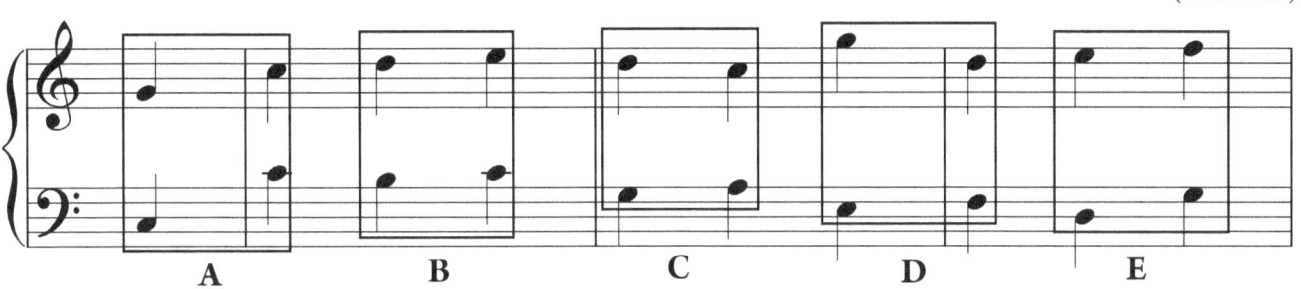

a. Add the correct time signature directly on the music.

b. Name the key of this piece._____

c. Name the composer of this piece. _____

d. Name another composition by this composer. _____

d. In what musical era was this composed? _____

e. This piece is: ❑monophonic   ❑polyphonic

f. Identify the motion at:

	contrary	parallel	similar	oblique
A:	❑	❑	❑	❑
B:	❑	❑	❑	❑
C:	❑	❑	❑	❑
D:	❑	❑	❑	❑
E:	❑	❑	❑	❑
F:	❑	❑	❑	❑

Music Terms and Signs

Terms

accelerando, accel.	becoming quicker
accent	a stressed note
ad libitum, ad lib.	at the liberty of the performer
adagio	slow
agitato	agitated
alla, all'	in the manner of
allargando	getting slower and broader
allegretto	fairly fast, a little slower than allegre
allegro	fast
andante	moderately slow, at a walking pace
andantino	a little faster than andante
animato	lively, animated
arco	for strings return to bowing after pizzicato or col legno.
attacca	begin immediately, proceed without a break
a tempo	return to the original tempo
ben, bene	well
bewegt	with movement, agitated
calando	becoming slower and softer
cantabile	in a singing style
cédez	yield, slow down
col, coll', colla, colle	with
comodo	at a comfortable tempo
con	with
con brio	with vigor
con espressione	with expression
con fuoco	with fire
con grazia	with grace
con moto	with motion
con sordino	with the use of a mute

©San Marco Publications 2022

crescendo, cresc.	becoming louder
da capo, D.C.	from the beginning
D.C. al fine	repeat from the beginning and end at *Fine*
dal segno, D.S.	from the sign
decrescendo, decresc.	becoming softer
diminuendo, dim.	becoming softe
dolce	sweetly, gentle
dolente	sad
e, ed	and
espressivio, espress.	expressive, with expression
fine	the end
forte, f	loud
fortissimo, ff	very loud
fortepiano, fp	loud, then suddenly soft
giocoso	humorous, joyful
grandioso	grand, play in a grand and noble style
grazioso	gracefully
grave	slow and solemn
langsam	slowly
largamente	broadly
larghetto	fairly slow, not as slow as largo
largo	very slow
léger	lightly
leggiero	light
lentement	slowly
lento	slow
l'istesso tempo	at the same tempo
loco	return to the normal register
ma	but
maestoso	majestically
mano destra, m.d.	right hand

mano sinistra, m.s.	left hand
marcato	play marked or stressed
martellato	strongly accented, hammered
mässig	moderately
meno	less
meno mosso	less motion
mesto	sad, mournful
mezzo forte, mf	moderately loud
mezzo piano, mp	moderately soft
mit Ausdruck	with expression
moderato	at a moderate tempo
modéré	at a moderate tempo
molto	much, very
morendo	dying, fading away
mouvement	movement, tempo, motion
non	not
ottava, 8va	the interval of an octave
pesante	heavy, play with weight
pedale, ped	pedal
pianissimo, pp	very soft
piano, p	soft
piu	more
piu mosso	more motion
pizzicato	pluck the strings, for string instruments
poco	little
poco a poco	little by little
prestissimo	as fast as possible
presto	very fast
primo, prima	first, the upper part of a duet
quasi	almost, as if
quindicesima alta, 15ma	play 2 octaves higher

rallentando, rall.	slowing down
risoluto	resolute, bold, strong
ritardando, rit.	slowing down gradually
ritenuto, riten	suddenly slower
rubato	flexible tempo with slight variations of speed to enhance musical expression.
scherzando	playful, play in a light-hearted happy manner
schnell	fast
sehr	very
secondo, seconda	second, lower part of a duet
semplice	simple
sempre	always
senza	without
sforzando, sf, sfz	sudden strong accent on a single note or chord
simile	continue in the same manner as has just been indicated
sonore	sonorous, resonant; with rich tone
sopra	above, indicates piano player crossing hands
sostentuto	sustained, play in a prolonged manner
staccato	play short and detached
stringendo	gradually faster, pressing forward
subito	suddenly
tacet	be silent, voice or instrument does not play or sing
tempo	speed at which music is performed
Tempo Primo, Tempo I	return to the original tempo
tranquillo	tranquil, quiet
tre corde	3 strings, release the left pedal on the piano
troppo	too much
tutti	a passage for the whole ensemble
una corda	1 string, depress the left pedal on the piano
vite	fast

vivace   lively, brisk

vivo   lively

volta   time, *prima volta*=1st time, *seconda volta*=2nd time

volti subito, v.s.   turn the page quickly

Signs

accent - a stressed note

common time - symbol for 4/4

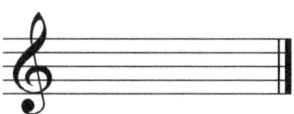

crescendo - becoming louder

decrescendo - becoming softer

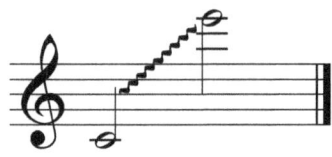

double bar line - the end of a piece

fermata - hold note or rest longer than written value

glissando, gliss - a continuous sliding up or down from one pitch to another

slur - play the notes smoothly (legato)

staccato - play short and detached

tie - hold for the combined value of the tied notes

repeat marks - at the second sign go back to the first sign and repeat the music from there. The first sign is left out if the music is repeated from the beginning.

pedal symbol - press/release the right pedal.

tenuto mark - when placed over or under a note, hold it for its full value.

dal segno, D.S. - from the sign.

8va - play one octave higher than written pitch.

8va - play one octave lower than written pitch.

down bow - on a string instrument, play the note by drawing the bow downward.

up bow - on a string instrument, play the note by drawing the bow upward.

breath mark - take a breath or a small break

©San Marco Publications 2022   Terms snd Signs

www.ingramcontent.com/pod-product-compliance
Lightning Source LLC
Chambersburg PA
CBHW081613100526
44590CB00021B/3427